D1564474

Sorrow and Consolation in Italian Humanism

SORROW AND CONSOLATION IN

ITALIAN HUMANISM

George W. McClure

PRINCETON UNIVERSITY PRESS

PRINCETON, NEW JERSEY

LIBRARY OF CONGRESS CATALOGING-IN-PUBLICATION DATA

MCCLURE, GEORGE, W., 1951–
SORROW AND CONSOLATION IN ITALIAN HUMANISM /
GEORGE W. MCCLURE.
P.   CM.
INCLUDES BIBLIOGRAPHICAL REFERENCES.
ISBN 0-691-05598-X (ALK. PAPER)
1. GRIEF.   2. CONSOLATION.   3. HUMANISM—ITALY.   4. RENAISSANCE—
ITALY.   5. PETRARCA, FRANCESCO, 1304–1374—PHILOSOPHY.   I. TITLE.
B780.G74M23   1990
152.4—DC20   90-36719

THIS BOOK HAS BEEN COMPOSED IN GALLIARD TYPEFACE

PRINCETON UNIVERSITY PRESS BOOKS ARE PRINTED ON ACID-FREE PAPER,
AND MEET THE GUIDELINES FOR PERMANENCE AND DURABILITY
OF THE COMMITTEE ON PRODUCTION GUIDELINES
FOR BOOK LONGEVITY OF THE COUNCIL
ON LIBRARY RESOURCES

PRINTED IN THE UNITED STATES OF AMERICA BY
PRINCETON UNIVERSITY PRESS, PRINCETON, NEW JERSEY

1   3   5   7   9   10   8   6   4   2

To Jennifer, Rosie, and David

CONTENTS

PREFACE

THE RENAISSANCE reclamation of the cultural heritage of antiquity sprang from a variety of impulses. The thirst for literary enrichment, philosophical breadth, and rhetorical refinement; the desire for secular models of historical grandeur and moral distinction; the yearning for literary expression and fame; the search for a rhetorical (as against a logical) idiom of human and divine wisdom; the growing concern for perfecting civic discourse and public persona—all these forces contributed to the emergence and success of Italian humanism. In terms of moral thought, classical literature and learning offered guidance in the art of living virtuously and happily. The psychological domain of grief and consolation—as it applied both to moral theorists and to rhetorical practitioners—was an urgent part of this realm of humane letters both in antiquity and in the Renaissance. My study has two general purposes. Delineating the contours of this important, but somewhat neglected, Renaissance psychological tradition, it attempts to establish the historical context for the origins and popularity of the Trecento and Quattrocento humanist interest in consolatory literature, theory, and rhetoric. More specifically, this book elucidates the thought of particular humanists as seen through or shaped by their consolatory endeavors. In examining this literature of sorrow, my purview includes a range of psychological concerns including grief or bereavement, fear, despair, general misfortune, and even physical suffering—problems treated either singly or sometimes collectively in humanist consolatory writings. Surveying this tradition from Petrarch to Ficino, this book is not meant to be a comprehensive catalogue of all such literature in fourteenth- and fifteenth-century Italian thought. Rather, focusing on selected prominent figures, genres, and themes, it attempts to define some of the salient currents in that tradition.

This study grew out of a dissertation completed in 1981 at the University of Michigan, under the direction of Charles Trinkaus. I am grateful to him for various suggestions concerning both general approach and specific sources. Marvin Becker and Thomas Tentler also contributed many helpful ideas. I would also like to thank Ralph Williams and Fr. John O'Malley, S.J., who read the dissertation and offered their thoughtful advice. Like so many students of the Renaissance, I owe my greatest debt to Paul Oskar Kristeller. He painstakingly read the initial two-volume study in 1982, offering a wealth of invaluable criticism, detailed corrections, and references. His suggestions and emendations have been my constant guide through the several years of revision. His generosity will long continue to be a source of inspiration to me and to the entire community of Renaissance scholars. Parts (or versions of parts) of the manuscript have been published in the *Journal of Medieval and Renaissance Studies* (Fall 1985), the *Renaissance Quarterly* (Fall 1986), and the latest Festschrift for Paul Oskar Kristeller, the *Supplementum Festivum*, ed. J. Hankins, J. Monfasani, and F. Purnell, Jr. (Binghamton, 1987). For their critiques and corrections of these pieces I am indebted to Ronald Witt, Benjamin Kohl, John Monfasani, and James Hankins. For their permission to reprint this material I am grateful to the editors of these publications, and to the Center for Medieval and Early Renaissance Studies, State University of New York at Binghamton. Finally, I wish to thank the Press readers, Margaret King and Jerry Bentley, for their suggestions—and I am also grateful to my copyeditor at the Press, Laura Kang Ward. I, of course, bear full responsibility for any errors that remain in the book.

I would also like to thank the cooperative staffs of the Biblioteca Apostolica Vaticana, the Biblioteca Medicea Laurenziana, and the Biblioteca Nazionale (Florence), who show such kindness to the foreign scholar. I am also grateful to the staff of the Harlan Hatcher Graduate Library at the University of Michigan—and, in particular, to the librarians in the Department of Rare Books. For microfilms of manuscripts and early printed sources I thank the BAV and BML as well as the Bibloteca Casanatense (Rome), the Biblioteca Civica in Verona, the Newberry Library (Chicago), the National Library of Medicine (Washington), and the Beinecke Rare Book and Manuscript Library (Yale). I also want to thank the University of Alabama for a University Research Grant in the summer of 1987 and for a Bankhead Fellowship in the spring of 1988. I am especially grateful to the Department of History for a flexible schedule in 1987–88, which allowed me a term of released time to put the manuscript in final shape.

Finally, I want to give special thanks to my wife, Jennifer. A constant source of conceptual, linguistic, and stylistic advice, she has led me out of the forest of confusion and despair several times. The book owes much to her intelligent, insightful suggestions and to her careful reading. If undoubtedly hoping for a sunnier topic next time, she has nonetheless been ever-patient and good-natured about this project. Our children, Sarah Rose and David William, operating under the assumption that silence can be more distracting than a steady din, have also been a great help. To Jennifer and to them I dedicate this book.

Tuscaloosa, 1989

ABBREVIATIONS

BAV   Biblioteca Apostolica Vaticana
BML   Biblioteca Medicea Laurenziana, Florence
BNC   Biblioteca Nazionale Centrale, Florence
BHR   *Bibliothèque d'humanisme et renaissance*
DBI   *Dizionario biografico degli Italiani* (Rome, 1960–)
GSLI   *Giornale storico della letteratura italiana*
IMU   *Italia medioevale e umanistica*
JMRS   *Journal of Medieval and Renaissance Studies*
L   Biblioteca Medicea Laurenziana, MS. Laur. 54, 10
PG   *Patrologiae cursus completus, Series Graeca*, ed. J.-P. Migne, 161
      vols. (Paris, 1857–1905)
PL   *Patrologiae cursus completus, Series Latina*, ed. J.-P. Migne, 221
      vols. (Paris, 1844–1904)
RQ   *Renaissance Quarterly*
SR   *Studies in the Renaissance*
V¹   Biblioteca Apostolica Vaticana, MS. Archivio di S. Pietro, H 13
V²   Biblioteca Apostolica Vaticana, MS. Vat. lat. 8764
Ve   Verona, Biblioteca Civica, MS. 1472 (B. Lett. 82. 4)

Note: All citations of the Bible (and the numeration of the Psalms) refer to the Vulgate. All
  English translations are from the *New Oxford Annotated RSV*, 1973.
Unless otherwise indicated, classical citations are from the Loeb Classical Library.
When citing others' translations, I have in some cases made minor revisions.

Sorrow and Consolation in Italian Humanism

INTRODUCTION

THE CLASSICAL AND CHRISTIAN TRADITIONS

T
HE THEORY and practice of proffering consolation commanded
a prominent place in humanist moral thought and literature. Reviving and furthering the tradition of the ancient *consolatio*, Renaissance writers formulated solace for such problems as bereavement, fear of
death, illness, despair, and misfortune. In the Trecento and Quattrocento
there appeared countless consolatory letters, a wealth of funeral orations,
and numerous consolatory dialogues and treatises. The coherence and importance of this consolatory tradition in Renaissance culture have not been
fully recognized. By studying this tradition more closely we can learn much
about the psychological functions of rhetoric and philosophy in Renaissance thought. Equally important, we can begin to see more clearly how
the history of ideas has been changed and enriched by its quiet counterpart,
the "history of emotions."[1]

For the historian this consolatory eloquence is a window onto prominent intellectual themes as well as onto more personal emotional currents
in fourteenth- and fifteenth-century thought. The aim of this book is to
establish the larger cultural context for this humanist interest in consolation. How did the consolatory impulse provide both a forum and inspiration for the discussion of certain timely philosophical, psychological, spiritual, and social issues? How did this pursuit of solace speak to the larger
moral and rhetorical interests of the humanists? How did it relate to wider
currents in the history of pastoral care and the history of friendship? How
did it signal a dramatic laicization of psychological theory and practice?

To explore these questions this study will examine both the social and
personal faces of humanist consolation. In some cases, humanists explicitly
directed their efforts toward others. In addition to letters, orations, or dialogues written to assuage the grief of a particular friend or patron, they also
composed general manuals for a larger audience. Besides these efforts on
behalf of others, humanists also took up their pens to console themselves
for personal tragedy or despair. In these instances, writing could serve to
express or ease a private sorrow: it could be a "salubrious soliloquy" (to
borrow one of Petrarch's phrases)[2] or an inward colloquy, articulating and
resolving the stages of personal grief. In a few cases these two faces of
consolation—the social and the personal—were implicitly joined into one,
as the motivations for formulating solace lay as much in the consoler's heart
as in his reader's despair.

In some instances, these writings illustrate how Renaissance humanists saw themselves in the role of specialized consolers, self-consolers, and "doctors of the mind." Like certain classical moralists, they sometimes perceived their "clinical" office as healers of mental *morbi* as analogous to the medical office of the doctor. Less stated, but culturally more dramatic, their efforts as healers also assumed a therapeutic relevance in relation to the traditional perspectives of the spiritual office of the priest. As doctors tended to the *body*, and as priests to the *soul*, a figure such as Petrarch wanted to fashion a therapeutic wisdom for the area in between, the *mind*. In doing so, he and certain other humanists staked out a discrete clinical domain, broaching the area of the lay psychologist.[3] Moreover, in general, Petrarch and his heirs were trying to unearth a wisdom and eloquence that dealt more realistically with the "art of living and dying," a wisdom that had not, in their view, been provided in the sterile disputations of scholastic philosophy and theology.[4] Rejecting dialectic and theoretical learning, humanist writers instead cultivated a practical eloquence that spoke to human emotion, the human will, the human psyche. Evincing a belief in the legitimacy of worldly grief, they provided a solace responsive to the vicissitudes of secular life, and they sometimes offered particular lay perspectives and solutions different from the sterner warnings and cures traditionally advanced by the confessor and pastor. Fully acknowledging the humanity of sorrow, they sought out comforts from neglected troves of Platonic, Stoic, Peripatetic, Epicurean, and Christian thought.

The humanist interest in despair, and the effort to open up this realm in both social and personal terms, signaled a shift toward a heightened secularization in European thought. The causes and implications of this shift become clear only when the Renaissance tradition is viewed against the backdrop of consolatory traditions and psychological assumptions bequeathed to it from the ancient and medieval world. Before turning to Petrarch, the seminal figure in the Renaissance tradition, it is important to review broadly the varied and sometimes conflicting legacies that he and his successors inherited from their secular and sacred past. Beyond a consideration of consolatory genres and therapeutic roles, such a survey must also include a reflection on a subtler issue of cultural mentalité: namely, the shifting meaning and "status" of sorrow in the ancient and medieval world.

The genres of Renaissance consolation—the *epistola consolatoria*, the *oratio consolatoria* or *consolatio* (longer and more ambitious than the letter), the *oratio funebris*, elegiac verse, the consolatory dialogue, the consolatory manual—were of course classical in origin.[5] The roots of this tradition of therapeutic *ratio* and *oratio* were to be found in treatises, dialogues, and diatribes of the classical Greek philosophers and orators. The rhetorical character of the tradition undoubtedly owed much to the Sophists and their heirs, who readily saw the psychological realm as part of their domain. Gorgias of Leontini argued that the potential effect of language on the soul was analagous to that of medicine on the body. His contemporary Antiphon acted on such a sentiment in an explicitly therapeutic context. According to Ps.-Plutarch he established a clinic at Corinth where for a time he treated all comers of their particular distresses.[6] In general, from among the philosophers and rhetors there emerged a flourishing literary tradition of Greek consolatory discourses. Cicero attested to the currency and specialization of such writings in his *Tusculan Disputations* (3.34.82):

> For there are definite words of comfort habitually used in dealing with poverty, definite words in dealing with a life spent without obtaining office and fame; there are distinctly definite forms of discourse dealing with exile, ruin of country, slavery, infirmity, blindness, every accident upon which the term disaster can be fixed. These subjects the Greek divide up under separate books; for they are on the lookout for subjects to work at.[7]

In concert with the coalescing of discrete philosophical schools naturally came the development of distinct psychological theories and consolatory approaches. The Platonic notion of the immortality of the soul and its separation from the body served as the principal *locus* for an otherworldly idealism, readily adapted later by Christian consolers. If not expressly consolatory in genre, nevertheless the *Apology* and particularly the *Phaedo*, both portraying the doomed Socrates' testament on immortality, became seminal sources for later consolations for the fear of death.[8] As for a more specific psychological doctrine, Plato also delineated the divisions within the soul between rational and irrational spheres, the former to triumph over the latter.[9] Whether in reference to the dichotomy between the body and the soul or to the divisions within the soul itself, Platonic and Neoplatonic thought stressed the importance of the necessary ascendancy of the spiritual (or rational) over the corporeal (or nonrational). If the Academy was the most mystical of the schools, the Stoa was the most psychologically austere. Insisting on a virtual impassivity, the Stoic notion of *apatheia* called for the sage's freedom from all *pathe*, the four perturbations of delight, lust, distress, and fear. Because virtue is the only good and vice the only evil, all worldly externalities and contingencies are simply indifferent and are to be contemned. The Peripatetics took a more moderate approach than their Stoic competitors. For them, the misfortunes of life and the tragedy of death have an inexorable and legitimate impact on man's equanimity. The "goods" of the body and the external world, as well as those of the soul, are all valid factors in the pursuit of human happiness (cf. *Nicomachean Ethics*). The Epicureans were most fully the champions of psychological naturalism, arguing that happiness is best assured through the ascendancy of pleasure over pain. Sorrow could be eased by redirecting the mind to pleasant thoughts or endeavors. Though there were other schools—for instance, the Cyrenaics with their regimen of the premeditation of all eventualities—these were the principal ones that shaped ancient and Renaissance debates on solace and tranquility.[10]

The Greek work that apparently most fully synthesized Hellenic literature and doctrines concerning consolation was the (*On Grief*) composed by the Academic Crantor, a student of Plato's pupil Xenocrates. Lost, but for fragments, this treatise consoled a bereaved parent, and perhaps more than any of its predecessors it reified the genre of the *consolatio* proper. It not only served as a model for Cicero's *Consolatio*, but also influenced the famous *Consolatio ad Apollonium* of the Ps.-Plutarch. Particularly important is a sentiment that both these later writers pass on from Crantor's work: namely, the anti-Stoic belief that moderate grief is natural and legitimate.[11]

Without question, Crantor's counterpart among the Romans was Cicero. In 45 B.C. his daughter Tullia died and he wrote his *Consolatio* in an effort to resolve his sorrow. Although, like Crantor's treatise, his also has not survived save for fragments, Cicero later refers to the work in his *Tusculans* Books 1 and 3. Both the urgency of his grief and his penchant for eclecticism inspired him to sample a range of *topoi* and techniques from the various schools. His description of his approach (*Tusc.* 3.30.75–76) is a succinct statement of the purpose and method in classical consolation:

> These therefore are the duties of comforters: to do away with distress root and branch, or allay it, or diminish it as far as possible, or stop its progress and not allow it to extend further, or to divert it elsewhere. There are some who think it the sole duty of a comforter to insist that the evil has no existence at all, as is the view of Cleanthes [Stoic of the third century B.C.]; some, like the Peripatetics, favour the lesson that the evil is not serious. Some again favour the withdrawal of attention from evil to good, as Epicurus does; some, like the Cyrenaics, think it enough to show that nothing unexpected has taken place. Chrysippus [Cleanthes' Stoic successor] on the other hand considers that the main thing in giving comfort is to remove from the mind of the mourner the belief already described, in case he should think he is discharging a regular duty which is obligatory. There are some too in favour of concentrating all these ways of administering comfort (for one man is influenced in one way, one in another) pretty nearly as in my *Consolation* I threw them all into one attempt at consolation; for my soul was in a feverish state and I attempted every means of curing its condition.[12]

Despite its loss, the very fact of Cicero's *Consolatio* was of enormous influence in the Renaissance, as various writers from the fourteenth to the sixteenth centuries cited, imitated, or, in one case, even forged his treatise.

The *Consolatio* was only Cicero's entrée into the world of moral philosophy. Unhappily removed from the political stage, the former consul ventured deeper into moral theory, his efforts culminating in the *Tusculans*. As a synthesis of Greek philosophy, as a manual of psychological theory, this set of dialogues was possibly the single most comprehensive and influential source for Renaissance psychological theory. As an eclectic member of the New Academy, Cicero's perspectives ranged over several schools as he discussed some of the principal subjects pertinent to the consolatory tradition.[13] The first book, treating the problem of death and the nature of the soul, challenges the belief that death is an evil.[14] The second dialogue provides a regimen for the endurance of physical pain. The third book, the most important to the consolatory tradition proper, discusses the problem of *aegritudo* (distress). The most explicitly clinical of all the books, it proposes a psychiatric discipline to treat the diseases of the soul: having sanctified the medical art for the treatment of body, why has mankind been so reluctant to develop a comparable "medicina animi"?[15] The dialogue debates the question of whether the sage is vulnerable to *aegritudo* and surveys the various remedies for preventing or curing sorrow.[16] The fourth and fifth books are more general in their scope, the former examining the remaining disorders of the soul, the latter debating whether or not virtue alone can assure happiness. With its specific treatments of particular ills and with its general discussion of psychological theory, the *Tusculans* served both as a sourcebook for later consolers and as a model for subsequent theorists. In both capacities it fulfilled its promise as a systematic philosophical guide to psychological health, acting on Cicero's belief that *philosophia* "heals souls, removes vain anxieties, frees us from desires, banishes fears."[17]

The genres of the *Consolatio* and the *epistola consolatoria* (also practiced by Cicero)[18] were continued and refined by Cicero's great Stoic successor, Seneca. Sometimes railing against the uselessness of logic and natural philosophy, he stressed the importance of a useful, preceptive wisdom, one directed to the achievement of the virtuous, happy, tranquil life.[19] In his *Epistolae ad Lucilium* 94 he lauds that salutary advice that sustains, rouses, and confirms the soul; *consolatio, dissuasio, adhortatio, obiurgatio, laudatio* are the agents that effect that "perfectum animi statum."[20] In the manner of the "professional" resident philosophers retained by political and military notables in his day, even more than Cicero he activated the role of the practicing moral rhetor, offering substantive advice to friends and acquaintances.[21] His letters to Lucilius are the apex of the Roman moral letter, filled as they are with counsel and solace.[22] He also left three treatise-length consolations: the *De consolatione ad Marciam* and the *Ad Polybium*, both on bereavement, and the *Ad Helviam*, written for his mother concerning his own exile. Culling a wealth of philosophical precepts (*solacia*) and historical *exempla*, these treatises, along with Ps.-Plutarch's *Consolatio ad Apollonium*, served as the principal guides for the genre of the longer *Consolatio*.[23] Seneca's legacy as a rhetorical consoler was also assured by a work now generally thought to be pseudonymous, but considered genuine by Renaissance writers. This dialogue, the *De remediis fortuitorum*, is a spare colloquy between "Ratio" and "Sensus" on a variety of misfortunes, death in particular.[24]

Though the philosopher and the rhetorician were the principal shapers of the classical consolatory tradition, they were not the sole ones. The love poet also had an influence, particularly on the perceptions of sorrow and the genres of self-consolation. Ovid's poetry, dealing not only with lovesickness (e.g., the *Amores* and *Heroides*) but also with his own bitter exile (*Tristia* and *Ex Ponto*), offers rich literary depictions of sadness and despair. Earlier, Cicero had recognized the malady of love, offering suggestions for its cure in *Tusculans* 4.35. Ovid devoted a treatise to the subject in his *De remediis amoris*. Despite its specifically amatory focus, such literature nonetheless contributed toward a wider sensitivity to psychological experience in general.[25] In antiquity as in the Renaissance, the poetic maladies and cures of the lovesick offered a literary model for sorrow that could be applied to other types of emotional experience and healing.

As is clear from Cicero's *Consolatio* and Ovid's poetry, the classical consolatory tradition had an autobiographical strain. The culmination of this genre came in Boethius' *Consolatio philosophiae*, the most famous embodiment of the consolatory genre in the Western tradition. Imprisoned by Theodoric, Boethius wrote of his misfortune in a dialogue between himself and Lady Philosophia, who consoles him in gradual stages of psychological care. A work both of prose and verse, the dialogue harvests the therapeutic models of poetry, philosophy, rhetoric, music, and medicine, blending them to create a comprehensive regimen of healing.[26] In the course of the dialogue the specific consolation for Boethius' adversity and despair yields to more abstract discussions of happiness, good and evil, divine providence and human free will. Boethius (c. 480–524) straddled the classical and Christian worlds, and the issue of the Christian elements (or lack thereof) in the dialogue has long been a matter of discussion, from the Carolingian to the modern period.[27] Obviously suggesting that the work is more one of philosophy than theology, the title bore a secular connotation and may itself have worked toward stunting the vitality of the *consolatio* in the Christian tradition. It is noteworthy that by the fourteenth and fifteenth centuries, clerical writers such as Johannes von Dambach and Jean Gerson attempted to Christianize the genre with their works on the *Consolatio theologiae*.

In the letter, the treatise, the dialogue, the oration, the elegy, and the manual, classical philosophers, rhetors, and poets established a diverse canon of consolatory genres. In some cases they formulated a distinctly therapeutic definition of rhetoric and philosophy to respond to the assaults of Fortuna and the contingencies of mortal existence. Platonic mysticism, Stoic virtue, Academic and Peripatetic naturalism, Epicurean diversions, and Cyrenaic premeditation were among the solutions singly or jointly explored by the ancient consoler. Drawing from these fonts, classical writers and orators endeavored to heal minds of the diseases of sorrow, despair, and fear. The classical doctrines and genres of consolation in place, it was for Christian writers to adapt, correct, or ignore that tradition as they variously pondered "what Athens has to do with Jerusalem."

How did Christian thought transform the consolatory legacy? How did it view the realm of human adversity? How did Church Fathers and medieval pastors view the role of consolation? How did the priestly *cura animarum* compare to the classical cure of minds? Underlying such issues concerning Christian consolation and institutional care is a fundamentally different spiritual perception of human misery, suffering, and death. The Bible offered its own version of worldly adversity, one that assigned some meaning and function to temporal tribulation. Both the Old and New Testaments described a drama of human sorrow—even, particularly in the Psalms, Lamentations, and Job, gave distinct literary form to that drama. Judeo-Christian thought generally gave spiritual meaning to suffering in terms of both its origin and purpose. Death and suffering are just punishment for Adam's Fall. Labor and sorrow are the wages of sin, the agents of divine retribution. Worldly tribulation, moreover, can also be a vehicle for divine correction, and thus ultimately an adversity such as illness can be salutary, recalling the afflicted back to piety. In general, the earthly experience of the Christian *viator* is minimized; the future life of true beatitude, glorified. One can fairly say that the assumption that temporal existence is inevitably miserable has a more prominent place in Christian than in classical thought.

Rather than being a handmaiden to a random Fortuna, Judeo-Christian suffering serves a stern but purposeful Master. This divine scheme, moreover, is not completely without its consolations, for adversity and death are keystones in a system of redemptive suffering. The spiritual fruits of tribulation are promised in such Pauline passages as " 'power is made perfect in weakness.' . . .For the sake of Christ, then, I am content with weaknesses, insults, hardships, persecutions, and calamities; for when I am weak, then I am strong" (2 Cor. 12:9–10) and "we rejoice in our sufferings, knowing that suffering produces endurance, and endurance produces character, and character produces hope" (Rom. 5:3–4). In fact, the afflicted are among God's chosen: "For the Lord disciplines him whom he loves, and chastises every son whom he receives" (Heb. 12:6). Thus, where "pagan" adversity has only a mundane, temporal context, "spiritual" tribulation has a divine context, as a test of patience and piety. Such a concept of redemptive suffering resonates in that literature on the "tribulation of the just."[28] With his worldly losses, bereavements, and physical afflictions, Job is the archetype—if not the caricature—of Judeo-Christian suffering. A pawn in a strange, divine duel, he is nonetheless rewarded twofold for his troubles.[29] The Old Testament sorrows of Job and the New Testament Passion of Christ and the persecutions of the Church martyrs offer a powerful imagery for a vision of holy suffering.

With such a divine context for human suffering and death, what became of the specific perceptions of sorrow, its expression, and its remedy? Is temporal sorrow—a sorrow over the human condition—a fully legitimate, sanctified emotion? Paul's implicit answer was crucial to subsequent attitudes toward sadness. In 2 Corinthians 7:10 he writes of a distinction between divine and worldly sorrow: "For godly grief (*tristitia secundum Deum*) produces a repentance that leads to salvation and brings no regret, but worldly grief (*tristitia saeculi*) produces death."[30] That sorrow over sin leading to contrition is beneficial; that sorrow of the world, harmful. Such a construction not only diverts emotions of sorrow to the divine sphere— much as had been the case, for instance, in David's sorrow—but also it proscribes the realm of temporal sorrow.[31] Moreover, the expression of despair could reveal an impiety in its very suggestion of a loss of spiritual hope and belief. Among early Christian consolers a popular *locus* came from Paul's 1 Thes. 4:13, where he warns the persecuted Thessalonians: "But we would not have you ignorant, brethren, concerning those who are asleep (departed), that you may not grieve as others do who have no hope."[32] The unbelieving may have occasion for grief, but the faithful must not, given the promise of resurrection.[33] Thus, Paul largely proscribes the experience of sorrow as unbefitting the Christian.

If suffering is but the result of Adam's Fall, worldly sorrow but an unworthy emotion, tribulation but the test of piety, death but a welcome deliverance from this ephemeral earthly state, then the tenor and parameters of Christian solace must necessarily differ from those of classical consolation. Exactly how did Christian pastors and writers perceive and perform the consolatory office? If the pagan consoler forewarned of the contingency of Fortuna or tried to diminish its force, the theistic consoler was bound to explain something of God's plan. Job's miserable friends, the "first" biblical consolers, proved how dangerous a task this could be. Anti-models of the pious consoler, these bumblers became yet poor Job's last affliction with their sometimes indelicate, judgmental, and presumptuous arguments.

Not only was Job vexed by them, but so also apparently was God, who spared them punishment only because of Job's prayers. God's plan cannot be plumbed by men, neither by a Job who suffers nor by comforters who would console. The content and narrative drama of the Book of Job is a compelling argument for the futility of mortal or rational solace; one cannot justly question or explain human suffering.

Nonetheless, a tradition of Christian consolation does emerge, beginning with Paul's Epistles. Despite his caveat concerning *tristitia saeculi*, he still recognized the travails of persecuted Christians,[34] and his letters to besieged congregations not only represent a substantive effort at pastoral consolation but also recommend a type of fraternal love and care. For instance, his admonition about hopeless grief in 1 Thes. 4:13 was itself intended as a consolatory exhortation to be used as a brotherly consolation in the community: "Therefore comfort one another with these words" (4:18). More famous, and used by Christian consolers from the patristic to the early modern period, was his injunction to the Romans that they "rejoice with those who rejoice, weep with those who weep" (12:15). Moved by Paul's eloquent example and by the literary richness of the classical tradition, Greek and Roman Fathers cultivated a consolatory tradition that included the classical genres of the funeral oration, the letter, the treatise or dialogue on death, as well as the Christian genres of the sermon, the congregational letter, and the theological treatise.[35]

The potential continuity between classical and Christian consolation in patristic thought is well illustrated by Jerome, whose letter-collection offered probably the most important model for the Christian consolatory letter. Jerome wrote numerous *consolatoriae* for bereavement, including the well-known *Ad Heliodrum consolatoria* (*Epist.* 60).[36] Jerome begins this letter acknowledging Paul's warning (1 Thes. 4:13) that Christians ought not to grieve for the dead, but then admits that despite the hopeful doctrine of resurrection he nevertheless cannot restrain his sorrow.[37] His apologia for grief extended, he then offers a lengthy consolation of Christian and classical arguments and *exempla*. And despite Jerome's famous visionary divine scourging for being a "Ciceronian," this letter certainly betrays the lingering spirit of an ardent classicist. In his search for *topoi* he reveals his own wide reading in a rhetorical tradition extending back to Cicero and, earlier, to the Greeks:

> What shall we do, O my soul? Whither shall we turn? What theme shall we choose first? What shall we omit? Have you forgotten the precepts of the rhetoricians, and are you so preoccupied with grief, oppressed with tears, and hindered by sobs that you cannot keep to any ordered narrative? Where now is that love of literature which you have cherished from childhood? Where is the saying of Anaxagoras and Telamon which you always used to praise: "I

knew that I was born a mortal"? I have read Crantor, whose treatise written to comfort his own grief Cicero imitated. I have perused those minor works of Plato, Diogenes, Clitomachus, Carneades, and Posidonius, in which by book or letter they have tried at different times to lessen the sorrows of various persons and to console their grief.[38]

Jerome thus squarely placed himself in a classical tradition, one which he easily adapted to a Christian context.

Sometimes adapting classical themes, sometimes introducing distinctly new ones (e.g., resurrection),[39] sometimes offering different perspectives on the nature of suffering,[40] the patristic writers continued and Christianized the pagan tradition, leaving an important body of Christian literature that would appeal to Renaissance and early modern consolers. But despite the vitality of this consolatory tradition among the Fathers, also to be found were currents militating against a full-blown Christian recognition of sorrow. In both personal and theoretical contexts, these currents surfaced in Augustine, easily the most influential of the Fathers in the Renaissance. In his *Confessions* Augustine offers a study of his differing responses to bereavement, first as a pagan and then as a Christian. In Book 4, after the loss of a friend, he describes an excessive, indulgent sorrow, not unlike the superficial emotionalism found in classical theater and literature.[41] In Book 9, following his conversion, when he recounts the losses of two friends, his son, and, most famously, his mother, he shows a decidedly more tranquil, restrained face.[42] His grief over Monica was still great, but rather than relish it, he fought it, confined it, and he regretted it. As a Christian, Augustine acknowledged that he should know better than to lament the dead, and, when he found himself inexorably vulnerable to such human sorrow, that became itself a new source of divine sorrow: "I grieved for my grief with another grief, and I was tormented by a twofold sadness."[43] Though not using the Pauline vocabulary, Augustine perhaps reflects the view that the *tristitia saeculi*, if partly inevitable, is unbecoming to the believer. By the same token, so much of the intense emotionalism of contrition in the lachrymose *Confessions* exemplifies that salutary *tristitia secundum Deum*.[44] Certainly, for Augustine the process of conversion meant a dramatic shift in his perception and experience of grief.

Moreover, in Augustine's thought, from a theological point of view, consolation's general fate was tied to sorrow's demise. In the *De civitate Dei* 22.22, he makes a telling observation on the Christian vision of human misery and its cure. At the end of this chapter detailing the miseries of life, which have all been occasioned by the Fall,[45] he argues that consolation is not the proper domain of theology. Theology is not concerned with ministering to the fluctuations of this life, but rather with heralding the serenity of the next:

From the hell, as it were, of this miserable life no one is freed except by the grace of our Saviour Christ, our God and Lord (for his very name "Jesus" means "Saviour"). . . . For though in this life there are great consolations to be found in the cures of holy things and holy men, nevertheless even these benefits are not always granted to those who ask, lest religion be sought for their sake. Religion is rather to be sought for the sake of another life, where there will be no evils at all, and to that end even in the midst of these present evils all good men are helped by grace, so that, as they endure them with greater faith, they may find their courage so much the greater.[46]

Augustine would seem to proscribe any "consolations of theology." Human misery does not justly warrant such solace, given Adam's transgression, nor does it ultimately need it, given Christ's grace. Evils will be bravely borne only through faith. For Augustine, the nuances and labors of classical philosophy and rhetoric, which availed only a philosophical elite, are replaced by a simple vision of grace.[47] In sharp contrast to Cicero's view of a "philosophy" that "heals souls, removes vain anxieties, frees us from desires, banishes fears" stands Augustine's view here of "theology" that attends to "another life." Such a view of otherworldly theology and soteriological solace perhaps absorbed and precluded mundane concerns with particular misfortunes and comforts. Augustine's position here would suggest that a finely developed theological rhetoric of solace is largely superfluous for the Christian experience.[48]

Aside from the flurry of consolatory writings in certain patristic figures, what place did consolation generally find in the institutionalized cure of souls in the pastoral tradition? In examining Ambrose's *De officiis ministrorum*, Chrysostom's *De sacerdotio*, Gregory the Great's *Regula pastoralis*, or Isidore of Seville's *De ecclesiasticis officiis*, one does not find an expansive, detailed notion of a pastoral consolatory role.[49] There are, it is true, some general comments on the obligation to provide comfort to the afflicted and grieving. For instance, Ambrose's *De officiis* includes among the duties of friendship the obligations to sustain, console, and admonish; and Chrysostom's *De sacerdotio* cites the pastor's responsibility to "visit the sick, console the grieving, exhort the sluggish, aid the afflicted."[50] Also, the entire third book of Gregory's *Pastoral Care* contains admonitions and exhortations for a variety of moral and circumstantial conditions, though, still, the emphasis here is moral and corrective rather than consolatory.[51] Medieval pastoral literature does not yield a manual concerning the duty and method of consolation, such as that which Cicero provides in his *Tusculans* Book 3. Rather, the prevailing emphasis in medieval pastoral care was to be increasingly sacramental. The rhetorical realm of consoling, fairly strong in certain Fathers, gave way to the offices of communion, confession and penance, extreme unction. Certain of the "events" of human tragedy—namely, illness, dying, and death—were of course addressed, but in the largely ceremonial context of last rites, Requiem (and other) Masses, the Office of the Dead, vigils and prayers for the dead. These rites and offices treated human crises in a manner predominantly liturgical and formal rather than rhetorical and informal. As in the case of the Eucharist, marriage, and baptism, liturgy books and breviaries presented relatively set formulae for these situations, just as penitentials and confessors' manuals prescribed forms of penance for sin.[52]

The closest sacramental care came to dealing with the problem of despair was perhaps in the treatment of *accidia*, which became one of the seven deadly sins. This sin was long connected with *tristitia*, which, after Paul's censure of *tristitia saeculi*, was easily drawn into the net of sin. Initially a disease of the solitary, dejected, sluggish Egyptian hermit, *accidia* shared many of the psychological features of *tristitia* (such as dejection), and though, in fact, Gregory preferred *tristitia* in his battery of sins, *accidia* triumphed in the medieval canon. Moreover, despite its original psychological features, it largely became associated with the vice of sloth, its subtler emotional dimension yielding to a more banal pathology. In any event, what small place sorrow thus had in this sacramental tradition was one in which, after Paul, sadness was viewed more in a penitential and corrective framework than in a consolatory one.[53]

In a word, particularly once the penitential and sacramental tradition coalesced, medieval pastoral care did not fully cultivate the consolatory realm explored by the classical orators and moralists.[54] In spiritual sensibility, as in the practical *cura animarum*, the remedies of sin took precedence over the remedies of sorrow (itself linked to sin). The identity of the pastor as healer and consoler focused on that contritional sorrow and guilt.[55] Even the connotation of the term "consolation" perhaps partially shifted, as is illustrated in a title such as that given to Johannes Nider's (d. 1438) manual for confessors, the *Consolatorium timoratae conscientiae*.[56] By the high Middle Ages, literary currents colluded with institutional ones in the hardening of an ascetic temper reified in the emergence of the genre of the *contemptus mundi*, most famously represented by Innocent III's late twelfth-century treatise, the *De miseria humanae conditionis*.[57] Such a *contemptus* concerning the miseries of fallen man obviously militated against a "classical" sympathy for the misfortunes of worldly experience. *Tristitia saeculi* contemned, medieval theological and pastoral attention focused on that worthier *tristitia secundum Deum*.[58]

In reclaiming and relegitimating the domain of worldly sorrow, Trecento and Quattrocento humanists drew upon or reacted to these various psychological and spiritual traditions of the classical, patristic, and medieval period. A writer such as Petrarch was alive to various constructions of sorrow, misery, and psychological health articulated by figures such as Cicero, Ovid, Seneca, Boethius, Paul, Ambrose, Augustine, and Innocent. But aside from the major philosophical, theological, sacramental, and ascetic traditions, there were also other currents that anticipated or shaped the early Renaissance tradition founded by Petrarch and Coluccio Salutati: namely, the French protohumanism and Italian dictaminal, grammatical, and literary interests in the twelfth and thirteenth centuries.

As in the patristic period, so also in the "renaissance of the twelfth century," classical interests spawned a body of consolatory literature. In the case of the French cleric Hildebert of Lavardin (d. 1133), for instance, such writings included elegaic poetry on others' deaths and on his own adversity, a Boethian-like dialogue titled *Liber de querimonia et conflictu carnis et spiritus seu animae*, and a dabbling in the genre of the consolatory letter.[59] A more prominent figure was Peter of Blois, whose influence was assured by a popular letter-collection that has survived in over 200 manuscripts.[60] Peter was unusual in that, unlike other well-known letter writers who preceded him (e.g., Ivo of Chartres, Hildebert, Bernard of Clairvaux, John of Salisbury, Abelard), in the 1180s he organized and revised his collection.[61] Highly humanistic, the letters cite Seneca's letters and the works of such figures as Cicero, Quintilian, and Jerome. The collection includes numerous *consolatoriae* for bereavement,[62] as well as letters on illness, exile, and general hardship and affliction.[63] One theme surfacing in Peter's letters is that of the duty of the friend to be compassionate.[64] His larger interest in the *topos* of friendship is evident in his two-part treatise *De amicitia christiana et de dilectione Dei et proximi*, a work inspired by (and partly pilfered from) Aelred of Riveaulx's treatises *Speculum charitatis* and *De amicitia spirituali*.[65] Such writings on friendship reflect a blending of Cicero's notion of friendship in the *De amicitia* with Christian views of *caritas*.[66] Moreover, this heightened interest in friendship naturally led to a greater concern with both grief (as in the case of Laelius' for Scipio Aemilianus in Cicero's treatise)[67] and the social duty of consolation. In Peter as later in Salutati particularly, the consolatory impulse was fueled by such a social ethos.[68] Besides his letters, Peter also wrote a general work on adversity, the *De duodecim utilitatibus tribulationis*. This treatise assembled various Judeo-Christian assumptions concerning suffering (e.g., that tribulation is purging, that God castigates those whom He loves), citing of course the case of Job,[69] whose suffering Peter also discussed elsewhere in a discrete treatise.[70]

A growing interest in consolatory genres was also emerging in the rhetorical, grammatical, and literary culture of high medieval Italy. Kristeller first recognized the importance of the Italian *dictatores* as forerunners— even, as medieval analogues—to certain of the Renaissance humanists.[71] The roots of the *ars dictaminis* are found in the late eleventh century in the writings of the Benedictine cleric Alberico of Montecassino, and a strong tradition was established in Bologna by figures such as Hugo of Bologna. Closely tied to the notarial profession, the dictaminal art gained an important place in the administrative life of Italian cities. *Dictatores* served as professional rhetoricians for communal, princely, and ecclesiastical chanceries.[72]

In the thirteenth century such figures as Boncompagno da Signa, Guido Faba, Thomas of Capua, and Matteo de' Libri composed dictaminal manuals, which contained, among their treatments of epistolary genres, discussions of the consolatory letter.[73] For instance, Boncompagno, a leading Bolognese *dictator* and teacher, devoted a chapter of the first book of his manual, the *Rhetorica antiqua* (1215), to a discussion of consolation. This chapter, the "De consolationibus," contains 35 sections on the theory and practice of proffering solace.[74] He provides advice and *loci* for general and specific situations of bereavement;[75] he discusses the proper time for giving solace;[76] he reflects upon the nature and legitimacy of emotion;[77] he gives *exempla* of those who have borne loss with measured emotion or with calm;[78] he discusses those who do not require consolation;[79] he addresses other problems besides death (i.e., leprosy, blindness, mutilation); he treats the response to the *consolatoria*.[80] Though many of these sections are quite brief, such discussions illustrate how the dictaminal tradition addressed not only the mechanics of public correspondence but also, in a rudimentary manner, certain issues concerning emotional experience. In his treatment of weeping, for example, Boncompagno offers some fairly specific physiological and psychological observations. He cautions that excessive weeping, that "beyond the natural humor," can impair vision by blocking the optic nerve, and he argues that it is foolish "to weep excessively, because through immoderate grief many are made odious to God, feeling is lost, and human bodies are desiccated."[81] He also warns, however, of the danger of those who are unable to weep, suggesting that "when tears are kept inside, the soul is burdened with an indescribable weight and its actions are befuddled, whence in either case man is easily undone."[82] In his function as a rhetorician, Boncompagno thus was not merely a guide to proper epistolary style but also a source, if only a superficial one, of psychological theory.[83] As for the general tenor of that theory, Boncompagno's reliance on Christian themes is marked, while his *loci* make virtually no explicit use of classical sources[84]—though, in fact, Boncompagno's interest in Cicero's moral thought may well have heightened his general concern with the social duty and the psychological challenge of consolation.[85] As Boncompagno's treatise makes clear, the writings of the medieval *dictator* had a relevance beyond the courts, chanceries, and bureaucracies. His chapter "On Consolations" potentially spoke to a wider audience, offering guidelines for a general rhetoric of social discourse.[86]

Aside from the preceptive consolation in the rhetoric manuals, a more literary interest in consolation was also to be found in high medieval Italian culture, as can be seen in Arrigo da Settimello's (or Henricus Septimellensis, Henricus Pauper) *Elegia de diversitate fortunae et philosophiae consolatione*.[87] The poem was written in the 1190s by a Tuscan cleric who, apparently falling on hard times, may have intended the work to be self-consolatory.[88] A lament of misfortune, the first two books of the *Elegia* present a doleful dialogue between Arrigo and the goddess Fortuna; the last two his consolation by a lady (Philosophy). The classical tradition in which Arrigo places himself is well illustrated in the third book, when his consoler recalls to him the *exempla* of Seneca, Ovid, and Boethius, who similarly suffered misfortune.[89] This work, drawing widely from the Roman poets, is noteworthy not only for its Boethian genre, but also for its ostensible influence in the schools. In his *De origine civitatis Florentiae et eiusdem famosis civibus* (c. 1381–82), Filippo Villani remarked that the work was popular as a grammar primer.[90] Equally important, it was translated into Italian prose twice in the Trecento, and in this Tuscan version also was used as a literary textbook.[91] The currency of both the Latin and *volgare* versions assured that this work was an important predecessor to and possible influence on Petrarch's development of the Boethian genre in the *Secretum*.[92]

The twelfth- and thirteenth-century figures of Hildebert of Levardin, Peter of Blois, Boncompagno, and Arrigo exemplify how medieval protohumanism and rhetorical developments in some measure presaged the interests of Trecento consolers. As the writings of Petrarch, Salutati, and their successors make clear, however, these medieval currents were not merely furthered but transformed by the humanists' deeper classical revival, their more individualistic development of rhetorical genres, their more searching interest in the psychological domain. Moreover, in their exploration of the emotional realm, fourteenth- and fifteenth-century humanists dramatically expanded the legitimate bounds of worldly sorrow. Heirs to a variegated psychological and spiritual legacy from the ancient, patristic, and medieval world, they significantly readjusted the cultural balance between *tristitia saeculi* and *tristitia secundum Deum*. The origins, nuances, and complexities of that readjustment are most apparent in the thought of Petrarch, the architect of the Renaissance consolatory tradition. In his many guises as love poet, classicist, orator, moralist, letter-writer, minor cleric, penitent, and brother to a monk, he drew on a range of literary, intellectual, spiritual, and institutional traditions. He was to refract the shifting light of those traditions into an ever-clearer vision of consolation and rhetorical healing.

1

PETRARCH AS SELF-CONSOLER

THE *SECRETUM*

IN LETTERS to friends, in an exhortation to his cowled brother, in an interior dialogue with himself, in a manual for others, Petrarch broadly formulated for himself a special role as a consoler and rhetorical healer. His versatility in fulfilling this role makes him quite unlike his classical and medieval predecessors: his efforts as a consoler transcend genre and signify a more pervasive concern to become a *medicus animorum*, caring for the variety of ills besetting private and public man. By the time he completed his major consolatory treatise, the *De remediis utriusque fortune*, Petrarch had achieved an integrated vision both of the task of the verbal healer and of the language of therapeutic *oratio*. Exactly how and when he came to formulate this role is difficult to determine: his penchant for revising earlier letters and treatises defies the construction of a sure chronology of his thought. But *why* he formulated this role can more readily be explored, and can lead us to the center of Petrarch's endeavors as a moral philosopher and rhetorician. At the same time, it takes us to the heart of one of the principal contexts of the emergence of humanist moral thought.

In staking out a new territorial domain as a *medicus animorum*, Petrarch drew on several therapeutic archetypes of ancient and medieval culture: the remedies of the love poet, the consolations of the philosopher, the admonitions of the priest, and the salves of the doctor. Now in literal, now in figurative terms, strains from all these traditions find their way into Petrarch's vision of healing wisdom. Sometimes the influence of these earlier models is explicit and direct. Other times it is implicit or even, in some cases, antithetical, as when Petrarch sharpens his own therapeutic role in contradistinction to others he finds flawed or insufficient. Whichever the case, Petrarch's experimentation with varieties of *consolatio* and *remedium* is a significant Renaissance formulation of the therapeutic potential of moral wisdom and rhetoric. In this and the two following chapters we shall examine the form and content of Petrarch's many consolatory writings, with an eye toward establishing his larger view of remedial wisdom and the broader cultural implications of that view.[1]

Petrarch spent the first years of his life in Provence, where his father, in exile, had followed the Papal Court. Studying law at Montpellier and Bologna, he became devoted instead to letters and turned to a life of literature, in the 1320s beginning his study of the Latin classics and dabbling in Italian verse. A legal career abandoned, Petrarch turned to a type of clerical life: presumably taking the tonsure and possibly even minor orders, he availed himself of the opportunities of minor benefices. In 1330 he was appointed "household chaplain" of Cardinal Giovanni Colonna, a position he held on and off for seventeen years. Later he would receive a variety of benefices as canon, rector, or, archdeacon—holding these offices partly or fully in absentia. Not wishing (and technically ineligible) to assume the full pastoral duties of the *cura animarum*, he refused the offers of a bishopric.[2] His true career, of course, was his life as a poet, scholar, orator, and moral philosopher. Through the patronage of individual clerics or laymen and through the support of ecclesiastical sinecures, Petrarch was virtually free to be Petrarch, the famous poet and intellectual he quickly became. Certainly by the time of his invitations to receive laurel crowns in Rome and Paris in 1340, he could readily trade on his renown. The cost for him personally, however, would be the travails of such an impermanent and itinerant existence: the shuttling back and forth between benefices and patrons. But it was also the very nature of that sometimes precarious existence that must have deepened his investment in the surer world of study and writing.[3]

The ambiguity of Petrarch's vocation is perhaps central to our understanding of his cultural and social perspectives, his professional rivalries, and his subtle roles. He certainly internalized the competitive climate of the arts and disciplines of his day. He was enough of a lawyer to hate doctors. He was more than enough of a poet to contemn both of these. Finally, he was enough of a cleric and monk *manqué* to doubt the worth of any of these lay stations. Petrarch's "calling" was to be a new type of pious intellectual, giving cultural sanctity to the worlds of Roman moral thought, Tuscan poetry, and latter-day rhetoric, yet also sometimes painfully aware of the traditional spiritual limitations of secular endeavor. It was the nebulous and fluid character of Petrarch's professional and cultural role that allowed his remarkable synthesis of traditions and pieties. And it is that synthesis that evokes so many of the scholarly clichés about Petrarch: that he bridged the worlds "medieval" and "Renaissance," clerical and lay, spiritual and literary, penitential and poetic.

By virtue of his spanning these realms Petrarch forged new perspectives concerning the nature of the human psyche. One of his great contributions was his redefining of the categories of psychological health, both for himself and for others. Fusing poetic experience with other types of moral and spiritual experience, Petrarch moved beyond the formerly somewhat compartmentalized psychological worlds of the poet, philosopher, priest, and penitent. The result was a new outlook not only on the general psychology of human emotion, but also on the specific challenges posed by the human condition: particularly those of misery, illness, and death.

Certainly by the time of his writing *Fam.* 1.9 (in 1350),[4] Petrarch had established in his own mind the intimate connection between eloquence and moral health. In this letter fictionally addressed to Tommaso da Messina, Petrarch sets out a definition of eloquence, which begins by suggesting a link between the domains of moral philosophy and rhetoric: "The care of the mind calls for a philosopher, while the proper use of language requires an orator."[5] Language is not only the window on our own moral condition but also the social medium of moral exchange and influence. Through the "word," the orator instills virtue in contemporaries and in posterity. But even if the social value of the humanistic word should not inspire the study of eloquence, the private value must. For Petrarch, the written, spoken, and contemplative word is the true medicine for self-healing:

> I cannot tell you what worth are to me in solitude certain familiar and famous words not only grasped in the mind but actually spoken orally, words with which I am accustomed to rouse my sleepy thoughts. Furthermore, how much delight I get from repeating the written words either of others or sometimes even my own! How much I feel myself freed from very serious and bitter burdens by such readings! Meantime I feel my own writings assisted me even more since they are more suited to my ailments, just as the sensitive hand of a doctor who is himself ill is placed more readily where he feels the pain to be. Such cure I shall certainly never accomplish unless the salutary words (*verba ipsa salutaria*) fall tenderly upon my ears.[6]

It is revealing that in this, Petrarch's most direct definition of eloquence, the therapeutic purpose of rhetoric is stressed. Moreover, for Petrarch the "word" is the principal catalyst of a self-therapeutic regimen. Petrarch is deservedly famous for his capacity for introspection. His concern to know and cure the maladies of his own mind is the cornerstone for all his other efforts as a *medicus animorum*. Thus, it is with his efforts at self-healing that we must begin.

Petrarch's first literary experiences with psychological introspection were poetic. Like Ovid and Dante before him, he learned the habit of subjectivity through love poetry, where descriptions of lovesickness accustomed him to a pattern of emotional self-examination. As Ovid's *Metamorphoses* showed, the suffering of the lovesick could be literally transforming, and the bittersweet sorrow of the smitten could become comfortable and even nourishing: "Cura dolorque animi, lacrimaeque alimenta fuere"

(10.75).[7] Moreover, the cultivation of romantic grief could be tied to and even reified by poetic expression. Dante would make this plain, as he chronicled his own suffering in his *La vita nuova*, alternating metrical laments with a prose analysis of the anatomy of the lovesick poet. Like those of his predecessors, Petrarch's verses show him also feeding on tears, sighs, and swoons, indulging the pleasant pain of romantic longing.[8] The purpose and process of his poetry concerning Laura is the expression of a *voluptas dolendi*.[9]

Longing, however, was not the only source of Petrarch's grief. The habit of suffering formed in his love poetry extended to several types of emotional and spiritual experience, most immediately the torments of bereavement and the fear of death. In particular, the loss of Laura and several friends in the Black Death in 1348–49 plunged Petrarch into the cataclysm of the sorrows and horrors of death. In both Latin meters and Italian verse he followed the same regimen as the lovesick poet.[10] The sweet sorrow of writing has an effect that is at once wrenching and therapeutic. In the *Eclogue* 11, for instance, literary guise only thinly veils Petrarch's own fresh grief over Laura. When "Furca" asks a grieving "Niobe" why she willingly chooses the "lacrimis alimenta," Niobe's answer is that only this is the proper medicine for grief:

> Weeping is great comfort for a grave grief,
> sighs and laments relieve an afflicted soul.
> Contained grief destroys the mind;
> the greatest medicine for a sad heart is to weep openly.[11]

Likewise, in prose, several of the *Familiares* and other letters describe his grief over the death of friends. Confessing his need to exorcize his sorrow with writing and weeping, he sometimes used his letters as opportunities for literary catharsis—in one case (*Fam.* 4.10) even announcing tentative plans (never realized) for an entire treatise of self-consolation for a recent loss.[12] *Fam.* 7.12 charts his emotional experience in such a bereavement, portraying a despairing Petrarch's struggle with the conflicting demands of emotion and reason:

> Shall I indulge in tears and sighs and in place of my lost friend shall I embrace my sorrow incessantly? Or shall I strive to appease my mind and to escape from the echoing threats of fortune into the stronghold of reason? The latter appears preferable, the former more pleasing; virtue drives me to one; feeling bends me to the other.[13]

Emotion, it would seem, triumphed. At the end of this letter of plangent outpourings Petrarch exclaims: "But alas I am now proving what I read in Statius: 'Speaking is sweet to those in misery' [*Theb.* 5.48]. It is certainly so, for how many things did I, unawares, pour forth impetuously rather than through rational judgment!"[14] And, indeed, more than once, Petrarch's mourning sought escape in "sweet grief" and literary expression.[15]

Beyond longing, bereavement, and fear, Petrarch broadened the parameters of his self-healing to embrace larger problems of spiritual sickness and worldly despair.[16] It is, of course, in his *Secretum*, a three-day dialogue between himself and his divine "physician" Augustine, that he undertakes the most prolonged analysis and treatment of his soul. In this powerful work Petrarch first began to transform and reintegrate the disparate psychological strains in classical and medieval thought.[17] Delineating various layers of his maladies of mind and spirit, the dialogue most generally depicts Petrarch's guilt, but also sorrow, over his vulnerability to the vicissitudes of the *saeculum*. The dating of the work continues to be a subject of great debate. Though Petrarch's comments in the dialogue would suggest a fictive date of 1342–43, scholarly opinion is now justifiably leaning toward a later period of 1347–53.[18] This latter date would put the writing of the dialogue after an important moment in Petrarch's spiritual life: his brother's entrance into a Carthusian monastery in 1343. The magnitude of this event is reflected in several of Petrarch's writings, most explicitly in the *De otio religioso* and the "Ascent of Mt. Ventoux" (*Fam.* 4.1), and perhaps implicitly in the *Psalmi penitentiales* and the *De vita solitaria*.[19] It is not to our purposes here to try to solve the dating question concerning the *Secretum*, but suffice it to say that the dialogue was very likely written after Gherardo took the cowl, and that this fact partly explains the work's spiritual drama and its ascetic currents. Regardless, however, of whether Gherardo was the catalyst or not, Petrarch's crisis in the dialogue largely revolved around his concern to recognize and to heal his spiritual maladies. In doing so, he turns partially from a poetic model of healing to a penitential one, though, as we shall see, in a uniquely modified way.

Much of the historical importance of the *De secreto conflictu curarum mearum* lies in the ambiguity of its genre. Interestingly, various manuscripts and early printed editions of the work title it as a *contemptus mundi*.[20] That this dialogue would be thus categorized is understandable and somewhat justified: proclaiming the misery and vanity of the *saeculum*, the treatise does portray Christian scorn for the temporal realm. But unlike Innocent III's *De contemptu mundi, seu de miseria humanae conditionis*, the dialogue is also subjective and confessional. Though taking a markedly different tack, Petrarch is Augustine's successor in fashioning the genre of spiritual autobiography. But more than a *contemptus*, a *confessio*, and an autobiography, the dialogue is also a *consolatio*. It is this consolatory context of the *Secretum* that needs to be more fully elucidated. Both the general clinical framework of the dialogue and aspects of Petrarch's despair in the second book make the work a remarkable, almost contradictory fusion of *contemptus* and *conso-*

latio.[21] This ambiguity is perhaps partly revealed in the language of the title, where Petrarch settles on the term *"conflictus."* Besides presenting confession and self-consolation, Petrarch's dialogue describes a conflict between the spiritual and the secular man, a conflict not fully resolved even by the dialogue's end. The *Secretum*'s grounding in a tradition of *conflictus* literature needs further study.[22] Though Petrarch takes the genre much further, he may have been influenced by Hildebert of Lavardin's *De querimonia et conflictu carnis et spiritus seu animae*.[23] For Petrarch, the "conflict of his cares" might have been mirrored in his attempt to contemn worldly vicissitudes as he simultaneously sought to cure them with secular consolations.

The dialogue depicts Petrarch's (Franciscus') encounter with the figures of Veritas and Augustinus, who appear before him in a vision as he reflects on the nature of his life. His principal sources for this motif were Augustine's *Soliloquies* and Boethius' *Consolation of Philosophy*.[24] The motif of healing, found only partly in the former, he drew chiefly from the latter, in which Lady Philosophy engages the imprisoned Boethius to cure him of his despair. In the *Secretum*, Veritas brings in Augustinus, that "most excellent healer of passions he himself has experienced."[25] Because of his interest in classical thought, because of his own prolonged conflict over secular and spiritual concerns, Augustine is the perfect doctor for Petrarch. However, Petrarch makes of Augustinus an unusual and syncretic physician, ministering not only spiritual admonitions but also secular comforts.[26]

The dialogue moves from a general to a more specific treatment of Petrarch's maladies. In Book 1 Augustinus prescribes as a regimen for Franciscus' spiritual health an effective meditation on death and a true desire to rise from the earthly to the eternal. But he observes that Franciscus is held back from doing this by a weak will—similar to his own weak will prior to his conversion in the *Confessions*, a failing that reflected the dominance of secular over spiritual interests.[27] Augustinus further ventures the diagnosis that Franciscus' inability to meditate meaningfully is caused by an overload of sensual distractions, and Book 2 explores these worldly encumbrances, narrowing in on Petrarch's own particular moral and psychological afflictions. The final book concentrates on Franciscus' most serious spiritual ills, the vanities of love and glory arising from his poetic devotion to Laura and his classical quest for fame. The *Secretum*, then, portrays Petrarch's mortal, volitional weakness as "Everyman" (Book 1), his particular sins as a Christian penitent (Book 2), and his special temptations as a poet and celebrity (Book 3).[28] As a healer, Augustinus must move deftly between spiritual, moral, and emotional realms. Petrarch thus uses his fictitious physician to integrate several different types of healing.

The strains of the *contemptus* tradition are particularly noticeable in Book 1.[29] In this book, as in the dialogue as a whole, Petrarch outlines a spiritual and philosophical notion of health that calls for a scorning of the corporeal sphere. The idea of contemning the sensual and ascending to the divine is largely Platonic, or Ciceronian and Augustinian adaptations of Platonic thought.[30] In his stress on the eternal, Augustinus recommends the benefits of the meditation on death. And though the *meditatio mortis* is a familiar classical and Christian regimen, Petrarch's development of it here also suggests the influence of the more recent medieval flowering of the macabre.[31] Exploiting the graphic sensibility of the *memento mori*, Petrarch's Augustinus advises that a fruitful meditation on death can best be achieved through a frightful reflection on the *dying* with ". . . eyes sunken and weeping, every look filled with tears, the forehead pale and drawn, the cheeks drooping, the teeth yellowed, the nostrils stiff and pointed, the lips foaming" and so forth (in vivid detail).[32] There is a sure test whether this medicine takes effect, properly penetrating the psyche:

> [I]f in the act of meditation you find yourself suddenly grow stiff, if you tremble, turn pale, and feel as if you already have endured its pains; if, together with this, you imagine that your soul, immediately upon leaving its body, must appear before the eternal judge and must render an exact account of your whole past life, your actions, and your words, where you could have no hope of wit, eloquence, wealth, power, good looks, or worldly glory; . . . then you may be assured you have not meditated in vain.[33]

The medieval tradition of the *contemptus mundi* certainly must have provided an important source for Petrarch here. For instance, Innocent III's *De miseria humanae conditionis* used the motif of death's horrors—and, in particular, the theme of bodily putrefaction. And the tie between death and misery, fundamental in Innocent's work, is also central in Augustinus' regimen for Franciscus, which is initially characterized as a "meditatio mortis humaneque miserie."[34] In general the austere and threatening tenor of the ascetic attitude toward human life and death had a strong impact on Petrarch's thought. Not only the literary *contemptus*, but also monastic ritual seems to have influenced him, as Augustinus remarks on the institutionalization of a death-meditation:

> [I]n certain religious orders of the stricter kind, there has survived even down to our own time (which is so corrupt) the custom of allowing the members to watch the bodies of the dead being washed and put in shrouds for their burial, clearly so that the sad and lamentable spectacle placed before their eyes may be a memorable warning and may frighten the minds of the survivors from holding any hope in fleeting worldly things.[35]

Besides drawing on the medieval *memento mori*, Petrarch also turns to ancient thought, complementing the emotional excesses of the ascetic tradition with more dispassionate philosophical and poetic notions of death and temporality. This is particularly marked in the third book, in which

Augustinus tries to cure Franciscus of his vanities of love and glory. Against the allures of love he urges reflections on death, the shortness of life, and the passage of time. For the cure of glory he recommends, even against Franciscus' objections, the benefits of a recognition of worldly ephemerality (as found in *Dream of Scipio*), and he cites various other sentiments from Cicero and the Roman poets, closing with the cardinal maxim popularized in the *Tusculans* (1.30.74, from the *Phaedo* 67e) that "a wise man's life is a meditation on death."[36] To guide the ailing Franciscus in his ascent to the eternal, Augustinus thus joins to the frightful reflections of the *memento mori* these calmer musings of the *meditatio mortis*. The thought of death is thus fully a "remedy" in the *Secretum*. As we shall see later, however, Petrarch could also view death as a "malady" itself.

Having posed a regimen for the defects of the soul and will, Petrarch ends Book 1 by discussing the role of sensuality in this vision of spiritual psychology. He cites as a hindrance the distractions of the emotions, drawing on the notion of the fourfold assault of "desire," "pleasure," "fear," and "grief," which will be the underlying psychological scheme of the *De remediis*.[37] Book 2 then proceeds with an analysis of Petrarch's susceptibility to worldly vices and ills. Augustinus the physician now loosely assumes the role of the confessor, as he probes Franciscus' soul for the seven deadly sins. Between the time of the historical Augustine and that of the Petrarchan Augustinus, one can readily see the impact of developments in pastoral care—in particular, the coalescing of the traditional sin list. It is against this paradigm of spiritual health that Petrarch now measures himself.[38] Pausing substantively over the sins of pride (his hubris concerning his learning and eloquence) and avarice (to which is linked his vice of ambition), Petrarch moves through the list until he reaches a final sin: "the plague of the mind which moderns call '*accidia*' and which the ancients call '*aegritudo*.'"[39] In his discussion of *accidia-aegritudo* Petrarch constructs a timely formulation of despair, which draws not only on medieval moral theology and ancient moral philosophy, but also on modern poetic sensibility and personal experience. In this dramatic treatment of dejection Petrarch ventures out from the traditional territory of pastoral thought and care into a new area of secular psychology; Franciscus, appropriately, ventures from the realm of spiritual physician to the domain of secular consoler. In studying this malady we can begin to understand the genesis of the humanist revival of worldly sorrow.

In defining his affliction Petrarch draws upon the ancient malady of *aegritudo* and the medieval sin of *accidia*, though his despair conforms fully to neither.[40] One of the four affects in Stoic thought, *aegritudo* received its most extensive treatment in Cicero's *Tusculans* Book 3, certainly the principal single source for Petrarch's psychological theory.[41] Cicero discusses *aegritudo*'s many faces of grief, solicitude, anxiety, and vexation, dealing

chiefly with the problem of bereavement. *Accidia* is a much more complicated term. It is the deadly sin, and the part of Christian psychology that,
along with its sister sin *tristitia*, most approximated depression and melancholy.[42] As S. Wenzel argues, although *accidia* has been popularly associated with the mere vice of sloth, its history reveals a malady that had
spiritual and psychological dimensions. First codified by the Greek hermit
Evagrius Ponticus, *accidia* reflected problems endemic to the ascetic life in
fourth-century Egypt, namely, dejection and restlessness. Cassian included
accidia in his codification of the deadly sins and closely aligned it with the
sin of *tristitia*. Gregory the Great dropped it from the list of sins, using
instead the related sin *tristitia*. Cassian's *accidia*, however, survived in the
canon and by the late twelfth century *accidia* and *tristitia* were fused. Because the sin had eremitical origins, it was largely a monastic malady up
through the twelfth century. Yet attempts to "laicize" the disease began in
the eighth and ninth centuries, and in its confessional treatment *accidia*
became routinely associated with sloth, though more psychological views
of the sin could also be found, including scholastic interpretations of it as
a spiritual "tristitia de bono divino" and as a type of dangerous sorrow
concerning worldly things.[43]

Aspects of both the causes and the symptoms of Petrarch's malady expand the bounds of despair or dejection found in ancient *aegritudo* or medieval *accidia*. First, the pathology of Petrarch's disease appears to heighten
the emotional intensity of depression. After describing to Augustinus the
severity and duration of his bouts with despair, he ends by claiming that
the worst feature of his fits is that he finds a morbid pleasure in his grief:
"But, what one may call the climax of miseries is that I feed upon my tears
and sufferings with a morbid attraction (*atra quadam cum voluptate*), so
that I can only be rescued from them unwillingly."[44] And thus as Petrarch
transferred emotional patterns of lovesickness to the experience of bereavement, so also he grafts them onto a general experience of despair. That
lovesickness is indeed Petrarch's model here in Book 2 of the *Secretum* is
confirmed in Book 3, in which Augustinus describes Franciscus' bouts with
lovesickness in terms of the same "morbid pleasure (*funesta . . . voluptas*) in
feeding on tears and sighs."[45] In unifying these types of emotional experience Petrarch was breaking important ground in the history of ideas and
emotion. In fusing "love sorrow" with "life sorrow" he introduced possibilities for philosophers, literati, and theologians to explore more fully the
anatomy of sorrow. It is no accident that the great compendium of early
modern melancholy, Robert Burton's *Anatomy of Melancholy* (1621), has a
major section on love melancholy alongside those on humoral, circumstantial, and religious melancholy.[46] Petrarch, however, eschews the term melancholy, using it neither in his vernacular poetic works nor in the Latin
moral ones. In so avoiding the term in his philosophical works, he followed
the lead of Cicero, who essentially rejected it as a useful psychological con-

cept.[47] The fact remains, however, that just as "love melancholy" and "general melancholy" have some connection in late medieval and early modern culture, so also do Petrarch's "love despair" and "life despair."[48]

Just as the pathology of Petrarch's depression is revealing, so also is its etiology. Franciscus claims that his misery is caused by the continuous attacks of fortune. This general complaint, following as it does Augustine's treatment of Petrarch's vainglorious attachment to the blandishments of his life, essentially establishes in this work a framework parallel to that found later in the *De remediis*. In bewailing fortune's assaults, Petrarch could have drawn on various ancient models, most notably Boethius' *Consolation of Philosophy*.[49] In Franciscus' complaints about life and fortune, however, one finds a certain "existential" depth not so explicitly articulated in classical moral thought. That is, at times Petrarch refers to a general despair of life which is drawn less from the ancient philosophical tradition than from medieval religious thought. References to the *"conditionis humane miseria"* and the *"humane conditionis odium atque contemptus"* reveal the influence of the ascetic genre of the *contemptus mundi*.[50] Later, as we shall see in Chapter 3 below, Petrarch would return to treat this existential pessimism in the *De remediis*. But for now it is important to see how Franciscus' misery over fortune quickly turns to specific problems and woes.

As Wenzel argues, Petrarch completes the process of *accidia*'s laicization, richly endowing it with a despair concerning his earthly life and circumstances.[51] The problems on which Petrarch dwells are strikingly secular: his failure to fulfill his desires and goals in life, his dependence on other people, his distress over city life.[52] In highly personal terms, then, Petrarch reintroduces worldly causes of grief and sadness, portraying a type of secular sadness of the world.[53] Moreover, his complaints reflect the harsher trials of his secular life, just as "love" and "glory" reflect the cardinal sins of his spiritual life.[54] Petrarch is giving voice not merely to the generic plight of temporal life, but also, in the spirit of Boethius, to the specific problems of his own mundane experience. Such concerns of personal frustration and discontent represent a significant development in the realm of psychological theory: worldly experience and sadness enter the clinical domain of fourteenth-century thought.

Franciscus laments that he has never attained even a mediocre position in life, never gained a sense of security, autonomy, and tranquility.[55] To this worldly complaint concerning "career" Augustinus, now consoler more than pastor, offers an equally secular solace: Franciscus should compare his situation to that of the many less fortunate around him and see his dependence, obligations, and poverty in the larger perspective of the lot of mankind.[56] Franciscus' grumblings concerning urban life reflect Petrarch's moral and psychological preference for the contemplative, solitary life.[57] He presents a vivid picture of the malaise of the city: noise, filth, disease, the juxtaposition of poor and rich. And though this urban contagion is

disparaged elsewhere in somewhat "moral" terms (as a source of temptation for Petrarch's "cupidity" and ambition),[58] here it is condemned largely
in "environmental" terms. The mundane, cloying annoyances of city life
foster in Franciscus the "tedium and daily disgust of my life."[59] Augustinus
counsels Franciscus that even if he must endure the unsuitable milieu of the
city, even if he must live in the midst of such sensual chaos, he nonetheless
should maintain mental composure. To achieve this equanimity Franciscus
might find therapeutic such sources as Seneca's *Ad Lucilium* 56 and *De
tranquillitate animi* and Cicero's *Tusculans* Book 3, which treats "mentis
egritudo."[60] He also urges that Franciscus in general begin to collect a mental store of such salutary readings, so that he may have on hand remedies
for any passions and maladies that might arise.[61]

At heart, Augustinus' consolations are nearly as secular as Franciscus'
despair. His solutions are not those of spiritual *contemptus*, but generally
those of worldly rhetoric and reflection. Not only does he recommend certain readings and collected maxims as an antidote for despair,[62] but also, in
his closing, he again urges the benefits of temporal comparisons, promising
Franciscus that, if he will examine his own lot and that of others, he will see
the many joys that balance the sorrows of his life.[63] Significantly, it is the
solace of worldly comparison that seems to have comforted Franciscus the
most, for he finally admits "your warning has profited me so much that,
comparing myself to the greater part of mankind, I find my condition not
to be so miserable as it seemed."[64]

Petrarch's discussion of secular frustrations and circumstances has considerable importance. Along lines similar to Seneca's counsel for Serenus in
the *De tranquillitate animi* and to Boethius' consolations for fortune, Petrarch reintroduces the worldly dimensions of despair. In particular, his
dejection bespeaks his life as a poet and humanist. His literary career was
one that persistently demanded unhappy compromises with poverty, dependence, and urban life. As a therapeutic treatment of the subjective ills
of earthly lot, Petrarch's discussion of his despair is matched only by Boethius'.

In the case of both symptoms and causes, then, Petrarch deepens the
contemporary "clinical" view of the malady of despair. In terms of symptoms he grafts emotional poetic experience onto a wider, vaguer experience
of dejection. In terms of causes, he fuses and possibly expands the ancient
and medieval categories of despair. On the one hand, he perhaps deepens
classical notions of *aegritudo* with the existential pessimism of the medieval
ascetic tradition.[65] On the other hand, he expands the medieval bounds of
accidia (and *tristitia*) with secular dimensions not fully explored in Christian thought.

The discussion of *accidia-aegritudo* reveals how Petrarch's dialogue can
shift from the realm of sacred admonition to that of secular solace. Au-

gustinus moves from the role of spiritual physician to that of philosophical consoler.[66] Not only, then, the general clinical framework of the *Secretum*, but also the specific problem of the consolation for personal misfortune recalls Boethius' *Consolation of Philosophy*. In Augustinus' treatment of his despair, Petrarch turns the *Secretum* from a *contemptus* into a *consolatio*.

If Petrarch was true to Boethius' spirit in the *Secretum*, could he also be true to Augustine's? Only partly. Like Augustine, he portrays the conflict between competing secular and spiritual wills. Unlike Augustine, his struggles seem to endure in a lingering *conflictus* rather than end in a conversion.[67] More importantly, Petrarch has taken Augustine's model of spiritual autobiography and charged it with strikingly secular perspectives in the treatment of personal sorrow and misfortune. In some measure, he has turned Augustine's spiritual tears to secular laments, his *tristitia secundum Deum* to a *tristitia saeculi*. Though voicing many of the spiritual pieties concerning worldly misery, *contemptus*, and the *meditatio mortis*, and though using the framework of temporal vanities and the seven deadly sins, Petrarch nonetheless makes an innovative effort to secularize the psychological perspectives of pastoral care. His syncretic *accidia-aegritudo* gave new laic psychological dimensions to the one theological "sin" that could possibly accommodate such poetic, philosophical, and secular sensibilities.

With the writing of the *Secretum*, Petrarch continued and expanded a habit of psychological instrospection acquired from his earliest efforts as a poet. His efforts at self-healing in the dialogue show him to be a burgeoning *medicus* alive to the varieties of spiritual, moral, and emotional ills. Augustinus tried not only to cure Franciscus of his spiritual failings (a weak will, worldly involvement, love, and glory), but also to remedy his secular disease of sorrow. Though taking literary liberties with the historical Augustine, Petrarch's dialogue began to reestablish the legitimacy of worldly consolation. The *conflictus* in the *Secretum* is signaled not merely by Petrarch's unwillingness to abandon "glory" and his ambitious literary pursuits. It is mirrored also in the very tensions of the dialogue, in which an ascetic *contemptus mundi* and *meditatio mortis* are challenged by the worldly therapy of a *consolatio philosophiae*.

In uniting poetic, philosophical, ascetic, and confessional models of healing, the *Secretum* inevitably suffered a measure of disjuncture. The work's tone is now stern, now sympathetic. Misery and death are now seen as "remedy," now as "malady"—sorrow, now as "sin," now as "affliction." The penitential current in the *Secretum* could still be a genuine one, but Petrarch was also groping for another psychological resolution. He was straining to find a framework to heal not only the afflictions of *homo peccans*, but also those of *homo dolens*. That framework would achieve full form only in the *De remediis*, where the mature rhetorician would complete the psychological explorations that the young poet had begun.

2

PETRARCH AS PUBLIC CONSOLER

THE LETTERS

ETRARCH'S SUPPLENESS as a *medicus animorum* extended beyond his efforts as a self-consoler to his many endeavors as a "public" consoler, as he sought to comfort friends, patrons, and his un-
named reading public. Forever the letter-writer, he left two expansive collections: the *Familiares* and the later *Seniles*.[1] In these familiar letters
Petrarch cultivated the ancient role of the epistolary consoler, exhorter, and
sage. He comforted acquaintances in times of bereavement, exile, sickness,
absence of friends, fear of death, aging, and misfortune. Like Seneca he also
assumed the role of moral adviser, writing letters to friends on such topics
as adultery, drunkenness, and matters of spiritual health. Our chief interest
is in those consolatory letters in which he sustains friends in their trials of
grief, hardship, and fear.

Petrarch's letter-collections are not only a record of his enduring commitment to rhetorical consolation, but also, when he chose to write of his
own grief, a window onto his own state of mind. But whether as solace for
others or as expressions of his personal sorrows, the letters reveal some
larger patterns in Petrarch's psychological and literary life. Revised and
fictitious as some of the letters are, however, they are not always reliable
reflections of any given moment in Petrarch's life or thought.[2] In the process of selecting letters for his major collections, Petrarch had occasion to
review the ebb and flow of his epistolary past, and he sometimes made
comments on patterns he found there. As Petrarch knew, the act of choosing and editing letters could be an "act" of autobiography. Gaining some
perspective on his past, Petrarch sometimes acknowledged the life he saw
and sometimes tried to conceal it. Much can be learned not only from those
letters he admitted to his collections but also from those he did not.

The sources for Petrarch's view of epistolary consolation were essentially
Roman. After distancing himself from the influence of the *ars dictaminis*, in
the 1340s and early 1350s he began to cultivate a studied, classical style,
composing letters "addressed" to classical authors and inventing letters for
the first book of his *Familiares*.[3] Clearly, the principal sources for his mature style were Cicero and Seneca.[4] But what of Petrarch's exact view of his

role as a consoler? It varied. In some letters one finds the notion of the consoling philosophical friend: the friend whose counsel and authority aids in restoring tranquility.[5] In one instance Petrarch described his consolatory duty almost in professional terms. For a period of seventeen years, he served irregularly as household chaplain ("capellanus continuus commensalis") to Cardinal Giovanni Colonna.[6] This quasi-religious appointment, however, was certainly more social than pastoral. Whatever Petrarch saw as the obligations of his "office," one duty he apparently tried to fulfill for his patron was the office of consolation. In *Fam.* 7.13 of 1347–48 Petrarch wrote a *consolatoria* to Colonna in which he began,

> I shall freely confess (for although I may not be solvent I am a trusted debtor) that I owe you everything, certainly my talent and this little body that I inhabit as a pilgrim, and whatever external goods fall to my lot. For your palace contributed no less to my mind than to my body and to my destiny. Because I was brought up by you since my youth, grew up under you and was educated by you so far as the malevolence of intervening misfortunes or the mediocrity of my talent allowed, it is only right that I must persist in directing this pen, this hand and my mind, however humble, to the consolation and solace of your mind. I remember having done so to the best of my ability in other misfortunes of ours, and I do not believe that you have forgotten.[7]

In various earlier letters proffering solace and guidance Petrarch had done just that, assuming a role as a type of private "philosopher-in-retainer," a role perhaps not unlike that filled by certain Stoic "philosophical directors" in the ancient world.[8] In providing consolation in return for patronage, Petrarch broached the realm of the professional consoler. That he did so in the context of a "household chaplain" raises one other question. Did this position of chaplain in any way suggest a religious dimension in his role of consoler and adviser to Colonna? This domestic chaplaincy would be the closest Petrarch came in his life to providing any type of pastoral care. This is not surprising, as such a type of informal, rhetorical care would suit him more readily than any sacramental *cura animarum*.

Whether as friend or "professional," Petrarch at times characterized his task as a consoler in highly rhetorical or medical terms. As he remarks in *Fam.* 2.1, consolation requires particular artifice, "for in order to have consolation pierce the mind of a sorrowing listener, it needs great majesty of words, as well as weighty and bold sentences."[9] A vocabulary of rhetorical "healing" also appears in Petrarch's *consolatoriae*. He exploits such a medical terminology (of *morbi animi*, *antidota*, *medicamenta*) in *Sen.* 10.4, where, as we shall see, Petrarch carefully delineated and most dramatically developed a therapeutic approach, treating a friend's bereavement in the "authoritative" context of his own grief over a similar loss.[10] Whether for their studied rhetorical style, their learned *sententiae*, or their clinical detail, Petrarch's familiar letters of consolatory eloquence represented to him a challenging, specialized craft.

For the structure and content of these consolatory letters, Petrarch turned chiefly to the ancient models of the *epistola consolatoria* and the larger *consolatio* (Seneca's *Ad Marciam, Ad Polybium, Ad Helviam*) as well as the consolatory lore in Cicero's *Tusculans* and *De senectute*. Most numerous are his letters on bereavement, which structurally include many of the literary components of the ancient Roman *consolatoria*: the eulogy and *laudatio* of the dead, *exempla* of those who have grieved, philosophical *topoi* of the futility of grief, the inevitability of death, the miseries of life, the hope of immortality. To these classical consolations he adds Christian ones: the solace of otherworldly beatitude and resurrection.[11]

As was seen in the previous chapter, Petrarch sometimes used letters to describe his own bouts with grief. In one instance, he confesses that his personal need to lament could betray his public duty to console. During the ravages of the Black Death in 1349 he wrote a doleful letter to his "Socrates," Ludwig van Kempen. A plangent expression of his own despair, *Fam.* 8.7 reveals Petrarch's vulnerability to the emotional horrors of the plague. Condemning his own laments, he chides himself for being a consoler who cannot himself achieve calm and tranquility:

> Alas, dear brother! I am deeply troubled from within and take pity on myself. What would anyone who hears these words say? "You who seem to offer comfort and aid to others, who had promised us things that were superior, who ought to have formed a thick skin from your constant misfortunes and to have become callous against all the blows of fortune and hardened to something like a flintstone, see how weakly you bear your burdens, see how often you direct your frequent wailings to us. . . . Where are the magnificent words, which if intended rather to extol your genius than as advice for life, can be no more than empty sound and curious charms for the ear? . . . What we considered letters are laments, where we sought ingenious combinations of words, new molds for language, and sweetly ordered rhetorical colors, we behold nothing but mournful exclamations and indignant tones and tear stains."[12]

The "chastiser" continues, telling Petrarch that "lamenting the fate of all mortals" is an enormous and useless task, and he challenges him to bear his grief well, rather than "offer poison to your friends to whom you had promised a cure."[13] Thus helpless and forced to resort to his poetic regimen of weeping and writing, Petrarch the "comforter" fears that he has failed in his duty to others.

This theme recurs, or rather continues, in *Fam.* 8.9, which originally formed one long letter in conjunction with the preceding letters 7 and 8.[14] Petrarch presents in this letter a painful account of the violent death of a friend, confessing that, in the very recounting, "undergoing something miserable and deadly and yet pleasing," he is simultaneously tortured and healed.[15] Having sought refuge in the therapy of his bittersweet narrative, he ends with an apologia to his readers: "Thus far, dearest Socrates, indulging in my grief in an undignified manner, I have unburdened my mind of its complaints as best I could. I had to do so in order not to crack under the weight of my misfortune. Forgive me, dear Socrates, and let others who may read this also forgive me."[16] A reluctant victim of his emotions, Petrarch asks that his readers not judge him too harshly.

Around the time he completed these revised versions of *Fam.* 8.7 and 9, Petrarch apparently began to review and reconsider his penchant for excessive mourning. This period, beginning in 1350, marks a turning point in Petrarch's psychological life and, consequently, in his treatment of others' sorrows. In general, the mature Petrarch seems to have moved toward a less emotional attitude toward grieving. Though some self-criticism of his sweet grief and excessive emotion can be found in his earlier letters,[17] generally the younger Petrarch freely resorted to the remedy of tears. But the older man began partially to renounce such habits. As R. Watkins suggests, the dedicatory letters to the *Familiares* and *Seniles* collections offer Petrarch's larger perspectives on his own emotional past. Both dedications refer to his response to the tragedies of epidemic loss: *Fam.* 1.1 discussing his despair in 1348–49; *Sen.* 1.1, his determined composure during the renewed ravages of 1361.[18] In the former (1350) he confesses that letters of the 1348–49 plague years show him to be prey to a "serious disease," that he is now "ashamed of a life fallen into excessive softness."[19] He apologizes that, whereas early letters in the collection would show him to be manly, those of the plague era expose him as crumbling into despair, "descending to these lamentations which now displease me."[20] But he also defends himself by continuing, "My affection for my friends may perhaps excuse me, for while they were secure I never moaned at any of the wounds of fate. But when almost all of them were swept away in a single calamity, it seemed inhuman, rather than strong, not to be moved."[21] Because "Socrates" himself has copies of these letters, Petrarch is unfree to rearrange or to eliminate them. But he does promise a manly ending to the *Familiares*, one that can match its manly beginning, "because as I grow older I seem to become stronger against the blows and injustices of fortune. . . . This much is true, however, that right now my spirit is such that I shall never succumb to anything further: 'If the world slips into destruction, / the crumbling ruins will find me fearless'" [Horace, *Carm.* 3.3.7–8].[22] The vulnerable mourner of 1348–49 is being transformed into the Stoic opponent of Fortuna. *Sen.* 1.1 echoes this sentiment; reflecting on his doleful reactions to the earlier plague and the present recurrence of epidemic in 1361, he promises,

I would hope not again to be forced to laments unsuitable to this age, to these studies, and to myself. I then permitted myself many freedoms which I now deny myself. I hope fortune will not further find me weeping. I shall stand upright if I can: if not, fortune will lay me low dry-eyed and silent. Lamentation is more shameful than destruction.[23]

Though there are some lapses, Petrarch fulfills that promise fairly faithfully, as the indulgent behavior of the earlier years abates in the *Seniles*.[24]

Moreover, Petrarch's tack as a consoler, like his regimen as a mourner, also shifts. In the *Familiares* one can find Petrarch reminding the bereaved of the possible benefits of salutary weeping. He does so on two occasions in *consolatoriae* to his patron Cardinal Colonna. In 1342 (*Fam.* 4.12), comforting Colonna for the loss of a brother, he encourages a release of sorrow and a recognition of its inexorable course.[25] Consoling Colonna over several family losses a few years later in 1347 or 1348 (*Fam.* 7.13) Petrarch warns against the dangers of repressed grief, recommending that, rather than hiding one's emotion in private, "it is much safer to confess one's grief and to weep openly."[26] A few years later in a *consolatoria* of 1352 to the French cardinal Gui de Bologne, Petrarch again allowed for the natural course of mourning. Hearing of Gui's grief over the death of his mother, Petrarch sanctions one night of tears not unlike the irrepressible but finite grief Augustine experienced in the *Confessions* Book 9.[27] Though allowing for emotion in these letters of the 1340s and 1350s, Petrarch took a far sterner approach many years later in the premier *consolatoria* of his later years. In this letter (*Sen.* 10.4) he condemns his own earlier regimen of weeping and urges the one true remedy of patience.[28] In order to understand fully the context of this work, however, it is first necessary to examine several epistles of the intervening period that reveal Petrarch's "conflict" concerning tears.[29]

Petrarch's shifting and sometimes ambivalent attitude toward grief can also be seen in letters he excluded from his collections. As reviser and editor, he was mindful that his "private" letters would gain a "public" stature: they not only would represent a type of autobiography but also would constitute part of the larger corpus of his literature of moral healing and wisdom. Perhaps as a result, Petrarch withdrew various epistles from the official collections. Some of these letters deal with grief and are important missing pieces in any effort to reconstruct Petrarch's attitudes toward sorrow.

One such letter, now *Variae* 32, suggests that Petrarch may have learned that the dangers of grief go deeper than he first realized. The story behind the letter is a particularly sad one. In 1355 the son of the Roman noble Paolo Annibaldeschi was killed in battle. When Paolo beheld his son's mutilated body he himself died of grief.[30] Petrarch's letter to Neri Morando is a simultaneous lamentation and critique of this tragedy. In the first part of the letter, Petrarch admits that, though he thought he had a mind "hardened and armed against all assaults," this unique tragedy was one the likes of which he had never heard, read, thought, or contemplated.[31] As it is futile to blame deaf Fortuna or Paolo's weakness, Petrarch can only lament and discuss the tragedy. He thus falls back on a familiar regimen of weeping and writing. Perhaps, then, he fails in his earlier resolutions of 1350 (*Fam.* 1.1) to impassively endure such sorrow: "Oh savage sweetness! It helps to indulge and to nourish misery by speaking. For what is more suited to a sad mind than to write of sad things? For sadness has its pleasure, a pleasure indeed harsh but suited to it. In the *Ars poetica* [105–6] it is written: 'Sad words befit a sad face.' "[32]

But oddly, Petrarch's "indulgent" discourse concerning the tragedy is more a diatribe of indignation than a dirge. He is shocked by Paolo's unprecedented reaction to the loss of his son, for though many fathers "have followed their sons to burial with tears, and some even have followed them to the kingdom of the dead by turning their swords upon themselves, no one, that I know, before our Paolo has followed his son into the grave because of immoderate weeping (*fletu immodico*): and this is the reason for my new, rare, and inconsolable grief."[33] And though Petrarch had thought earlier tragedies of the Roman Colonna family had exhausted his supply of tears,[34] he will retap the reaches of emotion by the act of writing:

> However, you, most worthy man, will not be without my tears, which by speaking I will unearth from the deepest and hidden recesses of my soul, and through which I will attend your sad funeral from afar—rather, in fact, drenched in tears and as if present before your sad remains I will thus speak: "Alas! what have you done to me? A man shrewd and vigorous in other things, what have you done?"[35]

The speech that ensues is a long address to Paolo. And, in part, Petrarch's discourse represents his dutiful act of mourning *in absentia*; like the letter as a whole, the speech is a type of tearful commemoration which Petrarch owes to the memory of his lost friend. But as it unfolds, the address to Paolo is clearly less a commemoration than a condemnation, less an empathic lament than an angry indictment. Petrarch berates Paolo for dying: it was an ignoble "choice" for such a noble man. Paolo could have dignified his son's death in far more worthy ways: he could have shed (controlled) fatherly tears, could have shown a spirit of fortitude, could have had a sense of hope for his son's resurrection, could have begotten new sons, could have offered Christian prayers for the dead, could have taken vengeance for his son's killing.[36] But rather than honor his son's memory with any such "constructive" emotions or gestures, Paolo has dishonored it, endowing it with the infamy of having caused his own death. Petrarch offers a wealth of Stoic *exempla* of parents—both fathers and mothers—who have borne loss bravely. He ends by saying that, though there are cases that illustrate the extremity and dangers of violent grief, he has no knowledge of any other man thus literally dying of grief. On such a note, Petrarch admits that he himself has "perhaps been carried off by emotion (*impetus animi*) longer than I should. Forgive me, I beg: it was a bitter sweetness and a sweet bitterness to contend with a friend already buried as if he were present and able to respond to me."[37] While it is true that, like a wise man, he had always tried to foresee all tragedies and to arm himself against all eventualities, he did not foresee such a unique tragedy. Finding him unprepared, the shock left him "worn down and dejected. Gradually I am beginning to revive my mind and to collect the scattered [mental] arms."[38]

In tone and motivation *Var.* 32 is an anomalous work. What was the real motive behind Petrarch's writing of the letter? Did he compose it to commemorate Paolo or to resolve his own grief and anger? Certainly, this letter of the mid-1350s found Petrarch testing his Stoic resolve to stand firm against Fortuna's assaults. Unprepared for this remarkable type of tragedy, he retreated somewhat to "weeping and writing" about it. But his lamentation was perhaps voiced somewhat out of social duty, as a commemorative act of mourning. As an almost angry condemnation of Paolo, however, it was a bitter tribute to his memory. It is no surprise that Petrarch left this letter out of his official collection. It is a dark account of the dangers of unrestrained grief, an account ironically itself symptomatic of Petrarch's own irrepressible, unresolved emotion. The newly "converted" Stoic of the 1350s condemns Paolo's death, becoming now fully aware of the potential danger of sorrow. At the same time, however, the structure of his letter reveals his own lingering need for cathartic expression. Reflecting at once the impulses of poetic sorrow and the convictions of Stoic impassivity, *Var.* 32 is a contradiction.

Perhaps Petrarch suppressed the letter simply because of its uncharitable, judgmental treatment of a broken man. On later reflection he may have fully recognized the damning tone of this letter ostensibly conceived out of sympathy for the departed Paolo. But perhaps Petrarch withheld the letter also because its emotional tenor damns himself. He knows he has failed in his earlier Stoic promises. He knows he has been too dejected for too long. He knows Fortuna has caught him unprepared. He knows this doleful and angry discourse is partly a necessary remedy for his grief. Though on a lesser scale, Petrarch indulges in the similar passion he condemns in Paolo. Though we can never fully know why Petrarch excluded *Var.* 32, of one thing we can be sure: the example of Paolo made a firm impression on Petrarch, as we shall see in *Sen.* 10.4. This case of Paolo's fatal grief may have further convinced the budding Stoic that emotional excess should be controlled.

If the death of the grief-stricken Paolo was a sober warning to Petrarch, it did not cure him of his doleful ways. Letters of the early 1360s show him still indulging in the remedy of tears. In *Var.* 19 he laments the death of his patron Azzo da Correggio.[39] In *Var.* 54 to Bartolomeo di Pace he explains that his recent bouts with despondency (about which Bartolomeo had inquired) were due to the death of friends—and that his remedy is "*flere largiter et queri.*"[40] The most dramatic commentary on Petrarch's conflict over weeping is found in the content and fate of *Var.* 58. This letter of 1363 (or thereafter) was sent to Gasparo dei Broaspini, who was then transcribing Petrarch's *Familiares.*[41] He opens the letter with a medical analogy: "There are those who are so affected and overwhelmed with sorrow that, as in the case of bodies—unless a noxious humor is first purged, outside remedies are applied in vain—so also in the minds of such people it occurs that, unless a hardened grief is first released through laments and tears, you cannot heal them with the consolations of words."[42] This is a rather skeptical stance toward the "consolations of words" for a Stoic who, by this time, had possibly written a major portion of a massive manual *De remediis*.

As was seen above, Petrarch had briefly discussed the theme of catharsis in two letters (*Fam.* 4.12 and 7.13) to Cardinal Colonna in the 1340s. Now he expands upon it, harking back to another letter of the 1340s, this one to the aging patriarch of the Colonna family, Stefano the Elder. Petrarch wrote this letter (*Fam.* 8.1) in 1348 or 1349 after Stefano had lost the same Cardinal Giovanni, his son and Petrarch's longtime patron. This loss was only the last of many tragedies for Stefano, who in the course of his life had lost five brothers, his wife, seven sons (including Giovanni), and some number of grandsons. Approaching the age of one hundred, he is left virtually heirless and alone. Petrarch's letter to Stefano, aptly identified as a "consolation filled with tears," is a review of these many tragedies and is perhaps the saddest of all of Petrarch's *consolatoriae*.[43] In *Var.* 58 Petrarch now returns to this old *consolatoria* with a comment concerning his purpose in writing it, and Stefano's response in reading it. He says, "I spoke to him in that letter, not so that I would suppress his tears—which if I had done so would have killed him—but [I spoke] so that I would call forth and completely drain him of his tears and thus purge a soul filled with excessive grief."[44] Hearing an eyewitness report of Stefano's reactions, Petrarch then claims that the cure was effective:

[I]t [the letter] succeeded. As the messenger who delivered it reported back to me, Stefano read that letter with so many tears and such great sighs, that he

[Stefano] feared harm would come to him, his friends charging me with bringing on some harmful and fatal condition. But, to the contrary, after having read the letter Stefano wiped his eyes and swore he would never weep again, not even if the whole world should crumble, because he had wept to satiety and had exhausted whatever source of tears there was in his heart.[45]

In retrospect at least,[46] Petrarch thus envisioned *Fam.* 8.1 as a consolation that was meant to provoke a sad heart to spend its grief. It was a dangerous but potent cure: if the purgative did not destroy the patient it would completely heal the disease. The report of Stefano's reaction must have had a powerful impact on Petrarch. Not only must it have enhanced his sense of the potential power of one of his consolatory letters, but also it surely reinforced his belief in the salutary effects of catharsis. The example of Stefano proved to Petrarch that there were others—others besides a poet such as himself—for whom effusive grief is therapeutic.

Petrarch's discussion of grief in *Var.* 58 drew not only on this letter of the late 1340s but also on the recent experience in the 1360s. He confesses that he, like Stefano, has often availed himself of the remedy of tears.[47] In fact, he says that he discussed this point in a recent letter—namely, *Var.* 54 to Bartolomeo di Pace. It is a sad irony that having recently described to Bartolomeo his remedy for weeping he must turn to this regimen again as he now mourns the loss of Bartolomeo himself. Petrarch encloses a copy of no. 54 for Gasparo's transcription.[48] Petrarch then suggests that another recent loss, that of Azzo da Correggio, provided the greatest occasion for his resorting to the regimen of weeping. To be fully rid of his grief over Azzo, Petrarch knew he must exhaust his font of tears once and for all, and so he sought to pique his sorrow. As a spur he wrote a letter (*Var.* 19) to a friend of Azzo's, a letter that brought him to tears both as he wrote it and reread it. As he had hoped, this cure worked. As Stefano had been cured by unrestrained grief, so had Petrarch.[49] But despite the salutary effects of no. 19, Petrarch was ashamed of its unmanly strains, fearing such a letter was unbecoming to his age and reputation. He was probably particularly struck by the irony that this emotional, non-Stoic letter lamented the loss of Azzo, that very person to whom he dedicated his manly *De remediis*.[50] Clearly, Petrarch knew what could be said of his grievous letter: "Physician, heal thyself!" Having urged Azzo to bear all the assaults of Fortuna with tranquility, the Stoic *medicus* himself lapses into a deep grief. Perhaps as a consequence of this, Petrarch suppressed the letter. At some point, however, Gasparo obtained a copy, and Petrarch approved his including it in the transcription of the *Familiares*. Now in *Var.* 58 Petrarch wishes to issue a caveat concerning the emotional letter. He wants to warn Gasparo and all future readers that the content of *Var.* 19 was self-directed; it was peculiar to Petrarch's own process of mourning, in which he hoped to provoke himself to an exhaustive sorrow. Feeding on his misery with a type of *voluptas dolendi*, Petrarch galvanized and completed his grief: "I was in such a state [of indulgent grief] when I wrote that letter, and in such a state I would have remained had I not written it: by writing and weeping I achieved what I had not been able to achieve by reasoning."[51] Petrarch is thus warning his readers that they will not find traditional consolations in this letter, but only what has proved comforting to him.

In a word, *Var.* 58 is an apologia for weeping. Still aware of his earlier promises to be more Stoic, perhaps still stunned by the consequences of Paolo Annibaldeschi's grief, Petrarch thinks it meet to explain to his readers why such sorrowful self-consolations are still to be found in his collection. A mirror of his public *persona*, Petrarch's letters could thus show him faltering in his philosophical resolve: continuing in the 1360s to seek comfort in tears, Petrarch was backsliding from his earlier promises to be constant in the face of tragedy.

Perhaps it was that sense of philosophical "failure" that decided the ultimate fate of *Var.* 58, as well as that of no. 19 and no. 54. Though approved and included in Gasparo's transcription, all three letters were later withdrawn by Petrarch from the final corpus of the *Familiares*.[52] Why did Petrarch change his mind? We cannot know with certainty, but he may have reconsidered the letters in light of his overall philosophical program. He may have wanted to maintain a consistency—or, rather, the appearance of a consistency—in his Stoic development. In addition to *Var.* 19, 54, and 58, Petrarch also suppressed no. 32, dealing with Paolo Annibaldeschi's fatal grief. Part lament for and part attack of his noble friend, this letter revealed not only the dangerous side of grief but also Petrarch's own contradictory attitudes. Almost angrily damning Paolo's vulnerability to sorrow, he nonetheless also reveals his own. Taken as a whole, these four letters chronicle Petrarch's enduring need to weep and to write. All reveal his failure to follow his own Stoic resolve.[53] Increasingly committed to Stoic solutions as the author of the *De remediis*, the mature Petrarch must have felt that the safer course for his reputation was to withhold these letters. Moreover, he may have come to see the potential danger of grief for those who were not of his poetic ilk. It is true that Stefano Colonna was healed by his violent response to Petrarch's *Fam.* 8.1, but the purgative almost overwhelmed the patient. In Paolo Annibaldeschi's case, Petrarch found that unbridled grief could overwhelm—it could even kill.

Returning to those letters Petrarch chose to retain in his collections, we find that he again had occasion in the 1360s to reflect on the remedy for sorrow. This time, in perhaps the greatest *consolatoria* of his career, Petrarch would again return to his Stoic convictions. This letter, *Sen.* 10.4

(1368), not only offers a clear statement of Petrarch's mature, public views on mourning but also represents his most sophisticated attempt at epistolary consolation for bereavement.[54]

Petrarch structured *Sen.* 10.4 as a joint consolation. Hoping to comfort his friend Donato Albanzani on the death of his son Solone, he centers the letter around the therapeutic principle that those who suffer are most readily healed by consolers who also suffer:

> [A]nd therefore, as much as I am able, I console you and equally myself, also in need of comfort. Indeed, many people have consoled others and indeed themselves with books and treatises; I endeavor to do both at the same time, which I hope will be pleasing to you. And whatever remedy will result, will be aid *to* the sick *from* the sick. And whereas it is easy for the well to console the sick with words [cf. Terence, *Andria* 309], the solace of no one penetrates a sad mind more effectively than that coming from one suffering similarly . . .[55]

In this case, Petrarch's similar "sickness" sprang from his grief over the loss of his grandson Franceschino, a loss he describes early in the letter. Part self-consolation and part *consolatoria*, the letter then proceeds with a personal and historical critique of mourning practices and an exhortation toward emotional restraint.

Both the spirit and the language of this letter bespeak the determined Stoicism of the *De remediis*.[56] Perhaps more than in any other *consolatoria*, he attempts to be the careful moral *medicus*. Time and again damning the remedy of tears, he urges patience and reason. As he had done in *Fam.* 1.1, he abjures his own earlier penchant for weeping, telling Donato,

> [T]oday I am ashamed of many letters which, in a younger age, I poured forth piously but too effeminately when I was conquered by grief over the deaths of my friends. I hope myself at least to be freed from so many womanly habits, so that let the whole world conspire as if against me alone and it will find me perhaps not happy or unmoved, but neither querulous or dejected. I learned that complaints are of no avail, that nothing is so useful as patience.[57]

Thus denying himself a show of tears for his Franceschino, Petrarch instead chooses to build a monument. He tells Donato that he erected an engraved marble sepulcher in honor of his grandson. This deed perhaps epitomizes Petrarch's larger message in the letter: rather than retreat into tears, the bereaved should seek more constructive comforts.[58] Petrarch then proceeds with such a constructive consolation aimed at comforting both Donato and himself.

Fully in the tradition of Cicero's *Tusculans* and his own *De remediis*, Petrarch emphasizes the importance of arming the mind with fortitude and courage, turning it from the sensual. Achieving such a rational calm is a challenge for the sage and a test of virtue for those who would win glory.

Petrarch gives little quarter to tears. It is the refuge of the weaker sex. It is the way of those who follow vulgar opinion. Arguing that "it is easy to weep, difficult to be consoled," Petrarch reviews the history of mourning practices: "Inveterate and immutable is the custom of weeping over the loss of our loved ones, a custom covered with the veil of piety, excused and even praised in that name, and reinforced not only by the folly of the crowd but by the wisdom and example of illustrious individuals."[59] He then presents a few examples of misguided ancients and moderns who have thus wept too much. Not surprisingly, his modern example was the dramatic case of Paolo Annibaldeschi, who died of sorrow.[60] The strong-spirited and the wise, however, will ignore the pedestrian customs of mourning and the pusillanimous *exempla* of such famous grievers. Interestingly, Petrarch would later continue and even intensify his attacks on common mourning practices. In 1373, in *Sen.* 14.1 to the Paduan tyrant Francesco da Carrara, he roundly condemns the excessive mourning rituals he sees in Padua. He particularly objects to the public weeping and lamentation of women— something he also comments upon in the Preface to Book 2 of the *De remediis*.[61] And though Petrarch would probably have differentiated such "public" lamentation from his, or others', "private" weeping, nonetheless he may have come to recognize a potential hollowness in both: one as ritually banal, the other as emotionally futile. Clearly, in *Sen.* 10.4 he condemns his younger self as he does the larger customs of mourning he finds in society. His message is plain: though it may be difficult to remain tranquil in the face of loss, it nonetheless is praiseworthy, desirable, and virtuous. Petrarch then reflects at length on the happier state of the dead, the brevity and misery of life, the assaults of Fortuna, and the importance of "living well" and "dying well." He reiterates the Stoic attack on emotion: "I therefore repeat, why cry? It is time to rejoice and to dry your tears, which you can do if only you wish it and if you do not willingly indulge in your misfortune. For you must know that these sobs and laments do not come from nature, but only from the cowardice of certain individuals."[62]

Petrarch then proves that such weeping is not innate. Drawing upon classical, biblical, and modern examples, he argues that not all people weep, or weep in the same way, for their losses.[63] From the moderns, he contrasts the tragic grief of Paolo Annibaldeschi to the manly bereavements of Stefano Colonna and King Robert of Naples.[64] Thus sorrow is a matter of choice. Petrarch ends by exhorting Donato (and himself?) to cultivate "positive" rather than "negative" emotions. He does not forbid paternal feeling, but only sorrow: "[Y]ou are not denied paternal love and memory: only grief, sighs, and laments. I want you to speak of him, think of him, love him, recall him not bitterly but sweetly, and, as befits a Christian, [think of him] not as one who is dead but as one who is now beginning to live, who, escaping a brief exile, reaches the homeland."[65] Petrarch thus complements his sterner Stoic exhortations to fortitude with a happier solace of Christian beatitude.

Perhaps inspired partly by the presence of his fellow writer Boccaccio, who was then visiting him,[66] Petrarch attempted to make *Sen.* 10.4 an epistolary masterpiece. His own loss perhaps also moved him to make this his premier *consolatoria* for bereavement. Moreover, the autobiographical character of the letter underscores its therapeutic potential. A sufferer himself, Petrarch's words will more readily comfort Donato. This and so many other "medical" perspectives in the work indicate how fully Petrarch was under the influence of the *De remediis*. The voice of the Stoic *medicus* is clearly triumphant, that of the poet almost silent. *Sen.* 10.4 reveals Petrarch's renewed convictions concerning the weakness and futility of tears. He renounces the plangent letters of his younger years; he implicitly abrogates his earlier advice concerning the benefits of emotional release.[67] As both a self-consolation and a consolation, this letter is a forceful public statement that weeping will not be his remedy, nor should it be anyone else's. He has overcome his backsliding of recent years. In fact, he has learned from these years the important lesson drawn from the tragic example of Paolo Annibaldeschi.[68] Now cured of his proclivity to indulgent grief, Petrarch is able constructively to join his roles as mourner and as consoler; the tension he felt between these roles in the plague letter *Fam.* 8.7 is now resolved.

Sen. 10.4 thus represents the culmination of a long and sometimes tentative development in Petrarch's thought: namely, his rejection of poetic remedies for philosophical ones. If this letter marked the end of a psychological journey for Petrarch, it may have also signaled the start of a literary tradition for later humanists. His autobiographical discussion of the loss of a child here might well be a source for several similar writings in the Quattrocento. As we shall see in Chapter 5, Petrarch's discussion of personal bereavement and his exploration of the psychology of parental loss will be continued and challenged by later writers.

. . . . .

Besides his letters on bereavement, Petrarch also wrote consolations for such woes as exile, aging, fear of death, illness, and dejection. Sometimes he proffered consolation in the diffuse context of a response to the general problems and misfortunes that friends had suffered. For instance, *Fam.* 6.3 to Friar Giovanni Colonna is a *consolatoria super quibudam vite difficultatibus*, dealing with old age, poverty, and gout.[69] Another letter, *Fam.* 21.9, is a response to the despair of his friend "Socrates" over current difficulties and misfortunes. This *consolatio cum consilio* offers exhortations to fortitude and tranquility in the face of hardship and the raging of Fortuna.[70]

In the tradition of Seneca, Petrarch also counseled others on the problem of the fear of death.[71] His most dramatic and urgent such letter was addressed to his famous friend Giovanni Boccaccio. Unlike Seneca's somewhat abstract counsels to Lucilius on death, Petrarch's advice to his fellow poet responded to a particular crisis. In trying to calm his frightened cohort, Petrarch assumed an important and timely role as lay comforter, offering new perspectives on the old problem of the proper preparation for death.[72] In 1362 Boccaccio had written Petrarch telling of an ominous prophecy he had received: a Carthusian monk from Siena had brought him word that a dying fellow brother had prophesied the imminent deaths of himself, Petrarch, and others in Italy and abroad. All these notables should rectify their ways and turn to God. A trafficker in pagan and scandalous letters, Boccaccio must renounce his involvement in secular literature.[73] This spiritual warning found a vulnerable target in Boccaccio, who wrote Petrarch of his plans to abandon his sinful literary interests and of his intention to sell his library, offering the collection to Petrarch. In his reply (*Sen.* 1.5) Petrarch rallied with a *consolatoria* for the fear of death and a defense of the study of secular letters in old age.

Petrarch's consolation for Boccaccio's fear of death is an easy blend of classical and patristic thought: time and again, he complements a classical *locus* with an Christian one.[74] But appropriate to Boccaccio's spiritual crisis and urge for renunciation, Petrarch's citations are weighted more toward the Christian than the pagan world. He draws most heavily on the second book of Ambrose's *De excessu fratris sui Satyri*, an important source for Christian consolation concerning death.[75] At one point, Petrarch presents two opposing views of the nature of human existence. One is the gloomy maxim cited in Cicero's *Tusculans* (1.48.114) that "non nasci homini longe optimum esse, proximum autem quam primum mori," which supports Ambrose's comments on such a theme in the *De excessu* Book 2. But, as a balance, Petrarch also offers Lactantius' exegesis of the "non nasci," which criticized Cicero's pessimism, refuting this negative appraisal of human life. Having set forth both positions, Petrarch then in Senecan fashion urges the psychological middle ground between fearing and desiring death.[76] He also poses the familiar regimen of the frequent meditation on death, citing both the Platonic-Ciceronian maxim that "tota philosophorum vita commentatio mors est" and the Christian advice to meditate on Christ's death and victory on the Cross.[77] He ends his consolation, appropriately and somewhat sarcastically, by citing a maxim from Vergil, illustrating by example how the forbidden fruit of pagan wisdom can be salutary. And with this he thus pointedly introduces his defense of poetry and secular studies.

To counter Boccaccio's intention of renouncing secular literature, Petrarch then turns to the question of the legitimacy and value of literary studies in old age. He argues that, though one who is unread should not try to begin cultivating letters in old age, one who like Boccaccio is well versed in them should not forsake this source of joy and "solace and support in old age."[78] Looking to the Fathers for spiritual support, Petrarch asks what would have happened if such a prohibition of literature had been heeded by a Lactantius or an Augustine. It is no doubt purposeful that the preceding consolation fully exemplifies the continuity between classical (or "literary") and Christian responses to the problem of death. Boccaccio should meet his death by renouncing worldly thoughts, desires, and bad habits, but not by abandoning literary studies: "[W]e must not, as a result of an exhortation to virtue or the pretext of approaching death, be deterred from letters, which, if they are received into a good soul, excite the love of virtue and either extinguish or mitigate the fear of death."[79] Allowing for the possibility that his plea might fail, Petrarch ends the letter by offering to buy Boccaccio's library, hoping to preclude its dispersal and to ensure its being joined with his own and eventually passed on to some "pious and devout place."[80] This reference to a religious bequest of their libraries perhaps subtly underscores Petrarch's belief in the sanctity of their secular studies.

Sen. 1.5 is an important document both for understanding the spiritual and cultural climate of early Italian humanism as well as for studying the potential psychological and social function of the familiar letter. Boccaccio falls prey to ascetic warnings of late-life repentance issued by a monk who himself lay dying. An alarmed, middle-aged Boccaccio confides his fears to Petrarch, who, in a special capacity as lay consoler and counselor, checks his friend's impulse toward renunciation. Petrarch expands the legitimate boundaries of human pursuits. It is bad habits that must be forsaken, not literature; Boccaccio ought not to relinquish that world of letters that can be such a great comfort for aging *literati* such as themselves. Petrarch's defense of classical literature relies chiefly on his citation of patristic humanists, the Renaissance humanists' true cultural ancestors. Certainly, Petrarch provides his fellow humanist and writer with a timely lay defense of secular learning and literature. As will be seen in Chapter 4, Coluccio Salutati will also offer counsels against secular renunciation, though in a more social than intellectual context.

Sen. 1.5 to Boccaccio and the later 10.4 to Donato Albanzani represent the rich potential of Petrarch's mature style of letter-writing. The exhortation to Boccaccio is a dramatic piece of lay comfort and counsel; the *consolatoria* to Donato, his greatest attempt to be a philosophical *medicus* for a grief-stricken friend. Certainly, these letters of the later years show how fully Petrarch had left behind the formulaic dictates of the *ars dictaminis*. Transformed by his reading of Seneca's and, later, Cicero's letters, he revived the genre of the familiar letter as a forum for literary discourse, for reflection, for confession, for self-examination, for catharsis, for "professional" healing, for friendly consolation and advice.

But as this new epistolary style evolved, Petrarch at times perceived a conflict between his roles as mourner and as consoler. His public duty to comfort was sometimes vitiated by his private need to weep. Increasingly uncomfortable with this tension, Petrarch promised a Stoic maturity and fortitude in both the dedicatory letters to his *Familiares* and *Seniles*. But he could not fully honor that resolution. He ultimately suppressed several backsliding letters of the later years in which he still sought those doleful comforts of indulgent grief. Petrarch the editor of his public letters was also the curator of his public *persona*. In the last analysis, he decided that his permanent collection should reaffirm his intention to show a Stoic face to the world.[81] Thus, though his emotional instincts sometimes fought it, the mature Petrarch sought to replace the remedies of the poet with those of the moral philosopher. His greatest effort toward that end came in his psychological encyclopedia *De remediis*.

3

PETRARCH AS UNIVERSAL CONSOLER

THE *DE REMEDIIS UTRIUSQUE FORTUNE*

FROM the particular misfortunes of friends Petrarch the epistolary consoler ventured forth to brave the universal contingency of Fortuna. Undoubtedly his most ambitious and systematic effort as a *medicus animorum* was his writing of the *De remediis utriusque fortune*. Its voluminous scope testifies to its purpose: to gather the many strands of healing wisdom in Petrarch's world; to universalize this wisdom for a wide range of readers and situations; to complete Petrarch's growth as a constructive Stoic healer. The *De remediis* not only at times expands upon earlier consolatory themes in Petrarch's thought but also transforms them. Moreover, Petrarch's role as humanist *medicus* also crystallizes, taking ever clearer shape against the competing types of healers of his day. Despite its importance for an understanding of Petrarch's thought and despite its early modern success, the *De remediis* has been sorely neglected. Its relationship to Petrarch's earlier writings has not been sufficiently examined, nor has its place in Renaissance thought been fully established.[1]

Begun sometime in the mid-1350s and completed in 1366, the *De remediis* complements and crowns several of Petrarch's previous efforts as a consoler and moralist.[2] First, it explores several of the psychological problems set forth in the *Secretum*. The manual provides an extensive treatment of the four passions of *Spes, Gaudium, Metus,* and *Dolor,* to which "Augustinus" referred in the *Secretum* Book 1.[3] It also fulfills the therapeutic mission begun, in personal terms, in the *Secretum* Book 2, which treated Petrarch's vanities, sins, and fortune. More specifically, in its very format, the *De remediis* also develops an idea first mentioned by Petrarch in the second book of the *Secretum*. Here Franciscus complained that he could not effectively retain and use the therapeutic wisdom that Augustinus, naming works of Seneca and Cicero, had argued would be helpful in curing his *accidia-aegritudo*. Franciscus claimed that, in his experience, the benefits of these moral studies were not permanent, their effect disappearing soon after his readings were completed. Augustinus responded that it is the problem of many readers that the wisdom of the *ars vivendi* is not actively put to use. He urged Franciscus to make notations during his reading, to glean in his mind a trove of healing truths:

> Whenever in your reading you come upon salutary maxims, by which you feel your mind to be stimulated or restrained, do not trust in the power of natural

wit, but hide these maxims in the interior of your memory and make them familiar to yourself with great study. In this way, just as the expert doctors are accustomed to do, in whatever place or time a sickness befalls you requiring immediate attention, you may have, so to speak, the remedies written in your mind.[4]

Augustinus thus called for a manual of mental remedies; the *De remediis* gives literary form to that therapeutic ideal. Petrarch hopes to collect and to activate the salutary maxims of the moral tradition, to compile a permanent store of remedies that can be applied to cure the many passions and maladies of the mind.

In the dedicatory letter addressed to Azzo da Correggio, Petrarch defines the nature of his task of formulating such a therapeutic philosophy. Typical of his many attacks against scholastic philosophy, he argues that the true philosophy is not one that is borne on the "windy pretense of sterile disputations" but one that in "certain modest steps leads toward health."[5] As K. Heitmann suggests, also in *Fam.* 12.3 Petrarch rejected that "loquacious, scholastic, windy kind [of philosophy] with which our [modern] men of letters ridiculously pride themselves" and quoted Cicero's argument that the true purpose of philosophy is that it "medetur animis, inanes sollicitudines detrahit, cupiditatibus liberat, pellit timores" (*Tusc.* 2.4.11).[6] Given the goals of the *De remediis* and its debt to the *Tusculans*, it is clear that this definition of philosophy readily became Petrarch's own. In his preface to Book 1, Petrarch points out that his manual of remedies is not meant to replace Azzo's more serious literary endeavors but to provide interim maxims that are brief and precise, that can be remembered, and that, "like expeditious and permanent arms," can be used "against all insults and every unexpected attack."[7] Augustinus' call for mental salves is thus answered by Petrarch's literary "arms" for Azzo.[8]

Petrarch's letters, of course, also set the stage for the *De remediis*. Conveying solace and counsel, they show how Petrarch tendered healing words to individual friends, much as a somewhat sterner "Ratio" administers them to "Spes," "Gaudium," "Metus," and "Dolor" in the all-purpose remedy book. Moreover, some of the problems discussed in various letters, such as those concerning gout or the prophecies of soothsayers, appear as chapters in the manual.[9] Thus, the *De remediis* reflects Petrarch's actual experience as a consoler and adviser. In fact, it could even be used to supplant, in part, the need for epistolary consolation. In 1360 Petrarch wrote a *consolatoria* for gout (*Fam.* 23.12) to his friend Guido Sette, in which he lamented that he did not yet have a copy of his *De remediis* to send him.[10] Obviously, Petrarch recognized that his remedy book could relieve and enhance his efforts as a serial consoler.

Besides the *Secretum* and the letters, Petrarch's Lenten treatise *De otio religioso* also anticipated the *De remediis*, although, heretofore, scholars have not fully recognized the possible importance of this treatise as a formative influence.[11] Written to confirm his brother Gherardo in his monastic vocation, the *De otio* provided Petrarch with an opportunity to participate vicariously in his brother's holier life.[12] It afforded the poet a chance to define a monastic, thoroughly spiritual *otium* that paralleled his own conception of *otium* in his life of solitude and letters.[13] The work is centered around an exegesis of a passage from Ps. 45:11: "Be still and see [that I am God]" (Vacate et videte).[14] Among the themes Petrarch discusses in the *De otio* are those concerning worldly mutability, human misery, death, and the meditation on the eternal—themes he would also treat later in the *Secretum* and the *De remediis*. In some measure, these themes have an implicitly therapeutic context: they are part of a regimen for spiritual health. And though the *De otio*'s tone is wholly ascetic, nonetheless the treatise may have honed Petrarch's therapeutic perspectives.[15] This is particularly the case in a section of scriptural remedies in Book 1. Petrarch drew the idea for this small manual from Augustine's *De vera religione* 3.4, in which there are scriptural cures for ills such as avarice, lust, pride, and wrath.[16] But whereas Augustine's brief discussion treats only a few conditions, Petrarch signficantly expands upon this theme, claiming that "there are an infinite number of other similar [scriptural] examples aimed at the consolation and guidance of souls (ad consolationem animarum et consilium)."[17] He then lists a set of further scriptural remedies and consolations for a variety of moral, psychological, and physical states—38 other conditions in all.[18] This compilation of scriptural cures constitutes a brief monastic handbook of remedies for Gherardo and his fellow Carthusians.[19] In structure, it not only mirrors the warnings and consolations in Book 3 of Gregory the Great's *Regula pastoralis*, but also anticipates Petrarch's later admonitions and comforts in the *De remediis*.

As we shall see, however, there is a distinct difference between the fully scriptural character of the *De otio*'s "manual" and the eclectic, more laic content of the *De remediis*. It is no accident that in the former Petrarch speaks of consolations for the soul (*anima*) while in the latter he discusses more those for the mind (*animus*).[20] Despite such differences, however, this remedial section of the *De otio* may nonetheless have been an important model for Petrarch's later book of remedies. Pushing the argument back one step further, the *De otio*'s grounding in the *De vera religione* is also noteworthy. That is, the skeletal set of scriptural remedies in Augustine's treatise may thus have been an important source for Petrarch's concept of verbal remedies. In part, then, the inspiration for the *De remediis* should possibly be dated as far back as the 1330s, when Petrarch first discovered the *De vera religione*. His annotated manuscript of the work, which has been examined by Rico, shows that he took notice of the remedy section (3.4) of Augustine's treatise. In the margins of this section of the manuscript Petrarch wrote "Medicina data avaris," "Luxuriosis," "Superbis,"

"Iracundis," "Discordiosis," "Superstitiosis," "Curiosis," "Omnibus generaliter."[21] Petrarch perhaps saw this section of Augustine's work as a model of spiritual medicine. In fact, this manual of scriptural remedies may have inspired the regimen of mental remedies recommended by "Augustinus" in the *Secretum* Book 2. The historical Augustine of the *De vera religione* together with the literary Augustinus of the *Secretum* may thus have joined to provide Petrarch with part of the framework for the manual of remedies. He would transform Augustine's scriptural "medicina" into rhetorical medicine, a process he began in the *Secretum* Book 2 and completed in the *De remediis*.

In sum, Petrarch was urged on to his task in the *De remediis* by several other interests and endeavors in the realm of rhetorical care. The *De remediis* also reflects the determined Stoic spirit that Petrarch began to articulate in the 1350s and 1360s. More than once he promised to endure his sufferings more bravely than he had in younger years: let the whole world crumble about him and he would remain calm, patient, and "dry-eyed." The remedy-book explores all the contingencies of such a troubled world, and offers warnings and comforts to moderate Petrarch's own spirit and that of any reader.

The *De remediis*, then, is a culmination of various strains of psychological experience in Petrarch's thought. The models of the poet, the penitent, the confessor, the philosopher-orator all had some part in the evolution of Petrarch's vision of such a manual. But with its writing, it would appear that the emotional excesses and the near nihilism of poetic and ascetic sensibilities are now being countered by more "constructive" attempts to respond to life's sorrows. The emotional indulgence of the poet and the graphic *contemptus* of the sinner do effectively speak to the larger psychological challenges of lay experience. Tragedy, hardship, illness, misfortune, despair, and death need their consolers—they need their own healing wisdom. Petrarch had begun to find it in the realm of therapeutic rhetoric and moral philosophy. Certainly, in large measure, his efforts as a *medicus* were inspired by classical and patristic models of healing in Cicero, Seneca, Boethius, and Augustine. But his forceful and determined endeavors as a "healer" may also reflect the indirect influence of another therapeutic model, a modern-day one. To understand fully the *De remediis*, one must first understand Petrarch's attitude toward his rivals in the contemporary medical world.

In letters to a pope, to friends, and to physicians, Petrarch complained of the preoccupation with eloquence he found in contemporary medical care.[22] His bout with the doctors began with a letter in 1352 (*Fam.* 5.19) to Pope Clement VI advising him to beware of the crowd of disagreeing physicians at his sickbed and to find one "outstanding not because of his eloquence but because of his knowledge and trustworthiness."[23] Petrarch condemns doctors' zeal for speaking:

> For now, unmindful of their profession and daring to emerge from their own thickets, they seek the groves of poets and the fields of rhetoricians, and as if called not to heal but to persuade, they dispute with great bellowing at the beds of the sick. And while their patients are dying, they knit the Hippocratic knots with the Ciceronian warp; they take pride in any unfortunate event; and they do not boast of the results of their cases but rather of the empty elegance of words.[24]

This letter sparked a confrontation between Petrarch and an unknown doctor of the papal court. At least one side of this polemic is recorded in Petrarch's *Invective contra medicum* of 1352–53, the first book of which is Petrarch's response to the letter that the doctor wrote in reply to Petrarch's warning to Clement VI; the last three, his response to the reply that the doctor, in turn, had given to Petrarch's *Invectiva* Book 1.[25] These invectives reveal Petrarch's construction of the many potential conflicts and contrasts between fourteenth-century medicine and humanism: polarities pitting the mechanical vs. the liberal arts, dialectical vs. moral philosophy, the "active" vs. the "contemplative" life, Averroistic vs. Christian thought, the health of the body vs. the health of the mind. As E. Garin suggests, these invectives and Petrarch's clash with the physicians should be seen in the larger cultural context of the "dispute of the arts" that raged in Trecento and Quattrocento thought. This dispute found humanists and doctors competing to dignify and defend the various professions and disciplines.[26] The *Contra medicum* reflects not only such a struggle for cultural primacy but also a measure of hostility between Petrarch and the doctors. Like the later *De sui ipsius et multorum ignorantia*, the invectives vividly reveal Petrarch's objection to scholastic logic, natural philosophy, and Averroistic Aristotelianism; in particular they show his correctly identifying doctors with all these aspects of scholastic learning.[27] Part of the *Contra medicum* deals with Petrarch's refutation of the doctor's claim to be a philosopher. But the dispute concerned not only opposing views of *ratio* but also those of *oratio*. Petrarch describes contemporary doctors as "perorating and altercating and clamoring" and cites Vergil's characterization of medicine in the *Aeneid* (12.396–97) as a "mute art."[28] For his part, the doctor claims that rhetoric is an art subordinate to medicine. In Book 3 Petrarch refutes this contention and argues that the doctor should have no use for rhetoric—except in certain ironic ways: to "excuse" himself from blame (by "accusing" the patient, attendants, and nature) when a patient dies and to "console" the survivors.[29]

Perhaps partially fired by his polemic with the papal doctor, Petrarch continued his attacks. Later, in numerous letters in the *Seniles* he registered various complaints about doctors and medical eloquence—directing several to doctors themselves. To the physician Guglielmo da Ravenna he addressed an entire epistle, *Sen.* 3.8 (1361–), on the matter of medical eloquence. In this letter Petrarch accepts Guglielmo's invitation to friendship only by first warning that Guglielmo should not be inspired by his own example to pursue eloquence. He recalls his experience in Milan with a doctor who, in treating him, "pummeled my head weary with words and, intent on eloquence, as much as he was able, certainly indeed much more than he was able, he wove marvelous and inextricable fables."[30] Petrarch argues that all verbosity is "odious" to a patient and that doctors should use "herbs not words." They should tend to the cure of bodies and "leave the cure or moving of minds to the true philosophers and orators."[31]

Undoubtedly, enmity and resentment partly animated Petrarch's fight with the doctors. Numerous letters reveal his perception of them as incompetent, audacious, pompous, greedy, and fraudulent.[32] Some of these negative sentiments could have been sparked by an underlying competitive and resentful attitude toward doctors' social and cultural pretensions. Moreover, contemporary doctors often trafficked in intellectual pursuits antithetical to those of Petrarch. As sometime students and teachers of natural philosophy and logic, they were disciples of that world of Aristotelian learning for which Petrarch had so much contempt.[33] Suffice it to say that Petrarch's attack was motivated both by a hostile attitude toward physicians and a possessive attitude toward eloquence. Whether scientific or humanistic, the doctor's use of studied discourse is proscribed. For Petrarch, "words" do not pertain to a medical craft that he views as mechanical and mute by nature.[34] They do pertain vitally, however, to humanistic pursuits and to the psychological "craft" of the moral philosopher and orator.[35]

Petrarch's bout with the doctors perhaps helped to clarify his sense of purpose in the writing of a *De remediis*. Though seeds of his manual can be found in earlier works—the *Secretum*, the letters, the *De otio*—his outlook toward medical practice and learning may also have urged him on, urged him to supply the moral medicine and healing wisdom his age sorely lacked. It is perhaps no accident that the *De remediis* contains Petrarch's clearest definition of the "philosopher" as the "animorum medicus."[36] The medical world had increasingly become a foil for Petrarch. Now in his remedy-book he fully details a new type of therapeutic wisdom. He challenges the science of the physical and natural world with a new science of moral man and his psychological world.

The *De remediis* provides a useful collection of maxims that can aid in the assaults of both good and bad fortune—"fortune" being a term that, in proper Christian doctrine, Petrarch argues (or feels obliged to argue) is merely a figure of speech rather than a reality.[37] There are 122 chapters detailing the temptations, vanities, and distractions of good fortune, 132 the miseries of bad—life being apparently 10 chapters more adverse than favorable. Of Petrarch's Latin works this one was for long the most popular—the earliest to be printed (1468) and the one having the most editions (over 70 Latin and vernacular editions through the mid-eighteenth century).[38] In fact, B. Kohl has argued that the *De remediis* was the most popular philosophical work to come out of the Italian Renaissance.[39] Petrarch's manual likely responded to some vital psychological interests in early modern literate society.

If the idea of conquering the emotions was essentially Stoic, nonetheless Petrarch's manual perhaps was unique in presenting what was until then the most comprehensive humanist response to the threats of the affects. In the prologue to the first book, Petrarch places his work in a particular intellectual and historical context. Disagreeing with Aristotle (*Nic. Ethics* 3.9.2.1117a) and Seneca (*Ad Luc.* 66.49) that bad fortune is harder to handle than good,[40] he intends to expand the remedial treatments found in [Ps.-] Seneca's work, the *De remediis fortuitorum*, which dealt only with bad fortune. He will add remedies for the temptations of good fortune and include a discussion of vices and virtues which, though not aspects of fortune, are part of the world of the human affects.[41] Besides its partially Stoic roots, Petrarch's major treatment of good fortune here, like the admonitions of "Augustinus" concerning prideful conceits in the *Secretum* Book 2, also reveals partially the influence of the Christian themes of *vanitas* and *contemptus mundi*.[42] In combining the realms of morality and the seven deadly sins, the vanities, emotions, and both domains of fortune, the *De remediis* is a complete manual for the care of soul and mind.[43] And in dealing with some particular, highly secular interests such as "love," "eloquence," "books," and "fame"—concerns all personally important to Petrarch—the treatise mirrors the wide landscape of Petrarch's psychological world.[44]

Our interest lies not in analyzing the entire manual, but in focusing on three areas: Petrarch's general psychological theory; his definition of the art of rhetorical care; and his particularly substantive treatment of certain problems in Book 2. As for the first area, the prologues to both books contain theories concerning the human mind. The notion of the four Stoic affects, referred to in the *Secretum* Book 1, is the keystone to the work. This is evident not only in both prologues but also in the very structure of the work in which Ratio ministers to Spes and Gaudium in Book 1 and to Metus and Dolor in Book 2.[45] In both prefaces Petrarch develops this classical paradigm of the turbulent psyche in some anthropological detail. In the first preface he opens by saying that man's gifts of intelligence are turned against him in that, unlike ignorant animals, he can be solicitous of the past, present, and future.[46] In the second preface Petrarch discourses on the natural sources of man's state of emotional and psychological chaos. Developing the Heraclitean notion that "flux" is the engine of nature, he describes the natural phenomenon of strife and contention to be found in the skies, seas, cities, animals, angels, and, finally, man.[47] It is a world of perpetual unrest and disquiet. Moreover, this natural dynamic of strife applies to man not only externally but also internally:

> [H]ow great is the internal contention? Indeed man contends not only against other species but also, as I said, against his own; not only against another individual but against himself. In that corporeal shell of yours, which is the vilest and lowest part of us, and in the intimate interiors of the soul, everyone assiduously wars with himself. In what way this body seethes and is disturbed by contrary humors we can learn from those they call "natural philosophers." In what way the mind fights with itself with so many diverse and adverse affects, one need only ask himself and respond to himself how with varied and shifting impulses of the mind he is seized now here and now there, never whole, never placid, contradicting and fragmenting himself. To mention a few impulses: to wish, not to wish, to love, to hate, to flatter, to threaten, to ridicule, to deceive, to feign, to joke, to weep, to pity, to spare, to grow angry, to placate, to slip, to be brought down, to be raised up, to waver, to halt, to progress, to regress, . . . and emotions that are of this kind, which assuredly are more uncertain than anything that can be imagined, and with which mortal life fluctuates from beginning to end without any respite.[48]

Petrarch draws the Heraclitean strife of nature into the psychological domain, constructing a theory of mental experience that can complement the scientific studies of the natural philosophers. Though tame here, this comment should be seen as part of Petrarch's ongoing response to scholasticism: his humanist exploration of the anatomy of the human mind will provide a much-needed analogue to the scholastic discussions of the anatomy of nature and the human body. An examination of the human psyche reveals a pattern of relentless unrest. The subsequent dialogues of the *De remediis* act on this theory of constant chaos by responding to almost every imaginable vicissitude found in human psychological experience. As Diekstra argues, the treatise testifies to Petrarch's thoroughgoing participation in and recognition of the affect-ridden world of temporal experience.[49]

Itemizing this mundane psychological world, which he had only begun to explore in the *Secretum*, Petrarch sought not only to identify but also to remedy these myriad ills of the human condition. In the preface to Book 1 he presents his definition of the eloquent healer. Turning to a medical analogy, he sets out his theory of therapeutic rhetoric:

Neither am I ignorant that, as in the bodies of man, so also in their minds that are affected with sundry passions, the medicines of words (*medicamenta verborum*) will seem to many to be without effect. But it does not escape me that as the diseases of the mind (*animorum morbi*) are invisible, so are their remedies invisible also. For those who are assailed by false opinions must be liberated by true maxims, so that those who fell by hearing may rise up by hearing. He who willingly offers to a needy friend what he has, however small it is, fulfills the full office of friendship.[50]

This definition of his task as healer reveals not only Petrarch's idea of the medium of medicinal *verba* but also his sense of the social impulse behind such endeavors. As he had said earlier in his prefatory letter, his attempt to console Azzo is analogous to [Ps.-] Seneca's effort to comfort Gallio in his *De remediis*. Having suffered exile, illness, and bereavement, Azzo certainly was an appropriate recipient. For Petrarch, then, his book of remedies generally fulfilled the office of friendly care which the moralist performs more narrowly in the consolatory letter. But it was perhaps less the obligations of friendship than Petrarch's enduring fascination with therapeutic eloquence that prompted him to embark on this herculean project.

Misery and Sadness

Our study of the body of the *De remediis* will focus on the consolatory Book 2 rather than the monitory Book 1.[51] Of particular importance here are the preeminent treatments of misery, illness, and death. From Petrarch's point of view the most innovative and dramatic remedy in the entire manual would almost certainly have been his consolation for misery. Several chapters of Book 2 deal with the specific realm of mental disquiet or despair: "On the Discord of a Fluctuating Mind" (75), "On a Doubtful State" (76), "On the Tedium of Life" (98), "On Madness" (115), "On Misery and Sadness" ("De miseria et tristitia") (93). Though all of these chapters illustrate Petrarch's fascination with psychological unrest, it is in Chapter 93 that he fully develops the problem of despair.

This chapter completes an investigation of sadness begun in the *Secretum* Book 2. But rather than use the terminology of "*accidia-aegritudo*," Petrarch chooses that of "*miseria-tristitia*." "*Accidia*," in fact, has disappeared from the *De remediis*, as Petrarch represents this deadly sin now as "*torpor animi*," treating it merely as sloth.[52] Petrarch looks elsewhere for his vocabulary of despair, and develops some dimensions of misery only touched upon in the malady portrayed in the *Secretum*. He again breaks new ground in dealing with the problem of despair. But whereas his contribution in the *Secretum* lay chiefly in his treatment of the symptoms and causes of sadness, in the *De remediis* 2.93 it rests chiefly in the cure.

In the "De miseria et tristitia" Petrarch explores an aspect of despair only hinted at in the *Secretum*: namely, that of "existential" misery. In his discussion of *accidia-aegritudo* in the *Secretum*, Petrarch briefly made reference to the generally miserable, contemptible nature of the human condition, but he focused his discussion on several specific, individualized causes of despair enumerated by "Franciscus." In the "De miseria et tristitia," however, he is more concerned with the general problem of misery. Perhaps largely because the many dialogues of the *De remediis* Book 2 address the gamut of circumstantial woes, Petrarch is free here to turn his attention to this intangible, causeless woe.[53] "Ratio" will now concentrate his efforts on the fundamental misery of man *qua* man, as "Dolor" utters such global complaints as "Huius vitae miseria moestum sum."[54] The source of this despair over human existence is unknown but its symptoms include the familiar *voluptas dolendi*:

> At times, moreover, there is no wholly apparent cause—not sickness, losses, injuries, ignominies, poor conduct, or, in general, any unexpected rumor of such things—but only a certain pleasure of grieving (*dolendi voluptas quaedam*) which makes the soul sad. It is a plague all the more deadly in that its cause is more unknown and thus the cure more difficult; therefore Cicero [*Tusc.* 3.11.26] suggests that this malady, like a crag to the soul, ought to be fled with every aid of sails and oars.[55]

Petrarch thus informs this existential sadness with the same pathology of indulgent brooding found first in his *Rime* and later in the *accidia-aegritudo* of the *Secretum* Book 2. The emotional patterns of the poet, first transferred to Franciscus as depressed individual, are now given to Dolor as universal man.

But more important here is Petrarch's treatment of the "malady" of the human condition. Dolor's complaint of a "*tristitia*" prompts Ratio to make the Pauline observation that a sadness concerning sin, the *tristitia secundum Deum*, is useful. But Dolor's sadness over the misery of the human condition, the harshness of fortune, and the brevity of life is clearly closer to that opposing worldly malady *tristitia saeculi*.[56] The language of Dolor's despair is revealing: the lament over the "miseries of this life" clearly reveals the influence of the *contemptus mundi*.[57] Petrarch's remedy for this "misery of the human condition" is his famous praise of the dignity of man, celebrating man's capacities, his arts, his intellect, his bounteous natural environment, his divine similitude, his dignity in the Incarnation, the immortality of his soul, his hope of resurrection.[58] Formulated "partly philosophically and partly theologically"[59] as Ratio admits, the discussion draws largely on the positive traits of man found in Augustine's *De civitate Dei* 22.24 and Cicero's *De natura deorum* 2.54 ff.[60] Marshaling a range of theological and natural evidence, Petrarch makes a forceful statement concerning man's favored place above the animals and, even, the angels.

Petrarch also dealt with the theme of human misery in his earlier monastic work *De otio*. In developing the topic there, he cited Pliny the Elder's *Naturalis historia* 7.6, Cicero's *Consolatio*, and Augustine's *De civitate Dei* 22.22.[61] Although these citations reveal the ancient and patristic sources for such a motif, it is essentially the medieval *contemptus* that informs Petrarch's notion of misery. And it is this later tradition that Petrarch principally draws on and reacts to in the *Secretum*, the *De otio*, and the *De remediis*. In the *De otio* Petrarch's solace for human *miseria* consisted largely of a praise of God's majesty and mercy.[62] His fuller, more secular response to misery comes, significantly enough, in the *De remediis* 2.93, where he lays considerably more stress on the dignity and majesty of man. And although many of the arguments are religious, the tone is anthropocentric rather than theocentric. The rhetorical Petrarch thus deftly varies his counsel according to audience and setting. To his brother he presents a traditional theological consolation concerning God's mercy; to Azzo and a wider laity he offers the solace of human happiness.[63]

Never one to conceal talent from his readers, Petrarch points out the importance of his remedy in Chapter 93. Ratio opens his oration on human felicity by suggesting that no author has successfully written on this subject due to its relative difficulty. Commenting that certain writers had made false starts in this area, Ratio alludes to Innocent III, who never produced his promised treatise, *De dignitate humanae conditionis*, a work meant to complement his famous *De miseria humanae conditionis*. Petrarch confirmed this connection between his own discussion and Innocent's contemplated work in a letter (*Sen.* 16.9) to the Grand Prior of the Chartreuse, who had requested that Petrarch write a treatise on Innocent's proposed topic of human dignity. Petrarch replies that he has just begun working on such a topic in his chapter "De miseria et tristitia" in the *De remediis* when he received the Prior's letter:

> There is a book of mine in progress, the *De remediis ad utranque fortunam*, in which I strive to the best of my abilities to mollify or, if possible, to extirpate my own passions and those of my readers. Moreover, by chance, it just so happened that when it had come time for me to work on the section "de tristitia miseriaque" and I was occupied in that endeavor to console this kind of sadness arising from no certain causes, which the philosophers call sickness (*aegritudo*) of the mind, to console this sadness by opposing to it its contrary, which cannot be more effectively accomplished than by seeking out the causes of happiness, which is indeed nothing else than examining the dignity of

the human condition—on that same day your letter urging this very topic arrived.[64]

One never knows whether to believe Petrarch concerning such coincidences.[65] But whether inspired by a clerical friend or, in fact, by the very structure of his own remedy-book, Petrarch clearly saw his efforts in Chapter 93 within the literary context of Innocent's two works. But, as is clear, he also framed the discussion in psychological terms, viewing *miseria* as a mental malady like ancient *aegritudo*.

Thus, Petrarch draws into his net the notion of "misery" popularized in the medieval ascetic tradition. Mortal misery is now seen not merely as a well-deserved spiritual trial, but as a psychological condition requiring a remedy. In his writings Petrarch treated misery in both of these lights. In the *Secretum* Book 1 Augustinus' regimen for Franciscus was a "meditation on death and human misery"; misery, here, was a remedy, a cure for vanity. Also, however, partly in the *Secretum* Book 2 and particularly in the *De remediis* 2.93, misery was a malady, a psychological despair over the human condition. Petrarch thus moves misery from the purely spiritual plane of the *contemptus mundi* to the emotional plane of worldly dejection. In Chapter 93 misery is part of that long-neglected, long-scorned *tristitia saeculi*, and yet Petrarch treats it as a legitimate type of sorrow.[66] In placing such a worldly psychological focus on this once fully otherworldly notion of human misery, Petrarch's consolation represents a signficant departure. No longer solely a punishment for Adam's Fall, no longer solely a contemptible mortal passage preceding a blissful immortal state, misery is an emotional ill, a causeless woe, linked to "sweet grief" and to *accidia-aegritudo*. In his remedy-book Petrarch thus dramatically moves misery from the world of the religious panegyrist to that of the lay consoler and rhetorical *medicus*.

As Petrarch himself seemed to realize, his Chapter 93 broke new ground in the history of ideas. The medieval ascetic lament of misery now had a consolation rooted in the majesty of man rather than in the transcendence of God. As Trinkaus has shown, Petrarch's praise of human dignity and happiness launched what later became, as is well known, a prominent Renaissance theme developed by Quattrocento writers such as Giannozzo Manetti, Aurelio Brandolini, Marsilio Ficino, and Pico della Mirandola.[67] This theme had considerable historical significance: the formulation and articulation of a more positive view of human existence marked an important shift in emphasis away from prevailing medieval views of man. It is fitting that this praise of man came in a lay consolation manual meant to provide comfort for sorrows somewhat neglected by dominant currents in the ascetic tradition and in pastoral care. Sensitive to the multitude of worldly cares, Petrarch saw the need for a more sanguine, ennobling view of the very nature of man. His consolation for the human condition completed a process of his redefining the contours of Christian sorrow. In the *Secretum* Book 2 he informed medieval *accidia* with highly secular concerns of personal misfortune and travail. In the *De remediis* 2.93 he fully shifted *miseria* from its status as an ascetic remedy to that of a worldly malady, offering as its long-awaited cure the anthropocentric consolation of human dignity.

Illness and Pain

Though most of the *De remediis* treats moral, spiritual, and psychological ills, some chapters deal with physical ones: "On Adverse Health" (3), "On Gout" (84), "On Mange" (85), "On Toothaches" (94), "On Leg Aches" (95), "On Blindness" (96), "On Deafness" (97), "On Obesity" (98), "On Dumbness" (103), "On Fevers" (112), "On Colic and Fainting" (113), "On Various Pain and Illness of the Whole Body" (114). The last of these chapters ("De totius corporis dolore ac languore vario") is the longest and most substantive of all such chapters—in fact, it is the longest chapter in the treatise. In this chapter Petrarch fully addresses the problem of pain (and overall bodily affliction such as leprosy), presenting theories of healing eloquence on both a general, theoretical level and on a specific, prescriptive level. If Chapter 93 is, in some measure, Petrarch's rejoinder to those more ascetic medieval theologians, Chapter 114 is his answer to contemporary physicians. He uses this chapter to formulate his own type of healing eloquence, one that can replace that spurious kind of the doctors. In this effort, Petrarch moves out from the realm of the moral *medicus* and encroaches on that of the physical *medicus*, clearly hoping to best his professional foes, the physicians.

In Chapter 114 Petrarch squarely confronts the problem of the efficacy of words in the face of pain. Dolor repeatedly objects to Ratio's attempts to provide verbal remedies. In Chapter 117 ("On the Fear of Death") "Metus" makes a similar objection to the usefulness of philosophical remedies for treating the fear of death.[68] But there is an important difference in the degree of skepticism in the two chapters. In Chapter 117 there is only a single objection to philosophical remedies, but in Chapter 114 Dolor complains continuously about the value of "words" or philosophy in a time of pain. In fact, Dolor's part here is the most vocal and combative in all of the *De remediis* Book 2.[69] This is no accident. Although the dialogues in Cicero's *Tusculans* Book 2 and the Book of Job included some protests to the academic treatment of suffering, it is almost certain that Petrarch's Dolor is fired by something even more. Writing Chapter 114 certainly after the *Contra medicum* and very possibly after other epistolary attacks on the doctors, Petrarch may have been heeding his own warnings to physicians that words are *molestum* in the face of pain and useless in the treatment of the sick.[70] Dolor's challenge to Ratio's eloquence echoes Petrarch's challenge to doctors' eloquence. Very combative and skeptical, the fictitious Dolor voices the objections earlier made by the real Petrarch, complaining throughout the dialogue: "Alas, I suffer and you dispute," and "I trust not in the trifles of philosophers but in my senses," and "Alas, how you torment me and add tedium to my grief; may you produce a remedy; now neither you nor philosophy with you ever will make it so I do not feel what I feel."[71]

Certainly, Ratio has his work cut out for him. In his consolation, Petrarch presents a considerably Stoic, but eclectic, exhortation to forbearance, proclaiming the power of virtue, patience, strength of mind, and inspiring *exempla* to vanquish pain.[72] Significantly, Petrarch frames his labored therapeutic speech—largely an adaptation of the second book of the *Tusculans*—in the context of a contrast to scientific learning. It is entirely fitting that, in this chapter in which Petrarch implicitly counters the medical use of *oratio*, he also presents one of his criticisms of the uselessness of natural philosophy, which no doubt was meant partly to allude to the scholastic *ratio* associated with doctors *qua* philosophers. After a lengthy dialogue in which Ratio carefully and sensitively tries to convince the doubting Dolor that wisdom and virtue can strengthen the mind against pain, Dolor finally starts to become more receptive, asking Ratio to elaborate on the "arms of the mind" that can be used to fight pain. Ratio replies:

> I have hope of your health, for as it is womanly to weep in the face of adversities, it is moreover manly and effective in overcoming them to strive, to resist, and to seek counsel and help. Indeed the arms of the mind and arts of battle are many and varied because of the diversity of enemies. Nor is any gift of philosophy more useful and holy than to treat these things which I think pertain to us somewhat more than to know what the stars do, what nature-gazing Jupiter promises, what Mars joined with Saturn threatens, . . . whence comes rain and heat, whence earthquakes, by what power the deep seas rise and [regrettably] not to know whence comes the passion, rage, trembling, and weakness of minds, and with what remedies passion may be calmed, rage confined, and trembling and weakness strengthened and confirmed.[73]

The subject of true philosophy is the wisdom concerning the problems of the human mind and psyche—not the trivialities of astrology or natural philosophy. As a doctor of minds investigating the fluctuations of the spirit, Ratio pursues a wisdom superseding that of the natural scientist.

At the end of Ratio's lengthy consolation Dolor still repeats his objections: "It is possible to be as you say, but now even I lack much that health of mind toward which you aim; and I am in great doubt, whether pain is alleviated or removed by all these things, or whether words filling minds and delighting ears are nothing to pain."[74] Petrarch responds with his theory of rhetorical therapy for the afflicted. Ratio argues: "I admit that words do not heal bodies, unless perhaps incantations and old-womanish songs merit any credence; but they do heal sicknesses of minds, the health of which truly either extinguishes or mitigates bodily pain."[75] Curing and manipulating the mind can aid or effect the cure of the body. Ratio's goal, thus, has been to try to instill a mental health that indirectly can heal the physically ailing Dolor.[76] In doing this, Ratio uses a carefully crafted moral eloquence epitomizing Petrarch's vision of a new wisdom that can replace the irrelevant, sterile learning of his day. In his dialogue of Christian Ciceronian persuasion, Petrarch formulated his own specialized therapy for pain. By virtue of his role as a *medicus animorum* he ventured, in some sense, to become also a *medicus corporum*.[77]

Petrarch's techniques to heal and fortify a sufferer's mind entailed his new vision of rhetorical, moral (particularly Ciceronian) philosophy. It is likely that Petrarch would have argued that his philosophical "healing eloquence" could be administered only by a few.[78] With a special expertise he could fulfill the role of the rhetor-psychologist that he forbade to doctors in his *Sen.* 3.8 to Guglielmo da Ravenna. Using *oratio* to "cure and move minds," he practiced a technical craft that properly belongs only to the "true philosophers and orators."[79]

Death

Besides "misery" and "illness," Petrarch's other great challenge in the *De remediis* was "death."[80] Bereavement, fear of death, the act of dying, concern over one's affairs after death: these problems command the greatest number of chapters in the treatise. The dialogues on bereavement, dealing with the loss of a wife (18), a father (46), a mother (47), a son (48), an infant (49), a brother (51), and a friend (52) offer some traditional *solacia* and *exempla* on grief and are not particularly noteworthy. As seen in Chapter 2 above, his more substantive treatment of bereavement would come later, in 1368, in the consolatory *Sen.* 10.4 to Donato Albanzani. Much more important in the *De remediis* are those chapters concerning one's own death. As Cicero's *Tusculans* Book 1, Seneca's letters to Lucilius, and the Ps.-Senecan *De remediis* all reveal, the problem of death had been a prominent one in the Latin moral tradition. And though much of Petrarch's effort here can be characterized as a humanist revival of the Stoic treatment of death, there is also a more timely historical context for his dialogues on death. As the *Secretum* and the *De otio* clearly show,[81] the ascetic, macabre image of death and the concern with human mutability had a powerful hold on Petrarch. In fact, a medieval "meditation on death and human misery" was a central cure in the *Secretum* Book 1. But it was not only as a page from the *contemptus mundi* but also as a tangible threat that death had a highly charged emotional context in the fourteenth-century world. Petrarch certainly had seen the specter of death many times in his life: this is quite evident in the despairing letters and verse of 1348–49, when he lost Laura, Cardinal Colonna, and various other friends. Events of the 1360s only deepened his awareness of death's physical and psychological presence. In 1361 he lost his son Giovanni and his "Socrates." In May of 1362 he wrote his lengthy *Sen.* 1.5 to Boccaccio, who was frightened over the prophecy of death. In 1363 the rumor of Petrarch's own death began circulating, and, even worse, he lost his beloved friends "Laelius" and "Simonides." *Sen.* 3.1, which he wrote concerning the latter losses and the endemic ravages of plague over the past decade and a half, is the most doleful letter of his later years. Reflecting at some length on his bouts with his persistent nemesis Fortuna, Petrarch confesses to some of the old habits of the *voluptas dolendi.*[82] At the same time, however, he declares his determination to hold fast to "a recently formulated proposition, fashioned from true and solid maxims, a proposition I have relied upon like a rudder in the sea of life: namely, the thought that *death* and all mortal things must be borne by mortal beings with equanimity."[83] Moreover, he also voices a resolve to scorn hope, fear, happiness, and grief—clearly a reference to the categories of the *De remediis.*[84] Acknowledging that "the day draws near when will vanish all those things that now becloud and delight our life with such great intensity," Petrarch seems to be contemplating his old age: "For us now the sole task is to be firm against the terrors and blows of sorrow, because the contrary, namely, either anxious hope or unbridled happiness, offers no threat to us these days."[85] Should Petrarch die, only his Boccaccio now remains to be caretaker of his works in progress.[86] Clearly Petrarch is increasingly looking toward a lonely senescence, looking toward the end of his life.

Is it possible that Chapters 117–132 were, in full or in part, Petrarch's last effort to defend against Fortuna? Were they his attempt to face the fearful last threat his old enemy would bring?[87] Certainly his mood of the 1360s might have set him to such a task. In addition to these various tragedies and letters of the period, one last letter is particularly pertinent. On his sixty-second birthday, July 20, 1366, Petrarch wrote again to Boccaccio discussing his state of mind as he entered the frightful sixty-third year of his life. Astrologers saw in this year the unhappy marriage of the numbers "7" and "9." Petrarch resolves to meet this year with a brave face, and he debunks the buffoonery of the stargazers. But though he may have professed

to dismiss the danger of this superstitious year, perhaps he was still somewhat frightened by it, as Boccaccio had been by the divine prophecy of his
impending death a few years before.[88] Certainly, his letter (*Sen.* 8.1) is a
searching reflection on his old age and, in some measure, a self-exhortation.
Citing the Davidic "Et si ambulavero in medio umbrae mortis" (Ps. 22), he
consoles himself with the twin hopes of immortality and resurrection.[89] In
early October of 1366, only shortly after the writing of this letter in July,
Petrarch completed the *De remediis*.[90] Were some, or even all, of these
death chapters his philosophical remedy for the fear of his own death in this
sad decade, and in this particularly scary year of his life? Indeed, mounting
personal crises and fears may well have informed these powerful last chapters on the philosophical art of dying.[91]

Petrarch presents sixteen chapters on death and dying. Some treat topics
discussed in the Ps.-Senecan work,[92] but others have a more contemporary
and personal cast. One, "On Dying in Sin" (126), elucidates the particular
Christian dangers of improper death. Some chapters, such as "On Premature Death" (120) and "On Concern for Fame after Death" (130), treat
topics that reflect Petrarch's own past and present concerns.[93] Some enu-
merate various pragmatic and highly secular concerns attending death:
"On Dying Worried about What Will Become of Patrimony and Children"
(127), "On Dying Anxious about What Your Wife Will Do after Your
Death" (128), "On Dying without Children" (131). In all, except for some
of the sacramental aspects of dying,[94] Petrarch covers almost every facet of
dying in the fourteenth century.

The most important chapters are "On the Fear of Death" (117) and "On
Death" (119), in which Petrarch deals with the fear and acceptance of
death. In these two discussions he presents one of the fullest philosophical
and consolatory treatments of death since Cicero's *Tusculans* Book 1.[95]
Moreover, in Chapter 117, as in the earlier Chapter 114 on affliction, discussed above, Petrarch also makes a plea for a more meaningful moral philosophy, one that can minister to the problems of human life. In Chapter
117, after Ratio has offered some consolations concerning death, Metus
complains about the inefficacy of philosophical wisdom: "These things are
trite and common among the philosophers and they are pleasing while they
are heard, but let a silence fall, and the fear returns."[96] Ratio's answer is a
powerful plea for a revival of a true moral wisdom. He chides Metus for
clinging to the fear of death innate in common people, and then counters
Metus' impugning of philosophy:

> For I marvel at what you say concerning philosophers, since you seek advice
> on sailing from sailors, on sowing from farmers, and on fighting from military
> leaders, and yet you contemn advice obtained from philosophers concerning
> the art of living. And I marvel that for the cure of the body you invoke doc-

tors, but for the cure of the mind you do not go to philosophers, who, if they are true philosophers are certainly doctors of minds (*animorum medici*) and experts on living. For if they are false and only puffed up with the name of philosophy, not only must they not be consulted but they must be avoided— nothing is more troublesome and insipid than such philosophers, of whom no age is more abundant than our own, since it is so lacking in good men.[97]

As he did time and again throughout his life, Petrarch here attacks the uselessness and vanity of modern-day scholastic philosophy.[98] In its place he would summon the salutary wisdom of the true philosophers, the *medici animorum*. It is that ancient moral learning that must now be recaptured and tapped: "And since from the present-day philosophers there is nothing you can hope for except pure trifles, if, returning to the ancients (*ad priscos*), you would find anything among them that might relieve your distress, do not spurn it and do not [pejoratively] say, as the ignorant do, that you obtained these things from the philosophers."[99]

Having called for a renaissance of remedial philosophical *content*, Petrarch then discusses the problem of rhetorical *form*. He defends his own part in the ongoing mission of rhetorically gleaning, restating, and applying ancient consolation:

[A]nd if, like treasures, these [philosophical truths] are discovered by and hidden amongst the philosophers, these same truths nevertheless can be brought into the open by others and can be expressed either more concisely, more clearly, more distinctly, more briefly, or, finally, differently, such similar things bringing hope to all who hear them and bringing success to a few. Such is the power of order and combination which, as Horace also teaches most elegantly in the *Ars poetica*, affects minds often in various ways and sometimes in various degrees. So great can be the charms of telling even the most well- known thing! Such newness can be added to the old; so much light to the shining, so much grace to the beautiful![100]

Chapter 117, then, serves as a forum for Petrarch's proclamation of his endeavors as a latter-day moral orator seeking to provide effective, useful philosophy through his rhetorical art. Ratio's speech is a blueprint for Petrarch's vision of the proper joining of moral philosophy and rhetoric: the ancient *ratio* of the true philosophers and "doctors of the mind" must be reappropriated and refashioned in ever-changing strains of modern-day *oratio*.

Why did Petrarch choose this chapter to present a theory of remedial eloquence which in some ways could apply to the entire *De remediis*? Possi- bly it is simply because death has always posed such a formidable challenge for the consoling philosopher: it certainly had pride of place in Cicero's *Tusculans* and Ps.-Seneca's *De remediis*.[101] Recognizing the difficulty and importance of treating the problem of death, Petrarch thus is at pains to explain that the only effective cure would be a new formulation of moral maxims mined from the lode of true philosophy.[102]

Having thus underscored the significance of Ratio's task, Petrarch then presents a truly complete consolation for death and dying. For the most part his *solacia* are drawn from discussions in Seneca's letters and in Cicero's *Somnium Scipionis* and *Tusculans* Book 1. He essentially argues a Stoic view of dying, commending a tranquility that avoids both the fear of death and the lust for it. Separating the Chapters "On the Fear of Death" and "On Death" is one "On the Taking of One's Own Life" (118), which, focusing on Cato, warns against this solution as a escape from life's harshness.[103] As a whole, Petrarch's chapters on death emphasize the importance of dying well; they represent a thoroughgoing revival of the Stoic concern with the *ars* or *scientia moriendi*.[104]

A key element in this humanist "art of dying" is the familiar regimen of the reflection on death. As the *Secretum* and the *De otio* reveal, Petrarch's sources for such a remedial meditation are found both in the classical philosophical tradition and in the medieval ascetic tradition. In "On the Fear of Death" Ratio warns Metus that "there is nothing more damnable in human evils than to be forgetful of God, of oneself, and of death."[105] Recommending a type of Platonic-Stoic anticipation of death, he invokes the maxim that "vita omnis meditatio mortis est," locating that regimen both in "*philosophia antiqua*" and now in "*nova pietas*."[106] Though joining classical and ascetic strains of the death meditation, Petrarch's approach here must draw more on the former tradition than on the latter. The graphic horrors of a *memento mori*, such as those "Augustinus" prescribed to "Franciscus" in the *Secretum* Book 1, would not be helpful here: the macabre warnings of the *contemptus mundi* would only intensify the fears of Metus and the reader of the *De remediis*. As in Chapter 93 on misery, in these chapters on death Petrarch must shift the focus of the meaning of human suffering: rather than as a remedy for vanity, suffering must be seen as a malady itself. Consequently, Petrarch has to soften the tone of the death meditation. The harsh admonition of the "meditatio mortis humane-que miserie" in the *Secretum* Book 1 is now shorn of its threatening asectic quality. Instead Ratio cultivates here more that Platonic-Stoic facet of the death meditation that calls for a calm anticipation and acceptance of one's death. Petrarch uses the *meditatio mortis* as part of the revival of a Stoic concern with dying well, the rational art of meeting death with prepara-tion, obedience, and a ready will.

Besides the death meditation, Ratio offers various other consolations that unite classical and Christian perspectives. That death is neither good nor evil, that it brings a release from temporal chains (a *locus* Petrarch cred-its to Plotinus), that the soul is immortal: all these philosophical remedies

are confirmed by Christian thought. For instance, in the discussion of immortality in the "On Death" Petrarch sanctifies Cicero's reflections on that
theme:

> The same Cicero . . . disput[es] [in the *Tusculans* Book 1] sagaciously among
> his friends whether the soul dies or is transferred so that there would be either
> nothing evil or very much good in death; among us there truly is no doubt of
> this not only among philosophers but even among the crowd. Nor do I be-
> lieve, by Hercules, that there was any doubt for Cicero himself—concerning
> whom we often speak—who declared it most magnificently in many places,
> but who heeded the doubts of his disputant or of that age. Therefore, main-
> tain this truth to the highest degree so that you may know that the soul is
> immortal, because not only the harmonious opinion of your people but also
> that of all the most excellent philosophers maintains this truth.[107]

Ratio thus gives added weight to the classical philosophical doctrine of
immortality by affirming its theological familiarity to the ranks of all Christians. As a latter-day consoler Petrarch was attempting to revive and bap-
tize the somewhat neglected *consolatio* for death in *Tusculans* Book 1. Of
course, the fuller rebirth of the theme of immortality would come with the
revival of Platonic thought in the following century.

In addition to philosophizing on the nature of death, Petrarch also details the proper method of dying willingly, obediently, triumphantly. In the
spirit of Seneca's "bene autem mori est libenter mori" (*Ad Luc.* 61.2) Ratio
urges the dying "cupias quodcunque necesse est";[108] he counsels obedience
to the orders of the heavenly commander and to the laws of nature; he
exhorts the dying to rise in spirit at the time of death. Petrarch's remedies
for death thus join philosophical attitudes with psychological acts. In combining the Ciceronian consolation for death with the Senecan "science of
dying well," Petrarch's treatment perhaps surpasses any single classical response to the problem of death and dying. In a climate of late medieval
asceticism and epidemic mortality, Petrarch fully provides a response to
death as a psychological threat. Though alert to the macabre *memento mori*,
he could also draw on softer classical currents to offer a reassuring guide, an
art of dying calmly and well, for the fearful experience of death.

Petrarch's thought thus mirrors the two faces of death in late medieval
culture. On the one hand, Augustinus' frightful death meditation in the
Secretum Book 1 reflects the prevailing "irrational" reaction to the threat of
death. On the other, Ratio's remedies in *De remediis* 2.117–32 attempt to
offer a "rational" response to death's tyranny. In both cases, Petrarch's outlook has much in common with the later northern flowering both of the
danse macabre and the *ars moriendi*.[109] The similarities between his *De remediis* and the later *ars moriendi* are limited but very revealing.[110] In the early
fifteenth century there emerged a *Tractatus artis bene moriendi*, a work gen-

erally thought to be from the hands of a Dominican. Drawing largely on Jean Gerson's *De scientia mortis* in his *Opusculum tripartitum*, the *Tractatus* was intended as a manual to instruct the faithful in their last moments. It contained sections on the commendation of death; on deathbed temptations, interrogations, and obsecrations; and on instructions and prayers for those attending at the deathbed. In manuscript and printed editions this work appeared in Latin, German, Low German, Italian, Spanish, Dutch, French, and English. A shorter, illustrated version, the famous block-book titled *Ars moriendi*, enjoyed a wide popularity in the fifteenth century. The genre of the "art of dying" had a considerable currency in Renaissance and early modern Europe, with versions appearing from Italian figures such as Savonarola, Pietro Barozzi, and Roberto Bellarmino, and northern writers such as Erasmus, Thomas Lupset, Thomas Becon, and Jeremy Taylor.[111]

Petrarch's *De remediis* 2.117–32 is not as spiritual and liturgical as the *Tractatus artis bene moriendi*, but is more concerned with psychological and secular problems. There are, however, sections that correspond to the concerns of the *Tractatus*. The chapters "On the Fear of Death" and "On Death" serve as a type of commendation of death and as a guide to accepting death. "On Dying in Sin" corresponds roughly with the *Tractatus*' concern with the temptation to despair. Petrarch's Ratio seeks to guide Dolor to the proper spiritual state in which he would have sufficient contrition for his sin, but not so much as to despair of his salvation.[112] The concern with dying willingly and gladly, the exhortation to entrust oneself to God, the treatment of spiritual despair, the anxieties over various secular issues concerning one's estate and surviving family: all these matters in the *De remediis* find some treatment or mention later in the *Tractatus*. True to its consolatory purpose, however, Petrarch's manual goes far beyond the *Tractatus* in its rhetorical treatment of the fear and acceptance of death. This is no accident. Even by the time of the emergence of the *ars moriendi*, pastoral writers generally did not substantively deal with the problem of consoling for death: for the theologian, the secular psychological threats of death were far less pressing than the spiritual dangers of a sinful or improper departure.

Yet, like the *De remediis*, the *Tractatus* also represents an attempt to temper the harsh climate of necromania in later medieval culture. As Beaty and O'Connor suggest, the *Tractatus*, in contrast to the *danse macabre*, presented a more positive and comforting view of death. It provided some balance to the excesses of dancing icons of putrefaction as well as to the literary vision of wretchedness in the *contemptus mundi*.[113] The first chapter, titled in an English version "[C]ommendacion of deth and cunnynge for to dye well," deals most explicitly with consolation.[114] Citing Aristotle, Seneca, Ecclesiastes, Wisdom, Paul, Cassian, and other sources, it urges the acceptance of death. It draws upon some of the same arguments found in the *De remediis*, including the Senecan *locus* that one dies well who dies freely. This consolatory component in the *Tractatus*, however, is only a minor prologue to the fuller quasi-sacramental treatment that dominates the handbook. By contrast, Petrarch's treatment of dying has much more consolatory, philosophical, and psychological depth. With its many *solacia* (e.g., immortality), with its various *exempla*, with its regimen of a classical death meditation, with its call for emotional readiness and anticipation, and with its treatment of the related secular anxieties attending death, Petrarch's remedy for death offers a comprehensive guide for meeting the terrors of the end.

Petrarch's "*ars moriendi*" may be compared to a work Beaty character-izes as a "humanistic" version of the genre, the sixteenth-century *Waye of Dyenge Well* written by Thomas Lupset, an associate of John Colet's and Erasmus'.[115] His treatise, if broadly grounded in the *Ars*, develops the genre in a highly classical manner, dealing most thoroughly with the prob-lems of the fear and acceptance of death.[116] Though Lupset's *Waye of Dyenge* contains much more traditional religious content than Petrarch's remedies, nonetheless, classical moral and philosophical concerns prevail. Like Petrarch, Lupset presents a major treatment of the fear of death, de-veloping many of the same arguments posed by Petrarch, attempting to formulate a highly psychological Christian-Stoic manual for dying.[117] Though some early modern pastoral tracts in the tradition of the *Ars* do treat somewhat the "Stoic" psychological problem of the fear of death,[118] it is perhaps not until the seventeenth century, in a work such as Charles Drelincourt's *Les consolations de l'âme fidèle contre les fayeux de la mort*, that one finds an extensive religious response explicitly competitive with the Stoic treatment of death.[119]

Petrarch's sixteen dialogues on death anticipated the need for a psycho-logical "art of dying." The fear of death; the despair of dying in sin; the worry over estate, wife, children;[120] the frustration of premature death; the insecurity of fame after death: Ratio's remedies for all these ills constitute a lay manual for dying.[121] Possibly, part of the printed success of the *De remediis* can be explained by its function not only as a general psychologi-cal handbook but also as a particular guidebook for death and dying. J. T. McNeill rightly sees the *ars moriendi* as a part of the laicization of psycho-logical and spiritual care. Conceived as a layman's manual for guiding a dying friend or relative, it represents a shift from clerical to lay care, a shift partially necessitated by the scarcity of priests during plagues, but also par-tially encouraged by the interests of an increasingly literate urban laity and the emergence of printing.[122] Petrarch's *De remediis*, and particularly those sections on death, perhaps struck a chord in the psychological sensibilities of an early-modern reading public. But in contrast to the *Tractatus artis bene moriendi*, his remedies, like Lupset's *Waye of Dyenge* later, offered more fully a psychological, rather than a spiritual and liturgical, response to death. For Petrarch, the regimen for dying well was part of a broader revival of the role of the Roman moral philosopher acting as a *medicus animorum*. In practicing this craft of physician of minds, Petrarch did not expressly compete with the priestly *cura animarum*. Yet, in several ways his remedies for death provided a much-needed, alternate source of care for a problem that soon became an important concern also for the clergy.[123] As in the case of "misery," so also in that of "death," Petrarch helped to reshape the medieval categories of psychological experience.

· · · · ·

Petrarch forged a new role of comforter and healer for the latter-day moralist and rhetorician. His formulation of this role came by virtue of a literary and intellectual versatility, or even ambiguity. Petrarch imaginatively harmonized the voices of the poet, the penitent, and the philosopher. He was something of all of these, and yet not fully any one. He had the subjectivity of an Ovid (*Tristia*), an Augustine (*Confessions*), and a Boethius (*Consolation of Philosophy*), yet he was not bound to any one of their categories or "genres" of personal sorrow. His autobiographies of despair ranged from the woes of lovesickness, to those of spiritual disquiet, to those of world-weariness. Beyond his own sorrows, Petrarch also healed those of others, fashioning an array of specialized cures for the layman, the monk, the despot, the fellow poet, the prelate, the nameless reader from any station in life. For this social role as healer, Petrarch could draw on the therapeutic roles and approaches of the classical moralist and the medieval confessor. To his friends both lay and clerical, he could be a versatile epistolary comforter and adviser; to his brother, a spiritual director for the life of the novitiate; to his patrons, a quasi-professional consoler.

Whether in the genre of the Boethian *consolatio*, the *epistola consolatoria*, or the remedy manual, Petrarch's writings have much more probing psychological and philosophical depth than do those of his protohumanist or dictaminal predecessors. A remarkable diary of vanities, woes, and spiritual ills, the *Secretum* was part religious confession, part secular self-consolation. The dialogue had all the volitional struggle of Augustine in the *Confessions*—but without the conversion! Appropriately, the tentative penitent did not dare make his confessions to God, as did the African saint, but negotiated instead with a mortal confessor and literary cohort. Moreover, the ascetic admonitions of Augustinus never fully defeated the worldly sorrows of Franciscus. And this was the key to the "secret conflict of his cares."

Petrarch rebelled against the harsher medieval categories of emotion, giving his *accidia-aegritudo* a dramatically secular cast. He implicitly questioned those Pauline, Augustinian, and subsequent confessional assumptions concerning the illegitimacy of *tristitia saeculi*.

Petrarch's remedy book fully particularized the sorrows of the *saeculum*, from the menace of fleas to the formless despair of the human condition. Anticipated by his earlier efforts as an epistolary consoler, by the manual of Scriptural remedies in the *De otio* Book 1, and by Augustinus' call for a mental collection of ready cures, the massive handbook capped Petrarch's efforts to acknowledge and to cure the myriad travails of worldly existence. As he had grown older, Petrarch had promised to grow braver, more tranquil in the face of tragedy. His *De remediis* was, in large measure, the product of that resolve, serving as an exhortation to himself and as a Stoic roadmap for others.

But the historical importance of Petrarch's thought lies not merely in the formulation of innovative genres but also in the exploration of psychological experience. The *accidia-aegritudo* of the *Secretum* Book 2 and the *miseria-tristitia* of *De remediis* 2.93 represent historically pivotal treatments of the problems of despair and depression. Joining the general problem of classical Fortuna and medieval *miseria*, Petrarch's treatment of sadness transcends any one treatment found in the ancient or medieval traditions of psychological or spiritual care. In the *Secretum* he assigned his *accidia-aegritudo* an essentially secular cause: the woes of urban life, his dependence on others, the frustration of not achieving his just station in life. Though working within the pastoral framework of the seven deadly sins, Petrarch emphasized secular Boethian sorrows rather than more traditional moral and theological views of *accidia* and *tristitia saeculi*. In the *De remediis* Book 2, myriad worldly woes themselves comprised the array of chapters, thus freeing Petrarch to focus one chapter (93) on the general state of human *miseria*. Endowing this misery with psychological status and symptoms, Petrarch enriched the therapeutic view of despair beyond what could be found in such ancient works as Cicero's *Tusculans* Book 3 and Seneca's *De tranquillitate animi*. His remedy, heralding the long-neglected aspects of human dignity and happiness, though drawn largely from Augustine's *De civitate Dei*, was a timely positive affirmation of the human psychological condition. Petrarch's approach to the problem of human despair thus combined both his own subjective secular frustrations and the generically miserable human condition publicized in the *contemptus mundi*. In both cases, he added vital ingredients to fourteenth-century psychological theory. In the *Secretum* the Stoic side of the confessor Augustinus fully engaged the realm of secular sadness—and thus partly legitimated it. In the *De remediis* Ratio treated misery not as a spiritual punishment but as a psychological condition now worthy of remedy. Petrarch thus responded to the various levels of human sadness, both the "secular" misfortune of the world and the "sacred" misery of fallen man.

As he changed the contours of misery, so also did Petrarch alter the perspectives on death, giving it due status as a psychological threat rather than a spiritual opportunity. His *De remediis* 2.117–32 consciously attempted to revive a neglected philosophical and consolatory treatment of the fear of death. In what was perhaps thus far the major postclassical statement on the "art of dying" Petrarch provided a timely counterpoise to the prevailing horrors and images of fourteenth-century death.

Thus, in a sense, Petrarch straddled two psychological worlds in his treatment of human misery and death. On the one hand, the ascetic dictum to meditate on death and misery constituted the spiritual regimen in the *Secretum*: that is, mortality and misery were, in theological terms, corrective spiritual conditions. On the other hand, Petrarch also came to frame them elsewhere in psychological terms as two of the principal maladies inherent in the "sorrow of the world." And in so doing, this lay consoler spoke to a realm of psychological care partially neglected by Christian pastoral thought.

Besides his treatment of the causes and cures of despair, Petrarch's writings also dealt significantly with its symptoms. Undoubtedly, the love poet's emotional patterns were a source for the humanist's fascination with sorrow. In the bouts of bereavement, described in the letters, in the *accidia-aegritudo* of the *Secretum* Book 2, and in the *miseria-tristitia* of the *De remediis* 2.93, Petrarch described an indulgent grief. He adapted the bittersweet swoons of his "vernacular" lovesickness to the *voluptas dolendi* of his "Latin" forms of sorrow, as the emotional intensity of the poet was transferred to those wider circumstantial, philosophical, and "existential" types of despair. Petrarch's symptoms of sorrow represent an important contribution to European attitudes toward despair. As scholars have suggested, his "sweet sadness" should be viewed in the light of the later flowering of the cultivated melancholy of the early modern era.[124] Though not using the term "melancholy," Petrarch in various contexts explored and described an emotional condition similar to that which would later appear under the label of melancholy. As we shall see, Marsilio Ficino would also draw on personal aspects of his philosophical experience when he sought to treat the "heroic" melancholy of the literati. By the time of Robert Burton's remarkable *Anatomy of Melancholy* in the seventeenth century, the many threads of humoral, circumstantial, love, heroic, and even religious melancholy are all woven together.[125] Petrarch marked an initial phase in this psychological movement in that he translated specific poetic emotions into more general types of sadness, reifying and dignifying the despair of the *saeculum*. Ushering in to the world of letters a renaissance of worldly sorrow, he partially dismantled the emotional paradigm, implied by Paul and reinforced by subsequent Christian theology, that would validate only that *tristitia secundum Deum*.

At the same time, however, that Petrarch was long enslaved by poetic sorrow, he also sought to be free from it. His letters on bereavement, both those he retained in his collections as well as those he did not, are a record of a struggle to escape from the clutches of *voluptas dolendi*. As he aged, the refuge into doleful "weeping and writing" must have increasingly seemed to be a bottomless pit, an experience too circular, futile, and emotionally hopeless. A case in point is the older Petrarch's perspectives on the charms and sorrows of love in the *De remediis*, where he makes a symbolic departure from the regimen of his earlier poetic years. In his chapter "On Pleasant Love" (Book 1.69), which he includes among the vanities of good fortune, Ratio warns a love-stricken Gaudium that sorrows will soon come his way. At this Gaudium vaunts his confidence in the curative powers of love poetry: "Indeed I will not weep but I will sing, and I will console myself with verses in the manner of lovers."[126] Ratio, however, gives no quarter to such a remedy: "By speaking and singing, love is nourished and kindled, not quenched and assuaged, so that those songs and verses of which you speak do not heal, but hurt, your wounds."[127] He then offers such remedies as change of scenery, avoiding the beloved, new projects or distractions, a sense of shame, an act of the will, a reflection on human ills.[128] The stern physician of the *De remediis* thus rejected poetic solutions for "constructive," commonsense, sober remedies. This chapter mirrors a larger quest in Petrarch's life. Though ever alive to the emotional sensibilities piqued by lovesickness, he gradually attempted to conquer them with more Stoic cures. Later humanists would perhaps draw upon or react to both legacies in Petrarch's thought—namely, that legacy of emotional awareness and expression as well as that of Stoic consolation and equanimity.

Petrarch's imbroglio with the physicians only sharpened his focus on the therapeutic potential of rhetoric and philosophy. By the time of the writing of the *De remediis* Petrarch had fully come to see his role as a rhetorical healer, replacing the defective or deficient efforts of other healers of his day. Both the prefaces and the dialogues themselves represent Petrarch's attempt to delineate a science of the human mind. It was in this treatise that Petrarch explicitly articulated the role of the philosopher as *medicus animorum*. And, certainly, what theologians and confessors had done for the *cura animarum*, what natural philosophers and doctors had done for the *cura corporum*, Petrarch tried to do for the *cura animorum*. With the notable exception of the *Consolatio theologiae* of a German contemporary,[129] the pastoral *cura animarum* had little attended to this psychological world. Petrarch's treatment of misery, death, and the countless woes of worldly

vicissitude helped to fill a void left by medieval religious care. If not acci-
dentally as massive and detailed as a contemporary confessor's manual, his
handbook nonetheless aimed to supply a markedly different type of therapeutic wisdom.[130] From a close acquaintance with varied poetic, penitential, philosophical, and medical traditions of psychological experience and
healing, he forged a new Renaissance tradition of rhetorical healing. Legitimating and popularizing the forgotten reaches of man's emotional experience, he shaped the contours not only of humanist consolation but also of
early-modern psychology.

4

CONSOLATION AND COMMUNITY

COLUCCIO SALUTATI
AS FRIEND AND COMFORTER

IN 1390 a physician in Faenza, Antonio Baruffaldi, took up Petrarch's admonition that doctors not interest themselves in eloquence. Baruffaldi wrote Petrarch's admirer, the Florentine chancellor Coluccio Salutati, asking him to address the question of whether *verecundia* (shame) was a virtue or a vice. Opening his letter by referring to a *Seniles* letter—presumably *Sen.* 3.8—in which Petrarch dissuaded a doctor from pursuing eloquence, he expressed his hope that Salutati would not similarly lecture him on this matter, as he disavowed any claims of being eloquent. Having thus duly renounced any designs on the humanists' turf, he then asked Salutati, whom he considered an expert in moral philosophy, to discuss the problem of *verecundia*.[1] Salutati responded not only with the requested moral discourse, *De verecundia, an sit virtus aut vitium*, but also with a brief tractate *Quod medici eloquentie studeant* (That Doctors May Study Eloquence). In this latter treatise, Salutati showed himself to be at odds with what he saw as Petrarch's joking argument, and he made the counterargument to the medical world that it may indeed pursue humanistic interests and use rhetoric as a therapeutic tool.[2] He would de-emphasize rhetoric's status as a distinct art inaccessible to the nonhumanist. Though agreeing with Petrarch that doctors are sought "for curing" and not "for persuading," Salutati nonetheless argued that they should not be deprived of the use of "ornate and impressive speech," the faculty that distinguishes man from the animals.[3] Viewing rhetorical skill as largely innate, he allowed that, should a doctor have this natural talent, he should cultivate and use it. He even suggested that the doctor's speech could have a therapeutic effect upon the patient's dejection in the same way that music can assuage and mitigate anger.[4] Rhetoric is man's peculiar medium, the mark of his *humanitas*.

This vignette captures the contrast between Petrarch and his follower Salutati. Whereas Petrarch was a great snob, Salutati was not. Whereas Petrarch would restrict the world of eloquence to the "true philosophers and orators," Salutati would open it up. Whereas Petrarch marked out a highly specialized domain for the "doctor of minds," Salutati envisioned a universal realm of Christian consolers. Salutati was unquestionably Petrarch's most important Trecento successor as a consoler. And, although he shared many of his predecessor's moral and spiritual interests, Salutati's formulation of the comforter's role had a significantly different emphasis. Given his liberal position on doctors' use of "healing eloquence," it is not surprising that Salutati would likewise have a nonexclusive idea of the consoler's office. Both his vision of that office and his specific counsel as a consoler have much to teach us about the potential social face of Renaissance solace. Salutati offered to the world a truly catholic idea of consolation, breaking down some of the walls of specialization that characterized the classical philosopher, the medieval priest, and the Petrarchan "*medicus animorum.*" Moreover, in the content of his consolations, Salutati forged a rich synthesis of ancient and medieval consolatory traditions, and offered some innovative perspectives concerning the resolution of worldly sorrow.

In contrast to Petrarch's highly literary career, Salutati's life was rooted more firmly in the traditional structures of late medieval society. A family man, notary, Tuscan officeholder, and Florentine chancellor, his world was more "institutional" than Petrarch's. His livelihood, his obligations, and his perspectives were tied to the larger, daily demands of the domestic, social, and political world. And although less prolific than Petrarch, Salutati still found time for humanistic pursuits. Besides his study of classical texts and his sponsoring of classical learning (he was largely responsible for bringing the Greek scholar Manuel Chrysoloras to Florence), he wrote a voluminous collection of private letters, a few poetic compositions and commentaries, and treatises on the religious life (*De seculo et religione*), classical poetry and mythology (*De laboribus Herculis*), moral themes (*De verecundia*), philosophy and theology (*De fato et fortuna*), the disciplines (*De nobilitate legum et medicine*), and politics (*De tyranno*)—all this in addition to his output of public writings as chancellor of Florence.[5]

Whereas Petrarch's consolatory writings ranged over various genres, Salutati's were confined to one: the private letter. Ranging from the 1360s on into the early 1400s, Salutati's corpus of familiar letters reveals his concept of the consolatory role, his specific "practice" as an epistolary consoler and adviser, and even his own encounters with grief.[6] His letters of consolation represent a more complex epistolary genre than do Petrarch's *consolatoriae*. Petrarch's letters reflect more the studied rhetorical and philosophical style of the classical familiar letter. Salutati's collection, on the other hand, represents a truer hybrid of classical and medieval traditions. Practicing as a professional rhetorician in his notarial and chancery career, Salutati perhaps continued to adhere more closely than Petrarch to the vocabulary and themes of the *ars dictaminis*—even in his private letters.[7] Moreover, as Witt suggests, Salutati was less of a classical purist than Petrarch and more accepting of medieval Latin writers. Perhaps partly because of this and partly because of developments in his own thought, his mature letters have more traditional religious content than Petrarch's.[8] In their moral and spiritual tone, some of his letters in large measure resemble those of a patristic writer such as Jerome or those of a twelfth-century "protohumanist" such as Peter of Blois.[9]

Besides having a more religious character, Salutati's letters also have a more social emphasis than those of Petrarch: they reflect a marked concern with the social properties of letter-writing and consolation. In order to understand Salutati's motivation and role as a consoler, we must begin by carefully examining the assumptions and pieties underlying his view of this social dimension.

Time and again Salutati's letters emphasize the value of friendship. He perceives his letter-writing largely in terms of the duty (*officium*) of friendship and love. Whether it is to answer someone's question or to console a friend's grief, his letters express his intention to fulfill variously the "officium amicitiae," the "officium caritatis," the "officium amoris," the "officium dilectionis." An interest in the classical notion of friendship—and its role in the duty of letter-writing—can be traced back to the twelfth century. Aelred of Riveaulx's *De amicitia spirituali* and *Speculum caritatis* and Peter of Blois' *De amicitia christiana et de dilectione Dei et proximi* reveal a theoretical concern with both classical and Christian conceptions of friendship.[10] Peter's popular letter-collection, furthermore, contains various epistles that articulate the role of friendship in letter-writing, communicating, and sharing grief. In his own letters Salutati reveals a familiarity with Peter,[11] and, though it is uncertain which—if any—of Peter's works he actually knew, it is possible that Peter's social ethic could have influenced him; as epistolary consolers they certainly share similar notions of the nature of friendship. Also, in all likelihood Salutati knew the more recent treatise on friendship by the thirteenth-century *dictator* Boncompagno.[12] Thus, in general, Salutati's theory of friendship must be seen in terms of a larger development that began to emerge in twelfth-century moral discussions and letter-writing. And if his views are not necessarily unique to him, nonetheless they reflect the emergence of a prominent social sensibility in medieval and Renaissance moral thought.

In a letter of 1375 to Andrea Giusti da Volterra, Salutati ended a discussion of friendship with a definition of the friend's several roles:

[F]or you are able to treasure among mortal things no greater and more perfect good than friends. Friends indeed confirm us in prosperity, assist us in our efforts, oppose themselves in our danger, mitigate calamity and adversities, make us merrier in happy times and effectively console us in sad ones; they bridle adolescence, accompany youth, make themselves useful in old age, and assist in declining years, opportunely supporting the weakness of age.[13]

Among a friend's duties, then, is that of "effectively consoling" others in their sorrows, a responsibility Salutati frequently shouldered.[14] In a letter (11.8) to Bernardo da Moglio discharging his very "office of consolation," Salutati articulated what his task as a consoling friend should be. Should he not fulfill the duty of sharing his friend's grief, he argues, he would be thought remiss in the obligations of friendship. For Salutati, shared grief was an important aspect of friendship, love, and true consolation.[15] But here to Bernardo he argues that, in sharing his friend's tears, he would fail the dictates of virtue and corrupt the "office of love," for sometimes it is one's duty to correct or even, if necessary, to abandon an errant friend.[16] There is no friendship where there is no virtue. One is bound, then, to drive out the errors or the "corrupted emotions" he finds in a friend. In this case Salutati chooses to reason rather than to weep with his friend, and he defines his task of chiding, reasoning, and assuaging in terms of the general duty of friendship.[17]

Salutati's notions of the character and obligations of friendship were drawn largely from ancient moral philosophy. From classical works such as Cicero's *De amicitia* and *De officiis* and from Aristotle's *Nicomachean Ethics* (Books 8 and 9)[18] he borrowed ideas such as those concerning the role of virtue, reciprocity, and mutual identification in true friendship. Salutati also, however, deepened his concept of friendship with religious dimensions. In a letter of 1377 to Alberto degli Albizzi he responded to a letter in which Alberto praised friendship and compared it to God. Salutati in turn delivered a praise of friendship in which he took the cue to define it in religious terms, equating friendship with *caritas* (love), and *caritas* with God.[19] He then exalts *caritas* as the most important, fundamental social and religious virtue:

> This [*caritas*] alone glues mankind [*conglutinat*] together in a natural associa-
> tion so that, since man was created for the sake of man, we observe the dispo-
> sition and rule of that highest maker by embracing it. This alone, which low-
> ered God to the insignificance of man through the mystery of the Incarnation,
> raises man almost to the sublimity of God through his enjoyment of it. This
> alone, then, vivifies virtues. . . . This alone fosters the family, enlarges cities,
> maintains kingdoms.[20]

Later, in 1404, Salutati again took up the question of the religious character of friendship in a more focused context. Galieno Palmieri da Terni wrote asking him to comment on Aristotle's and Cicero's notion that it is difficult to have true friendship with many—a notion about which Galieno expressed his own doubts. Salutati supports Galieno's reservations by rejecting the classical idea of exclusive, limited friendship and by posing what, in some way, is a Christian concept of universal friendship. He asks why it is thought that friendship cannot exist among members of civic, political society. If the ancients doubted this, it was because they did not have the true Christian *caritas* that signaled the unity of mankind.[21] Declaring the possibility of the Christian ideal to love one's neighbor as oneself, he asks, "[W]ho would oppose the idea that, in the true head of all Christians, there can exist a true and perfect society and a most perfect friendship?"[22] Salutati also has to tackle the problem of the feasibility of fulfilling the several and sometimes conflicting *officia* of many friendships. Countering Aristotle's argument in the *Nicomachean Ethics* (9.10.5) that it would be impossible simultaneously to share happiness with one friend and tears with another, he argues that ministering to one friend's needs does not thus cut off one's friendship with another whom he must, at that moment, abandon. Then, he presents his vision of a society of friendship in which there is an adequate distribution of the friendly *officia* of consoling the sad, rejoicing with the happy, and suffering with the sick:

> Then if there would be the greatest multitude joined by the band of mutual friendship, they will divide themselves by way of *officia*, so that these assist the grieving, those congratulate the happy, these support the infirm, those defend the litigating. Nor in this society of friends, if it is genuine, could there be anyone who could lack what friendship will require.[23]

Salutati's society of friendship expands the classical vision of exclusive friendship and interaction into the vision of a universal society of friends mutually sustaining and supporting each other. Salutati's interest in discussing the expanding parameters of friendship can be found in his earlier letter of 1375 to Andrea Giusti cited above. He had suggested that various classical theories on the boundaries of friendship all miss the mark. Andrea's befriending and helping an acquaintance of Salutati's—which prompted Salutati's letter to Andrea—revealed to him the true "bounds" of friendship. Friendship concerns not merely one's ties to friends but also the friends of one's friends: "For the plenitude of friendship is overflowing which not only embraces the personalities of friends but extends itself in equal offices of love to the friends of friends."[24] Looking beyond more exclusive and restrictive classical friendship, Salutati heralds the open-ended, expansive bounds of the community of friends.

Salutati's vision of universal friendship was largely religious. His concept of catholic social bonds was built upon the notion of the universal Christian bonds of society. In his letter to Galieno he referred to Christian unity and *caritas*, and in the earlier letter on *caritas* to Alberto he praised, in largely religious terms, the love that is the cardinal feature of man's social and theological existence. Social love, social bonds, and social duty can have a Christian base. Salutati's commitment to his own social and Christian duty is evident in his *De seculo et religione* of 1381–82. Salutati's comments here complement the social attitudes found in the letters. He couches his concept of the office of religious exhortation in much the same terms he applies to the general *officia* of friendship, consolation, and love. Salutati promised to write such a treatise after visiting a Niccolò Lapi da Uzzano not long after this friend entered the Camuldensian monastery of Santa Maria degli Angeli in 1379.[25] In the preface of the work he suggests that the treatise fulfills not only his promise but also his natural Christian social obligation:

> Indeed we owe it to our neighbor—as much for the natural reasoning that we are all as mankind bound together at the same time, as on account of the glue (*gluten*) of the Christian religion by which we are all brothers in Christ—so that we should help the errant by correction, raise the lapsed, warn the ignorant, and, through our exhortations, aid him who elects the way of salvation through the grace of God. In this thing, I affirm that, although occupied in many things, within the limits of my slight ability (I would that it were not so slight) I nevertheless have been able to honor promises and to fulfill the precepts of that natural obligation through the office of exhortation.[26]

Both natural human bonds and Christian human bonds urge Salutati to meet a "natural obligation," the office of exhortation. Later (1392?), writing to Bernardo da Moglio, he reiterates the idea of the natural and Christian bonds of society:

> [F]or indeed there is nothing more human than to love those who love us. For, just as most perfectly the Christian religion orders that even enemies ought to be loved with a certain overflowing of love, thus nature, which creates us political and associative, since man was created for the sake of man, secretly makes it so that we naturally love all those by whom we are loved or presume to be loved.[27]

Emerging in Salutati's writings is an unmistakable language of community, a syntax of social ties. Time and again he describes people as being "glued" together by *caritas*, by the Christian religion, by friendship.[28] Salutati's interest in social bonds would certainly have been at the heart of a work entitled *De vita associabili et operativa*, a treatise on which he claimed to be working in 1372 but which he never completed.[29] His conception of such a work, however, indicates that his interest in social bonds extended beyond his role as a consoler to his thought in general. Whether it be united by the bonds of nature or by the glue of Christianity, Salutati's ideal world is a society of friends, tightly bound by mutual love, care, and obligation.

Without question, then, Salutati's view of himself as a consoler accented more the social dimension underlying his "office" than the rhetorical, literary, and philosophical dimensions. In fact, one can find in his letters statements suggesting that consolation follows more from the power of social ties than from the force of rhetoric. Though it was a common rhetorical gambit to play down the efficacy of mere words in a consolatory letter, still it is telling that Salutati discounted the effect of words numerous times, questioning their worth in comparison to the efficacy of friendship, of time, or of God. Important in such statements extolling friendship over language is not his diminution of "healing discourse" but rather his praise of "healing friendship." One such remark comes in a letter of 1369 to Stefano da Bibbiena. Salutati speaks of joyfully hearing from Stefano that he has recovered from his illness, and then he presents another of his praises of friendship, which he calls the most pleasing, joyful, and dear of all things.[30] Then, responding to Stefano's statement that he found Salutati's letters medicinal in his time of illness, Salutati takes care to explain that the medicinal power came from friendship, not from the letters:

> I do not know why it came to your mind to affirm that my letters have been medicinal: for in my view this [medicinal] result comes from the hidden power of friendship. For it is a fact of nature that things given with beloved hands are not only more welcome but also more efficacious. Thus it happens that my letters brought consolations and medicine to you by virtue more of the sender than of themselves.[31]

It is friendship that heals. Consolation cures through the hidden power of social bonds.

In one other important instance Salutati affirmed the distinction between the healing power of the consoler and that of consolation. In 1400 he responded to a consolatory letter Francesco Zabarella had written to him concerning the death of his son Piero. In his letter, Zabarella had disavowed any ambitions to offer consolation and suggested only that he might lessen Salutati's sorrow by sharing in his grief.[32] In his reply Salutati develops this theme, acknowledging Zabarella's emotional empathy as the mark of a genuine friend and consoler: "You are a singular and true friend to me; I know, even if you are silent, that, on account of the identity of love, all my things—whether they are happy or sad—are yours and that they move you as much as they move me."[33] Salutati then argues that the social character of consolation is rooted in the very structure of the word. He defines the true nature of the "*consolator*" as one who gives solace both to himself and to another, as one who is not merely an "*ad*solator" for someone else but must also be a "solator" for himself because of his own sympathetic grief.[34] For Salutati, the shared experience of grief and solace is essential to true consolation. He affirms that Francesco is correct in suggesting that grief is diminished by the fellowship of grievers. Elaborating this highly Peripatetic notion,[35] Salutati insists that it is the consoler's empathy alone that is therapeutic. Even the silent co-sufferer, without words but with compassion alone, can alleviate grief:

Therefore I am able to have as many consolers as I have condolers, yes indeed I have as many as grieve with me; since, as you affirm—which moreover is true—griefs are mitigated by the fellowship of grievers; so great is the power of such a thing, that compassion alone, although the co-sufferer (*compatiens*) neither speaks nor administers the liniment of discourse, may lighten and lessen the suffering.[36]

Salutati's stress on the efficacy of compassion—of others' shared emotion and empathy—again signals his belief in the power of human ties and in the social character of consolation. Just as he underscored the healing power of friendship in the case of sickness, so also in the case of grief he stresses the healing power of the *cons*oler's *com*passion. In an earlier letter (9.8) in which he replied to Jacopo Manni's letter of consolation to him, Salutati also affirmed the importance of the mutual, associative act of grieving. The letter contains a vocabulary of shared, social grief—a vocabulary that depicts the true friendly consoler as one who "*con*flevit," "*con*dolet," "*com*plangit."[37]

Though Salutati expressed a belief that *caritas* and compassion alone could bring comfort, nonetheless his letters also conveyed a wealth of consolatory maxims and advice. What philosophical, theological, and psychological solutions did he offer in his actual "practice" as a consoler? What problems did he address? What balance of "classical" and "medieval" themes informed the content of these letters?

Like Petrarch, Salutati composed consolatory letters not only for death but also for a miscellany of other problems. He ministered to friends who had suffered setbacks (1.3, 1.8, and 4.4), pressing on them the Stoic advice to overcome fortune with *virtus* or offering the commonplace that adversity teaches and warns, whereas prosperity deceives.[38] In a letter (4.15) to the Bolognese chancellor, Giuliano Zonarini, he addressed the latter's complaint of "melancholy," treating the malady in both its physiological and psychological contexts. In another instance (4.17) he responded to Benvenuto da Imola, who had recounted to him various aspects of his personal and family life. Benvenuto apparently included a regret about his old age, for Salutati answered with a consolation on aging, which employed classical *topoi* as well as detailed spiritual comments concerning the divine plan and the human life cycle.[39] For illness Salutati could present either a Stoic exhortation to patience (in 3.13) or the more spiritual consolation (in 7.1) that physical frailty fosters spiritual introspection.[40] Thus, in the content of his consolations, just as in his view of the Christian consoler's role, Salutati comfortably drew on both the Stoic and Christian traditions.[41]

Like Petrarch, Salutati also lived through a period of recurring epidemics. In various letters he dealt with the question of the proper response toward the threat of death—specifically, whether it is proper to flee plague-infested cities. In these letters Salutati tried to serve as a counselor and consoler concerning the crisis of death. It is instructive to study these letters in some detail because they portray the evolution of Salutati's particular vision of consolation and counsel for the problem of death. In the early 1380s he began to deal substantively with the question of those who would flee Florence during its periods of epidemic.[42] In these letters—to figures such as Antonio di ser Chelli, Guccio di Francesco Gucci, Ubaldino Buonamici, Pellegrino Zambeccari—he argued that those who would flee pestilence are wrong. His arguments are very revealing in that they reflect his attempt to deal with both the social and religious implications of fleeing Florence. In terms of social concerns, Salutati sees this flight as a breach of social and civic duty.[43] For him, it is shameful to abandon the dead and to desert one's city. But he also frames the problem in theological terms by dealing with questions of divine predestination and human choice.[44] To those who fled Florence he argues that Providence foresees all things, including one's death. Actions to avoid death are futile. Those who think the circumstances of death are random, those who think "divine providence does not order all things," follow that "detestable and rejected opinion of Democritus and of the Epicureans."[45] Appropriately enough, Salutati's principal theological perspectives are drawn from the cardinal Judeo-Christian *exemplum* of suffering: Job. He turns most consistently to Gregory's exegesis of Job 14 in the *Moralia*, citing also, however, certain discussions of Augustine's concerning divine providence.[46] In one such letter Salutati complements his theological consolation and counsel with classical *loci* drawn from the *Dream of Scipio* and Seneca's letters.[47] In a letter to Ubaldino Buonamici he adds to his theological discussion concerning death a set of classical and religious *exempla* of those who have borne death bravely.[48] In dealing with the crisis of the climate of death, Salutati thus takes a number of tacks, presenting social, theological, and philosophical arguments as well as offering both Stoic and sacred examples.

Growing out of Salutati's dialogue with those who advocated flight is a consideration of divine providence and human free will.[49] And although Salutati had expressed an earlier interest in this question in connection with another problem,[50] it is likely that the central impetus behind his philosophical and theological treatise, the *De fato et fortuna*, lay in the considerations emerging from this crisis concerning the proper response to the plague.[51] The *De fato* deals with the problems of causation, predestination, fate, fortune, and free will on an abstract level, but these problems, in large measure, have a concrete grounding in reality—and, now seen in this context of epidemic and critical human decisions, the *De fato* takes on a certain pointed relevance and immediacy. The plague letters thus provide an important insight into the origin and context of one of Salutati's major intellectual works.

Besides treating problems concerning the hardships of life and fear of death,[52] Salutati of course wrote numerous *consolatoriae* for bereavement.[53] From these letters emerges the subtlest and most complex picture of Salutati's role as a consoler. In them we find how Salutati could exhibit a certain flexibility in developing and posing solutions to grief, and, in one particular case, we see how he could make a remarkable shift from the role of formal consoler to that of informal psychological counselor.

Although many of Salutati's consolatory letters reveal considerable classical content and arguments, some reflect a predominantly spiritual perspective. One such letter was sent (c. 1383) to Petrarch's former friend Donato Albanzani, now the Ferrarese chancellor. Many years earlier the recipient of Petrarch's preeminent *consolatoria* (*Sen.* 10.4) for the death of his son Solone, Donato had now lost his eldest son Antonio. Salutati begins his letter with a discussion of his motivation of love in writing. Saying that he intended to fulfill his "ardor of love" with a light and jocular letter, he intimates the futility of this aim by bewailing instead the sad state of earthly life. He then presents a capsulized version of the *contemptus mundi* theme, lamenting life's vanity and mutability and presenting a homily on 1 John 2:16 that all worldly things involve either "desire of the flesh, desire of the eyes, or pride of life." The last of these, the "pride of life"—which is proved to be vain by the fragility of the human condition—leads to Salutati's consolation on death. Extrapolating the biblical passage and providing some classical examples, he then turns to the specific case of the death of Donato's son Antonio. He muses on Antonio's happy transition from the corruptible and mutable to the immortal and eternal; he mentions his welcome release from the temptations and sins of earthly life. He closes by exhorting Donato to be as strong as those ancient figures who suffered bereavement—figures, in fact, who were deceived by the "blind superstition of the gentiles," unlike Donato, who is a "knower of the true God and fortified by the admonitions of the Christian faith."[54] Finally, he tells Donato to number him among his friends and declares his love for him. Thus, besides reflecting his interest in the ideals and bonds of love and friendship, this letter also shows Salutati drawing more on Christian than on ancient thought. Traditional spirituality informs not only the prefatory "contempt of the world" but also the greater part of the death consolation. Its conventional religious tone far more pronounced than that found in Petrarch's analogous *consolatoria* to Donato, this letter reveals Salutati's potential contrast to Petrarch as a consoler: its homiletic, ingenuous piety stands in contrast to the more classicizing, studied therapeutic rhetoric of Petrarch's letter.

A comparison of earlier consolations (of the 1360s, 1370s, and early 1380s) to later ones (of the later 1380s and 1390s) reveals Salutati's increasing emphasis on one particular consolation: the consideration of divine omnipotence, wisdom, and goodness and a consenting to divine will. The consolatory letter (7.1) of 1390 to the Lucchese chancellor Antonio da Cortona is illustrative. After presenting a highly spiritual *consolatio* for illness, Salutati turns to console his fellow chancellor for the death of a child whose loss caused a grief which Antonio suggests has not been cured by reason, by the exhortation of friends, by study, or by reading. Salutati's counsel is that Antonio is too absorbed in the sensual and needs to look to the spiritual:

> Raise yourself for a while; if you are able, elevate your eyes from worldly things. Return with your whole mind to your Creator; consider his majesty, consider his omnipotence, wisdom, and goodness. Consider that he is making all things, ruling all things, and arranging all things; and dare, if you are able, in the view of his glory and in the presence of that infinite wisdom and goodness, to reprove or to change anything concerning the series of his disposition. I believe if you will thus compose yourself, if you will thus elevate your mind, that you will be ashamed to have grieved in whatever manner concerning your infirmity or your wife's sickness or the death of your son. And consenting to that incomparable wisdom and goodness you—who wished to know more than that wisdom, who even thought to be evil what that infinite goodness ordained for you—you will judge yourself foolish and, not only not good, but even evil. And you who missed him will see that you feel stupidly as well as wickedly concerning your son, since he departed from his carnal to his spiritual father and was carried from corruptible to eternal things.[55]

Here, as in the later consolations generally, there is a new emphasis on divine power, divine goodness, and divine will. The language of divine omnipotence and providence which comes to fill Salutati's letters on the plague also begins to appear in his letters of consolation. His fideistic treatment of the fear of death thus inspired a similar treatment of the grievous reality of death.[56]

This aspect of Salutati's response to death reveals his innovative and supple quality as a consoler. He developed as a consolation and psychological solution a belief in the divine plan. The plague had forced him to deal substantively with the question of the theological implications of fleeing death. The ensuing consideration of cause, fate, and providence led him to a heightened conviction about God's infinite wisdom and about the critical emotional importance of yielding to the divine plan. The development and application of this divine consolation reflects the fluid character of Salutati's psychological sensibilities and "therapies." Moreover, he was himself later to rely fundamentally on this divine solution in his own confrontation with family deaths and personal grief.

As a consolatory theorist Salutati also addressed the issue of the therapeutic power of time. His view of "time" as healer, for the most part, represents a skeptical outlook on the adequacy of "reason" or "consolation" as healer. The most detailed discussion of time comes in a letter of 1399 (11.1) to Malatesta di Pandolfo Malatesta. Here, he prefaces any consolatory arguments with a thorough discussion of time as the ultimate and inevitable remedy and as a prerequisite for establishing a psychological state receptive to reason and consolation. The "course of time," conquering and mitigating all things that afflict the human mind, is the most efficacious cure. The notion of healing time is an old one and, in itself, is not so significant.[57] What is perhaps important, however, is the context of Salutati's interest in this theme. The letter to Malatesta falls after his own sad encounter with grief in the death of his wife Piera—an encounter he described in the responses to various *consolatoriae* written to him.[58] Likely, there was a connection between this discussion of the psychology of grieving and his own experience. In the next chapter we shall consider how the death of his son Piero triggered from Salutati a significant discussion of the psychology of grieving, in which, in a skeptical attack on Stoic thought, he would again argue for the efficacy of "time" over "reason." In this later exchange with Francesco Zabarella[59] as well as in the one to Malatesta, his detailed and insistent emphasis on the role of time reveals a very realistic, almost "clinical" approach to grief that possibly mirrors his own experience. In elaborating on the futility of trying to console a fresh grief, he tells Malatesta that a mind disturbed with passions cannot receive consolations from without or respond to reason from within:

> Thus, when the turbulence of the passions is seething, the mind does not receive things posed from without and whatever reason attempts from within it does in vain. The persuasion of consolation requires ears that are empty, not full and dulled from the clattering of the passions; otherwise, just as what you pour into a full vessel spills, thus efforts of consolation labor in vain, and what is said in warning does not completely reach the core but disappears on the surface if it is not accepted when the passions have been made peaceful. The sickness does not respond to the remedy of medicine until after the illness begins to diminish.[60]

Salutati thus presents the notion that psychotherapeutic medicine can take effect only after the malady has begun to diminish as a result of the natural effect of time.[61] The letter to Malatesta not only reveals a fairly specific and possibly exploratory interest in defining the psychological "structure" of grieving, but also suggests the possibility that Salutati integrates personal emotional experience into his consolatory *officium*.

Salutati's most dramatic effort as a consoler came in 1393, when he wrote a set of three consolatory letters to the notary and public official Andrea Giusti da Volterra—the same Andrea whom in 1375 he had praised as an exemplar of the true "friend."[62] Salutati would now himself take up exemplary duties of friendship and attempt to steer Andrea through what must have been the roughest passage of his life. Exemplifying the historically pivotal potential of Salutati's solace and advice, these letters are invaluable documents for studying the nature and significance of lay humanist psychological care. Dealing with the enduring problem of human grief and resignation, they reflect both traditional spiritual pieties and solutions as well as emerging new lay perspectives and aspirations.

The letters (8.17, 18, 19) fall consecutively in the months of May, June, and July of 1393. Andrea had lost six children and six grandchildren, and Salutati sought to provide solace. In the first letter he reveals his capacity to take two very different and seemingly opposed tacks as a consoler and adviser. On the one hand, he reminds Andrea of the inevitability of death, and he counsels him on the need to conquer and transcend the sensual. One of Salutati's consolations is particularly otherworldly: these family members being gone, Andrea is relieved of some of those temporal family concerns that impede one's spiritual health.

> You are relieved of a heavy burden, my dearest brother Andrea. The promise
> of eternal beatitude is made not to the lovers of the world, but to all "who
> relinquish home or brothers or sisters or father or mother or wife or sons on
> account of my name," the Truth says, "[who] will receive a hundredfold and
> [who] will possess eternal life" [Matthew 19:29]. The grace of God relieved
> you of this burden.[63]

This sentiment echoes the ascetic perspectives found in Salutati's *De seculo et religione*, written a little more than a decade earlier.[64] This treatise reveals how fully Salutati valued the traditional medieval perspectives concerning the evils of the secular life and the sanctity of religious vocation. Confirming a Camuldensian friend in his choice of the monastic life, the treatise is Salutati's *contemptus mundi*; it closes with an explication of the same passage from Matthew that Salutati cites to Andrea: those who forsake family and friends for God will reap the greatest heavenly rewards for their deeds.[65] In the case of Andrea, Salutati uses this ascetic judgment to cast a positive light on family deaths, which, in such a context, could represent a partial release from worldly burdens. At the end of the letter, however, Salutati abruptly changes directions. When he finishes his consolation he then chides Andrea for turning down a Sienese public office offered him. He argues that such an office affords him the opportunity "to profit legitimately so that you may aid the poor, and to be employed honorably and piously so that you may benefit many."[66] Thus, having first consoled Andrea that family losses allow him a greater chance for spiritual quietude, Salutati then chides him that he ought not relinquish those worldly duties that remain for him. This advice is not contradictory—to the contrary, it is creative. Salutati aptly uses otherworldly perspectives when discussing loved ones who are gone; he marshals worldly perspectives when confirming Andrea in the Christian social duties that still await him. A clever rhetorician and casuist, he adjusts his persuasions to the situations and choices at hand, now proclaiming the piety of the "contemplative" life, now that of the "active" one.

In the two letters that follow, the treatment of Andrea's grief continues. The formal consolation is surpassed: a dialogue between laymen concerning grief, the acceptance of death, and psychological resignation begins. To Salutati's letter of May, Andrea apparently responds that although now "I thus 'wish' what happened in the sense that I do not wish it not to have happened," still his grief lingers, as "the flesh desires against the spirit."[67] He would seem, then, to acknowledge an intellectual but not an emotional acceptance of the deaths. Salutati argues that Andrea's mind is prey to the senses and is too softened. Whatever weaknesses afflict the mind can be fended off by virtue and reason. He then includes the familiar argument that the lost loved ones have escaped the temporal dangers and evils that the living must endure.

But the most important point comes near the end of the letter, where Salutati counsels Andrea not to flee the active life and, again, not to reject the offer of public office. Apparently, Andrea expressed to Salutati the wish to change life-status, to withdraw from the active to the contemplative or monastic life:

> Therefore wipe your tears and may it shame you, a learned and Christian man, not to put an end to your grief and thus to damn the remaining portion of your life, because you will be thought unwilling to live, because you will seem to have adhered to God because of a certain desperation and nausea of the world and not because of choice, which a good action demands.[68]

Though not specifically designated, some sort of monastic or religious retreat surely is what is meant by this "adherence to God."[69] Exactly what connection this retreat has with Andrea's refusal to accept the Sienese position is somewhat unclear. But because Salutati consistently links the two issues, it is fair to conclude that Andrea was generally seeking secular renunciation and that Salutati was trying to dissuade him from this course. After telling Andrea not to flee secular life, Salutati urges him not to reject honors or honest gains—again referring to the Sienese offer. He argues the spiritual legitimacy of secular status: "It does not befit all to remove sins with penance, but it is suited to many to delete them with alms."[70] Then Salutati explicitly relates both of these aspects of Andrea's secular renunciation to his grief, suggesting that his motives for seeking the solitary life and for rejecting public honors are illegitimate: "You seek to change your life and you long for solitude so that you may indulge your grief. Do not wish to bury yourself while you live; live, while the fates allow. Nor on account of the grief and sadness over your sons should you renounce that honor which is offered."[71] Thus tied together here are grief, despair, and renunciation. It would seem that Andrea is tempted to resolve an emotional crisis of grief and despair with a religious solution of renunciation and withdrawal. The importance of this therapeutic dialogue grows. As a counselor Salutati tries to respond not only to Andrea's specific problem of mourning but also to what he sees as the more general psychological and even behavioral repercussions of his grief.

The third and final letter of Salutati's treatment of Andrea's crisis is most important because in it he expands upon his arguments for the value of Andrea's maintaining his active, secular status. The letter begins with Salutati's response to Andrea's continued failure to accept the tragedy. Andrea had written him again—since Salutati's letter of June—describing attitudes in which Salutati sees signs of a certain emotional backsliding. Salutati chides him for retreating from the claim in his previous letter that he had truly become able "not to wish that what had happened had not happened."[72] He then launches the now common discussion of the importance of accepting divine will, proclaiming the justice, goodness, and immutability of God's will and suggesting that Andrea's tears reveal his resistance to God's will, his misjudging God's infinite goodness to have done evil, and his vulnerability to sensual concerns. Finally, Salutati discusses how Andrea should react—whether he considers the tragedy a "trial" or a "punishment"—and closes with a reproof of his lack of resolve in fully accepting the tragedy.

At this point Salutati again deftly moves from the heavens to the *saeculum*. The exhortations concerning divine will, sensual vulnerability, and sin now give place to a remarkable defense of the legitimacy of the secular, *negociosa* (busy) life. Again turning to the question of Andrea's refusing public honors and office, Salutati presents a praise of secular life based upon theoretical arguments of spiritual lay piety[73] as well as upon the personal testimony of his own lay experience. Andrea having bridled at his recommendation that public honors not be refused,[74] Salutati counters with an argument for the legitimacy of the busy, associative life and a defense of secular riches and honors:

I know also that different people have walked toward God in different ways: some, such as the hermits, anchorites, and cenobites of which we read, elect the secret and solitary life; nor am I unaware that many following the busy and associative life also have attained to the glory of God. Nor did many riches corrupt Abraham or his son Isaac or his grandson Jacob; nor did dignity corrupt Moses and Aaron or Joshua (who succeeded him in rule) and many others whom the Old and New Testaments consider holy. For although the solitary life is considered safer, virtuously to have time for virtuous employments is perhaps not less holy and more holy than to be in solitary leisure. Certainly rusticity benefits only itself, as that one [Jerome] affirms. Indeed busy holiness (*negociosa sanctitas*) edifies many, because it is manifest to many and it leads many with itself toward the entrance to the heavens because it supplies an example to many.[75]

Unlike private retreat, public endeavor can have an impact on many. Later Salutati returns to the question in terms of the specific aspect of Andrea's attitude toward public honors and office. He gives Plato's argument that the wise have an obligation to govern the state, and he expresses his belief that Andrea has, in his public career, helped to promote good and to avert evil. Then, Salutati turns to discuss his own experience in public service, saying: "I have been able, indeed often, to oppose evil efforts and to favorably aid the most virtuous desires of the best citizens."[76] Then he returns to what is perhaps his key argument, saying that the greater value lies in those pursuits that benefit many. Agriculture, for instance, may be a worthy occupation, but it concerns only the private domain. He continues: "More divine, however, are those things that are done for many. And I would not wish that you accept honor, nor that you reject it for the sake of glory, but only that you live virtuously, profit harmlessly, help many, and that you live not only for yourself, but for your country, your relatives, and your friends."[77]

Thus, we are brought back to the central concern of much of Salutati's thought: social ties and purpose. This defense of the active life is fundamentally linked to the notions of friendship and social bonds discussed earlier. Historians justly identify Salutati—the would-be author of a treatise *On the associative and busy life*—as a proponent of the active, civic life. His bias toward the "social" over the "private" can also be seen in his *De nobilitate legum et medicine* (1399), where he ranks law over medicine—in part, by arguing for the priority of the concerns of man and society over those of nature, and for the supremacy of the active over the (scientific) contemplative life.[78] As such a champion of secular and civic duty and purpose, Salutati opposed those who would flee Florence during epidemics, and it is perhaps somewhat in this same context of secular purpose that he attempts to dissuade those who seek to flee from social, lay life to solitary, monastic retreat. Besides his exhortation to Andrea to maintain secular status, Salutati made a later, similar appeal to the Bolognese chancellor, Pellegrino Zambeccari, who considered entering monastic life. Here also he argues the spiritual legitimacy and piety of lay endeavor, trying to restrain a friend's temptation toward renunciation.[79]

In the case of Pellegrino, the "crisis" of renunciation seems to turn largely on the problem of love. In a set of letters Novati dates between 1392 and 1394, Salutati counseled his Bolognese friend about his love for a certain Giovanna, rebuking him for his excessive affection for her. In 1398 Pellegrino wrote him of his intention "to forsake the distresses and frenzies of vain love and to confirm the mind in him who suffered on the cross for the salvation of mankind." In his retreat he will flee "the courts and profits that have deprived me of true freedom up until the present day."[80] He reveals his intention to substitute the Virgin Mary for Giovanna as his bride. Pellegrino offers an interesting challenge to the moral adviser: Salutati must try to unknot a confused tangle of sensibilities involving "vulgar" and "divine" love,[81] romantic sorrow, and religious guilt and piety. In his handling of the problem Salutati presents another vigorous defense of the active, secular life. He tries to break down the traditional assumptions about monastic retreat and piety, arguing that piety is not necessarily linked to religious or secular status. He maintains that the true drama of piety is played out in the heart, the mind, and the soul and that religious station does not guarantee spiritual health just as secular status does not preclude it. Pellegrino must not relinquish his obligations to family, community, and country, which God prescribed for him.[82] Then, as in the letter to Andrea, Salutati lists those pious religious figures who were engaged in the world rather than withdrawn into solitary retreat. Drawing on an Augustinian precept—that those concerned with worldly affairs can lift their hearts to God just as those devoted to heavenly works can drag theirs down to earth—he defends his personal station in life as well as secular status in general.[83] In the familiar terms of social duty he portrays his own experience of a pious lay existence:

> Clearly your fleeing the world can draw your heart from heavenly things to earth, and I, remaining in earthly affairs, will be able to raise my heart to heaven. And you, if you provide for and serve and strive for your family and your sons, your relatives and your friends, and your state (which embraces all), you cannot fail to raise your heart to heavenly things and please God.[84]

For Salutati, a spiritual worth is found in one's lay responsibility to family, friends, and country. In an earlier defense of the active life to Pellegrino (in 9.4) he contends that the spiritual value of lay experience is a necessary part of the divine scheme of human existence: "[S]ince we were born for eternal glory and, as we believe orthodoxly, appointed to refill the seats of the angels, nature would not have produced us political, that is, associative, if association (*conversatio*) did not at all direct us toward salvation."[85] Man must be able to attain salvation through the fulfillment of his natural role as a political and associative being.

The importance of Salutati's counsel cannot be overstated. Sensitive to spiritual perspectives but also confirmed in his own "pious" lay life, he is an invaluable source of counsel. With Pellegrino he attempts to combat the medieval uneasiness with the *saeculum*: the guilt over secular love and wealth. As a true lay spiritual counselor he plays a vital part in shaping a world that is able to find itself spiritually more at home in secular pursuits.

As for the letters to Andrea Giusti, one finds a defense of lay life made more strictly in the context of psychological counseling. For here Salutati tries to confirm in civic life a friend who seeks to resolve grief and resignation with the traditional solution of renunciation. In the third letter to Andrea, as in the second, Salutati chides Andrea for having the wrong motives for seeking the contemplative life. A love for God, not grief for the dead, should motivate a flight from the active life:

> Then not on account of tedium, not on account of the tumult of adversities, should the world be fled, but it must be abandoned on account of love. You, angry with the world and contemplating a quieter life, because the hand of God touched you, seem to desire a change; this, however, is to be thrown out rather than to leave. I wish that the love of God, not the grief over dead sons, would suggest to you a new mode (*institutum*) of living and that you would not seek hiding places for your grief and waste away in mournful tears. Believe me, I see what moves you, what you are thinking or what you desire. Do not wish to boast further of great things to me: you wish to flee the annoyance of hardships and you wish to avoid the dangers of the world.[86]

Andrea must be made aware of his emotional motives for retreat. He must not try to solve this type of psychological problem with a religious solution. Salutati's three-month dialogue with Andrea wrestles with those emotions hindering a true acceptance of the deaths and prompting a desire for renunciation: the exchange truly transcends the formal bounds of the *consolatoria*. Moreover, the letters reflect an intriguing mixture of spiritual pieties and burgeoning new "secular" values. On the one hand, Salutati comforts Andrea with otherworldly arguments concerning his partial release from mundane, familial responsibilities; he also ministers the spiritual consolation concerning the importance of accepting divine will which he has formulated. On the other hand, Salutati vigorously counters Andrea's temptation toward renunciation. Now, he turns to the value of serving family, friends, and country. Now, he proclaims the sanctity of lay life, drawing on the theological arguments and personal experience that support the case for the possibility of a pious lay existence. Andrea's "medie-val" spiritual response to grief is answered by Salutati's bold, lay argu-ments. Grief has made Andrea vulnerable to the emotional and spiritual uncertainties of secular experience, but the monastery should not be used as a haven for indulging and resolving grief. The offices, wealth, and hon-ors of this world are legitimate, because they can be honestly pursued and because they can even be, sometimes, morally imperative. Both in his role and in the nature of his advice, Salutati acts as a lay adviser. A pastoral adviser, by contrast, would probably have provided a very different re-sponse. In fact, clerical assumptions and perspectives would probably have supported Andrea's impulses.

Thus, Salutati proves that he can urge the pursuit of both the secular and religious lives. As was shown earlier, his *De seculo et religione* to Niccolò Lapi is a fraternal, Christian exhortation to one who has taken monastic vows. His rejection of the evils of secular life in this treatise would have won him praise from the most ascetic spiritual thinkers. On the other hand, his letters to Andrea Giusti and Zambeccari reveal his ability to exhort and confirm other friends in secular vocation as well. In both cases Salutati fulfills the same function: the friendly duty of exhortation. A layman, he nonetheless sees it as appropriate and charitable to step into the monastic world of his Niccolò and give him Christian encouragement. Also as a layman, he dares give spiritual advice to an Andrea who doubts his place in and obligations to the secular world. As a consoler and counselor Salutati does not see himself constrained by any traditional divisions of "monastic" vs. "worldly," "priestly" vs. "laic." Though no party to the anticlericalism informing Protestant thought, Salutati perhaps anticipates the ideas of the "priesthood of all believers" and fraternal correction. He is the "complete" lay exhorter and adviser: alive to both spiritual and secular sensibilities, he flexibly and carefully ministers to the variety of psychological needs and circumstances in the Christian community. As a comforter and mentor he is a thoughtful casuist, offering to some friends empathic tears; to some, rational solace; to some, rebuke; to some, encouragement; to some, a la-ment of this world; to some, a new, laic praise of its sanctity.

· · · · ·

Salutati imaginatively continued the tradition of the epistolary philoso-pher, consoler, even "theologian," which he had seen develop in the Latin West from such ancient figures as Cicero and Seneca, from Church Fathers such as Jerome and Gregory, from twelfth-century writers such as Abelard and Peter of Blois,[87] to the renaissance of letters he finds in his own day in Petrarch. More than in the case of his famous predecessor, however, the revival of letters in Salutati represents an easy blending of medieval and

Renaissance perspectives.[88] Often grounded more in traditional religious thought, Salutati's letters imparted a more fully spiritual eloquence than did Petrarch's.

Salutati's vision of the office of the consoler should perhaps be seen in the larger context of a medieval revival of the tradition of the friendly letter-writer that had been emerging since the twelfth century. In his letters the "duty" of the consoling friend and the social character of shared grief reflect the full Renaissance flowering of the Peripatetic and Ciceronian social ethic of friendship and Christian views of *caritas* and universal bonds and obligations. Where Petrarch strove to fulfill the role of orator, moral philosopher, and *medicus animorum*, Salutati sought to fulfill the role of friend. His view of the *officium* of consolation or exhortation drew on his vision of a society united in natural and Christian bonds of association, friendship, and love. Given his strong convictions concerning mankind's tightly knit social bonds, it is not surprising that one of Salutati's principal views of solace is found in the idea of shared grief, the community of consolers all mutually *compatientes, condolentes, consolantes, confleventes, conplangentes*.

Beyond observing the office of compassion, however, Salutati also assiduously sought to pursue those friendly duties of chiding, persuading, and advising—acting very much as a Christian Seneca. His capacity for innovation as a consoler is evident. His formulation of a fideistic consolation concerning divine providence attests to this. So also does his exchange with Andrea Giusti, in which he clearly steps out of the formal bounds of the consoler and enters the informal province of the lay adviser. Here he not only drew on his new convictions concerning divine will but also put forth his first major epistolary defense of the active life. Just as Petrarch provided lay counsel for Boccaccio's temptation to renounce his literary career, so Salutati ministered vital lay dissuasions of the urge toward secular renunciation that he found in Andrea and, later, Zambeccari. The same demands of the Christian community that time and again prompted Salutati to assume the role of epistolary comforter also beckoned him to defend the sanctity of lay status in persuasive appeals to grieving or impulsive friends. An important measure of the increasing valuation of social, secular, and civic life, the affirmation of the active life is particularly strong in Salutati's moral voice.

In his sense of purpose and in his perspectives, Salutati shows us the dramatic social possibilities of a lay Christian consoler. Not an ancient sage, not an ordained priest, not a Petrarchan *medicus animorum*, he was a different kind of consoler, more adaptable and less "specialized" than all of these. His was the consolation of universal community. Salutati's imaginative use of the private letter did not end here. As we shall see in the following chapter, his importance in the history of Renaissance consolation lay not only in his creative role as consoler but also in his sad experience as mourner.

5

THE ART OF MOURNING

AUTOBIOGRAPHICAL WRITINGS ON
THE LOSS OF A SON

A S PETRARCH illustrates, Renaissance consolers, like certain of their classical and Christian predecessors, wrote not only to console others but also sometimes to comfort themselves. This literature of personal sorrow can be quite revealing, as it sometimes ventured further from the realm of genre, and closer to the reaches of individual emotional experience. In his letters and *Secretum*, Petrarch went far in legitimating psychological autobiography, leaving a legacy that flowered in the fifteenth century. Shorn of the highly poetic dimensions Petrarch breathed into it, the autobiographical genre gained a wider currency when it was taken up by others who, if less literary than Petrarch, nonetheless pursued intensely some of the same problems he had engaged.

As was seen in Chapter 2, in letters both public and suppressed Petrarch discussed the problem of mourning not only in terms of others but also in terms of himself.[1] Several of his humanist successors continued his exploration of that realm, focusing on one of the most common, yet most challenging, occasions of self-consolation, that of parental bereavement. Between 1400 and 1461 four major humanists wrote on the death of a son: Salutati, Giannozzo Manetti, and Giovanni Conversini da Ravenna wrote directly in response to the loss of their children; Francesco Filelfo, though writing to console a patron's bereavement, also made pointed reference to his own.[2] It is highly probable that there were links among three and, possibly, all four of these works. Together these writings constitute a particular Renaissance tradition of self-consolation, a humanist formulation of the "art of mourning." Our greatest concern will be with two of these writings: Salutati's epistolary exchange (1400–1401) with Francesco Zabarella and its impact on the most important self-consolatory writing on bereavement in the Italian Renaissance, Manetti's *Dialogus de filii sui morte consolatorius* (1438). But we shall also briefly consider the writings of Conversini, Filelfo, and others as variations on a theme. For the historian, such writings constitute a sensitive source of evidence, affording us an intimate glimpse of psychological, philosophical, and spiritual sensibilities.

Petrarch wrote of his grief both in his vernacular poetry on Laura and in several of his letters on the loss of friends or family. In one case, *Fam.* 4.10,

following the death of a friend, Petrarch contemplated (but never produced) a self-consolatory treatise on the model of Cicero's *Consolatio* on
Tullia and Ambrose's *De excessu* on his brother.[3] Later, in *Sen.* 1.3, in a
reply to a consolatory letter sent him by Francesco Nelli, he reflected on
the deaths of his son Giovanni and longtime friend van Kempen.[4] His
most substantive prose comments on personal loss, however, came later,
in *Sen.* 10.4, in which he comforted Donato Albanzani for the death
of his son and, at the same time, consoled himself for a similar loss of a
grandson. As was shown in Chapter 2, this letter represented the culmination of Petrarch's transition from a highly emotional poet to a confirmed
Stoic. Couched in a clinical language of rhetorical remedies, it vaunts a
confidence in the power of reason and patience. Invoking the dangerous
modern-day example of Paolo Annibaldeschi, who died from his parental
grief, Petrarch sternly warned against the dangers of unbridled sorrow.
With its autobiographical overtones, albeit in reference to a grandson
rather than a son, Petrarch's letter was likely influential in the later tradition
of parental self-consolation fully launched by Salutati.[5]

Like Cicero and Petrarch, Salutati responded to those who had written
consolatory letters to him.[6] In a set of letters of 1396, Salutati replied to
friends writing to console him for the death of his wife Piera. In these
letters Salutati reflected an attitude that he had substantively begun to develop in the 1380s, when he counseled acquaintances not to flee the
plague—namely, that individuals should accept divine providence and re-
frain from any effort to flee death.[7] Later, in the 1390s, he brought this
conviction to bear upon his own resolution of grief. To Roselli de' Roselli
he wrote that, as he quickly accepted divine will, he not only endured grief
but was made content.[8] To Jacopo Manni he recounted that during the
fourteen days of Piera's illness, he grieved and he begged God for her re-
covery. At her death, however, he recognized God's will, accepted reality,
and fully recovered from his sorrow:

> But, in the emission of the last breath, seeing my prayers not to be in agree-
> ment with God's will, I made a "will" out of a "necessity." I dried the tears,
> ended my weeping, and, delivering thanks to God, I, with that One granting
> it, thus composed myself, in such a way that although aware of the loss I was
> made wholly insensible to grief. I remained without tears and in that tranquil-
> ity of mind in which I had been when she was alive.[9]

In a letter written a week later to his friend Pellegrino Zambeccari, Salutati elaborated on his attitude toward the death. First he discussed the importance of accepting fate, clearly revealing a connection between particular intellectual concerns and his own resolution of grief. As F. Novati
points out, it was around this time that Salutati was working on his *De fato
et fortuna*. And drawing on his philosophical and theological theory he

discussed in this letter questions of fate, causation, and divine providence.[10] The fate or course prescribed by divine providence must be followed and endured. He repeats the sentiment that it is because of God that he conquered his grief, and he again affirms that the key to consolation rests in one's fully willing God's will: "Indeed, all the power of this misery is in us: if you will decide to will what God wills, you bear not only patiently and calmly but freely and happily whatever happens."[11]

Salutati's most detailed record of grief resulted from the tragedies of the summer of 1400, when he lost his two oldest sons: the eldest, Piero, died in late May; Andrea, a couple of months later.[12] In letters replying to those who wrote him concerning Piero's loss, Salutati reassured his consolers of his peace in the matter.[13] In one case, answering someone who had written him of the death of a child, he reported his own loss of Piero and offered consolation concerning their mutual bereavements.[14] But the most intense account of Salutati's mourning came in late August, in a letter (11.23) to the Paduan canon lawyer Francesco Zabarella. Zabarella had written Salutati a highly Stoic letter, citing some of the traditional rational *solacia*, referring to Salutati's own many similar such counsels as a consoler, praising his reported fortitude in the death of Piero, comparing him to certain ancient figures who bore grief bravely.[15] Clearly, Zabarella's intention was charitably to give back to Salutati the same type of reasoned solace he had ministered to so many others in their grief. Unfortunately for the well-meaning Zabarella, his letter piqued the chancellor's psychological indignation, though, in so doing, it also prompted from him a remarkable autobiography of psychological experience.[16] Salutati reproves Zabarella for his ill-conceived praise of his composure, which would seem to attribute to him a fortitude greater than that found in such figures as Job, grief-stricken over the death of his sons, or Christ, who wept over Lazarus. Moreover, what calm Salutati did in fact find following the loss of Piero (and now that of Andrea as well) should be credited not to himself but to God.[17]

Salutati then recounts, step by step, what he experienced when Piero became ill. He lamented his plight as he watched his son, his hope, his glory, the "crutch of his old age," slip away.[18] Piero's sickness turned his thoughts to his own aging and decline as his seventieth birthday approached. Then, he says, he began to seek consolation for the imminent death first from the precepts of pagan philosophy. At this point Salutati begins systematically to cite and then discount certain Stoic *loci* concerning death. In *Tusculans* 3.32.77 Cicero presents a set of arguments to be used in consoling the bereaved. Rebelling vigorously against the rational character of such psychology, Salutati dismisses, one by one, Cicero's *solacia* for grief: he disputes the notion that death is not an evil; he discounts the consolation that death is the common lot of all; he refutes the contention that it is foolish to grieve when there is nothing to be gained by it.[19] Although this is not Salutati's first attack on Stoic consolation, it must certainly be his most comprehensive.[20]

Having fully rejected "rational" classical solace, he then describes the structure of his spiritual mourning, providing a detailed model of a Christian experience of consolation. He says that, discarding the ineffective counsels of the pagans, he turned to the true source of comfort: God. He spoke to God in the familiar language he had used in consoling others:

> I know, Lord, that you rule all things; that you foresee and govern all things; in fact, that, since you are the first cause, you make all things; and that not a leaf is moved from the trees that you do not move. I know you are good and the infinite goodness, whereby you love me far more than I myself. . . . Now, however, will I, mere ashes and your figment, dare to stand against whatever your wisdom, goodness, and omnipotence has wished, or to bear badly what you do or stupidly not to wish what you wish? May your will be done, Lord.[21]

In a lengthy entreaty Salutati pleaded with God to help him accept His will. God would be his true healer and consoler, as it was through God's grace and aid that Salutati sought to accept divine will: "Give me grace so that I may wish what you wish or at least so that I may not oppose it." And: "Indeed, without your grace, I, oh! so wretched, am only able not to wish what you wish, since I am flesh . . . so great is your kindness, you will perhaps strongly grant that I would not wish that it had not happened."[22]

His prayers were apparently answered by the time of his son's death. Called to Piero's deathbed, he comforted him and ministered a benediction "without tears and commotion." He consoled the family. When Piero died he closed the eyes and lips of his dead son, folded the arms in a cross, gazed at the calm face, and departed "neither mournful nor sad." His resolution of grief, his acceptance of the death, his consolation, are credited to God, "who showed me such as I had not been able to imagine. In that One, indeed, is my hope and consolation, who made the bile empty of bitterness and who cleansed the inestimable wound with such great consolation."[23]

In this subjective description of grief and consolation, the grieving chancellor defined the structure of his mourning and clearly outlined his own emotional and spiritual resolution. He turned to the consolation of divine will to which he had become intellectually and psychologically committed. He chose the religious over the secular, the divine over the human. He rejected rational secular psychology as emotionally ineffective. He denied the strictly human capacity to resolve grief, placing it in the hands of God. He rebelled against ancient rational psychology and confirmed his own spiritual solution of God's helping man accept divine will. At the heart of Salutati's consolation was an act of the will. His search for solace mirrored a conviction developed in much of his thought—namely, the belief in the supremacy of the will over the intellect.[24]

Interestingly, Zabarella rose to defend secular consolation against this attack, drawing Salutati into a dialogue concerning the psychology of consolation.[25] In a return letter, Zabarella praises Salutati's reliance on divine solutions, but he also proceeds to defend the legitimacy of Cicero's thought. Noteworthy in Zabarella's defense of Cicero are his remarks concerning the immortality of the soul. Prior to discussing the three *Tusculan* consolations, Zabarella proclaims the existence of a "higher" level of Ciceronian solace. In the rejection of Ciceronian for Christian thought, Zabarella sees Salutati as too quick to dismiss the former as merely mundane, worldly, and pagan. He suggests that Cicero ministers to the afflicted not just worldly arguments, but that, to the contrary, many of his works deal with the immortality of the soul. He points out that discussions or comments in the *Tusculans* Book 1, the *Somnium Scipionis*, the *Ad Atticum* (10.8), and the last part of the *De senectute* all reveal Cicero's belief in immortality. Such discussions represent a subtler, loftier type of consolation; the maxims of *Tusculans* Book 3 are only for those who are unable to see this vision of solace. Zabarella then defends each of the three *Tusculan* maxims, supporting them largely with Stoic arguments. Essentially providing a staunch defense of humanistic ancient thought and ideals, Zabarella concludes by saying that if Salutati can be consoled by his own theological vision he should not, however, think that others—those who are less able to comprehend the consolations of immortality, beatitude, and divine providence—may not be assuaged by these philosophical and secular consolations.[26] He argues for two possible levels of solace: otherworldly remedies for the most wise; mundane consolations for the less astute.

The following February, Salutati responded to Zabarella with another, expanded attack on Stoic thought.[27] Now challenged by his Paduan colleague, he moves the discussion even more fully to the theoretical, philosophical, and theological realm. The personal response to Stoicism in the first letter is buttressed thoroughly by Judeo-Christian theology and by Peripatetic doctrine. To call death "good," as Cicero and others would, is to contradict the divine scheme in which a benevolent God created man "everlasting and in his image and likeness" and meted out death as punishment for Adam's sin.[28] Salutati also invokes the philosophical quarrel between the Stoics and the Peripatetics. Citing arguments drawn from the *Nicomachean Ethics*, he counters the Stoic position that death is not an evil with the Peripatetic argument that it is an evil of a certain kind.[29] For him, Peripatetic thought is much more realistic than Stoic: "Greater is the Aristotelian authority and moderation of the Peripatetics than that severity, indeed that harshness and inaccessible reason, of the Stoics."[30] He draws on Cicero's occasional anti-Stoic notions that the emotions must not be eradicated in man. Then he turns to certain ancient and Christian examples to argue that it is natural to grieve at a loved one's death or at the thought of one's own.[31] To Cicero's argument that it is useless and foolish to grieve at an irreversible tragedy, he opposes his own psychological maxim. As in his earlier letter to Zabarella, he says that such a sense of immutable reality and finality of death only worsens the grief: "hopelessness concerning the thing that you lost increases and aggravates the grief."[32] Venturing further into the realm of psychological theory, the second letter makes several comparisons between the body and the mind in an attempt to identify the natural elements in the healing process. He formulates his own "clinical" maxims: the premeditation of death aggravates one's tranquility; the recognition of the finality of tragedy exacerbates grief; the consideration of others' similar griefs—another classical suggestion—can sometimes worsen one's own composure.

He closes his attack on rational psychology by suggesting that it is therapeutically important to consider when philosophical consolations should be administered. Reiterating a point he had made in an earlier consolatory letter (11.1) to Malatesta di Pandolfo Malatesta,[33] he argues that consoling a fresh grief is futile. For Salutati, applying reason and consolation to a distressed mind is useless. And should such cures be plied, any healing or improvement must be credited to time, not to philosophical consolation.[34] Presenting the familiar discussion of divine omnipotence, divine will, and human acceptance of divine decree, Salutati ends with the declaration that his true source of consolation rests in God.

Salutati's letters to Zabarella, then, reveal a highly personal quest for solace that ends in the formulation of certain clinical laws of grieving. In the negative sense, Salutati rebelled against the psychologically ineffective counsels of Stoic philosophy. In the positive sense, he embraced the divine consolation that he had, in recent years, been developing. In the second letter the notion of "healing reason" was rejected for that of "healing time." Grief is a very real and natural affliction that can be remedied only by time and, especially, by an absolute reliance on God's aid, a belief in God's goodness, and an acceptance of God's will. Provoked by the cool impassivity and psychological naiveté of Zabarella's *consolatoria*, Salutati's first letter concerning Piero charted the entire drama of mourning and resolution. From the time of his son's sickness through to his death he recounted stages of despair, prayer, and resolution. And the intermediate stage of rejecting Stoic remedies perhaps allowed Salutati to vent his anger: rather than raging at the harsh reality of death he instead attacked the superficial and inadequate arguments of worldly psychology and his Stoic consoler. Rejecting secular solutions for divine ones, Salutati's quest for comfort reveals an intensely personal probing of the dynamics of grieving.

Salutati's letters to Zabarella laid the groundwork for a later dialogue that would be the most famous Quattrocento work on personal grief, Giannozzo Manetti's *Dialogus de acerba Antonini, dilectissimi filii sui, morte conso-latorius in monasterio cartusiensium habitus.*[35] Manetti, the Florentine scholar and ambassador who studied Greek under Ambrogio Traversari, was a humanist of considerable learning and versatility. As a Graecist he translated the New Testament and several of Aristotle's works including the *Nicomachean Ethics*, which according to Vespasiano was one of his fa-vorite books. He wrote biographies of ancients and moderns, including a set of lives of Dante, Petrarch, and Boccaccio and a portrait of Salutati in his *De illustribus longaevis*. He presented state, wedding, and funeral ora-tions. Most famously, he was the author of the major study *De dignitate et excellentia hominis* (1452), which expanded upon the theme explored ear-lier in Petrarch's *De remediis* 2.93.[36] His *Dialogus consolatorius* was written in 1438 following the death of his son Antonino. The dialogue purports to record a conversation between Manetti and Angelo Acciaiuoli, who had summoned him to the Florentine Certosa (at Galluzzo) for the purpose of consoling him for the recent loss. And though an enounter perhaps actually took place, the *Dialogus* should be seen largely as Manetti's own literary creation. Manetti uses the dialogue to complete his mourning, joining themes that may actually have been discussed at the monastic retreat with lingering issues of unresolved grief.[37]

As the *Dialogus* shows, Manetti was fully aware of such ancient and pa-tristic consolatory works as those of Cicero and Ambrose, but it is the Renaissance context of the work that warrants further attention. It is virtu-ally certain that Manetti's treatise was inspired by Salutati's letters to Za-barella. The figure of "Manetti" in the Certosan meeting drew on the gen-eral and sometimes even the specific arguments of Salutati's rebellion against Stoic laws of consolation. Besides thematic and textual similarities between Salutati's letters and Manetti's *Dialogus*, there is other evidence that Manetti was familiar with Salutati's discussion of bereavement. In his section on Salutati in his *De illustribus longaevis*, Manetti cited Salutati's description (to Zabarella) of his consolatory experience in the death of Piero—clearly, Salutati's epistolary discussion of grief made an impression on him.[38] In fact, I believe, Salutati's autobiography of mourning was a model for his own. The types of questions raised in the epistolary dialogue between Salutati and Zabarella were given full philosophical treatment in this literary dialogue.

In the opening section of the *Dialogus*, Manetti recounts that, following the death of Antonino, he went to his villa at Vacciano to be alone and to console himself. Acciaiuoli visited him and persuaded him to come to the Certosa.[39] As the conversation begins, Manetti admits that the "death of my son was more grievous for me than ever before I would have thought."[40] Angelo responds by chiding Giannozzo that all his humanist studies have apparently not helped him to meet his adversity calmly, and he summons the (Cyrenaic-Stoic) truism concerning the wise man's premeditation of all possible things.[41] Giannozzo responds with his central position "that it is, however, not possible that fathers—if truly they are fathers—are not grieved at least somewhat by the loss of children dear to them." He insists that "the pain that fills me is due to my humanity rather than to frivolity."[42] Angelo, drawing heavily on Seneca's *De consolatione ad Marciam*, then presents a long *consolatio* built essentially around the Stoic position that bereavement is an evil *of opinion*, not *of nature*. He gives various arguments, anthropological as well as intellectual, supporting this stance: funerary customs prove that grief is not universal; young boys are often not grievous over death; time's having a healing effect proves grief to be subjective; and since premeditation is therapeutic, then, likewise, sorrow must be mental. Then, turning a Senecan argument to Christian ends, he accuses Giannozzo of grieving not over the misfortune of his son, who enjoys now a happier fate, but of lamenting his own loss, showing a potential ingratitude for those blessings God bestowed while his child was alive. Closing with a few other Stoic *loci*, he then offers a spate of *exempla* of figures who have borne grief well.[43]

Challenging this Stoic *consolatio*, Giannozzo begins by discussing the opposition between the Stoics and the Peripatetics in this matter:

> Most erudite and friendly man, we saw that this controversy of ours was formerly more fully debated by—and not yet resolved by—the Stoics and Peripatetics, the greatest leaders of ancient philosophy. For the Stoics, harsher than other philosophers, say that grief and other perturbations of the mind are evils of opinion, not of nature. The Peripatetics, truly a little more humane, argue that sicknesses of the mind at first arise from nature but that they are worsened afterwards by opinion. Which of these positions was true is worthily debated among us. Our Angelo indeed approves the *sententia* of the Stoics. I, however, follow and approve the position of the Peripatetics, which accords more truly with human life.[44]

Each of the major precepts that Angelo has presented he counters with his own arguments concerning the naturalness of grief, citing some of the very sources that Salutati had cited.[45] He ends with Crantor's condemnation of a dispassionate "*indolentia*" which occurs with "great cost of savageness in the mind and stupor in the body."[46] Having posed his counterprecepts, Giannozzo then offers his own set of counterexamples of classical figures who reveal the legitimacy and naturalness of suffering—including Cicero's grievous reaction to the loss of Tullia.

Manetti's dialogue thus brings into full focus the conflicting ancient theories as to whether death and bereavement are evils of opinion or evils of nature. Although Angelo did briefly invoke Christian shame, the argument thus far has been largely secular. Now, however, some observers who have heard the discussion take the matter to the prior of the monastery, Niccolò da Cortona. Entering the discussion as an arbiter, Niccolò adds a theological weight to the dialogue, developing a Christian theory of grief and solace that supports Giannozzo's secular theory. As did Salutati in the Zabarella letters, this priest presents the theological argument that death is clearly an evil that represents man's punishment for sin; he summons myriad citations and *exempla* from the biblical tradition that prove death to be a grievous evil.[47] Finally, focusing on patristic and medieval thought, he cites instances of grief in Augustine's account of the death of his mother (in *Confessions* Book 9); in Ambrose's consolatory letters and orations; in Jerome's *consolatoriae*; in Gregory's remarks on the suffering of Job (in the preface to the *Moralia*); in the example of Bernard's grief over the death of his brother (in the *Sermones super Cantica Canticorum* 26).[48] Thus the psychology of the Stoics is repudiated by Christian theology and history. Niccolò thus fully naturalizes the Judeo-Christian experience of loss and sorrow:

> Wherefore, to conclude finally (omitting, as we said at the start, the inane arguments of the philosophers), if it stands that so many patriarchs, so many kings, so many fathers of the Old Testament grieved the death of children with such great sorrow; if even Christ, the savior of mankind, when moved to pity by the tears of Mary and Martha lamenting their dead brother, was not able as a man to hold back tears; if the Virgin mother is said to have done likewise in the death of a son; if then Saint Augustine and other doctors of the Catholic Church and many other holy men (whom it would take too long to name) did the same, then what ought we—who are humble men (in comparison to the memorable founders of the church militant)—what ought we to do? . . . Therefore, if it is not possible to be done, if nature does not allow that parents not grieve at least somewhat over the loss of children, then sorrow (*egritudo*) arising in parents from the death of sons must be considered to be an evil of nature, not of opinion.[49]

Giannozzo's philosophical rejoinder and now Niccolò's theological corroboration thus fully develop and complete the Peripatetic and Christian repudiation of Stoicism that Salutati began.

Finally, the abbot suggests that after Giannozzo's experience of legitimate, grief, he should strive for a moderate equanimity, he should give thanks to God, and he should ask his departed Antonino to pray for him.[50] Giannozzo follows this advice. When the priest's speech ends, he releases his pent-up tears. When "*ille naturalis humane fragilitatis impetus*"[51] subsides, he turns to God in a speech that bears some resemblance to Salutati's address to God and discussions of divine goodness and wisdom in his letters to Zabarella.[52] Giannozzo then turns to his son to ask that he make divine intercessions for him.

The dialogue thus presents the entire process of grieving. Guided by his own emotional experience, by his own philosophical learning, and by the counsels of a clerical adviser, Giannozzo comes to learn and to brave the stages of mourning: to experience a legitimate, natural, human grief; then to achieve an equanimity admirable in the eyes of man and God; and then to turn to God and to his Antonino. Like Salutati, he offers his own model of grieving and consolation that he believes conforms more truly to the emotional realities of human nature; but whereas Salutati refuted Cicero, Manetti challenged his greatest Stoic successor, Seneca. Basically, the debate between "Manetti" and "Angelo Acciaiuoli" was a completion and formalization of the debate between Salutati and Zabarella. That is, Salutati first rejects Stoic thought as unrealistic and then turns to a thoroughly fideistic solace that he derives from his trust in God's omnipotent and divine will. Similarly, Manetti argues the case for the Peripatetic and Academic "stage" of natural grief and then outlines subsequent stages of spiritual solace and colloquy. Like Salutati's epistolary exchange with Zabarella, Manetti's dialogue also served as a rhetorical framework for his resolution of grief: with Angelo he has a colloquy of anger and emotion; with God, a colloquy of acceptance and thanksgiving; with his son, a colloquy of divine entreaty. Perhaps chiefly a symbolic voice for a larger cultural prejudice, the figure of "Angelo" was by turns naive and harsh in his position that grief does not befit a humanist or a Christian. Seeking to substantiate fully the inexorable and legitimate realm of grief that is part of man's *humanitas*, Manetti's response drew on classical and Christian thought in meticulous detail to make the fullest counter-Stoic statement concerning grief yet found in the humanist tradition. And complementing this regimen of natural grieving with the devotions of divine thanksgiving and colloquy, the *Dialogus* offered a realistic Christian and humanist guide to the crisis of bereavement.

As a major compilation of both secular and religious *loci* and *exempla*, Manetti's dialogue is an unusual work of psychology, philosophy, history, theology, and anthropology. What Crantor and Cicero had done for their eras, surveying the remedies for sorrow, Manetti did for his. He replaced their lost works and updated them, naturally broadening his sights to include the Judeo-Christian tradition. His treatise was a work of considerable learning, bringing to light many pertinent Greek sources: passages from such as Homer, Herodotus, Aeschylus, Euripides, Plutarch, and Diogenes Laertius grace its pages. The burgeoning revival of Greek learning is clearly in evidence, though Plato is noticeably absent.[53] He also culled the rich patristic sources of consolatory lore such as found in writings of Augustine, Ambrose, and Jerome. Thus marshaling a wealth of cultural and spiritual evidence, Manetti continued the philosophical and historical discourse on the rites of grieving undertaken by Petrarch (*Sen.* 10.4) and Salutati. Extending the latter's argument, he challenged the legitimacy of a Stoicism that the aging Petrarch came to champion, that Zabarella presumed for Salutati, and that his Certosan consoler pressed upon him. When "Angelo" proffered the Roman Stoicism of Seneca, "Manetti" countered with a Greek Peripateticism, which "Niccolò" complemented with a biblical, patristic, and medieval catalogue of sorrow.

The singularity of his work was not lost on Manetti. Recognizing its potential social importance, he soon after composed a vernacular version.[54] His motivations in this were noteworthy, because they spoke to his own perception of the purpose and relevance of the treatise. As he explained in a preface to the *volgare* version, he made this translation partly

> in order that merchants, rulers of the republic, and anyone whatsoever—who, because of the various occupations of everyday affairs, are not able to attend to the study of the Latin language—would not be entirely deprived of reading this material so worthy, so charming, and pertaining nearly to the majority of men.[55]

Manetti anticipated the efforts of Leon Battista Alberti to bring substantive moral discourse to the larger community.[56] His message to that community was one of intense psychological realism and measured hope. On the one hand, he wanted his *Dialogo* to explicate a truth that he felt had been neglected or denied in his culture—namely, the truth (confirmed by nature, by secular culture, and by religious tradition) that there is no greater tragedy than parental bereavement. On the other hand, however, he insists,

> And although this paternal love is so great that nothing greater can be found in this world, nonetheless I have also endeavored to make clear in what way and with what mind, *without offense to God and without denying nature*, one ought to bear the vexation that commonly afflicts fathers after the loss of their dear children.[57]

His treatise thus is both a manifesto on the emotional intensity of bereavement, as well as a practical guide to enduring this saddest of worldly tragedies. Moreover, as the statement above reveals, Manetti wanted to show how his art of mourning not only conformed more truly to nature but also remained safely within the bounds of Christian piety. In the dialogue, in one of his Senecan precepts Christianized, "Angelo" impugned Manetti's devoutness, a charge that elicited a forceful denial later from "Giannozzo."[58] Clearly, Manetti saw the issue of grief not only as a matter of disagreement among philosophers but also as a matter of concern among proper Christians. Unquestionably, he wished to show his contemporaries that there is no impiety in tears, no sin in sorrow. With only seven vernacular manuscripts of the dialogue extant (the printing press still some years away), Manetti's hopes for a popular impact were perhaps not realized. But judging him by his intentions, we find a learned humanist committed to providing his contemporaries with an engaging record of his own grief and with an authentic guide to the process of mourning.

· · · · ·

Though the most important Renaissance dialogue on bereavement, Manetti's was not the first. In the fall of 1401 Giovanni Conversini da Ravenna composed his *De consolatione de obitu filii*, dealing with the loss of his son Israele.[59] At various times a notary, tutor, chancellor, and professor of grammar, rhetoric, and poetry, Conversini was an admirer of both Petrarch and Salutati. As Sabbadini suggests, his lengthy autobiography, the *Rationarium vite* (1401), reflects a subjectivity similar to that found in Petrarch's *Secretum*.[60] And Conversini's dialogue format in the *De consolatione*, a conversation between Mestus and Solator, possibly drew upon Petrarch's format of Dolor (or Metus) and Ratio in his *De remediis* Book 2. Moreover, because Conversini corresponded with Salutati and because he was residing in Padua at the turn of the century and was friends with Zabarella, it is likely that he saw both of Salutati's letters to Zabarella concerning the loss of Piero.[61]

Like Manetti, Conversini used the dialogue to define and resolve grief. His interlocutors, however, do not have the focused and sustained "adversarial" exchange found in the debate between Salutati and Zabarella or in that between "Manetti" and "Acciaiuoli." In fact, the speakers Mestus (the bereaved) and Solator (the consoler) do not exclusively perform the roles their names would suggest. Although Solator often attempts to console Mestus, sometimes the reverse occurs. The principal function of the dialogue is to provide a framework for Conversini's attempt to express, dispute, and resolve certain aspects of his bereavement. The literary speakers give voice to an inward colloquy of emotional, philosophical, and spiritual issues—among them, the legitimacy of grief; the character and history of the child; the irreparability and particular pain, frustration, and disappointment of losing a child; the nature of life and death; the loss of a continuator and heir; the acceptance of divine will; the nature of heavenly beatitude; the continuation of "ties" between the living and the dead. In its structure the work illustrates again the humanists' experimental use of rhetoric to deal with emotional experience. Through a regimen of debate, remembrance, and rumination, Conversini too gave quarter to his sorrow by fashioning a literary framework for mourning.

In all three of these cases of humanist writings on bereavement, we have seen the role of Renaissance innovation in the "rhetoric of mourning": no extant ancient source fully provided an explicit model for any of these epistolary and literary dialogues on grief. This interest in autobiographical testimony also filtered into the more formal, traditional genre of the oration, in a work that was probably the lengthiest, most published Italian *consolatio* of the fifteenth century. In 1461 Francesco Filelfo, the noted Greek scholar and literary free-lancer, composed his well-known *Oratio consolatoria ad Iacobum Antonium Marcellum de obitu Valerii filii*, which he sent to Jacopo Antonio Marcello for the loss of his son, who died in January of that year.[62] Possibly under commission from Marcello, Filelfo in December completed this, his greatest of consolatory writings, a treatise running to about 80 pages in the Basel edition.[63] Filelfo infused into this work a strikingly personal frame of reference. He opened his work with a discussion of his own recent loss (in March) of his son Olimpio Gellio.[64] Here, and in other places, Filelfo clearly sought to compare the experience of grief he and Marcello shared.[65] In fact, this autobiographical framework for the *Oratio*, resembling that found in Petrarch's *Sen.* 10.4, perhaps derived from that same rhetorical precept that Petrarch exploited—namely, that the most effective solace is offered by one who also suffers. But Filelfo, like Petrarch before him, may also have been using the situation to compose a speech of collective consolation.[66] Even if writing on commission, Filelfo may have also seen this *Oratio* as an opportunity to enact his own process of grieving, to articulate his own program of mourning and resolution.[67] The lament over Olimpio found in the *Oratio* was followed by others later in Filelfo's life: in 1470 he wrote a doleful letter on the death of his thirty-seven-year-old son Senofonte; in 1475–76 he wrote several letters in which he reflected on the loss of seven- and eight-year-old sons and the death of his third wife. The comments concerning Olimpio can thus be seen as part of Filelfo's enduring concern with discussing personal loss.[68]

Moreover, in his opening remarks on Olimpio's death, Filelfo perhaps reveals that, aside from Petrarch, he may also have been influenced by other, more recent Renaissance writings on personal bereavement. Recounting his grief during his son's decline, Filelfo's language is not unlike Manetti's in the *Dialogus*: "I was not able not to be moved in my mind—which is a quality of fragility and of human nature—in such a recent and such an unforeseen sharpness of grief."[69] Filelfo's acquaintance with Manetti is confirmed by their correspondence and by Manetti's presence as an interlocutor in Filelfo's *Commentationes florentinae de exilio*.[70] Also possible is Filelfo's borrowing from Salutati's letter concerning the death of Piero. Like Salutati, Filelfo describes his grief and despair at his son's deathbed, bewailing his son's loss in terms of his own old age.[71] In describing his deathbed lamentation over Olimpio, Filelfo says that he turned to a consolatory passage in Menander dealing with the variability of human affairs. Providing a Latin translation of the Menander fragment (531K),[72] he continues:

> Therefore, first having been admonished by the verses of Menander as to what is the law of nature, what is the infirmity of man, and how we should evaluate

and endure however great a misfortune that may occur, and then having turned to the more valid remedies and aids of reason, I was helped and confirmed by them so that I plainly know no evil to have occurred to me, and that I did not so much send *away* by death as send *ahead* my Olimpio whom indeed I considered as dear as my life. Moreover, what is the nature of these arguments I will briefly show in consoling you.[73]

Again, this preface to the consolation suggests Filelfo's effort to identify himself to Marcello as a cosufferer and to characterize his oration as a personally tested "cure." In so doing, Filelfo was likely influenced by Petrarch's greatest Stoic *consolatoria*, *Sen.* 10.4, a work intended as a mutual consolation for sender and receiver. Though Filelfo does not identify this motive in his *Oratio*, we must still wonder whether he did not also see his speech partly as an effort at self-consolation, doubling as an external persuasion for Marcello and as an internal discourse for himself. Thus, for several reasons, it is possible that Filelfo's oration for Marcello perhaps drew on the Renaissance tradition of discussions of parental bereavement extending from Petrarch to Manetti. It is certain that it adapted the motif of autobiographical testimony to the broader domain of consolation literature.

· · · · ·

The importance of this Renaissance tradition lies not merely in its form but also in its content. These writings articulate some significant cultural themes and sensibilities in Renaissance thought, as the consolatory genre was a forum for experimenting with certain emotions and for formulating certain ideas. First and foremost, these writings represent a vital part of the humanist exploration of the emotional world. Salutati's brief Peripatetic and Christian defense of grief inspired Manetti's major anti-Stoic statement. Conversini also addressed the question of emotionalism in his dialogue. When "Solator" argues for the need for restraint and equanimity, "Mestus" proclaims the naturalness, inevitability, and piety of weeping, citing *exempla* of those who have wept.[74] Later in the dialogue the matter of grief comes up again, but this time the positions of the interlocutors have reversed. When Mestus suggests that "*tristitia*" can be harmful, Solator argues that weeping can have its benefits:

> Thus grief steeps the mind more dangerously in that person in whom it is concealed. Where, indeed, it is openly released from the recesses of the mind, it recedes, ceases, and gradually vanishes. Therefore, allow him who is raging with a just grief to lament, to wail, to weep, and to sigh. Indeed, grief has its solace and pleasure. Just as periodic quiet lessens labor, thus the release of tears, lamentation, and wailing lessens, tempers, and settles a fluctuating mind.[75]

Curiously, then, these humanists circle back to a position found in an earlier phase of Petrarch's writings on grief and emotion. Before his Stoic conversion was complete, Petrarch had indulged in the release of tears and, in some cases, had counseled others to do likewise. The (particularly Ovidian) sensibility of *voluptas dolendi* informed various writings of his. But Petrarch's interests in weeping largely sprang from poetic fonts. As he became more committed to acting as a *"medicus animorum,"* however, he sought out more constructive solutions in Stoic reason, virtue, and patience. Those of his humanist successors whom we have examined here, however, did not have his initial poetic frame of reference. They lacked his literary predisposition to emotionalism and his literary license to express it. Instead, their psychological starting point was a more philosophical one— one that derived largely from a predominant Roman Stoicism in which Petrarch, and the revival of Ciceronian and Stoic thought generally, had schooled them. Like Petrarch, these figures were interested in psychological exploration, but instead of heading toward Stoic *apatheia*, Salutati, Manetti, and, to some extent, Conversini were interested in moving away from it, charting new Peripatetic (and other) territory. And yet, ironically, it was Petrarch who had especially prepared the way for their interest in the emotional realm: it was he who popularized autobiographical Latin literature on such issues; it was he who legitimated the discussion of secular sorrow; it was he who aggressively sought to examine the psychology of the human condition. But although Stoic solutions spoke effectively to his own emotional evolution, these successors of his found them untenable.

What does this revolt against impassivity mean? In some way, it is tied to the emerging sensitivity to the nature and sanctity of the active life.[76] Grief was increasingly seen to be a worthy part of the world of friendship and charity, an inevitable result of an emotional investment in the worldly community. Salutati implied this in his famous letter of 1398 to Pellegrino Zambeccari, in which he vigorously opposed his friend's plans for a religious retreat from the world.[77] In his letter, a bold defense of the secular station, Salutati compared the active and contemplative lives. He argued that the two must never be fully distinct: the active life should not be devoid of all contemplation; the contemplative life should not lack all human intercourse. In explaining the worldly involvements necessary to the latter, Salutati cites the inevitability and charity of grief:

> [N]or can a contemplative, if he lives as a man, be completely dead to secular matters. . . . [H]e must live and help his neighbor on God's behalf. . . . Will he be a contemplative so completely devoted to God that disasters befalling a dear one or the death of relatives will not affect him and the destruction of his homeland not move him? If there were such a person, and he related to other people like this, he would show himself not a man but a tree trunk, a useless

piece of wood, a hard rock and obdurate stone; nor would he imitate the mediator of God and man who represents the highest perfection. For Christ wept over Lazarus and cried abundantly over Jerusalem.[78]

If a pious contemplative life thus cannot be without grief, obviously neither can the more social active life, so zealously championed by Salutati in this letter as in earlier ones to the grief-stricken Andrea Giusti da Volterra. Sadly, Salutati's own encounters with worldly tragedy reminded him of the truth of his comments: a couple of years after this letter to Zambeccari, he used some of the same language and the same example (of Christ's weeping for Lazarus) in his correspondence with Zabarella on his loss of Piero and Andrea.[79] In his family losses, Salutati himself felt the inevitable pain of the "active life." As a measure of worldly involvement, grief must be seen as an unavoidable and worthy part of man's social experience.

Of course, the revival of Peripateticism informed this new vision of psychological and social reality. The *Nicomachean Ethics* advocated a more realistic view of human happiness and experience; the *Politics* celebrated the centrality of the social order.[80] In their revision of Stoic thought Salutati and Manetti both called upon the former, and Manetti even summoned the latter. When rebutting the position of "Angelo," Manetti drew on both works to advance a truer anthropology of naturalism, affirming that "man by his nature is a social and civic animal, capable of smiling, born for doing and acting, even to be a certain type of mortal god."[81] Those who do not grieve the death of their children are like that asocial creature Aristotle characterized as being either a god or a beast, but truly no man (*Politics* 1.1.12.1253a).[82] For Manetti, such a being, like Aristotle's isolated "nonman," was simply beyond the pale. By nurturing a keener sense of psychological and social naturalism, the Peripatetic revival thus helped shape humanist approaches to mourning.

As in most such questions of intellectual cause and effect, it is difficult to assert with any certainty exactly in what way the Peripatetic revival led in these new views of grief, and exactly in what way it followed. We do know, however, as Garin would suggest, that the attack on Stoicism was not contained just to the followers of Aristotle, as the case of the Epicurean Lorenzo Valla illustrates.[83] Certainly, the intellectual revival of debates between the philosophical schools provided some basis for the discussion of emotional issues. But we should not minimize the role of psychological curiosity and experimentation that perhaps fueled the liveliness of these debates.

As Salutati's letters show, the humanist revolt against "reason" sought refuge not only in "emotion" but also in "time" and, particularly, in "volition." Salutati's final resolution of grief for his wife and children became entirely an act of the *will*. An intellectual reflection on Stoic truths was ineffective—it was instead a volitional embrace of divine will that thoroughly healed him. Salutati's concern with the will was also manifested elsewhere in his thought, as can be seen in his *De nobilitate legum et medicine* (1399), in which he places law over medicine because the former deals with a higher moral, volitional, social realm.[84] In his letters on grief Salutati shows how the will is ascendant not just in philosophical, social, and cultural domains but also in the private world of sorrow. Gradually developing his idea of a fideistic trust in divine will in his letters concerning the threat of plague, he eventually adapted this outlook to his own resolution of sorrow. Thus, in the world of grief, as in the worlds of philosophy, theology, and learning, we find the humanists formulating the position that a volitional experience is more powerful than an intellectual one—the position that, as Petrarch famously put it, "it is better to will the good than to know the truth."[85]

Salutati and Manetti notwithstanding, "reason" still, however, had a strong defender in Filelfo, whose *Oratio* for Marcello aspired to be an intellectual *tour de force*.[86] His consolation was a rich compendium of philosophical and Christian remedies, but its principal focus was on the immortality of the soul, a theme that became a major concern in fifteenth- and sixteenth-century thought. As is well known, Marsilio Ficino presented the fullest philosophical treatment of immortality in the Quattrocento in his *Theologia Platonica de immortalitate animorum* (1469–74).[87] Prior to Ficino's massive treatise, there were a few humanist writings on the topic. As di Napoli, Kristeller, and Trinkaus have shown, the themes of human immortality, dignity, and divinity had a considerable currency in the works of mid-century figures such as Fra Antonio da Barga, Bartolomeo Fazio, Giannozzo Manetti (*On the Dignity and Excellence of Man*), and Pier Candido Decembrio.[88] What has not been sufficiently stressed is that it was the consolatory or "remedial" genre that inspired some of the earlier humanist discussions of this topic. In his chapter "On misery and sadness" in his *De remediis* 2.93, Petrarch prescribed human dignity and immortality as two of the important remedies for despair. Also, in the chapters "On the fear of death" and "On death," he advanced immortality as a consolation, in the latter chapter citing Cicero's discussion in the *Tusculans* Book 1. In consolatory letters Petrarch and Salutati also sometimes addressed this theme. Salutati's friend Zabarella was Petrarch's first successor in proclaiming Cicero's consolatory interests in an otherworldly immortality. In their debate over Stoic solace Zabarella argued that in Cicero's discussions of immortality there was a "higher level" of consolation than that found in the *Tusculans* Book 3. Carlo Marsuppini, largely in imitation of Ps.-Plutarch's *Consolatio ad Apollonium*, also cited the argument of immortality in his *Consolatio* of 1433 to Lorenzo di Giovanni and Cosimo de' Medici.[89]

It was Filelfo, however, who first sought to compose for his time a comprehensive rhetorical consolation concerning immortality. Very likely, he drew his inspiration for this project partly from Marsuppini, who admittedly only broached the subject.[90] (Filelfo was probably moved by the spirit of rivalry in this. A personal, academic, and political adversary of Marsuppini's in Florence in the 1430s, Filelfo had once been a vocal foe, caviling at Marsuppini's literary shortcomings.)[91] Filelfo's discussion of immortality, commanding almost a third of his treatise, drew arguments from "nature," from "reason," and from "divine justice."[92] The argument from "reason," by far the most extensive, is probably the most substantive treatment of immortality that can be found in Trecento or Quattrocento consolation.[93] With the goal of formulating a philosophical proof concerning the soul's immortality, Filelfo presents an encyclopedic survey of the various definitions of the mind found in ancient and medieval thought, including figures such as Thales, Anaxagoras, Heraclitus, Democritus, Pythagoras, Plato, Aristotle, Dicaearchus, Zeno, Epicurus, Chrysippus, Posidonius, and Averroës.[94] He ends his discussion by arguing that the human soul is the image and likeness of the divine mind and that

> [o]ur mind has nothing mixed in it, nothing concrete, nothing corporeal, nothing external, but it stands by its own nature and power, by which it feels, knows, lives, and flourishes; by which it is most similar to God; whence it is not able to be dissolved, divided, or destroyed, but rather is immortal and distinctly everlasting. Why, therefore, Jacopo Antonio Marcello, should we grieve for sons snatched from us? Why do we cry so long? Why do we lament? At last, these broke away and, light and pure, they passed through the foggy, misty sky; and thither they are carried where there are no blasts of wind, no showers, no tempest; where there is no cold, no heat, no mutability, but all things are tranquil, serene, and full of ineffable joy.[95]

Thus a theme only partly explored as a consolatory topic by such figures as Petrarch, Zabarella, and Marsuppini, finds its fullest eclectic rhetorical development in Filelfo. As we shall see in Chapter 7, the particularly Platonic revival of this theme, only nascent in Marsuppini, will flower in Florentine consolation in the second half of the fifteenth century. What is the significance of the renaissance of "immortality"? Its causes perhaps ran deeper than the revival of classical texts and schools. As Kristeller argues, there was perhaps a larger cultural context for the popularity of this theme—namely, the preoccupation with fame. That is, the interest in the philosophical concept of divine immortality may have burgeoned in part owing to growing secular aspirations for worldly immortality.[96] This link is perhaps manifest in the content and the ambition of Filelfo's *Oratio* for Marcello. Known for his hubris, Filelfo clearly saw his works as vehicles for secular immortality.[97] The monumental scope and intended originality of his *Oratio* can be attributed partly to his quest for renown. It was not coincidence that, in the dedicatory letter of a collection of his consolatory orations, Filelfo boasted that his discussion of immortality was a noteworthy contribution.[98] Appropriately, the philosophical *topos* of immortality mirrors a worldly concern with fame.

There was perhaps yet another related motive for Filelfo's composition of the *Oratio*. At one point in his treatise Filelfo discussed the idea that children are a vehicle for secular immortality.[99] Very possibly, Filelfo sought in his *Oratio* to "replace" his lost son with a literary monument. Robbed of one kind of immortality, he created another. This was undeniably a motive behind Conversini's *De consolatione*. In his dialogue Conversini deals with the particular poignancy of the loss of a child. Unlike a possession that can be recovered, a child represents an irreplaceable extension of the self. Conversini discusses the connection between man's desire for immortality and parents' attitude toward their children. The urge toward immortality is one of man's innate features: some people hope to achieve a lasting name by founding cities, some by erecting monuments, some by pursuing the study of letters.[100] However, the surest and truest form of secular immortality is to be found in children:

> Truly, no thing, edifice, work, or fame is more personal and immediate to anyone and more mirrors and resembles the author than a child born of oneself. The love of children is the greatest love. Indeed, in the face of the son there shines the image of the father, in his mores the father's virtue, in his studies the father's glory. All those single works of mortals are produced from art and represent a dead image of the creator. A son, however, a gift of nature, represents the parent as a live image, so that a son, viewed as your likeness and effigy, assures that you are acknowledged, seen, recognized, and remembered.[101]

We might ask if larger cultural sensibilities in the Renaissance were beginning to affect attitudes toward children. That is, the growing interest in fame could have influenced a new view of children: like one's works, deeds, studies, or virtue, children perhaps came to be seen more consciously as a part of one's secular identity. Moreover, we might ask whether humanist ideas of man's dignity and divine image and likeness were eventually transferred to the notion of the child as an image and likeness of the parent. In a word, did the Renaissance theme of the "dignity of man" promote a greater sense of the "dignity of the child"?[102]

Toward the end of the dialogue, Conversini returns to the theme of the child as cultural heir and extension. Though he still had an estranged son who lived in Venice, Conversini felt that Israele's death left him with no true filial heir.[103] Mestus complains that he fears dying with no successor "to shine among posterity" (and with no one to inherit his library).[104] For

Mestus' solicitude concerning worldly immortality Solator offers the consolation that literary works are a much better assurance of fame than children: "The pen, which you have laudably made active, will guarantee you a longer and more splendid [name] than will a son. For, from sons praise is mortal, brief, and vanishing; from literary monuments it is eternal."[105] This is the perfect solution for the humanist teacher and scholar. His child is gone; the investment in Israele's education and character is gone; the hope that Israele would inherit his library is gone. Conversini thus turns to letters—the steady assurance that his name can endure. The bereaved, aging scholar must find his consolation in the thought of his immortal works. By creating a literary progeny, the *De consolatione*, Conversini can partially calm his fear of losing his purchase on immortality.[106]

What is clearly true for Conversini may be equally or partially true also for our other three humanist writers. That is, they perhaps all sought to immortalize their grief with their literary artifices—giving timeless life to their timely sorrow. Moreover, in the case of Filelfo, the concern with immortality informed not only the scale of his *Oratio* but also its philosophical content, which gave pride of place to the theme of immortality.

. . . . .

There is a strong case here for the emergence of a particular Renaissance tradition of parental self-consolation, one anticipated by Petrarch's *Sen.* 10.4, launched by Salutati's letters to Zabarella, formalized by Conversini's *De consolatione*, perfected by Manetti's *Dialogus*, and popularized by Filelfo's *Oratio*. It is probable that there were various links among some of these writings. But putting aside the question of specific lines of influence, all these writings clearly represent an important development in the Western consolatory tradition in general: they all chronicle the subjective experience of the loss of a child (or, in Petrarch's case, a grandchild); they all offer personal constructions of crisis and resolution in such a situation. Cicero's *Consolatio* lost, they flesh out a genre largely undeveloped in the extant literature of their ancient and medieval predecessors.[107]

The loss of children was a commonplace in premodern society: Filelfo, for instance, lost twenty of his twenty-four children.[108] Perhaps as a result, parental bereavement was not given its due as a subject of special literary or pastoral concern. Partly driven by their own greater interest in the subjective realm, these humanists imaginatively addressed the problem. Their various solutions of "emotion," of "will," of "immortality" show them groping for consolations that reflect significant personal or cultural perspectives. Particularly in Salutati and Manetti, the rebellion against prevailing ascetic Stoic and Christian assumptions reveals an attempt to reformulate the process of mourning. Salutati's effort to redefine the contours of grieving culminated in Manetti's dialogue. Manetti, in turn, presented a prescriptive manual for the entire process, lending to his own Peripatetic regimen of mourning the full authority of a "revised" Christian perspective, articulated by a Carthusian prior, "Niccolò da Cortona."

For Petrarch and for these successors of his, save perhaps Filelfo, whose motivations for writing were presumably varied, subjective experience was an important spur for probing the psychological domain.[109] In their resulting autobiographies of grief, these humanists use or manipulate ancient rhetorical and literary genres to describe personal bereavement and to formulate solutions for it. Whether in epistolary exhortation, epistolary debate, or literary dialogue, they reveal the rhetorical face of the humanist art of mourning. "Speaking is sweet to those in misery" (*Theb.* 5.48), as Statius and, after him, Petrarch would say.[110]

It is revealing to compare this humanist rhetoric of mourning to another early Quattrocento record of grieving that is left to us by a nonhumanist figure, the Florentine Giovanni di Pagolo Morelli, a "merchant writer," as C. Bec would call him. In his family memoirs, his *Ricordi*, Morelli recounted the first anniversary of the death of his first-born son, Alberto. Presumably written about a year after the loss, this account did not serve the purpose of resolving the immediate bereavement; instead, it seems to have served as a catharsis for unresolved guilt. It gives us a view of grief that is more "medieval" and spiritually traditional than that found in our humanists' writings. Morelli recounts that, long hoping his son would not die, he did not arrange for the administering of last rites for the boy. When the child died without benefit of sacrament, Morelli apparently became consumed with guilt, a guilt probably accounting for the troubling vision he had of his son stabbing him and his wife in the heart. Morelli attempts to resolve this remorse with a sacred ritual on the first anniversary of Alberto's death—or with a later account of such a ritual in his diary. In this ceremony Morelli organizes his mourning around sacral offices and prayers: he addresses the Virgin and St. John; he recites psalms, *laude*, the *Salve regina*, the *Credo*, the *Te Deum*; he embraces and kisses the *tavola*. His sorrow is more one of contrition for sin than one of grief for loss; weeping stems more from empathic meditations on the Virgin's and St. John's sorrows than from his own. Moreover, the final crisis and resolution is built around the appearance of dream visions, first of an accusatory Satan and then of the beatific Virgin and his own son. Clearly, the process of Morelli's mourning is structured around traditional concerns of guilt and sin, prayer and office, Satanic and divine visions.[111]

Besides being a fascinating record of mourning in its own terms, this account takes on added meaning as a counterpart to the humanist art of mourning. Like Manetti's conversation in the *Dialogus*, Morelli's anniversary celebration—or something like it—may well have taken place. But whereas Manetti and our other humanists wrote relatively soon after their losses to resolve grief, Morelli recorded his principal account of bereavement a "ceremonial" year after the event, hoping finally to resolve a lingering guilt. And whereas Morelli's solution lay in ritual and in spiritual visions, the humanists' answers were rooted in discussions of emotion, volition, philosophy, and theology.

The humanists were attempting to define a new structure for mourning based on rhetoric rather than ritual. They were searching to complement a medieval theological and institutional response to death which was not sufficiently consolatory, in the classical sense of the word, a response largely characterized by sacrament (last rites), the Office of the Dead, prayers for the dead. In their autobiographical accounts of bereavement, they fashion for themselves and for others a literary "ars maerendi," sometimes offering revised or new laws of mourning, sometimes developing particular theological or philosophical consolations.

A testimony to the cultural presence of this Quattrocento tradition of rhetorical mourning can perhaps be seen in its "counterfeiting." In one case, this special genre was perhaps commissioned or authorized by a bereaved parent to complete his program of mourning. The parent, whom we have already met, was Jacopo Antonio Marcello, the recipient of Filelfo's monumental *Oratio* and of numerous other consolations for the death of his son Valerio. Feeling that his consolers had failed him and had not recognized the legitimacy of his grief, Marcello either charged or permitted Giorgio Bevilacqua da Lazise, a student of Gurarino Veronese's, to compose on his behalf a response to his many comforters. Completed in late 1463, the proudly plangent reply was addressed to King René, Duke of Anjou, who also was to receive the collection of *consolatoriae* and was to be an arbiter in this dispute between Marcello and the orators.[112] This *Excusatio adversus consolatores in obiti Valerii filii* is thus a ghostwritten autobiographical writing on grief.[113] Like Salutati's letters to Zabarella and like Manetti's *Consolatory Dialogue*, Marcello's *Excusatio* is a substantive repudiation of all Stoicizing consolation. An epic record of parental grief, it vividly describes Marcello's sorrow,[114] presents a lengthy praise and history of the child,[115] recounts his illness and death, and firmly rebuts all overly rational assumptions, arguments, examples, and warnings advanced by his consolers.[116] Marcello felt that his consolers did not allow him his just sorrow, thus forcing him now to excuse himself for his profound grief.[117] The *Excusatio* is simultaneously an indictment of the failure of traditional consolation and an apologia for the legitimacy of Marcello's intense sorrow. As for his comforters, he found them to be "grave . . . [and] severe consolers and accusers of a despondent mind," who instead should have been more "indulgent and lenient."[118] Despite the herculean efforts of "the greatest orators" who sought to comfort him "not only with their most eloquent letters and orations but even with books," their rhetoric simply failed.[119] Though they assembled more arguments than probably were to be found in Cicero's *Consolatio* on Tullia, their efforts missed the mark.[120]

In countering the assumptions of his insensitive accusers, "Marcello" offers up both arguments and examples that suggest the inexorability and sanctity of tears. Examining the question "whether virtue can coexist with sadness," Bevilacqua challenges Cicero's argument that "sadness is a disease of the mind" (cf. *Tusc.* Books 3–4) and other Stoic assumptions with Peripatetic and Christian justifications and allowances for sorrow.[121] Addressing next the question "whether weeping or tears can be a remedy for mitigating or lessening sadness or grief," he explains the salutary benefits of emotional release.[122] He closes this section with a lament that his consolers did not turn their many efforts to a better end. If only they "had drawn [their consolations] from the school of the Peripatetics rather than that of the Stoics, and had tried to use on me not arms and weapons more appropriate for killing, but nets and snares more suited for saving life, and to cure me with the medicines, potions, and drugs that abound in the pharmacies of the Peripatetics."[123] Like Salutati and Manetti, "Marcello" seeks refuge in the more natural psychology of Aristotle's school. And like them he invokes examples of grievous figures not only from the classical world, but also from Judeo-Christian tradition. In one section, he presents a type of catalogue of Christian emotion, citing biblical *exempla* for the variety of pious feelings such as "the sharpness of grief, expansive happiness, great desire, immense devotion, vehement indulgence, true contrition" and so on.[124] Beyond grief, Bevilacqua wants to draw attention to the larger emotional history of the Judeo-Christian heritage. The *Excusatio* places Marcello squarely in that sacred, if somewhat neglected, tradition.

Notwithstanding the intentions of his consolers, perhaps Marcello's only remedy for his sorrow would be found in his "own" rhetoric of grief— a literary lament articulated, if not by Marcello himself, then by a humanist surrogate. In purchasing (or encouraging and participating in) such a vicarious rhetorical "art of mourning" he dramatically, if ironically, reifies this Renaissance tradition of autobiographical testimonies of loss and grief. Truly, it is a commentary on the place of consolation in Renaissance culture that such an anthology would be compiled by a mourner as a worthy expression of personal identity and experience, that it would be intended to be offered up for public judgment.[125] Marcello's grief is a source of pride; his bereavement and sorrow, a source of fame.[126] The consolatory tradition has been slowly transformed. Now challenging the status of the consoler's *consolatio* to the mourner is the mourner's reply to his consoler(s). Found only on a minor scale in Cicero's letters, this tradition was fleshed out by Salutati, continued by Manetti, and feigned by Marcello. Surely, grief has found a confident voice.

6

THE SCIENCE OF CONSOLING

A LITTLE-KNOWN CLERICAL MANUAL
OF CONSOLATION

THOUGH he possibly took minor orders and certainly held ecclesiastical benefices, Petrarch was, happily, not a priest and, albeit
somewhat regrettably, not a monk. Salutati was proudly laic in
status. Conversini, Manetti, and Filelfo were all laymen. If, in fact, lay humanists were providing a type of consolatory literature and care partly neglected by the medieval pastoral office, how did Renaissance clerical writers
adapt humanist perspectives to the pastoral domain? How did more traditionally religious writers aspire to compete with or complement the efforts
of their lay counterparts?[1] In a word, how did lay discussions of consolation prompt clerical responses? What perspectives emerge in such religious
writings? To which sources did Renaissance clerical humanists turn? In
exploring these questions this chapter will focus on two clerics, the Veronese Augustinian canon Matteo Bosso and a little-known Dalmatian, Nicolaus bishop of Modruš, both of whom composed revealing consolatory
works in the 1460s. Of particular interest is Nicolaus' manual, *De consolatione*, a handbook that attempted to systematize the consolatory office.
What had been loosely a rhetorical art, this Dalmatian cleric endeavored to
make a comprehensive science, uniquely joining the classical, patristic, confessional, and dictaminal traditions. His treatise not only reveals much
about the interplay among consolatory traditions in the fifteenth century,
but also dramatically illustrates the Renaissance interest in revitalizing, expanding, and popularizing the office of consolation.

As is well known, the classical revival met sometimes with clerical hostility, sometimes with clerical enthusiasm. Salutati had locked horns with the
vocal Giovanni Dominici on the issue of pagan learning. Naturally, his
apologia for the classics invoked the precedent of those liberal patristic figures such as Augustine, whose *De doctrina Christiana* (2.40) had urged that
the "spoils of the Egyptians" be robbed and adapted to better ends.[2] In
contrast to Dominici's conservative stance, many other religious figures
warmly embraced the new learning. In Florence in the first half of the
Quattrocento, the most notable such humanist in orders, or cleric of letters,

was Ambrogio Traversari, the Camaldolese monk who taught himself Greek and became a champion of classical and patristic studies.[3] The Latin Fathers, of course, had already been of considerable interest to Petrarch and Salutati, who drew upon them sometimes in a consolatory context—as famously seen in Petrarch's consolation of the fearful Boccaccio's threat to abandon secular studies.

Traversari, however, intensified this interest and enriched it with numerous translations of Greek Fathers such as Basil, Chrysostom, Athanasius, and Gregory Nazianzen. One of his lay disciples was Manetti, who in support of his sorrow in his *Consolatory Dialogue* culled the Latin Fathers. As for the neglected lore of Greek patristic sources of consolation, Traversari translated some of the letters, sermons, and treatises of Chrysostom, who was probably the most prolific consoler among the Church Fathers. Included in these translations was the three-book consolation *On Providence*, dealing with the despair of the monk Stagirius and the general problem of tribulation. Perhaps others besides Traversari recognized the relevance of this consolatory work, as his translation survives in numerous manuscripts from the Quattrocento.[4] In general, Traversari saw Chrysostom as an exemplar of Christian fortitude and pastoral duty. In the early 1430s he translated Palladius' dialogue *On the Life of Chrysostom*, dedicating the work to Eugenius IV. In his dedication Traversari explains the partially self-consolatory motive in his task, which he hoped would "lift up a withered soul sick with cares," and he testifies that he drew "great solace" from Chrysostom's biography.[5] Not only does he marvel at this Father's "invincible constancy amidst such grave and continual persecutions," but also he notes Chrysostom's dutiful effort to comfort his flock even in the midst of his own adversity: "Indeed even after having been driven into exile he still endeavored assiduously to console through letters those not able to bear the absence of their most skillful pastor."[6] In the 1430s Traversari also translated Gregory Nazianzen's *On the Death of a Father*, intending it as a consolation for an acquaintance recently bereaved of a father.[7] And like certain of his Quattrocento lay counterparts, Traversari wrote of his own experience with grief—in his case, describing the death of his brother Girolamo in 1433. Besides various letters on this loss, he left a detailed, emotional account of this tragedy in his autobiographical journal *Hodoeporicon*.[8]

As the example of Traversari illustrates, the fifteenth-century revival of Chrysostom and other Fathers perhaps both signaled and furthered a greater interest in pastoral eloquence and Christian rhetorical consolation.[9] Another case in point, from the second half of the century, was the Augustinian canon Matteo Bosso. Bosso had an impressive and varied exposure to humanist currents, both from lay and religious quarters. While in Milan in his early years he knew of Filelfo and studied under the latter's

pupil, Pierleoni da Rimini.[10] In Verona he fell under the influence of Timeteo Maffei, an Augustinian canon who penned a defense of humanist learning titled *In sanctam rusticitatem litteras impugnantem.*[11] In 1451 Bosso
joined Maffei as a fellow canon, and in the 1480s he made his way to
Florence, where he became abbot of the Augustinian order at Fiesole and
came into contact with Lorenzo de' Medici, Poliziano, and Pico. Among
his humanist writings is a highly Epicurean dialogue, the *De veris ac salutaribus animi gaudiis*, which, attracting the attention of Poliziano and Pico,
was published three times in the 1490s.[12]

Bosso also wrote a consolatory dialogue titled *De tolerandis adversis*
(1462–63), which, as part of an anthology of various writings, orations,
and a first book of letters, was also first published in the 1490s.[13] He wrote
the dialogue in response to a request from a fellow canon that he provide
something that could "raise and compose a mind . . . dejected and dis-
tracted by various cares and annoyances."[14] In defining his task, Bosso provides a clear picture of the philosophical and religious traditions in which
he places his consolatory task. He acknowledges the imposing heritage of
classical and Christian consolers:

> [I]t was disputed strongly by the Stoics that grief does not befall the sage, nor
> indeed that he is disturbed by any mental passions and that in virtue alone
> there is enough support against all ills. And indeed for soothing sorrow and
> patiently bearing the commotion of all of the most serious evils there exist
> many remarkable precepts of Plato, Posidonius, and Seneca. Also accessible
> are Cicero's five golden books of Tusculan questions concerning the contempt
> of death, the toleration of pain (*de tolerando dolore*), the easing of distress and
> the restraining of sicknesses of the mind and, finally, the power of a great and
> invincible virtue that helps and leads in the seeking of happiness and a blessed
> life—all these books ornate with all the flowers of eloquence, sparkling and
> brilliant like pearls. We also have many volumes of this kind from our [Chris-
> tian writers] illustrious through the glory of sanctity and singular doctrine,
> writers such as Chrysostom, Cyprian, and Jerome, to whose works clearly
> nothing—except our admiration—can be added in terms of eloquence and
> gravity and brilliance of thought.[15]

Disclaiming any intention to compose anything unique in the company
of such writers, Bosso argues that he is motivated not by the hope of
philosophical originality but by the goal of rhetorical efficacy. Acceding to
Solomon's adage that "there is nothing new under the sun," he maintains
that the repeating of well-worn truths can still be effective:

> In truth I am inspired to write by the same reason by which we are daily
> inspired to preach. For the recent and renewed mention of virtue, just like a
> perfume, smells more sweetly and always has something that brings new de-

light and benefit, according to the saying "Even after ten times repeated things can still be pleasing" (Horace, *Ars poetica*, 365).[16]

Bosso thus compares his role as a preacher to his role as a consoler.[17] Exhortation and consolation can inspire by presenting even old material. This statement, including the allusion to the *Ars poetica*, calls to mind Petrarch's discussion of remedial eloquence in his *De remediis* 2.117, where he explains his purpose in restating familiar truths in new ways.[18] Bosso also echoes Petrarch in his conscious avoidance of all esoteric scholasticism in his endeavor. Pointedly disavowing the propriety here of "intricate arguments, dialectical sophisms, or anything inextricable or tortuous," he suggests that his task requires rather an "open, guileless, sincere eloquence."[19] Bosso adapted a Petrarchan discourse of moral persuasion and comfort to a more pastoral genre—as, perhaps, he had also done in the pulpit. Undoubtedly, Bosso was influenced by developments in Renaissance rhetoric, including possibly both lay oratory and the recent resurgence of patristic sources.[20]

Bosso's dialogue portrays an exchange between himself ("Mattheus") and a group of Parmenese friends. Bosso's own suffering from a tertian fever provides the context for this discussion of adversity. His "Amici" approach him asking why such a good and God-fearing man would so suffer—why, in general, God allows the pious to be afflicted with "poverty, ignominy, pains, tortures, torments, servitudes, bereavements, exiles, afflictions, temptations, imprisonments, calamities, plagues, and violent deaths."[21] Mattheus responds with a discussion of why the "good" are beset with evils and why the "evil" are blessed with goods. Possibly reflecting contemporary discussions of "human dignity," he argues that man is truly divine, a "certain effigy of the divinity,"[22] and he warns that worldly blandishments distract him from his noble, eternal destiny. In fact, prosperity can be an obstacle to virtue, just as adversity can be its proving ground. Arguing that adversity is a necessary correction redirecting our sights toward heaven, Bosso invokes Paul's dictum that "virtus in infirmitate perficitur" (2 Cor. 12:9).[23] Adversity, moreover, is punishment for man's sin. It is also a worthy test of his righteousness. Bosso illustrates the sanctity of suffering by citing classical exemplars, Christ on the Cross, Christian martyrs, and modern-day figures who have borne tragedy gloriously, nobly, or meaningfully. Bosso's message, however, is not completely ascetic, as he softens his tone with a reflection on the beatitude of the afterlife. Drawing on Revelation, he describes the splendor, happiness, and *voluptas* of the future life—a theme bearing some similarity to the discussion of heavenly sensual qualities found in the third book of his *On the True and Salutary Joys of the Mind*.[24] One wonders if Bosso was influenced by the Epicureanism of Valla's *De vero bono* of the 1430s. In any case, having presented his amalgam of Stoic, Christian, and Epicurean remedies, Bosso closes the first book with an exhortation that both the false allures and the tribulations of the world should be contemned in the face of man's true spiritual end:

> Let us abandon, dismiss, and trample upon all these inferior goods which caress us with false delight, all those riches, honors, dignities, powers, sensual pleasures, and vicious and fatal enticements of glory and ambition. With a constant and invincible spirit let us bear poverty, ignominy, dangers, pains, tortures, even death if need be. For if the body is vexed or even extinguished, the mind still remains, that true and divine part of man, holy and eternal, which, its bodily chains broken, is about to fly to that place which receives souls divested and unburdened of all care into its spacious and blessed fold— the bodies to follow when, at the end of time, that terrible and powerful God will recall all flesh to life.[25]

Bosso thus offers his version of a remedy for both kinds of fortune, recast into a highly spiritual vision. The second book of the dialogue, grappling with the problem of the prosperity of the evil, considers the issues of divine providence, ponders the limits of man's knowledge of the ways of God, and reflects on the final disposition of the just and the unjust before the bar of divine justice.

Explaining the divine context for human misfortune, Bosso develops a distinctly Christian rhetoric of consolation. With its discussions of punitive, penitential, and virtuous suffering; of sin and free will; of the mysteries of divine providence; of the eternal justice awaiting all mankind; of the beatitudes of the afterlife, Bosso's pastoral dialogue is certainly more a "divine consolation" than a classical one.[26] Though he cites ancient arguments and examples, his reliance on classical content is far outshadowed by his interest in Christian themes. Citing Chrysostom, Cyprian, and Jerome as Christian antecedents for such consolation literature, Bosso was thus seeking to revive the patristic model of pastoral rhetoric and consolation.[27] In a framework that united the humanist concern with rhetoric with the pastoral tradition of preaching, Bosso tried to explain the problem of human suffering in a simple and persuasive manner. He chose the humanist dialogue as the form most suited to his fellow canon's request for a consolation book.[28] Perhaps more than anything else, Bosso was trying to compose a modern-day Christian counterpart to Cicero's secular psychological dialogues in the *Tusculans*. In some sense, the *On Bearing Adversities* was a pastoral complement to Petrarch's anthology of dialogues on fortune.[29]

A couple of years after Bosso wrote his dialogue on adversity, a ranking member of the secular clergy, the Dalmatian bishop Nicolaus of Modruš, composed his treatise *De consolatione*. Like Bosso, Nicolaus sought to integrate classical and Christian consolatory traditions, drawing especially on the Fathers. Like Bosso, he reveals the clerical interest in appropriating this psychological realm popularized by Petrarch and his successors. Though little-known and never published, Nicolaus' handbook deserves careful attention as a striking example of Renaissance innovation and synthesis in the history of consolation. It represents the fullest attempt, since Petrarch's *De remediis* of a century before, to provide a comprehensive handbook of remedies.[30] But Nicolaus' work differed from Petrarch's in significant ways. First, whereas Petrarch's *De remediis* dealt with both prosperous and adverse fortune, Nicolaus' was concerned only with grief and despair. Second, whereas Petrarch's manual was meant to be read for private benefit, Nicolaus' was intended to be used as a guide for administering solace—in addition, presumably, to its alternate function as a book of private reading and comfort. In its aim to be a complete handbook, it offered a thorough framework for the theory and method of consolation. Petrarch's treatise, though containing some general, prefatory remarks on the nature, purpose, and techniques of therapeutic wisdom, chiefly aimed to be a compendium of remedies. Nicolaus' work was unique, to my knowledge, in its attempt to construct, in an autonomous work, a systematic treatment of both the *topoi* and the administering of consolation.

Nicolaus Modrusiensis (or Nicolaus de Catharo, Nikola of Kotor, Nicolaus Machinensis, Nikola of Majine) was born in Kotor in the Venetian territory of Dalmatia in the first quarter of the fifteenth century. He studied under the theologian and philosopher Paolo della Pergola in Venice. Becoming a cleric, he held ecclesiastical offices in Dalmatia (e.g., at Modruš and Corbavia) and in Italy (e.g., at Viterbo, Ascoli, Todi, and Spoleto). Shortly after being named vice-legate to Cardinal Raffaelo Sansoni-Riario in Perugia in 1478, he served as Sixtus IV's emissary to Florence to try to win the release of the Cardinal who was imprisoned following the Pazzi conspiracy; in support of the pope in the ensuing conflict with the Florentines he wrote a *Defense of Ecclesiastical Freedom*. He died in Rome and was buried in S. Maria del Popolo.[31] Several volumes of his library passed to the collection of Sixtus IV. Thus, though not born in Italy, he was educated in Venice and had close ties to the Italian clergy and the Papal court. His works include a *De mortalium foelicitate* which he dedicated to Pius II; the *De consolatione* (1465–66) dedicated to Marco Barbo, then bishop of Vicenza; a *De bellis Gothorum* (ca. 1473); an *Oratio in funere Petri* composed (as was a eulogy by Niccolò Perotti) for the death of Cardinal Pietro Riario in 1474; the *Defensio ecclesiasticae libertatis* (1479); and a *De titulis et auctoribus Psalmorum* (ca. 1479). Of these works, the only one to be printed was the funeral oration for Riario.[32]

Nicolaus' book collection and his writings reveal both scholastic and humanist interests. Aristotelian commentaries by Alexander of Hales, Duns

Scotus, and Albert of Saxony, now found in the Biblioteca Angelica in
Rome, have been traced to his library.[33] But included in the books that
passed to the library of Sixtus IV in 1480 are not only several works of
Aristotle, but also a variety of more literary texts, such as philosophical and
rhetorical works of Cicero (including the *Tusculans*), Quintilian's *Institutes*,
Macrobius' commentary on the *Somnium Scipionis*, and Calcidius' on the
Timaeus; also found are works of Augustine, Jerome, and Lactantius.[34] As
for his own writings, the *De mortalium foelicitate* draws on both scholastic
and humanist sources.[35] Certainly the *De consolatione*, with its considerable
reliance on the ancient moralists and poets, shows Nicolaus to have been
well versed in the classical tradition.

The *On Consolation* was written in 1465–66 when Nicolaus was in Viterbo.[36] The genre of the treatise is that of a handbook, intended to deal
comprehensively with the science of giving solace by treating its theory,
method, and the major *loci communes*. It is a kind of *summa* for the *officium
consolandi*. In his prefatory comments, Nicolaus states his purpose in the
work and alludes to the traditions to which his treatise is related. His intended audience is not a scholastic elite but a more general population:

> I have therefore attempted in this work to explain the method of consolation
> not according to the precise standards of philosophy—for we are not now
> disputing about the nature of the world or about those subtler and finer
> points that must be discussed away from the crowd, in retreat with the wise—
> but in a broader and cruder fashion which can be actively used even before the
> people. It is indeed our purpose to pass on precepts by which, as in the case
> of other disturbances, so in the case of [adversities warranting] consolation,
> when the circumstances require it we may influence the mind of a hearer,
> succor those who are afflicted, and alleviate their distress as much as possible.
> And I do not think I have undertaken this labor in vain, even though there
> exist many distinguished works written by very skilled men about this
> method, as are widely available those books *On [the] Consolation [of Philoso-
> phy]* by the indeed renowned Boethius, Seneca's noted book *On Consolation*
> as well as that work he entitled *On the Remedies of Misfortunes*, and Isidore's
> shining little gem of *Synonyms*. If, indeed, the work that Cicero wrote on this
> subject were extant, perhaps we and all would have been freed from this task.
> There are extant, however, almost all of his worthy consolatory letters, as
> there are some of Cyprian, Jerome, Basil the Great, and many other very
> learned men both Greek and Latin. For many Greeks—Plato, Cleanthes,
> Crato, Diogenes, Epicurus, Dicaearchus, Posidonius, Carneades, Chrysippus,
> and Crantor whom Cicero followed—wrote on this subject.[37]

Embracing treatises, dialogues, and letters, this list is a good survey of
the Quattrocento view of extant, fragmentary, or lost sources in the consolatory tradition. Had Cicero's *Consolatio* survived, Nicolaus argues, it
might have relieved him of his present task: clearly, then, the genre of this

lost work must have been the central inspiration for his treatise. As for the other classical sources he names, one wonders if the Ps.-Senecan *De reme-diis fortuitorum*, a skeletal work, warranted mentioning not so much because of itself as because of Petrarch's notable, modern-day development of the genre. As for the patristic sources, Nicolaus cites not only the letters of Cyprian, Jerome, and Basil, but also a somewhat neglected treatise by Isidore of Seville. The *Synonyma*, subtitled *De lamentatione animae peccatricis*, is a dialogue between a "deflens homo" and an "admonens ratio." The "lamenting man" bewails various misfortunes: misery, unhappiness, exile, poverty, adversities, insults. The dialogue is a near-perfect blending of classical and Christian perspectives on the human condition. In dealing with the problem of adversity, Isidore presents classical remedies (such as the universality of tragedy and the anticipation of future evil), but he also develops various Christian themes (such as man's state of sin, divine retribution, and redemptive suffering). And although the dialogue deals with misery, much of it treats as well the general problem of sin, temptation, and spiritual health.[38]

Though these classical and Christian sources offer various consolatory genres and *topoi*, none (at least none of those extant) serves as a theoretical manual for the entire office of consolation. And this is what Nicolaus' treatise attempts to do. His nearest model for such a manual is the third book of Cicero's *Tusculans*, which discusses the malady of *aegritudo* and the method of consoling, and which, apparently, drew to some extent on Cicero's earlier *Consolatio*. Nicolaus in fact relies heavily on the *Tusculans*, despite his failure to mention it in his prefatory survey of the consolatory tradition.

Having discussed the literary legacy, Nicolaus continues his preface with a further explanation of his purposes in writing the work. He is careful to identify his task as one that requires not philosophical acuity but Christian *caritas*:

> Truly, all these authors [those ancient and patristic writers cited above] performed the office of consolation most worthily and most wisely. But how would others [later] also be able to fulfill the same office? A very few persons [i.e., the scholastic theologians] wished to teach, and, because of the admirable sharpness of their intellects, they perhaps did so abundantly enough, but [their teaching] in my judgment is too concise and spare for those not trained in philosophy. Nor certainly do I think these people to have been remiss in this because of an ignorance of [the nature of] sin—for what indeed did these divine intellects not know? . . . Rather it is due more to a certain negligence or carelessness and to a contempt for the very easiness of the subject itself.[39]

Nicolaus would thus suggest that there was something of a gap in consolatory thought from the time of Isidore to his own day. The teaching of the highly intellectual scholastic elite has been too cerebral to treat this

matter in any accessible way—Nicolaus' own *De mortalium foelicitate* bears
this out. Nicolaus, however, is careful not to insult his forebears or himself.
Rather than castigate scholastic teaching, as Petrarch had done, he excuses
it. The Schoolmen generally overlooked this topic, which perhaps seemed
to them intellectually too pedestrian and too simple to command their attention. While not daring to repudiate the scholastic heritage, Nicolaus
must nonetheless distance himself from it in order to justify his own efforts
as a consoler. Christian duty demands that all people minister to the sorrows of their fellow man:

> Nor ought it to be shameful to offer milk to the infants for whom Christ did
> not blush to die, especially since the Lord himself will ask all men, not only the
> philosophers, not only those who are considered wise, to visit and console
> him if he were in prison or tribulation [cf. Matthew 25:36]. Whence one can
> see with what great necessity mortals should try to undertake the office of
> consolation, [an office] of which the Lord threatens to make himself so severe
> a taskmaster. Therefore, wishing to benefit everyone and to show all the way
> for fulfilling that which is required of them equally by divine and human law,
> we have arranged in order the precepts of consolation, aided by the help of
> that One who is the greatest consoler of all those in misery.[40]

As all these prefatory comments indicate, classical and Christian influences informed not only Nicolaus' view of the genres and sources of consolation, but also his notion of the consolatory office: it is an *officium* fulfilled
by philosophers; it is also a duty that should be met by all Christians. Appropriately, Nicolaus' goal was to provide a practical, general guide that
might serve a wide range of people, including those who are not necessarily
erudite. He wanted to provide a useful manual that could help foster a
broader, more effective practice of this philosophical and spiritual duty.

Nicolaus could look to several classical and Christian sources for consolatory *topoi*, but for a model of a manual he could really turn only to
Cicero's *Tusculans* Book 3 or, more recently, Petrarch's *De remediis*. There
were, however, two other literary traditions that could have offered him
guidance in his task. The first was the dictaminal tradition, which spawned
various manuals containing models for the *epistola consolatoria* and, in the
case of Boncompagno's *Rhetorica antiqua* Book 2, general comments on
the nature of consolation, the proper time of administering solace, the
advantages of moderate weeping, funeral customs, and other matters.[41]
Though offering a less theoretical, less comprehensive, less humanistic
treatment of consolation than that found in Nicolaus' work, a rhetorical
manual such as Boncompagno's could have served as a model for his own
highly rhetorical treatise.[42] The second tradition on which Nicolaus might
have drawn was that of the confessor's manual. Given his scholastic background and his training and vocation as a cleric, Nicolaus was surely famil-

iar with the literature on confession, which began to flower in the thirteenth century with the appearance of massive *summae* for confessors and other handbooks of pastoral care.[43] Patristic-like consolation in eclipse, this confessional office was the central "therapeutic" legacy of medieval pastoral care. And though the theme of solace became somewhat absorbed by that of salvation in the confessional tradition, nonetheless, the confessor's *summa* could still provide a number of therapeutic perspectives germane to the consoler. While Nicolaus' manual was clearly more a rhetorician's *summa* than a confessor's, it still perhaps invoked some of the latter's clinical approaches concerning the overall therapeutic scheme, and possibly some of the specific details, required for psychological healing. In sum, Nicolaus' treatise represents a blend of the humanist, dictaminal, and pastoral traditions, and it is this hybrid quality that gives the work its special historical significance.

Though the consolation for death is perhaps Nicolaus' primary interest, he is also concerned with the general problem of solace, and in one section he explicitly discusses the problems of poverty, power, and fame. In defining grief and in prescribing solace, Nicolaus draws from Greek tragedians (such as Menander and Euripides), Roman poets (Vergil, Ovid, Horace, Terence, Juvenal), philosophers (Plato, Cicero, Seneca), Scripture, and religious writers (Jerome, Augustine, Isidore, and Gregory the Great).[44] Nicolaus builds much of his manual from letters, using consolations to and from Cicero and *consolatoriae* of Seneca and Jerome.[45]

In the tradition of Cicero, Nicolaus couches his treatise in a clinical framework. In his prefatory statement he says, "[W]hen we professed the art of curing souls, I decided that it was necessary for us, just as it is for physicians of bodies, to present certain general and principal methods of healing, but to leave particular methods and those that can occur to [any] diligent person to the prudence of the doctor, . . ."[46] Soon afterwards, he defines the tripartite scope of his healing manual: "It is expedient for the ideal consoler to know three things: first, how afflicted are those who need consolation; then, from which persons they especially want that consolation; thirdly, by what method the office of consolation ought to be undertaken and in what ways it ought to be performed."[47]

Nicolaus then proceeds with what is truly a *summa* for consolers—one intended, however, not for a specifically clerical audience but rather for a general one.[48] He opens with a detailed portrait of the nature and dangers of grief and *aegritudo*.[49] His chapter "What Dangers Distress May Bring" reveals a rich blend of literary sources and of psychological, medical, and religious traditions. Opening with the Scriptural citation that "*tristitia viri nocet cordi*" (Prov. 25:20), he discusses how grief can afflict the body with the melancholy humor, among other things. Citing Ovid's description of his own sadness that led to a loss of appetite and sleep (*Ex Ponto* Book 1), he then presents the medical cures of sleep, wine, and hot baths, arguing that Augustine availed himself of these cures in his grief over his mother's death (*Confessions* Book 9).[50]

He next turns to the problems of who best can receive solace and who best can administer it. In his discussion of the first, Nicolaus perhaps betrays the eye of the medieval confessor and casuist in his careful delineation of "Those Who Receive Consolation More Easily and Those Less Easily," where he explains: "For not all people are equally afflicted by this grief, but rather it varies according to factors of age, character, time, and misfortune. Some people indeed are cured more quickly, some more slowly, some in fact never."[51] Most receptive to solace are youth and women. For those not so receptive, Nicolaus includes separate chapters of special remedies: "Antidotes for the Old and Pusillanimous" (the latter condition a familiar one in the confessional tradition), "Antidotes for Those Overly Devoted to Worldly Things," "Antidotes for the Irreligious."[52]

In his chapter concerning "Those Most Suited for Consoling Others" Nicolaus begins by citing Servius Sulpicius' notion that consolation is to be given by one's relatives and friends.[53] He then elaborates with a subtle and perceptive psychological point concerning children's natural potential to be particularly effective consolers:

> Therefore the most able consolers are friends, parents, children, or persons connected by some other relationship; and among these the consolation of children is most special, particularly that of adolescents or little ones, when it happens that any of them might speak more appropriately, or weep with the parent: by the former, parents are greatly delighted; by the latter, after the satisfaction [of such weeping] parents are moved on account of their paternal piety to restrain themselves lest they upset or see suffer children whom they love to hold. For this same reason the consolation of a wife or dear friend avails greatly.[54]

Of course, he also cites the effectiveness of consolation given by the wise and pious whose words carry the meaningful weight of authority.[55] And as a highly rhetorical and philosophical treatise, the *On Consolation* is most directed toward the therapeutic techniques of the learned friend, the epistolary consoler, the funeral orator.

As for the techniques of proper consoling, Nicolaus shows himself to be a careful clinician. Presenting solace at the proper time; carefully approaching those severely depressed; assuring the bereaved first of one's friendship with him or her; using caution, skill, and humility in consoling the wise: all these concerns are given systematic analysis.[56] Time and again, Nicolaus' method is to use ancient, biblical, or patristic sources to illustrate or construct various methods, as in the case of the chapter "In What Way the More Severe Sorrows Must Be Approached," in which he mines Seneca's consolation to Lucilius (*Ad. Luc.* 63) to present the delicate techniques of ministering to those in deep grief. Other times he is highly eclectic in his formulation of such principles. For instance, in his chapter "On the Proper Time for Consoling," he draws, among other things, on theories of timely solace and psychological medicine found in Cicero (*Tusc.* 3.31.76) and Ovid (*De remediis amoris* 119–34), and he cites the case of Job, whose consolers made no attempt to console his vehement grief for an entire week (Job 2:13).[57]

After these sections on the nature of the afflicted, on consolers, and on the administering of solace, the treatise then turns to its principal subject: specific consolatory *topoi*, remedies, and techniques. Nicolaus presents ten sets of *loci* that as a whole attempt to embrace almost every conceivable philosophical, emotional, and theological argument and tactic of consolation. He collects all the many traditional *solacia*, such as those concerning the inevitability and universality of death, the shortness and misery of life, the varieties of fortune, the benefits of death.[58] Many of Nicolaus' topics have as their aim the Stoic goal of persuading the sorrowful that no evil has truly befallen them—thus those *loci* dealing with the miseries of life and the benefits of death.[59] In some of his chapters Nicolaus also recommends the Cyrenaic practice of premeditation, the habit of foreseeing all the possible adversities that life can hold.[60] In some cases, his themes are highly spiritual. For instance, in the second set of *loci* there is an "Argument from Justice," which draws principally on biblical examples and arguments to propose that misfortunes must be seen as just. Nicolaus quotes an extensive passage from Isidore's *Synonyma* (1.32–37) that deals with the divine plan and justice in the realm of human adversity. Christian perspectives in this set of chapters are also to be found in the "Argument from Divine Will" and the much lengthier "Argument from Utility," which explains the spiritual reward or "utility" that results from tribulation.[61]

One set of *loci* deals exclusively with the funeral oration, revealing the usefulness of Nicolaus' manual for the duties of public solace. This section "On the Six Funeral Arguments" suggests various rhetorical topics appropriate for the eulogist, such as the arguments "From [the Deceased's] Works," "From the Kind of Death," "From the Cause of Death," and others. Nicolaus would have occasion to avail himself of such conventions later in Rome when he delivered his *Oratio in funere Petri* following the death of Cardinal Riario in 1474. (It may have been a relief to have rhetorical guidelines to inspire him here, where perhaps sincerity could not: there is some evidence that Nicolaus had great disdain for the Cardinal, possibly alluding to him as a "Caligula" in a letter to a friend the previous year.)[62]

Beyond the comforts of reason and faith, there are other approaches open to the consoler. He can appeal to his patient's sense of shame concerning his grief or his fear of its repercussions. He can exhort him to virtue.[63] He can summon the force of *exempla*. One section of the treatise deals with the "diversion of grief" by which "we draw or lead out a mind from its sorrow to some other concern, endeavor, or pleasant (*voluptuosa*) thought."[64] It includes chapters on various social, psychological, and behavioral remedies such as the compassion of friends, lamentation, pleasant activity, the consideration of the good features of one's life, the hope of future good. In those chapters dealing with *voluptuosa* thought or activity, we can see Nicolaus' development of the Epicurean approach to consolation.[65] Of particular interest in this final section of the treatise is the "Argument from Lamentation," in which Nicolaus presents a lengthy argument concerning the therapeutic power of weeping and emotional expression. After illustrating the notion of cathartic weeping and writing with Ovid's *Tristia* (4.3.37–38), Nicolaus goes on to complement this poetic portrayal of *voluptas dolendi* with a highly clinical explanation of the phenomenon of lamentation. He suggests that *maeror* has both a bodily form (in the melancholy humor) and a mental one.[66] He says that some thinkers theorize that the physical melancholy is purged by weeping. Then, more importantly, he explains why the mental *maeror* is also cured by tears. Nicolaus may have considered particularly significant his ensuing discussion, because it is one of the sections of his emended copy that contains special markings in the margins.[67] He gives three reasons why weeping is therapeutic: it entails the bittersweet recollection of past goods; it releases and dissipates a grievous emotion which, pent up, tears at the mind; it encourages people to indulge in their own most suitable type of behavior (such as solitude, asceticism, doleful writings). Thus Nicolaus fully systematizes the notion of therapeutic weeping.[68]

Did Nicolaus know of any of the earlier writings on weeping by Boncompagno, Petrarch, Salutati, Conversini, Manetti, or Bevilacqua? We cannot know for sure. But the question of literary influence aside, his "Argument from Lamentation" certainly represents another instance of the substantive interest in the psychology of sorrow that can be found in dictaminal and humanist writings. In his effort to set forth the laws of lamentation he unites literary sensibilites of "sweet grief," medical notions of melancholy, psychological observations concerning the emotional and behavioral benefits of expressing sorrow. Most importantly, his chapter fully reifies in theoretical terms the Quattrocento fascination with grief evident in the writings of those humanists who would proudly proclaim the necessity of their sorrow. This humanist priest has gone far toward naturalizing the domain of secular emotion. Far beyond giving tears a mere Peripatetic legitimacy, he endows them, as the younger Petrarch had done, with Epicurean powers.[69]

Nicolaus ends his manual on a highly philosophical and spiritual note, offering a final set of topics that are aimed at the "most wise and religious men." The first is the thoroughly Christian "Devout Reflection on the Passion of the Lord," in which Nicolaus presents a meditation on the life of Christ. Against His suffering, all human tribulation is nothing; a pious contemplation on the Passion "so lightens our mind from all its distresses that in the place of sadness it brings a wonderful sweetness and wholly restores and strengthens the mind."[70] The second chapter in this set, the "Argument from the Meditation on Human End," is a *contemptus* of earthly temptation and tribulation and an exhortation toward man's moral and spiritual pursuit of his original beatitude.[71] The final chapter, the "Argument from the Reflection on Death," draws on classical and Christian notions of the death meditation, citing at length from Isidore's *Synonyma* (1.47–50). Like the earlier arguments "From Justice," "From Divine Will," and "From Utility," these last topics articulate the particular Christian contribution to the problem of consolation. It is interesting that this set of *loci* for enlightened and virtuous men is preceded by a rather cynical group of chapters, dealing with such matters as revenge, which Nicolaus suggests is generally unsuited for the learned and religious.[72] He thus ministers counsel to two extremes. A true rhetorician, Nicolaus addresses his manual to a whole spectrum of people—to the pusillanimous, unbelieving, overly secular, and vengeful; to the wise and virtuous; and to the array of people who fall in between.

Neither as a humanist nor as a cleric can Nicolaus be said to be a major figure in Renaissance thought. There is no evidence that his *On Consolation* or any of his other writings had any significant impact. And yet his consolation book is historically noteworthy, not only because it so clearly reifies the Renaissance interest in consolation but also because it represents an imaginative contribution to the general "history of the cure of souls," to borrow J. T. McNeill's phrase. In the first place, it completes the Quattrocento exploration of the challenge of consolation. Earlier humanists had emulated other consolatory and remedial genres: the consolatory letter, the oration, the dialogue, the remedy-book. Works such as Petrarch's *De remediis* or, to the north, Johannes von Dambach's *Consolatio theologiae* provided comprehensive collections of consolatory topics. But Nicolaus' treatise attempted to fully systematize the office of consolation by offering advice on general therapeutic problems, by gathering copious rhetorical *topoi*, by recommending various psychological remedies. Expanding and updating Cicero's *Tusculans* Book 3, Nicolaus provided a guidebook to help others fulfill better the moral and spiritual office of consoling. As a comprehensive manual, his discussion surpassed what could be found from ancient or patristic writers or from Nicolaus' more recent dictaminal and humanist predecessors. Culling precepts from both profane and sacred fonts, he isolates and develops many facets of the consoler's task: he deals with the nature of despair, the varying temperaments of the grief-stricken, the varying capacities of consolers; he codifies the therapeutic benefits of time, compassion, and (with notable detail) lamentation; he cites the techniques of friendly chiding, the exhortation to virtue, the use of *exempla*; he offers *solacia* and remedies that range from the mundane (pleasant distractions) to the sublime (a reflection on Christ's suffering). His sources include consolatory letters and an eclectic array of other literary, philosophical, and religious writings. Joining classical and Christian sources and perspectives, the *On Consolation* is the complete guide for the Quattrocento humanist and Christian.

Nicolaus' treatise filled an important gap in the history of moral, rhetorical, and spiritual care. Though there were many ancient consolatory writings, only the *Tusculans* Book 3 provided an extant skeletal manual for consolation. Likewise, in patristic thought, though there were numerous instances of consolatory letters, dialogues, and orations, there was no systematic manual to which the consoler could turn. The medieval literature of pastoral care did not offer a comprehensive manual for consoling.[73] The *ars dictaminis* manuals provided some guidelines for consolatory rhetoric and, at least in the case of Boncompagno, there was some general discussion of the problem of grief and consolation. But a dictaminal manual such as Boncompagno's lacked the theoretical scope, the range of therapeutic considerations, the autonomy of genre, and the humanistic content found in Nicolaus' manual. In sum, by composing such a thoroughgoing handbook, Nicolaus can be said to have filled a void found in ancient, patristic, and medieval thought.

As modern-day Christian rhetoricians, Matteo Bosso and Nicolaus of Modruš both drew inspiration from classical and patristic sources of consolation in their attempt to revive a type of psychological care that had fallen into neglect in the hands of their medieval clerical forebears. Both clearly reflect the impact of rhetorical currents that had been intensifying since the time of Petrarch. Both distinguished their efforts from the esoteric, intellectual endeavors of scholastic tradition. Moreover, these figures were not merely clerics who happened to be humanistic in their bent. They were clerics who attempted again to bridge a chasm between the world of Cicero and the world of the Church. The writings of such Fathers as Cyprian and Jerome, whom they both cited, served as a model for this endeavor. But they also perhaps drew upon more immediate aspects of their institutional background as men of the Church, Bosso explicitly referring to the pulpit, Nicolaus implicitly borrowing from the confessional. Their resulting efforts ended in interesting hybrids. Bosso's *On Bearing Adversities*, the more spiritual of the two, was a pastoral exhortation couched in the appealing, familiar format of the Ciceronian dialogue. His was a modern consolation

that truly marked the "Ciceronian" revival of a type of pastoral solace cultivated so richly by Chrysostom. Nicolaus' manual also drew principally on
the *Tusculans*, though his particular interest was not in adapting its genre
as a dialogue but rather as a manual. The resulting work was a handbook
of Ciceronian psychological advice and Petrarch-like remedies, joined with
the perspectives of early Christian consolers and possibly also with the rhetorical rules of the dictaminal tradition and the clinical insight and ambition of the confessional office. Nicolaus provided a guide to the treatment
of sorrow as comprehensive as those directed to the treatment of sin. His
effort would aspire to grant *homo lugens* a greater degree of parity alongside
his counterpart, *homo peccans*. Both Bosso and Nicolaus, like some of their
patristic predecessors, thus sought more fully to acknowledge the *tristitia
saeculi*. And in naturalizing the realm of human sorrow, they even went so
far as to cure it partially with Epicurean remedies of otherworldly or
worldly delights.[74]

The cases of Bosso and Nicolaus illustrate the Quattrocento clerical interest in the consolatory realm. Both figures evince a readiness to adapt the
revival of classical rhetorical concerns to more fully Christian ends. They
even adapt some of the classical moral content. Various other clerical writers, in Quattrocento Italy and particularly in the early modern north, were
less willing or able to blend classical and Christian thought: they drew
a greater distinction between sacred and profane consolation.[75] As for
fifteenth-century Italy, Bosso and Nicolaus, like Traversari before them,
urge us to explore more fully the question of the impact of humanist rhetoric and psychological thought on religious literature and pastoral care. Did
there emerge a greater measure of consolatory rhetoric in the pulpit, in
pastoral writings or pastoral letters, in the priestly offices of personal ministrations and last rites? One can fairly assume that Bosso's preaching, for
instance, may well have shown such an interest. Or, rather than reclaim
consolation for the pastoral domain, did these writings instead serve more
to break down distinctions between clerical and lay consolation? Certainly
in Nicolaus' manual one finds a forceful exhortation that all Christians
should take up the duty of consolation. And if perhaps partly drawing on
the medieval pastoral tradition, Nicolaus also stood outside of that tradition. He decidedly did not write his manual exclusively for clerics but for
a wider audience of Christian mourners and consolers. And though clerics
could have used his handbook for their ministrations to the sorrowful, so
too could have laymen. It may indeed have required a cleric to so fully
systematize the Renaissance science of consoling, but, ironically, Nicolaus'
manual codified an *officium consolandi* that was meant to extend beyond the
circle of the collar and the cowl to a community of consolers embracing all
humanists and Christians, clergy and laity alike.

7

GRIEF AND MELANCHOLY IN

MEDICEAN FLORENCE

MARSILIO FICINO AND THE

PLATONIC REGIMEN

I N 1462 Cosimo de' Medici, Florence's first citizen, provided Marsilio
Ficino with a villa at Careggi and with Platonic texts. The result, well
known to students of the Renaissance, was the birth of the Platonic
Academy. At Careggi Ficino continued his efforts, already begun in the
1450s, of translating and commenting upon various Greek writings. By the
end of his career he had translated not only the entire corpus of Platonic
dialogues, but also the works of Neoplatonic figures such as Plotinus, Porphyry, Iamblichus, and Proclus as well as works attributed to such pseudonymous figures as Hermes Trismegistus and Pseudo-Dionysius the
Areopagite.[1] From his studies he reconstructed the history of an "ancient
theology" that included such culturally diverse figures as Zoroaster, Trismegistus, Orpheus, Pythagoras, and Plato. His major work, the *Theologia
Platonica de immortalitate animorum* (1469–74), represents his own formulation of that ancient religion.[2] The major intellectual force in Laurentian Florence, Ficino drew into his net not only Cosimo's famous heir but
also literary and philosophical figures such as Cristoforo Landino, Angelo
Poliziano, and Pico, as well as other figures from the ranks of doctors,
jurists, clerics, merchants, and statesmen.[3]

One consequence of this Platonic revival was the marshaling of Platonic
thought to the world of consolation and psychological experience. As has
been shown, there had been similar adaptations of Stoic, Peripatetic, and
even Epicurean thought in Christianized and eclectic visions of humanist
solace. With Ficino, however, we come to one who was more philosopher
than rhetorician, one who imposed an increasingly consistent philosophical perspective on several areas of psychological and even physical health.
His particular assumptions as a Platonic philosopher yielded a coherent set
of cures for bereavement, adversity, human misery, and the approach of
death. As a trained and practicing physician, as a guru for his circle of
intellectuals, and, from 1473 onward, as an ordained priest, Ficino sought
to offer physical, philosophical, and spiritual cures for his associates and

acquaintances. But, like Petrarch a century earlier, Ficino was important not only for his "remedies" but also for his "maladies." As Petrarch's experience as a love poet shaped his vision of sorrow, so did Ficino's experience as a Platonic philosopher mold his view of the intellectual's peculiar psychological constitution. That is, while Platonism could cure worldly woes, it could simultaneously spawn them, generating in its devotees the insidious affliction of melancholy.

The revival of Greek thought in Florence dated back at least to the appointment of Manuel Chrysoloras to teach at the Studio in the 1390s.[4] Like later Byzantine scholars, Chrysoloras found able students, such as Leonardo Bruni, among his Italian hosts.[5] A further surge in Greek studies was occasioned in 1438–39, when Gemistus Plethon and John Argyropoulos came to Italy for the Church Council of Ferrara and Florence. According to the testimony of Ficino, Plethon's Florentine lectures during this period sparked Cosimo's original interest in Plato.[6] In the second half of the century, the success of Ficino's Academy largely assured the primacy of Platonic thought over other schools in matters philosophical, spiritual, psychological, and consolatory.[7] As the leader of that movement, Ficino formulated a distinct and, in some ways, unique vision of solace and tranquility which he articulated in formal philosophical works as well as in didactic "sermons" and consolatory letters. To appreciate the historical context of Ficino's writings, however, it is important to review certain intellectual currents and works that anticipated this crystallizing of Platonic psychology in the latter part of the fifteenth century. In this task we have a rich source, which culling several consolatory writings from the 1430s to the 1460s, invites an assessment of the patterns in Medicean consolation during Cosimo's middle and later years.

The *Collectiones Cosmianae*

An important part of the history of fifteenth-century consolation can be seen through the fortunes and misfortunes of the Medici family. As patrons of learning and as, in turn, beneficiaries of humanist solace, this family's experience mirrors some of the prominent currents and shifts in Renaissance consolation and psychology. At some point after the death of Cosimo in 1464, the Medici associate Bartolomeo Scala compiled a collection of writings concerning the life and death of Florence's famous patriarch. Scala dedicated this commemorative anthology, the *Collectiones Cosmianae*, to Cosimo's grandson Lorenzo the Magnificent. Part of the collection consists of general material relating to Cosimo, such as letters or prefaces (to translations) from scholars such as Ambrogio Traversari, Leonardo Bruni, and

Argyropoulos. But a major portion of this manuscript consists of consolatory literature to or about Cosimo, including a lengthy dialogue by Scala
himself.[8] These writings cover the periods of 1433 (when Cosimo suffered
both the loss of his mother and exile from Florence)[9] and 1463–64 (when
his son Giovanni and Cosimo himself died). A reflection of the vitality and
variety of Renaissance consolatory and funerary genres, the collection includes six consolatory letters (and one reply to such a letter), a lengthier
treatise or *Consolatio* proper, a consolatory dialogue, a preface to a consolatory translation, a funeral oration, and elegiac verse. The consolers include
both lay and clerical figures; the addressees, three generations of Medici. It
is not to my purpose to examine all of these works but only to show how
certain of them help elucidate the intellectual setting for the triumph of
Platonic thought and psychology in Ficino's Florence.

The two consolations in the collection from the early period offer a symbolic contrast, one looking back to the Petrarchan legacy of the Trecento,
the other looking forward to new currents emerging in the Quattrocento.
In a letter from Rome, Poggio Bracciolini consoled Cosimo for his exile
from Florence in September of 1433. Taking a fully Stoic tack, he urged
the triumph of virtue over fortune, reminding Cosimo that the wisdom and
examples to be had from the *studia humanitatis* could steel one against the
vicissitudes of both good and bad fortune.[10] The influence of Petrarch's *De
remediis utriusque fortune* almost certainly is evident when Poggio praises
Cosimo for his equanimity: "We have seen you neither inflated or haughty
in prosperous things nor languid or dispirited in adverse ones, but instead
bearing both kinds of fortune with the same equanimity of expression and
mind."[11]

In contrast to the Roman Stoicism of Poggio's letter stands the highly
Greek tenor of the other consolation from this period in the anthology,
Carlo Marsuppini's well-known *De morte Nonninae matris consolatio*.[12] Following the death in April 1433 of Cosimo's mother Piccarda, Marsuppini
composed his lengthy *Consolatio* for Cosimo and for Lorenzo di Giovanni,
to whom Marsuppini had been tutor.[13] Significantly broadening the range
of Greek literary and philosophical sources, the *Consolatio* represents a
turning point in Renaissance consolation. Drawing heavily, as Ricci suggests, on Ps.-Plutarch's *Consolatio ad Apollonium*, Marsuppini opens with
an attack on Stoic psychology.[14] Taking Crantor's stance as recorded in the
Tusculans (3.6.12), Marsuppini argues that the Stoic ideal of insensibility
is too harsh and that moderate grief is legitimate.[15] A few years later in his
Dialogus consolatorius Giannozzo Manetti would cite the same *locus* from
Crantor. But though Marsuppini and Manetti both started with anti-Stoic
sentiments, their arguments moved in different directions. Manetti, like
Salutati before him, corrected Stoicism largely with Peripatetic thought.
Marsuppini, on the other hand, like Ps.-Plutarch, spoke more from an Aca-

demic position and improved upon Stoic thought with Platonic consolation. That is, he presented a number of arguments concerning the immortality of the soul, citing or drawing upon the *Apology, Phaedo, Republic, Gorgias, Phaedrus*, and *Letter 7*.[16] Manetti's *Dialogus* did not cite the Platonic corpus a single time. Through the influence of Ps.-Plutarch's *Consolatio*, and perhaps through his own study of Platonism, Marsuppini ushers in that strain of classical consolation which, as yet, has had only a limited influence in Renaissance thought.[17] He admits, however, that his discussion is rather cursory, and he defers the matter, saying that "this is not the place for philosophizing."[18]

As was suggested in Chapter 5, the mantle was taken up some years later in Milan in December of 1461 by the Renaissance maverick Francesco Filelfo. In his widely published *Consolatio* to Jacopo Antonio Marcello, Filelfo, like Marsuppini before him, drew heavily on Greek thought and endeavored, at even greater length, to develop the theme of immortality.[19] Undoubtedly, Filelfo was trying to best the earlier efforts of his erstwhile rival, attempting to develop fully this truly Greek philosophical theme only broached by Marsuppini.

As Filelfo's discussion of immortality, however, like his *Oratio* in general, was highly eclectic, we must look elsewhere to follow the specific course of Renaissance Platonic thought and consolation. We must return to Florence and to the consolers of the Medici. The death of Cosimo's son Giovanni in November of 1463 elicited sympathy from various quarters, both lay and religious. Alamanni Rinuccini translated the *Consolatio ad Apollonium* to console Cosimo for the loss.[20] In the *Collectiones Cosmianae* Cosimo's comforters include Pope Pius II and two local clerics who both enjoyed Medici patronage and benefices in San Lorenzo: Francesco da Castiglione and Antonio Agli.[21] The former's letter particularly warrants notice. A theologian and Greek professor whose students probably included Ficino, Francesco assiduously avoided classical *loci*, developing pointedly theological consolations. Expressing doubts about the efficacy of secular consolation, he draws upon biblical themes and sources, including the Psalms (on which he wrote a commentary).[22] Perhaps betraying a measure of clerical resistance to classical learning at mid-century, Francesco (who had earlier been secretary to the conservative Archbishop Antonino) attempts to offer a theological consolation, one more effective than that available from the works of the "orators."[23] In doing this, he turns first to the "divine doctor," to the Godhead as "paraclitus," a word whose very etymological Greek roots connote consolation.[24]

Our primary interest in this period of Medicean consolation, however, concerns not these letters, but an unusual consolatory dialogue portraying the aging and ailing Cosimo's state of mind in this time of bereavement. This work, Scala's *Dialogus de consolatione* or *Cosmus*, depicts a lengthy discussion between Scala and Cosimo. We cannot know how much of the *Dialogue* is simply Scala's own musings, how much it is truly Cosimo's worldview, and how much it is Scala's perception of the latter. Nonetheless, the treatise is a window onto prevailing currents in Florentine moral and psychological thought.[25]

Coming to Florence in the 1440s, Scala may have studied letters under Marsuppini, who had been appointed to the Chair of Greek and Latin in 1451. In 1454, Scala journeyed to Milan and continued his Greek studies under Filelfo. Returning to Florence, he became first Pierfrancesco's secretary and later an intimate of Cosimo's. In 1465 he obtained the prized position of Florentine chancellor. Most importantly for us here, he had occasion for ongoing "philosophical" contact with the aging Cosimo, who called upon him to read aloud Donato Acciaiuoli's notes on Argyropoulos' lectures on the *Nicomachean Ethics*. These domestic encounters must have given Scala a chance to plumb Cosimo's philosophical predispositions at the end of his life. In any case, these visits apparently put him in the patriarch's inner sanctum at the time of Giovanni's death.[26]

The exact purpose of the dialogue is somewhat vague. Dedicated to the young Lorenzo the Magnificent, who was apparently not present during Cosimo's period of mourning, the dialogue was ostensibly meant to record for Lorenzo the remarkable equanimity of his seventy-four-year-old grandfather.[27] It could, of course, also have been intended indirectly as a didactic consolation for the fourteen-year-old Lorenzo concerning the death of his uncle Giovanni. The dialogue, however, is weighty stuff for a teenager, and we should consider the possibility that Scala also intended the work to come back to Cosimo himself as part consolation, part affirmation of his philosophical outlook in his time of grief and old age. Certainly, with Cosimo still alive at the time of composition, Scala must have felt compelled to depict accurately the range of Cosimo's philosophical interests and perhaps even the tenor of his specific positions.

Scala opens the *Dialogue* by reflecting on his own grief over Giovanni and by expressing his concern over the bereaved, aging, gout-stricken Cosimo. A witness to the patriarch's brave composure as he was visited by the many people who came to console him, Scala marveled at his philosophical insights.[28] Deeming it important to record Cosimo's wisdom for posterity, Scala says that he will use the dialogue format for verisimilitude.[29]

As background, we should be aware, as Scala probably was, of another portrayal of Cosimo from the previous decade. In 1455 the aging chancellor Poggio Bracciolini composed a somewhat somber dialogue *De miseria humanae conditionis*, in which a Stoic Cosimo appears as one of the interlocutors.[30] Set against the recent fall of Constantinople, Poggio's dialogue has Poggio and Matteo Palmieri offering a litany of the misery of the human world, physical, moral, temporal.[31] Against this pessimism Cosimo champions the power of reason and virtue to protect "*adversus utranque fortunam.*"[32] Though the sanguine Cosimo has the last word in the discussion, his doleful discussants command by far the greater portion of the dialogue.[33] Poggio seemed to be retreating from his position of Stoic confidence, such as that he extended to the exiled Cosimo twenty-odd years earlier.[34] But even if he himself were starting to doubt the Stoic remedy for misery, it is interesting that he chose Cosimo as the voice of reason, confident in the capacity of rational and virtuous beings to contemn the vanities of good fortune, to be ever prepared to accept calmly the adversities of bad.[35] Was Poggio portraying a representative picture of Cosimo's psychological perspectives in 1455? It is certainly possible. In any case, at least partially this must have been Poggio's perception of Cosimo's outlook. Eight years later Scala composed his dialogue concerning Cosimo, and I think it very likely—almost certain—that Scala knew of Poggio's portrait of a Stoic Cosimo.[36] It is a measure of the sea change in Florence's intellectual climate—and possibly in Cosimo's own actual outlook—that Scala's depiction of Cosimo was centered not so much in Stoic confidence but more in Platonic resignation and mysticism.

Now to Scala's dialogue. Finding Cosimo alone, sighing, and pensive, Scala thought it meet to draw him out with conversation and solace. He begins by reminding Cosimo of the "many gifts of the immortal gods to mankind."[37] Citing Cicero's *De legibus* (1.7.22), he proclaims man's special greatness, capacities, and divine similitude. The consolation of human dignity, advanced by Petrarch in his *De remediis* 2.93, is now invoked again by Scala, who for this theme probably drew upon Giannozzo Manetti's *De dignitate et excellentia hominis* of the early 1350s.[38] Given these generic blessings mankind has received from the gods, should not Cosimo, with his special virtue and wisdom, be counted especially happy?

Cosimo's answer is first to correct Scala's polytheistic framework of the "gods," and then to delineate the tradition of an "ancient theology" in the classical world. He cites passages from Orpheus, Hermes Trismegistus, and Zoroaster, who, along with Plato, all espoused a vision of a single, incorruptible God.[39] As Brown argues, Scala's quotations and sources here reveal the impact of George of Trebizond's translation of Eusebius' *De preparatione evangelica* and Ficino's early translations of Hermetic and Platonic texts.[40] Scala adds that the Incarnation of the Christian God must be seen as one of the divine gifts to mankind. Drawing upon Lactantius's *De opificio Dei*, Cosimo then argues how human perfection, and in particular the mind, enables man to see and appreciate the nature of the Creator.

When Cosimo turns from the generic "contemplation of human dignity" to reflect on his own particular state, he is less sanguine. Acknowledging his considerable good fortune, he suggests that that very prosperity has always prompted him to beware the adversity that must inevitably be due to him. As a result, he is uncertain whether he is more happy or sad. Now that his Giovanni is gone, now that he himself is aging and weak, and his other son stricken with the family gout, he confesses that he is either blinded to the good in life, or else, in fact, the life of man is miserable. The figure of Cosimo henceforth in the dialogue becomes fairly pessimistic, eventually retreating into a Platonic and Christian contemplation on death.

When Scala tries to heal Cosimo's despair with the Stoic consolation that virtue can overcome all worldly misfortunes, Cosimo replies with an attack on Stoicism, an attack very possibly influenced by the similar position advanced by Manetti in his *Dialogus consolatorius*.[41] Scala's treatise, however, differs from Manetti's in that its focus is more diffuse. That is, after critiquing Stoic psychology, "Cosimo" turns to the Epicureans whose philosophy he also finds lacking.[42] Having dismissed these two schools, Cosimo then reflects on the Peripatetic paradigm of the goods of body, mind, and external things.[43] After Cosimo has contemned those vanities of the body and fortune, Scala asks him to reflect on those of the mind:

> Is not the mind—which is the true image of its creator, and which you have ennobled to such an extent that everyone agrees you have approached the essence of that image most closely—is not the mind a most outstanding thing, even greater than can be expressed with words or comprehended in thought? Therefore, because of the mind, is it not possible that human nature can be considered glorious and that much can thus be counterpoised to human misery?[44]

Cosimo acknowledges the nobility of the mind, and says that "until it returns whence it was sent by God it will find nothing but a certain shadow of the true and solid good."[45] He then launches into a highly Platonic discourse on the benefits of death, introducing his comments with the famous maxim that "true philosophy, as Plato also agrees, is a preparation for death."[46] He reviews the miseries of human life, drawing on, for instance, various *loci* assembled in the *Tusculans* Book 1. But his "Platonic" sources for this discussion extend beyond Cicero to a Christian work, Ps.-Eusebius of Cremona's *De morte Hieronymi*, which provided an *exemplum* of the "good death."[47] He cites the dying Jerome's comments lamenting the fragility of worldly life and welcoming the joys of death.[48] Later he quotes Jerome's consolation to his friends in which he exults in his imminent passage "from darkness to light, from danger to safety, from poverty to wealth, from battle to victory, from sadness to joy, from servility to lordship, from the temporal to the eternal."[49] This literary device of the dying sage who consoles his friends is a familiar Platonic motif, originating in Plato's portrait of Socrates' death in the *Phaedo* and found later in many variations, including Cicero's portrayal of Cato in the *De senectute* and the account of Hermes' death in the *Altividus de immortalitate animae*, an excerpt appended to some versions of Ficino's Hermetic translations.[50] Cosimo ends by saying that he counts the imminence of death to be one of the benefits of old age: "For this reason old age is to be preferred to all other ages, because it prepares us for the departure from the laborious vanity of living, and it leads us back to the celestial homeland where we may enjoy eternal life without cold, fatigue, toil, and grief."[51]

This discourse on death is the true consolation of the dialogue, and it would suggest that Scala was attempting to portray Cosimo's readiness for a "good death." If, in fact, the dialogue was meant to return to Cosimo, we might say that the work was as much a consolation for Cosimo's old age as for the loss of his son. The treatise leans decisively toward the Platonic school,[52] portraying Cosimo not as the Stoic optimist of Poggio's earlier dialogue, but as an otherworldly Platonic and Christian mystic, awaiting his final release from life's miseries.

Scala's dialogue thus reflects three important currents in Quattrocento consolation. First, in opening with the consolation of human dignity, it reveals the influence of this prominent Renaissance theme initiated by Petrarch and continued by Manetti and others. Secondly, it charts the on-going attack on Stoic psychology, begun at the turn of the century by Salutati and continuing in the consolatory writings of Marsuppini and Manetti, among others. Finally, like Marsuppini's *Consolatio*, Scala's *Dialogus* complements this critique of Stoicism with Platonic consolation. And if this consolation of otherworldly beatitude speaks partly to Giovanni's death, it perhaps bears even more fully on Cosimo's own approaching end. Scala portrays Cosimo as one scorning all the spiritual and psychological errors of the various classical schools, choosing that one tradition of an ancient theology found in Orpheus, Hermes, Zoroaster, and Plato that would lead to a Christian vision of an eternal God endowing his creature, man, with a noble mind seeking its return to the Godhead. The ultimate consolation for Cosimo's bereavement, for his illness, for his family's uncertain future in Piero, for his old age, was to be found in this prospect of a happy death.

How much was this truly Cosimo's state of mind? We cannot know for certain, but we can turn again to the *Cosmian Collections* for some further clues. In his reply to Pope Pius' consolatory letter to him for Giovanni's death, Cosimo cites a commonplace found in Cicero's *Dream of Scipio*: in speaking of Giovanni's death Cosimo declares that "this thing that we call life is death; that truly is life only which is eternal."[53] Alison Brown suggests that the *Dream*, a highly Platonic account of a conversation between the deceased Scipio Africanus and his grandson, was apparently a favorite of Cosimo's; Alamanni Rinuccini declared in 1463 that Cosimo seemed to know the work practically by heart.[54]

Of course, Cosimo's Platonic interests went far beyond such a Roman derivative to a commitment to the Platonic corpus itself. The *Collections* chronicles part of that commitment, including a letter of 1462 from Ficino referring to the founding of the Academy, and a version of another letter of 1464 in which Ficino outlines, for Cosimo, Plato's theory of happiness, drawing upon the *Euthydemus, Theaetetus, Philebus, Parmenides, Letter* 2, and the *Republic*.[55] Even more important for our purposes is Ficino's well-known account of Cosimo's last month of life, found in the preface to a translation Ficino made for Piero de' Medici. The work, the Ps.-Platonic *Axiochus*, or *De morte*, which Ficino attributed to Xenocrates, served as an oral consolation for Cosimo and as a written one for his son Piero.[56] In his preface Ficino describes Cosimo's intellectual interests in his old age, interests that included both the Aristotelian translations Argyropoulos made for him and those Platonic ones that Ficino provided. As for Cosimo's thoughts on his deathbed, Ficino reports:

> Twenty days before his [Cosimo's] pure spirit was released from its corporeal chains, . . . he began to deplore the misery of this life and to inveigh against the errors of mortals, so that he proclaimed death to be a certain advantage; and acutely and fully he discussed many things concerning the contempt of this life, since he already aspired to that supernal beatitude. When he had finished speaking I said: "These same things, Cosimo, were discussed by Xenocrates, the venerable and beloved pupil of our Plato." Then he said: "Marsilio, repeat in Latin what Xenocrates said in Greek." I did so, and he approved. He ordered it translated, and I have done so.[57]

The resulting translation Ficino sent to Piero. The *Axiochus* was an ideal consolation for the failing Cosimo. Whereas the more famous *Phaedo* grew out of the unusual circumstances surrounding Socrates' death, this dialogue addressed the more common, and in this case more appropriate, situation of imminent death at a time of serious illness. An ailing Axiochus has slipped into despair, and Socrates comforts him with arguments concerning the evils of earthly life and the prospect of the immortality of the soul.[58] The dialogue not only served the dying Cosimo but also, as Ficino indicates, should teach the surviving Piero "what [little] should be hoped for in this life and to what extent one's own death or that of one's parents or sons ought to be lamented."[59]

Ficino thus portrays Cosimo's own Platonic "good death" as he contemned life and embraced death. Moreover, Cosimo's own reputed Platonic sensibilities were reinforced by other deathbed readings that Ficino supplied. In this same prefatory letter to Piero, Ficino also reports that, not long after the reading of the *Axiochus*, Cosimo read (or, apparently, had read to him by Ficino) "the book of Plato on the origin of all things [the *Parmenides*] and that one on the highest good [the *Philebus*]—twelve days thereafter, as if about to return to enjoy that 'origin' and that 'highest good,' he was recalled from this shadow of life and drew near the supernal light."[60] It is as if those Platonic texts facilitated and even hastened his welcome departure from this life. Reading aloud consolatory literature at the bed of his patron, Ficino thus palpably assumed the role of a resident "philosophical director."[61] He reified the humanist "office" of consoling the dying, an office intimated, on a literary level, in Petrarch's dialogues on death in the *De remediis* 2.117–32. In contrast, however, to the rather eclectic rhetorical solace Petrarch presents through the figure of "Ratio," Ficino tenders a purely Socratic guide for dying. A Platonism only nascent in Petrarch's remedy-book now fully flowers in Ficino's comforting of Cosimo. Ficino, as reader, and Cosimo, as listener, together enact an ideally Platonic *ars moriendi*.[62]

With its variety of consolatory and funerary genres, Scala's compilation of Cosmian literary sources is a revealing record of Renaissance consolation. But more than that, this collection also chronicles larger patterns in Quattrocento learning and thought. The Platonic seeds found in Marsuppini's *Consolatio* of 1433 would begin to bear fruit in the 1460s, as Scala portrays "Cosimo" 's Platonic vision of consolation, and as Ficino confirms him in his Platonic death.

Of course, it was only after Cosimo's death that the Platonic revival truly triumphed. But the circumstances of his bereavement and death may have given that revival added life. As the *Cosmian Collections* reveal, the lessons of Platonic consolation were intergenerational, as they spoke not only to Cosimo but also to his heirs. His son Piero received the translation of the *Axiochus*. His fourteen-year-old grandson Lorenzo was the beneficiary of Scala's *Dialogus de consolatione*; less than a year later he attended Ficino's reading of the *Parmenides* and *Philebus* at Cosimo's deathbed.[63] Generally, in Renaissance moral thought, consolatory themes *followed* phases in the classical revival. And though this is certainly partly true for Platonic consolation, we might also ask whether in the case of Florentine Platonism consolatory concerns may partly have *led* in such a revival. An ideal philosophy for the aging, could Platonism have appealed to Cosimo chiefly on a psychological level? While his interests in Platonism supposedly date to the late 1430s, possibly whetted by Marsuppini as well as by Plethon, it was as a man in his seventies that he actually founded the Academy. And while it is true that Cosimo also sponsored Argyropoulos's Aristotle translations and had Scala read aloud to him notes on the *Nicomachean Ethics*, the weight of evidence at least in Scala's *Cosmian Collections* points toward a highly Platonic Cosimo at the end of his life.[64] Whatever the motivations for Cosimo's Platonism, this collection certainly shows him to be both the beneficiary and spokesman of Platonic solace.

· · · · ·

Ficino's efforts as a Platonic consoler and healer went far beyond his ministrations to his famous patron. In letters, orations, and treatises he provided a wide range of counsel and care for his associates, envisioning his Academy as a clinic for every facet of health. In a letter to one Francesco Musano, who had availed himself of the Academy's medical and musical remedies, Ficino explained the customs of Careggi, where his Platonic circle sought to combine the pursuit of medicine (for the body), music (for the spirit), and theology (for the soul).[65] As a doctor, musician, Platonic theologian, and eventually as an ordained priest, Ficino was ideally suited to lead the Academy in this holistic healing. Exactly how did he harness Platonic thought to the task of curing body, mind, and soul? In particular, how did he address, in theoretical and practical terms, the problems of tranquility, fortune, consolation, and melancholy?

The key, of course, to Ficino's philosophy centered on the nature and destiny of the soul.[66] As is clear from the subtitle of his magnum opus, the *Platonic Theology*, the "immortality of the soul" was for him a central organizing principle. There were, as seen in Chapter 5 above, various humanist antecedents to Ficino's interest in immortality, but it was Ficino who gave this theme its most famous Quattrocento treatment.[67] Throughout his writings we find that Ficino's Platonic assumptions concerning the nature of the soul led to a distinct vision of mental and spiritual health. For Ficino, the inspired and contemplative mind seeks to return to its eternal state by ascending the levels of metaphysical reality that comprise the graded universe.[68] That process of ascent from the temporal to the eternal, from the physical to the spiritual, from earthly shadow to heavenly Idea, is the keystone to all philosophical and psychological experience. Through a series of stages, the several branches of philosophy, "the medicine of human ills," heal and restore the soul.[69] The soul has an innate anxiety to return to its true end, a longing to transcend the distractions of the corporeal state and to regain the beatitude of its proper immortal essence.[70]

The soul's ascent is manifested by various types of "divine frenzy," a doctrine Plato discussed in the *Phaedrus, Ion*, and *Symposium*.[71] In a letter of 1457 to Pellegrino Agli, Ficino discussed the concept of the four frenzies of love, poetry (or music), mysteries, and prophecy.[72] In this letter, as in his thought in general, he is most concerned with the first two. For Ficino, as for Plato, the greatest of these frenzies was the amatory, which he adapted to his experiences both with his fellow man and with God.[73] The poetic frenzy also had a particular relevance to the life of the Academy. Poetry, identified with music as a gift of the Muses, imitates and recovers the celestial harmonies of the divine sphere; the notion of the divinely inspired poet—as well as perhaps that of the divinely inspired philosopher—was fundamental to Ficino's view of himself and his friends as devotees of the Muses.[74] Ficino's interest and expertise in music perhaps also tied him closely to the domain of the Muses and the experience of poetic rapture.[75]

Philosophical ascent and varieties of rapture thus were the staples of Ficino's Platonic psychology. Ficino's letter-collection is generally comprised of philosophical "abstracts" that reveal Ficino's interest in instructing his acquaintances in the way of such Platonic truth. Generally short and pithy, his letters are far less rhetorical than those of Petrarch and Salutati.[76] Usually they are epitomes of his positions on various philosophical positions.[77] Sometimes they are more explicitly prescriptive in nature. For instance, in a letter *De constantia adversus fortunam comparanda* to his close friend Giovanni Cavalcanti, Ficino applies the notion of Platonic ascent to the problem of bearing fortune calmly. He presents Socrates' advice in the *Theaetetus* (176a–b) that one must flee the evils of the mortal sphere and strive to emulate God. Ficino interprets this Platonic advice by saying that whereas the body is subject to the vicissitudes of fortune, the soul can and must remain aloof:

> Every soul should withdraw from the encumbrance of the body and become centered in the mind, for then fate will discharge its force upon the body without touching the soul. The wise man will not struggle pointlessly with fate. He will rather resist it by flight. You cannot rout misfortune, so flee. That is why Plato advises us to retreat from "here" to "there"—that is, from attachment to the body and involvement with worldly affairs, to the cultivation of the soul. Otherwise we cannot avoid evil.[78]

Attracted to the medical analogy, Ficino sometimes couched his advice in explicitly clinical terms. In a letter on worldly *dolores* he observes that from Apollo, the font of medicine, came two sons: Aesculapius, tending to the cure of the body, and Plato, tending to the cure of the mind. And just as the Aesculapians administer a medicament for the ills of the body, so do the Platonists prescribe one for those of the mind—namely, the maxim "*ubi dolor, ibi amor.*" The meaning of this adage Ficino makes clear: the source of all anxiety and grief is the misdirected love of earthly things; the source of all equanimity, the love of the "good."[79] Letter after letter expounds the basic tenet that all psychological evils result from man's failure to escape the corporeal for the spiritual, the temporal for the eternal. In an open letter in praise of self-knowledge he stresses the need to "separate soul from body, reason from sensual desire," and he recommends, "Therefore leaving behind the narrow confines of this shadow [the body], return to yourself; for thus will you return to spaciousness. Remember that there is immeasurable space in the spirit, but in the body, one could say, infinite constriction."[80]

As Kristeller has shown, the letter-collections also include moral and spiritual orations, or "declamations," delivered at the Academy. He observes that such speeches, among other evidence, suggest that the Academy should be seen in the tradition of the lay confraternity. Ficino's Platonic teaching thus had not only a philosophical or literary context but perhaps also a social and religious one as well.[81] One set of such sermonlike orations (Book 1.57–59) was titled *Stultitia et miseria hominum*.[82] In the first of these letters, Ficino condemns men for their obsessive concern with the body and their neglect of the soul. He exhorts mankind to disregard the corporeal and to cultivate the spiritual:

> Let us climb into the high watchtower of the mind, leaving the dust of the body below; then we will gaze more closely at the divine and view the mortal from a distance. The former will seem greater than usual, and the latter smaller. So, cherishing the divine and disregarding the mortal we will no longer be foolish or miserable, but indeed wise and happy.[83]

In 1478 Ficino translated these letters into Italian and included them in a collection of *Sermoni morali*,[84] thus enabling such Platonic counsel to reach a wider audience, and heightening its impact with the authority of the sermon.

Thus in theoretical, hortatory, and even more explicitly clinical formats, we find Ficino practicing his Platonic psychology. Not surprisingly, he adapted this regimen to the particular consolatory context of death. We have already seen how he shepherded Cosimo through his last days with a Platonic "art of dying." But he also administered Platonic solace to the sorrows of bereavement, consoling family and friends in both vernacular and Latin *consolatoriae*. The most noteworthy of all these letters was occasioned by the death of his brother Anselmo. Following this loss Ficino composed in 1462 a family consolation titled *Pistola consolatoria a' suoi propinqui della morte de Anselmo suo fratello dilectissimo.*[85] This letter is Ficino's account of a vision he had of Anselmo, who appeared to him offering consolation and reassurances, instructing him to record the encounter so that the rest of the family could share in it.[86] This motif of the dead consoling the living has various classical and Christian precedents.[87] It is particularly well suited to Ficino's consolation, which vividly stresses the life and beatitude of the soul after death.[88] "Anselmo" begins by explaining that when freed from the "earthly tomb" and ascending the heavenly spheres he "heard the sad tears and funereal din from your mournful breasts echoing through the air."[89] Compassion demanded that he interrupt his ascent to reassure his family of his fate. His speech exults in his deliverance "from servitude to freedom, from darkness to light, from sleep to waking, from death to life."[90] Why should they grieve? Certainly he, in his "better state," does not suffer; and they, to whom his earthly contributions were negligible, can benefit much more from his heavenly endeavors as intercessor for their own safe passage to the eternal realm. In this tender family letter the cerebral Ficino shows some capacity for more familiar cultural idioms, as he plays upon a commercial metaphor. In life a traveling merchant, "Anselmo" argues that his maritime voyages have won for him heavenly rewards and that he is far richer than those with earthly wealth. Furthermore, he exhorts: "Be content, my dear parents, who, having hoped for your son to be a merchant of worldly things, find that he turned out to be a trader in precious pearls, true goods, incorruptible possessions."[91]

Ficino's most important consolation in this letter, however, concerns his singular concept of communing souls. "Anselmo" discusses the possibility that his family might grieve that they can no longer see or live with him. His response is striking. His family in fact never truly perceived him with their merely corporeal eyes; they saw only his "appearance and entombment," his vile, bodily state. When, however, they looked to his soul, his spiritual state, they saw him with mental eyes. This true "seeing" they can continue to do now—just as before. The very structure of Ficino's vision of Anselmo hinges on a similar such communion, as he hears Anselmo's *"voce spirituale"* with his *"orecchi mentali."*[92] As for his family's lamenting their not being able to live with him, Anselmo describes the eternal communion between souls that death facilitates:

> The nature of bodies is such that two are not in one identical place, and that no one can be in more than one place at a time. And to the same condition are subjected the souls that are enclosed in bodies. But the soul free from earthly bonds, through the power of indivisible essence, is whole throughout the world and in every part of the world. For this reason, I—who before was for the greater part of the time far away and seldom and only briefly nearby—I am now always present in you, and in one identical place my soul is present with yours; and, there not being impediments of place, time, or distance, the one soul and the other are reduced into one nature. Therefore, do not search for me outside of yourselves, because I am alive in you and I think as you yourselves.[93]

Thus, the bereaved must look only into their own souls, where the souls of the departed can be found ever present.

This most impressive of Ficino's *consolatoriae* thus develops the theme of immortality both in dramatic structure and philosophical content. Ficino's vision itself affirms both Anselmo's afterlife as well as the possibility for a mystical, comforting communion of souls. Moreover, Anselmo's speech to the living testifies to the beatitude and promise of eternal life. It is the doctrine of communing souls, however, that is Ficino's special contribution to Renaissance consolation. This theme also appears in the other extant vernacular consolation we have from him, a letter to a cousin concerning the death of her sister. Building upon Platonic and Christian assumptions concerning the soul's release from its lamentable incarnation, Ficino responds to the problem of never seeing a loved one again:

> [A]ll the theologians and philosophers aver that each of us is not that which one sees and touches, but that the soul is the substance of each of us and the body the prison and tomb in which man is bound and buried the first day that he assumes the body; and when the soul departs from the body man does not die, but rather the prison is broken and the bonds loosed; the tomb opened in which it was occupied and obscured, the mind is free to return to the

eternal good, if it leaves the prison without debt. . . . And if you say that you grieve not being able any longer to see her and to be with her as you were accustomed, know that you are not able less now than before to see her and to be with her. Because with corporeal eyes you did not ever see her (you say the body, her enemy in which she was imprisoned) but you considered her with the mind. In that same way you are able now and always to consider her soul and to see her mentally as before and with more consolation than you were accustomed to. Because before your intellect considered her soul bound in a dark prison and deprived of true light; now it considers it free and re-splendent in divine light.[94]

Because of the eternal essence of the soul, consoling spiritual contact between the living and dead can be sustained.

This consolatory *topos* can also be found in Ficino's rather terse Latin *consolatoriae*. In a letter to Bernardo Bembo, he urges that Platonic contemplation will facilitate a reunion of his soul with that of his departed friend:

> You should never complain about his absence then, unless perhaps you object that it is not the way of the free soul to commune with the one now impris-oned in your body. Separate the mind from the body, Bernardo, if you can, and, believe me, your souls will quickly meet. But if you cannot do this, do not doubt they will meet a little later whether you will or no.[95]

He advocates a similar regimen for the bereaved Sigismondo Stufa, who lost his fiancée in 1473.[96] Using a familiar Platonic metaphor of the bodily "shadow," Ficino urges, "You will cease to weep, Gismondo, when you cease looking for your Albiera degli Albizzi in her dark shadow and begin to follow her by her own clear light. For the further she is from that mis-shapen shadow the more beautiful will you find her, past all you have ever known."[97] Again, the perception of her true spiritual essence can be achieved by a withdrawal into the soul, a withdrawal toward God: "With-draw into your soul, I beg you, where you will possess her soul which is so beautiful and dear to you; or rather, from your soul withdraw to God. There you will contemplate the beautiful idea through which the divine Creator fashioned your Albiera."[98] Thus, just as in his solutions for misery, misfortune, and worldly unrest, so also in his solutions for bereavement Ficino prescribed a "withdrawal" or "separation" of mind from body. In this case, the fruits of Platonic contemplation or ascent lie not merely in a quietist return to one's true self but in a comforting reunion with the dead.

As Petrarch adapted Stoic thought to modern Christian consolation, and as Salutati and Manetti developed a Peripatetic revisionism, so did Ficino, in turn, powerfully appropriate Platonic truth. These letters of his are perhaps the purest and most imaginative examples of Platonic solace to be found in Italian Renaissance thought. Relying little on rhetorical embellishment, devoid of *exempla*, uncontaminated by philosophical syncretism, they turn wholly on a Platonic conviction concerning the immortality of the soul.[99] Their message is spartan and clear—namely, souls of the dead endure and can forever commune with those of the living; the bereaved need but open their spiritual eyes and ears to regain the company of the departed. This message is Ficino's signal contribution to the Western consolatory tradition.

Ficino was not the only source of Platonic consolation emanating from the Academy. The Florentine cleric Francesco Bandini had been an involved member of Ficino's circle from the 1460s until his departure from Florence in the mid-1470s; in fact, he is named as the master of ceremonies in the Platonic symposium described in Ficino's *De amore*. In 1480 Bandini wrote a vernacular consolatory dialogue intended to console the family and friends of Simone Gondi, a young Florentine who had died in his company in Hungary.[100] Bandini, who had been a friend and teacher to his fellow Florentine abroad, attended to Gondi when he was stricken by the plague, and the dialogue purportedly records Gondi's tranquil comments to Bandini at his end.[101] In a letter to Jacopo Salviati, Gondi's last Florentine correspondent, Bandini says that before his death even "in such great danger he was not forgetful of his father or his brother and friends, all of whom he asked me to console with letters."[102] Intending the *Dialogue* to fulfill Gondi's deathbed request, Bandini sent it to Salviati with instructions to circulate it among Gondi's family. Titled *Dialogo di messer Francesco Bandini dun ragionamento avuto conlui Simone Ghondi il di avanti morissi*, the work thus employs the Platonic motif of the dying figure who consoles his surviving friends. As Kristeller argues, the consolation "Gondi" extends to Bandini includes not only such familiar *topoi* as the inevitability of death and evils of life, but also a discussion of immortality that might reveal the influence of Ficino.[103] "Bandini," who had instructed him in letters and philosophy, asks "Gondi," "in this misfortune of yours [imminent death], which you so readily make the means of freeing yourself from this prison to go to the other life, do you have any proof (beyond the usual) of the signs of the afterlife and of the immortality of our soul, a topic you know how often we have discussed."[104] The dying "Gondi" responds with a testimony of his nascent ascent from the temporal to the spiritual. He says,

> After I took most holy communion, like the worm enclosed in the cocoon of silk when the most noble part separates itself from the mortal caterpillar and becomes a butterfly ready to fly, so in me it seems that the mind closed up in me little by little separates itself from the mortal and prepares itself to fly away. And it seems that the more my body is beaten and dies, the more I feel my mind rise, grow stronger, and see not only some things that I was accustomed to know before, but also many things more. . . . I feel in myself that every

mundane thing is being abhorred and [I feel] a remarkable desire to break away from the corporeal prison.[105]

"Gondi" continues with a description of the sublime experience of his incipient ascent:

I seem to have truly seen here vigilant around me the most beautiful forms . . . and many other signs which presently I cannot narrate, but believe me, I have seen the most manifest signs of the afterlife. What evident argument for the immortality of the soul can be greater—beyond those other infinite arguments you narrated to me ever so often from Plato, Cicero, and others—than the things described above?[106]

Thus, rather than review theories of immortality that he and Bandini had discussed in the past, "Gondi" presents the testimony of the emerging blissful ascent to the divine.[107] His deathbed experience reveals to him the contrast between the mundane life of the body and the divine life of the spirit, verifying to him that "the more the mind is freed from the body, the more its divinity shows."[108]

Just as Ficino's *Pistola consolatoria* concerning Anselmo presented the cheering testimony of the dead, so Bandini's *Dialogo* portrays that of the dying. In both cases, the arguments center on the fortunate release of the soul from the body. As vernacular works, both of these consolations reveal that Platonic thought had a measure of popular adaptability to audiences wider than that found within the groves of Careggi. And in general, as has become clear, from Marsuppini's *Consolation* of 1433 to Bandini's *Dialogue* of 1480, Platonic solace proved itself to have a growing and enduring appeal to Florence's consolers and perhaps, in some cases, to its mourners.

· · · · ·

Platonic contemplation also had its costs. An important part of Ficino's contribution to psychology, or psychiatry, is his early recognition of the somatic liabilities attending the life of the philosophical mystic. His propensity to recognize and treat such conditions stemmed from his background as a doctor. This medical background gave him an added clinical perspective on the human condition, a perspective that he applied to the experience of the Platonic philosopher. The last major figure in this study, Ficino offers a notable counterpoint to the first, Petrarch. In his efforts as a *medicus animorum* Petrarch fully contemned the learning of contemporary doctors; in fact, he looked to it as a foil for his own remedial wisdom. Ficino, however, succeeded in blending the worlds of Hippocrates and Plato. In so doing, he drew "new" attention to an old disease, melancholy, an affliction that would increasingly fascinate the cultural elite not only in Italy but also in northern Europe as well.[109]

If Ficino's grounding in medicine set him apart from Petrarch, his interest in melancholy, ironically, linked him historically with his famous predecessor in a subtle but important way. Both took important steps in isolating, elevating, and publicizing certain types of personal psychological experience. For Petrarch, it was the *accidia-aegritudo* of the *Secretum*, a condition of personal despair that boldly secularized and legitimated worldly sorrow. In describing and reifying his affliction Petrarch turned to classical moral thought (*aegritudo*), medieval theology (*accidia*), and poetic sensibility (*voluptas dolendi*). It was perhaps this last, the predisposition to indulgent grief, that laid the foundations for his exploration of despair. Ficino's encounter with dejection tapped other sources, notably the medical tradition of black bile, a term assiduously avoided by Petrarch.[110] Like Petrarch, however, Ficino also brought a special cultural perspective to his vision of despair. But whereas Petrarch drew on the sweet sorrow of the poet, Ficino drew on the ecstatic abstraction of the Platonic philosopher.

As a trained physician Ficino was, of course, very attuned to the Hippocratic humoral theory outlining the necessary balance between the four bodily humors of blood, phlegm, yellow bile, and black bile. As Klibansky, Panofsky, and Saxl have shown in their magisterial *Saturn and Melancholy*, melancholy (black bile) has a complex history as a humor, disease, and temperament. Ancient medical theory recognized the debilitating psychological dimensions of this humor, which in medieval theology and late medieval literature came to be closely associated with *accidia*, lovesickness, and *tristitia*.[111] By the early modern period it had achieved a prominent, if not the prominent, place in the vocabulary and symptomatology of despair. Petrarch notwithstanding, Italian writers of the Trecento and Quattrocento seemed to be using the word as synonymous with sadness, sorrow, or unrest.[112] Boccaccio, for instance, in the Proem to the *Decameron*, uses "malinconia" in reference to a generalized romantic dejection or "gravezza di pensieri." And in Alberti's psychological dialogue *Profugiorum ab aerumna libri*, the term is fairly interchangeable with such words as "*tristezza*" and "*egritudine d'animo.*"[113]

In comparison to these literati, however, Ficino drew much more on melancholy's specific medical legacy, joining it with a related tradition of "heroic melancholy" found in Peripatetic thought.[114] The Ps.-Aristotelian *Problemata* 30.1 presented the argument that great figures (such as Ajax and Heracles), prominent thinkers (such as Empedocles, Socrates, and Plato), and all those who are outstanding in the creative or political realm are melancholic.[115] In the 1470s Ficino apparently became increasingly interested in the links between contemplation, frenzy, and melancholy. In the *Theologia Platonica* 13.2 he discussed types of ecstatic rapture common to such figures as poets, philosophers, priests, and prophets.[116] Their routine "abstraction" or separation from the body is the source of extraordinary powers of creativity or divination.[117] In fact, all genius derives from this flight from the corporeal: "Whoever achieved something great in any noble art did most when he withdrew from the body and fled to the citadel of the soul."[118] He then connects creative genius to the Platonic notion of ascent and the Peripatetic concept of heroic melancholy.[119]

He also came to identify his own "madness" and experience as a philosopher with this special affliction. Writing to Niccolò Michelozzi, he refers to a letter he had written to Lorenzo de' Medici, in which he showed himself "to have gone mad" in the manner of the inspired poet or philosopher.[120] Writing to his good friend Giovanni Cavalcanti, Ficino even more explicitly characterized himself as a type of melancholic, vulnerable to the influences of Saturn, the planet associated with the intellectual and the gifted. He bemoans a

> certain melancholy disposition, a thing which seems to me to be very bitter unless, having been softened, it may in a measure be made sweet for us by frequent use of the lyre. Saturn seems to have impressed the seal of melancholy on me from the beginning. . . . [I]f it should be necessary that it does issue from Saturn, I shall, in agreement with Aristotle, say that this nature itself is a unique and divine gift.[121]

In the 1480s Ficino wrote three books on the health, longevity, and astrological life of men of letters. In 1489 he assembled the treatises under the title *De vita*, dedicating the compendium to Lorenzo de' Medici.[122] Of most concern here is Book 1, *On Caring for the Health of Students, or Taking Care of the Good Health of Those Who Work in Letters*, in which Ficino suggested that a particular disease of scholars is melancholy. Melancholy facilitates contemplation; contemplation, in turn, can induce a pathological melancholy that has both physical and psychological symptoms. Notably, philosophers suffer owing to their abstraction of mind from body, for in "join[ing] the mind to bodiless truth, they are forced to separate it from the body," leaving the latter diminished and melancholy.[123] Though humoral in nature, the pathological type of melancholy can nonetheless have serious psychological consequences, engendering a "melancholy spirit, a sad (*moestus*) and fearful soul. Since these darknesses are much more inside than outside, they seize the soul with sadness and wear it out."[124] Though of different origins, this disease is certainly as fierce as Petrarch's *accidia-aegritudo* in the *Secretum* Book 2 or his *miseria-tristitia* in the *De remediis* 2.93. Moreover, unlike Petrarch's rather individualized poetic sorrow, Ficino's melancholy strikes that collective elite that serves the Muses, those given to Platonic frenzy.[125]

The scholar's melancholy is partly Platonic not only in its cause but also in its cure. In prescribing remedies for the malady, Ficino personally attested to one that he found to be effective:

> Mercurius [Hermes Trismegistus], Pythagoras, Plato claim that a dissonant or sad soul might be composed and cheered with the cithara and song both constant and pleasing. The holy poet David freed Saul from insanity with the psaltery and psalms. I too (if it is permitted to compare the lowest with the highest) have often found at home how much the sweetness of the lyre and song avail against the bitterness of black bile.[126]

Drawing on Orphic, Pythagorean, Platonic, and Hermetic traditions, Ficino had a profound interest in music. As mentioned earlier, he saw music as the embodiment of the poetic frenzy and as part of a clinical triad of the Academy in which body, spirit, and soul were ideally treated by medicine, music, and theology, respectively.[127] Moreover, because the spirit is the intermediary between body and soul, so music is potentially powerful on both physical and psychological levels.[128] In a letter *De musica* Ficino responded to a query concerning his interest in combining music with medicine. Defending his interdisciplinary interests as a healer, he presents a history of medicine in which he argues that the curing of the body and soul can be handled by one and the same person, as Chiron and David illustrate. He ends the letter by describing how music is a staple in his regimen as a Platonic mystic:

> For myself, to say something of your friend Marsilio, this is why, after my studies in theology and medicine, I often resort to the solemn sound of the lyre and to singing, to avoid other sensual pleasures entirely. I do it also to banish vexations of both soul and body, and to raise the mind to the highest considerations and to God as much as I may. This I do with the authority of Mercurius [Hermes Trismegistus] and Plato, who say that music was given to us by God to subdue the body, temper the mind, and render Him praise. I know that David and Pythagoras taught this above all else and I believe they put it into practice.[129]

Given its capacity to act on both body and soul, music is thus a particularly likely remedy for melancholy, but it is by no means the only one Ficino prescribes, as he recommended numerous other dietary, practical, and even (in the *De vita* Book 3) astrological remedies.[130]

In both its philosophical cause and its musical remedy, the scholar's melancholy described by Ficino affirms the presence of Platonism even in Ficino's medical writings. Most importantly, it was the fusion of Ficino's medical perspectives with his Platonic ones that led him to an influential psychiatric understanding that also had cultural consequences. Like Petrarch's *accidia-aegritudo*, Ficino's melancholy has been seen by scholars as part of a process by which the realm of despair was secularized, popularized, and, to some extent, legitimated in late medieval, Renaissance, and early modern thought. Melancholy's net came to embrace not only poets and philosophers, but also artists. In the sixteenth century the interest in melancholy found its most memorable iconography in Dürer's *Melancholia 1*, and proliferated in medical and moral handbooks, in drama, and presumably in general parlance. Its literary apogee came in the seventeenth century in Robert Burton's *Anatomy of Melancholy*.[131]

In the dedicatory letter of the *De vita* to Lorenzo, Ficino remarked on his dual clinical background and roles. As his father the physician had pointed him toward Galen, the *"medicus corporum,"* so Cosimo had "consecrated" him to Plato, the *"medicus animorum."* Honoring Cosimo, his Platonic translations and his *Theologia Platonica* had represented his duty to minister a "salutary medicine of souls." Now honoring his father, the *De vita* would tend to the health of the body.[132] And yet despite its focus on the physical, the *De vita*, as has been seen, was nonetheless also a work sensitive to the realm of the mind and to its inexorable ties to the body. The final chapter (26) of the *De vita* Book 1 explicitly addresses the problem of the relationship between physical and psychological health. In this conclusion Ficino acts as a Socratic doctor of souls for his literary friends, complementing the generally medical regimen of the manual with a thoroughly philosophical one. This chapter ("We should be Guardians of our Spirits") also is extant among Ficino's letters as an *Exhortation to the Moral, Contemplative, and Religious Life*.[133] Ficino advises that the soul must be cared for with the same diligence as the body—or, rather, with even more diligence. His source for this theme is Plato's *Charmides* (156d ff.):

> It is not all right just to take care of the body, which is only the servant of the soul, and neglect the soul, which is the king and master of the body. There is a saying of the magi, and of Plato, that the entire body so hangs from the soul that unless the soul is well the body cannot be well. This is why the founder of medicine, Apollo, decided that Socrates was the wisest of men and not Hippocrates, though Hippocrates was born of his lineage. As much as Hippocrates studied the health of the body, Socrates studied the health of the soul, although what both of these men tried to do only Christ brought about.[134]

Ficino the doctor, Platonist, and priest thus orders the healing disciplines, clearly affirming the preeminence of the health of the soul. Though also drawing on Christian thought, Ficino's vision largely describes a Platonic beatification of the will and the intellect. Blending Platonic and Christian images of "light," Ficino argues that the mind is created for seeking divine light and truth, just as the eyes are created for perceiving the

light of the sun.[135] Through the familiar regimen of purgation and philosophical preparation, the "eyes" can be awash with the splendor of divine
light:

> When someone purges his eyes and looks at that light, he suddenly finds its
> splendor pouring in, shining grandly with the colors and figures of things. It
> is the same when through moral discipline the mind is first purged from all the
> disturbances of the body, and is directed by a religious and most ardent love
> to divine truth, that is, to God himself. Suddenly, as the divine Plato says, a
> divine truth flows into the mind, and happily explains true reasons, which are
> contained in it, and in which all things exist. It surrounds the mind with as
> much light as the joy that it pours so happily into the will.[136]

Ficino thus closes the *De vita* Book 1 with the imagery of light, just as he
had opened the *Theologia Platonica*.[137] Entering a mind purged and prepared, this light illuminates man's intellect and overjoys his will, engendering that health of spirit that is necessary for the health of the body. As
Socrates would cure *Charmides*, so would Ficino his scholarly friends: even
as a doctor he prescribed Platonic remedies essential for spiritual health.

Ficino's early biographer, Giovanni Corsi, presents an account of Cosimo's
appointment of Ficino as a Platonic scholar. Summoning the elder Ficino,
a physician, Cosimo asked that he allow young Marsilio to forgo his intended medical career and turn his efforts to Platonic studies. As Corsi
describes it, Cosimo urged the father: " 'You, Ficino,' he said, 'have been
sent to us to heal bodies, but your Marsilio here has been sent down from
heaven to heal souls.' "[138] The story true or not, Ficino certainly envisioned
for himself such a role as a complete healer of souls.[139] To his family, to an
aging and dying Cosimo, to his fellow literati at Careggi, he ministered the
remedies of Platonic quietism, withdrawal, ascent. As a consoler and "psychologist" Ficino was far less eclectic and rhetorical than those humanist
predecessors of his whom we have studied. Completing the Florentine revival of Platonic consolation first substantively begun by Marsuppini, he
set forth a consistent vision of psychological experience, bringing to frui-
tion that which had begun to germinate in the *Cosmian Collections*. For
misfortune, for distress, for loss, comfort could be found through a withdrawal from the body, a retreat to the divine. In letters, in philosophical
abstracts, in orations, he perfected a holistic Platonic medicine of body,
spirit, and soul. As with many of our humanists, Ficino's vision of tranquility sometimes emerged in personal contexts, as was seen in his loss of his
brother Anselmo and in his periodic melancholy. Moreover, like his humanist counterparts, he translated that suffering—and his other psychological perceptions—into an accessible literature of consolation and advice for
others. As a translator, he instructed Cosimo in the Platonic art of dying.

As an imaginative consoler, he reassured family and friends of the possibility of the communion of souls. As a Renaissance *magus* he instructed his intimates in the ecstasy of frenzied ascent and cured them of its humoral side effects. For himself, for Florence's first family, for his Academy, he made a palpable reality of a lost healing art, the Platonic cure of souls.

CONCLUSION
THE ITALIAN RENAISSANCE AND BEYOND

FROM PETRARCH to Ficino, Trecento and Quattrocento literature reflects the interest in reviving consolatory genres in various
rhetorical, philosophical, social, and religious contexts. This humanist flowering of consolation was of course tied to the larger revival of
classical and patristic thought. But to acknowledge the mere fact of that
revival, as if somehow inexorable, is not to explain it. Timely cultural motivations inspired the rise and success of humanist learning and literature
generally, just as they shaped the emergence of consolatory writings specifically. To understand the cultural, spiritual, and intellectual context of this
consolatory revival is to understand better the reasons for the larger moral
and rhetorical interests of Renaissance humanism. The psychological impetus behind the development of humanist literary genres was considerable.
Moreover, that impetus sometimes reflected notable shifts in larger cultural
assumptions about the nature of psychological maladies, the sources of psychological care, forms of psychological discourse, and the content of psychological remedies.

The vitality of Renaissance consolatory literature, especially self-consolatory literature, certainly reflected a substantive recognition—even an embrace—of secular sorrow and misery. Whether urging that it be curbed,
purged, or diverted, humanist mourners and consolers recognized that sorrow was not merely to be contemned or overlooked. Moreover, the sources
of that sorrow came to include an increasingly secular canon of ills that
included not only the familiar tragedies of bereavement, fear of death, and
illness, but also those more esoteric or worldly sorrows of poetic sweet
grief, unrealized temporal ambition, and philosophical melancholy. The
writings of Petrarch especially illustrate how such attitudes toward temporal sorrow partly competed with divine sensibilities concerning the *contemptus mundi*. Himself alive to the ascetic and confessional traditions, he
nonetheless sought systematically to treat misery and death not just as spiritual punishments but also as secular woes. In doing so, he and others to
follow offered a cultural correction to the ascetic view of the deserved "misery of the human condition." Most importantly, the humanist exploration
of sorrow was often inspired by personal concerns. In the format of the
letter or the dialogue Renaissance writers gave new depth, legitimacy, and
popularity to autobiographical genres of consolation and psychological
discourse. Often such diaries of emotional introspection represented much
more than merely a straightforward imitation of classical or patristic mod-

els; rather they revealed an imaginative reshaping of extant genres or the invention of new ones. Petrarch, Salutati, Conversini, Manetti—all evinced a determination to create literary opportunities for emotional expression.

The treatment of sorrow was undertaken not merely in a personal context but also in larger social, generalized contexts, as humanists both lay and clerical assumed various roles as sympathetic friends, as grateful clients of ecclesiastical or lay patrons, as psychological theorists. And though such roles clearly showed classical and patristic influence, they also sometimes yielded creative attempts to further consolatory genres only nascent in or not existent in the ancient world. These roles also sometimes took on specifically contemporary casts in their particular cultural and social setting. Thus, for instance, in their role as epistolary consolers, Petrarch and Salutati can be found offering a type of solace-cum-advice that reflected timely new perspectives on secular endeavor. In his consolation of the fearful Boccaccio, who was contemplating flight from secular studies as a penitential preparation for his prophesied death, Petrarch tendered not only a consolation for the fear of death but also a Christian humanist defense of classical studies. In his consolation/chiding of the despondent Andrea Giusti da Volterra, who was contemplating flight from the *saeculum*, Salutati offered not only spiritual consolation for his grief but also a vigorous defense—Salutati's first—of the active, secular life. These examples illustrate how the laicization of psychological and spiritual care could contribute to a growing secularization in psychological perspectives. In both cases, secular renunciation, a presumably not uncommon ascetic solution for fear or grief, was rejected in favor of an affirmation of the sanctity of secular learning or work.

What of the general form of this humanist consolation? Naturally, the flourishing of consolatory genres reflected not only a new literary fashion but also, to some extent, the larger humanist belief in the power and function of rhetoric. As is well known, this general commitment to a rhetorical revival arose partly in explicit contrast to scholastic learning. The psychological dimension of that rhetorical revolt, however, should not be minimized. Petrarch long recognized the psychological power of rhetoric and acted upon that conviction in his many verse and prose efforts as self-consoler and consoler. Contemptuous of the vain intellectualism of the modern philosophers (to his mind, windbags, logic-choppers, natural philosophers in the main) he conceived his very identity in the *De remediis* as a new type of moral and psychological philosopher returning "*ad priscos*," culling the classical remedies and recasting them in new artful form. He defended such a recycling of the old in Book 2.117, suggesting that, in the proper retelling, familiar truths can assume new life and force. Rhetoric is thus the appropriate medium for psychological healing.

Petrarch's rhetorical critique of scholastic thought of course resonated in later humanist thought, sometimes again in the consolatory context. The Augustinian canon Bosso disavowed any pretenses to intellectual intricacy in his dialogue *On Bearing Adversties* and, like Petrarch, he cited Horace's *Ars poetica* in his praise of the power of rhetorical artifice. Another cleric, Nicolaus of Modruš, saw the need for a treatment of the consolatory realm in a style accessible to the nonphilosopher. Probably the most extensive Quattrocento praise of consolatory rhetoric came in Aurelio Brandolini's *Dialogus de humanae vitae conditione et toleranda corporis aegritudine* (c. 1489), written for King Matthias Corvinus and his sympathetic wife as a consolation for the King's gout.[1] Brandolini frames this treatise as a dialogue between Matthias and Bishop Pietro Razzano of Lucera, prefacing the exchange with the comment that "consolation is more effective" when presented in the dialogue format.[2] Later, "Bishop Petrus" begins one of his major consolatory speeches by explaining that his approach will be oratorical, not logical:

> And I will not (as either the ancient Stoics did, or as almost all the modern-day Philosophers and Theologians do) enclose you with those ever so narrow subtleties and triflings of the Dialecticians. For I judge to be circular that learning (*ratio*) of the Philosophers . . . but, if it please, I will approach you in that ancient and oratorical way . . . nor indeed will I assemble everything which could possibly be said by us, as if I were to recite some lecture—for I came here not as a Philosopher or a Theologian—but rather I will recall to your mind chiefly those things that I will deem most suited for consoling you.[3]

Unequivocally choosing to be neither a "Philosopher" nor a "Theologian," he thus aspires to be a new (or old) type of rhetorical Consoler, hoping to reunite rhetoric and philosophy in proper Ciceronian fashion, and thereby to correct the unhappy disjuncture of those two disciplines in scholastic thought.[4] Petrarch's *medicamenta verborum*, Bosso's holy reflections on adversity, Nicolaus' rhetorical *loci*, Brandolini's consolatory dialogue—all beckoned a wider rhetoric of solace that in its literary artifice, its verisimilitude, its more popular idiom, could appeal to the psyche and the will. This psychological potential of rhetoric must be seen as a vital and formative part of the wider moral and social appeal of rhetoric in Renaissance culture.

What of the content of humanist consolation? As befit Ciceronian rhetoricians, the humanists were generally eclectic, culling remedies from both classical and Christian thought, though they often favored one particular school or approach in the process.[5] Not surprisingly, the *loci* and arguments of fourteenth- and fifteenth-century works often reflected specific developments in the larger revival of the ancient schools. And though consolatory works often *followed* larger currents, they perhaps sometimes *led* in the process of reclaiming and popularizing classical thought. Petrarch was exposed to the Stoic strains in Cicero and Seneca at least as early as the 1330s,[6] but only later in his career did he substantively turn to the rock of Stoic patience and reason as a bulwark against the vicissitudes of life and the horrors of plague. Only later did he aggressively seek a philosophical substitute for the futile excesses of his lachrymose poetic past. Ever more intent on finding a consolation of reason, a battery of rational remedies, it was only in the 1350s and 1360s that he consummated the true revival of the *Tusculans* and transformed the meager dialogue of Ps.-Seneca in the writing of his massive and influential *De remediis*. His definition there of the philosopher as a *medicus animorum* certainly drew upon Cicero, but his purpose in reactivating such a therapeutic role had specific cultural contexts. Locked in conflict with the scholastic *cura corporum* of the medical world, and on the fringes of the pastoral *cura animarum*, his humanist "therapeutic" in this remedy-book offered a timely corrective to the scholastic learning of the doctors' world and to the asceticism of the priestly and monastic world. Petrarch's view of the need for a practical rhetoric and philosophy, as articulated in this remedy manual, was thus framed in clinical terms; Petrarch's personal and cultural identity as a moralist—in large measure, his humanist legacy—coalesced in therapeutic terms. In particularizing the psychological world in a strikingly detailed manner, and in attempting to redirect the intellectual and psychological currents of its day, the *De remediis* was not simply a classical imitation but also a new type of remedy manual from a new type of *medicus*. Yearning for a practical and constructive response to life's emotional turbulence, Petrarch sought out largely Stoic thought and genres as a framework for his modern-day humanist "therapeutic."

Psychological impulses may also have significantly sparked or intensified interest in other of the ancient schools. The revolt against Stoicism mounted by Salutati and Manetti perhaps resulted not simply from a growing revival of Aristotle's moral thought but also from their own emotional explorations. Though Aristotle was briefly invoked by both humanists, the *Nicomachean Ethics* was, of course, well known before the Greek revival, and Cicero's influential version of the Peripatetic position on emotion was already to be found in the ever-popular *Tusculans*. Now, however, finding in that Peripateticism a particular personal relevance, these grieving fathers embraced it, together with a neglected Christian tradition of weeping, in order to justify and sanctify their own sorrow. Finally, the triumph of Platonism in Medicean Florence perhaps also had hidden roots in psychological experience. Did Cosimo find the mysticism of Platonic ascent and immortality an increasingly attractive philosophy as he grew older? Certainly

Scala's and Ficino's consolation of the aging patriarch suggest that possibility. In short, psychological motivation and experimentation may have played more of a leading role than hitherto recognized in the larger history of the humanist revival of classical schools and genres.[7]

Aside from its interaction with the philosophical schools, consolatory literature was also tied to the emergence of specific philosophical themes in Renaissance thought. And here again there is some ambiguity as to how much consolation merely adapted prominent topics and how much it inspired them. The theme of the "dignity of man" is a case in point. Petrarch included his seminal treatment of the theme in his *De remediis* 2.93 as a cure for misery, admitting that he received a request from a religious to write on this theme (broached by Innocent) just as he was himself already embarking on his chapter. We can never know for certain whether Petrarch himself first conceived the idea to treat this topic, as he would have us believe, or whether this prior's request prompted him. Nonetheless, it is significant that he included his praise of man as a remedy for the ascetic existential misery of the human condition. In doing so, he partly drew misery out of the shadow of sin and into the light of psychology. Moreover, his remedies for misery, which had been theocentric in the monastic enchiridion for his brother, were now largely anthropocentric; thus, as Petrarch partly secularized misery, he also partly secularized its cure.

And though the theme of dignity would have an autonomous life in nonconsolatory genres, it also continued to have a consolatory function. This is best illustrated by the above-mentioned dialogue that Brandolini wrote for King Matthias.[8] As its title suggests, this *Dialogue Concerning the Condition of Human Life and the Bearing of Bodily Pain* ventured beyond the problem of illness to address the wider issue of the human condition in general.[9] The dialogue portrays "King Matthias" lamenting human misery (physical ills, old age, death, divine punishment for sin) and his consoler, "Bishop Petrus," offering a consolatory rejoinder.[10] The latter answers Matthias' *contemptus mundi* first with a praise of illustrious men, ending with a proclamation of the felicities and qualities of Queen Beatrice and Matthias themselves.[11] He then reflects on human happiness in general, the anthropocentric purpose of worldly creation, man's powers of mind and reason, his blessings of immortality and beatitude.[12] After this general consolation, Brandolini then turns to the particular issue of tolerating pain, drawing here, as Petrarch had done, on the *Tusculans* Book 2. Containing as it does specific *solacia* for illness, aging, and fear of death, as well as general human misery and evil, the *Dialogue* approximates a Quattrocento analogue to Petrarch's *De remediis* Book 2. Most importantly, Brandolini developed the theme of human dignity and happiness in a specifically therapeutic context. More than serving as a topic for abstract philosophical or theological debate, a sanguine contemplation on the human condition could be put to practical, consolatory use even for the treatment of the physically ill. In a letter-writing manual, the *De ratione scribendi*, possibly written prior to the *Dialogue*,[13] Brandolini hints at such a remedy. Containing discussions on various types of consolatory letters (e.g., for poverty, exile, death), this rhetorical handbook treats physical affliction in a chapter "De consolatione caecitatis et totius corporis imbecillitatis." Among the various remedies he suggests,

> Let us bring forward those things particular to the individual's wit, nature, discipline, virtues, mores, accomplishments, and other features attributable to people; in addition we could introduce into this consolation everything that can be said concerning the common condition of human life, concerning power, constancy, and every virtue.[14]

These consolations for blindness and affliction, which in their tenor and breadth resemble those offered to the ailing Matthias, may have been of particular relevance to Brandolini himself, as he suffered a lifelong eye problem.[15] In fact, his own affliction may partly have inspired him to develop a consolation concerning the blessings of human life. In any case, in terms both of epistolary theory and literary practice, he recognized the potential usefulness of this theme in practical, consolatory situations.

Regardless of Petrarch's original inspiration for his discussion of human happiness and dignity, he unmistakably linked this topic to the worldly psychological realm in *De remediis* Book 2.93, in which he explicitly joined "misery" to "sadness." This psychological perception of misery again surfaced in the following century in Poggio's *De miseria humanae conditionis*, which, if not sanguine, at least viewed misery in a therapeutic context rather than an ascetic one. Later, Brandolini also engaged "misery" in psychological terms and, like Petrarch, again offered the remedy of dignity. If it is true, as is likely, that the *topos* of misery reflected the strains of the *contemptus mundi* somewhat more than the influence of certain classical and patristic sources, then such humanist discussions offered a timely cultural counterpoint to the sensibility of the ascetic tradition. Misery is an emotional condition, not a moral one, its remedy to be found not in penitential *tristitia secundum Deum* but rather in an optimistic—even partly secular—recognition of human grandeur and bliss.

In their content, and in their very fact, consolatory writings perhaps also fed the Renaissance interest in immortality. Minor discussions of this theme can be found, for instance, in Petrarch, Salutati, Francesco Zabarella, and Marsuppini. It was, however, Filelfo who used the *Consolatio* to Marcello as a platform for a major rhetorical treatment of the theme. His was one of the more prominent Quattrocento discussions on immortality prior to Ficino's *Theologia Platonica*. Did such consolatory probes have a notable impact in the development of this topic? If Marsuppini's brief treatment of the theme interested his addressee, Cosimo, as much as it apparently inspired his rival, Filelfo, then we might argue that the consolatory forum for this theme was indeed a significant one. Moreover, on the broader level of genre, the flowering of funeral orations, elegies, funerary collections, and literary commemorations of the dead or bereaved perhaps implicitly promoted an investment in the concept of secular immortality, a concept that itself promoted the interest in the philosophical notion of divine immortality. Sometimes interpenetrating, the themes of dignity and immortality challenged the *contemptus mundi* with a markedly different view of human purpose and destiny—albeit a view often informed with spiritual perspectives.[16] It is not surprising, but nonetheless significant, that such a new view of the human condition began to take shape among the efforts of Renaissance consolers as they sought to engage and to heal the ravages of secular sorrow.

. . . . .

Trecento and Quattrocento consolers spoke not only to their own age but apparently also to future ones, both in Italy and in the early modern north. An example from the Cinquecento offers a revealing case in point. Petrarch's truest successor in sixteenth-century Italy was Gerolamo Cardano (1501–76), the Milanese doctor and sometime professor of mathematics, astronomy, astrology, and medicine.[17] From Petrarch's point of view, Cardano's scientific background would have made him an unlikely candidate as an author of consolatory and moral works, and yet he was a prolific one—a fact that itself is perhaps a commentary on the impact of fourteenth- and fifteenth-century humanist literary currents. A somewhat chaotic and tragic personal life inspired Cardano's endeavors in the consolatory realm. His most famous such effort, a *De consolatione*, appeared in Venice in 1542 and was translated and published in England twice in the 1570s.[18] Though identifying Cicero's lost *Consolatio* as his inspiration for this work, Cardano nevertheless developed the genre in broader terms than perhaps did Cicero, whose treatise presumably focused on bereavement. (The Renaissance fascination with Cicero's lost work culminated a short time later, when in 1583 a forgery of the *Consolatio* was published in Venice, attracting considerable attention and controversy.)[19] After presenting a general discussion on adversity in the first book, Cardano turns in the second to concentrate on what he considers to be mankind's major concern: namely, the fear of one's own death and grief over others'. This chapter is important because it clearly unites into one consolatory discussion the twin problems of fear and bereavement, a pattern that emerges in a number of consolatory manuals in the early modern period. In the third book, which treats a general set of problems including illness, poverty, exile, and imprisonment, Cardano attempts to place his treatise in its historical context. He concedes that there are various sources offering "*calamitatum medicinam*," citing as examples the works of Cicero, Plutarch, Boethius and, for his one modern reference, the "remedies of Petrarch."[20] He argues, however, that his work is notable for its personal authenticity, because, unlike these other writers (Cicero excepted), he has truly experienced misfortunes, which he then details in an autobiographical catalogue of his woes. In addition to thus identifying the self-consolatory quality of the treatise, such a statement suggests the extent to which subjective experience has continued to take on legitimacy and intellectual authority in Renaissance moral thought.[21] For Cardano, it is a major criterion for his qualification to compose a consolatory manual. As for the work's *solacia*, Cardano's leading consolation for the fear of death is a highly anthropological argument concerning the immortality of the soul. This theme preoccupied him in several of his other writings, and in his various discussions of the question he shows a considerable familiarity with the issues and principals in the fifteenth- and sixteenth-century debate on this subject.[22]

The *On Consolation* was followed by various other forays into the psychological domain,[23] the most comprehensive of which was a massive treatise *De utilitate ex adversis capienda*.[24] Opening with a discussion of the Cyrenaic regimen of premeditation, this manual presents books on corporeal ills (14 chapters), the goods of fortune (26 chapters), and the misfortunes of relatives and friends (12 chapters).[25] In its scope, the *De utilitate* is similar to Petrarch's *De remediis* Book 2, on which, probably, it was chiefly modeled. It is interesting to compare Cardano's chapter *De morte* to Petrarch's various chapters on death at the close of his second book of remedies. Like Petrarch, Cardano draws heavily on Cicero and Seneca,[26] and he seeks to provide a guide for the art of dying well. By the time of Cardano's work, however, the fifteenth- and sixteenth-century religious literature on this subject had flowered, and, in one instance, Cardano reacts to this tradition. He criticizes a work "de praeparatione ad mortem," probably meaning the treatise of that name by Erasmus, whom he often cites in his writings. Cardano then presents his own *ars moriendi*, outlining a model of deathbed solace, behavior, and prayer.[27]

In general, Cardano apparently saw his *De utilitate* as providing a source of psychological care neglected by the religious and intellectual establishment of his day. In the first section of the treatise he lobbies for a psychologically realistic response to human problems. And though the theologians might be expected to be the proper authorities in this area, they, and the philosophers with them, have failed to address such issues effectively:

[M]any would object that the Theologians would better be able to teach and persuade in these matters. But that is completely false. For they, like the Phi-

losophers, are engaged only in those things that seem paradoxical: for instance, where they teach that poverty ought to be embraced, we teach that it
ought to be fled. They praise sickness, disgrace, and calamities; we, on the
other hand, recommend that those things be avoided if possible or, if not, we
teach how they can be borne more easily or how, by counterbalancing evils
with goods, they may be made lesser and tolerable. Thus, whereas our whole
enterprise is built around things and acts, the Theologians only dispute,
changing or handling *things* minimally. Whence it happens that their arguments differ more amongst themselves than night from day.[28]

Here is truly a call for a secular psychology responsive to the palpable
woes of the world. Adversity and misfortune must not be cultivated as
penitential deserts or spiritual remedies; they must rather be cured and
assuaged as the worldly maladies that they are. Beyond being an unmistakable critique of asceticism, Cardano's comment also reflects a certain
antischolasticism similar to that which had animated Petrarch and Brandolini, and before them, the terms differing, Seneca. With its rejection of
asceticism and abstract intellectualizing, Cardano's outlook thus mirrored
two of the prominent forces that shaped Renaissance consolatory eloquence from the Trecento to the Cinquecento. Moreover, as Rice has
pointed out, in his treatise *De sapientia* Cardano further reified and elevated
the cultural stature of consolation by assigning it a place in his very definition of wisdom, referring the reader to his own treatment of this branch of
learning in the *De consolatione*.[29] And with the "exporting" of that consolatory manual (and other treatises) abroad, Cardano's new psychological
wisdom, like Petrarch's, was assured a cultural impact beyond Italy.

The Italian humanist legacy in fact found a fertile soil in which to germinate in the early modern north. As the classical revival moved across the
Alps, there appeared a growing number of editions and translations not
only of classical and patristic consolatory works but also of Italian Renaissance writings.[30] Most notably, between 1468 and 1758 Petrarch's *De remediis* appeared in Latin editions in Germany, France, Switzerland, Hol-
land, and Hungary; between 1501 and 1720 vernacular translations appeared in Bohemian, Spanish, French, German, English, Dutch, Swedish,
and Hungarian.[31] Other consolatory writings or collected works of
Petrarch, Filelfo, Bosso, Ficino, Brandolini, Cardano, and others also appeared.

A rich northern tradition emerged from lay and clerical figures alike, as
they too composed consolatory or self-consolatory writings on bereavement, fear of death, illness, misfortune, tranquility.[32] Sometimes, as in
Erasmus' *De morte declamatio* (pub. 1518), northern consolation showed
an Italianate blending of classical and Christian solace.[33] Sometimes, as in
Thomas More's *A Dialoge of Comfort agaynst trybulacion* (1534), there ap-

pears a greater effort to challenge the rather dominant forces of secular solace with a more exclusively Christian consolation.[34] As for Cardano's charge that the theologians had failed as consolers, one finds a remarkable flowering of consolatory writings among the northern pastoral authors. Particularly by the early modern period, pastoral writings reveal a truer sense of balance in the two faces of human despair than that which was found in medieval thought: *homo lugens* gradually achieved a greater prominence alongside his counterpart *homo peccans*. In the fourteenth century, this could already by seen in Johannes von Dambach's *Consolatio theologiae*, which in fact dealt far more with the temporal problems of adversity than with the spiritual concerns of sin.[35] In sixteenth- and seventeenth-century pastoral manuals the recognition of secular sorrow was ever more present.[36] For instance, the Anglican divine, Joseph Hall, composed a treatise titled *Heaven upon Earth, or of True Peace and Tranquillitie of Minde* (1606). Using the format of Stoic tranquility, Hall discussed not only the problems of conscience and sin but also those of misfortune, at one point making reference to Petrarch's *De remediis*.[37] John Downame's *Consolations for the Afflicted, or the Third Part of the Christian Warfare* (1613), provided a highly humanistic treatment of pain and affliction.[38] The pastor Martin Day published a *Meditations of Consolation* (appearing in 1630 in his larger work, *Monument of Mortality*), which dealt with the worldly problems (such as hardship, loss of honor, death, sickness, aging) before treating the divine problems of bad conscience and fear of judgment.[39] In some cases such manuals drew on classical solace; in some cases they criticized it, hoping to replace "pagan" remedies with spiritual ones; in some cases they did both. In a word, sometimes harvesting classical consolation and sometimes competing with it, early modern pastoral care was inspired by humanist thought to become more responsive to the problems of grief and sorrow.[40]

The writing, translating, printing, and reading of consolatory works commanded a prominent place in the Renaissance and early modern periods. As a result, one might expect changes in forms of psychological care. The rise of literacy, the development of printing, and the spread of consolatory literature would inevitably generate a rise in private readings. Such readings—along with public consolatory oratory and, possibly, private consolatory discourse—could signify a shift in the therapeutic "medium" employed in European psychological and spiritual thought and practice—a shift from an exclusively sacramental medium to a more rhetorical one. That is, the medieval paradigm of prayer, priestly administration, and liturgy was being complemented, or even partially replaced, by texts, by readings—by a "logotherapy," the healing persuasion of classical and divine texts.[41] Ritual was yielding to rhetoric, as both lay and pastoral writers attempted to make available a body of such consolatory readings.[42]

Aside from the lay and pastoral writings on death, illness, misfortune, and tranquility, there also emerged in the north a perhaps not completely unrelated fascination with melancholy, which culminated in England with the writing of Robert Burton's *The Anatomy of Melancholy* (1621).[43] Probably more than any other single work, this literary curiosity symbolizes the status of sorrow in the early modern world. The term "melancholy," scorned by Cicero and Petrarch, had now, at least in England, absorbed all its linguistic competitors. Besides discussing the traditional humoral face of melancholy, Burton examined its origins in various psychological and moral disorders, in the circumstances of misfortune, in the scholar's life (as expounded by Ficino among others), in the maladies of "love-melancholy" and "religious melancholy."[44] He completed the process of popularizing melancholy as a cultural disease. Moreover, the Italian Renaissance roots of Burton's endeavor extended beyond Ficino's medical book *De vita*[45] to the larger rhetorical and moral tradition of consolation popularized by Petrarch's *De remediis* and Cardano's *De consolatione*. The influence of both of these works can be seen in the Second Partition in "A Consolatory Digression, containing the Remedies of all manner of Discontents,"[46] an 80-page remedy-book culling consolatory speeches for a variety of misfortunes and moral disorders.[47] Even with its sometimes satirical literary tone, Burton's *Anatomy*, the work of a self-styled "melancholy divine," was far from that Pauline censure of worldly sorrow; rather, it was the consummate celebration of it.[48] Burton's elevation of melancholy as a legitimate, even fashionable, condition of modern man and society must be seen directly or indirectly as part of the same process of psychological exploration mounted by such figures as Petrarch, Ficino, and Cardano.

The legacy of Italian consolation and psychological theory warrants further study, but, as the case of Burton suggests, the psychological tradition became an increasingly refined and popular one in the north. In their various consolatory and therapeutic genres, Trecento and Quattrocento consolers offered a timely cultural idiom in which to explore the sorrows of self and others. The currency of such writings in the Italian Renaissance and beyond suggests that this new idiom spoke to the interests of writers and readers alike. The psychological activation of rhetoric and philosophy was a powerful force behind the emergence of humanist literature and moral thought. Descriptions of grief, debates on sorrow, exhortations to the bereaved, remedies for the afflicted—all gave voice to a long-silent world of sentiment. For the autobiographical writer such works offered new opportunities for cathartic reflection; for moral philosophers, new opportunities for psychological theory; for friends, new opportunities for social duty; for rhetors, new opportunities, yes, for display, but also for sustaining social discourse; for pastors, even, new opportunities for a more worldly psychological care. In each, and sometimes in a combination, of these contexts, humanist consolers evinced a recognition of the force and the legitimacy of temporal sorrow. That recognition was at once one of the urgent challenges and special appeals of Italian humanism.

NOTES

INTRODUCTION
THE CLASSICAL AND CHRISTIAN TRADITIONS

1. For an early, important study of Renaissance consolation see Paul Oskar Kristeller, "Francesco Bandini and His Consolatory Dialogue Upon the Death of Simone Gondi," in his *Studies in Renaissance Thought and Letters* (Rome, 1956), pp. 411–35. Also see A. Auer, *Johannes von Dambach und die Trostbücher von 11. bis zum 16. Jahrhundert*, Beiträge zur Geschichte der Philosophie und Theologie des Mittelalters, no. 27, pts. 1–2 (Münster, 1928); B. Langston, "Tudor Books of Consolation," Ph.D. Diss., University of North Carolina, 1940; F.N.M. Diekstra, "Introduction," in his *A Dialogue Between Reason and Adversity: A Late Middle English Version of Petrarch's 'De remediis'* (Assen, 1968); for other studies focusing on Petrarch see Chaps. 1–3; for scholarship on Giannozzo Manetti's *Dialogus consolatorius* see Chap. 5.

2. See his reference to "salubre soliloquium" in the *Invective contra medicum* IV, *Opere Latine di Francesco Petrarca*, ed. A. Bufano, 2 vols. (Turin, 1975), 2:968.

3. Most of the humanists treated in my study were laymen or, as in the case of Petrarch, effectively so (on the latter see Chap. 1, n. 2 below). As will be seen in Chap. 6, there were, however, clerical humanists who were interested in integrating classical and patristic consolation into a reshaped vision of contemporary pastoral care. For a broad survey (to which I am greatly indebted) of classical and Christian traditions of psychological and spiritual healing, see J. T. McNeill, *A History of the Cure of Souls* (New York, 1951).

4. See Eugene Rice's study of humanist notions of *sapientia* from Petrarch to Pierre Charron in his *The Renaissance Idea of Wisdom* (Cambridge, Mass., 1958); I hope that my study will complement his principal thesis that Renaissance thought reflects a shift from a medieval "intellectual" view of wisdom to a "moral" view.

5. Except in rare instances, my study will not address funeral oratory (which has a predominantly more laudatory than consolatory function); for a study and catalogue of Italian funeral orations from the late fourteenth to the early sixteenth centuries, now see John M. McManamon, S.J., *Funeral Oratory and the Cultural Ideals of Italian Humanism* (Chapel Hill and London, 1989). I shall also not treat the elegiac verse tradition (on which, in sixteenth- and seventeenth-century England, now see George W. Pigmann III, *Grief and English Renaissance Elegy*, Cambridge, England, 1985). For studies and bibliographies of classical, patristic, and medieval sources see, for example, B. C. Martha, "Les consolations dans l'antiquité," in his *Études morales sur l'antiquité*, 4th ed. (Paris, 1905), pp. 135–89 (also, on the funeral oration, see his "L'éloge funèbre chez les Romains," in *Études morales*, pp. 1–59); K. Buresch, *Consolationum a Graecis Romanisque scriptarum historia critica*, Leipziger Studien zur classichen Philologie, no. 9, pt. 1 (Leipzig, 1886); Sister Mary Evaristus (Moran), *The Consolations of Death in Ancient Greek Litera-*

ture (Washington, 1917); Sister Mary Fern, *The Latin Consolatio as a Literary Type* (St. Louis, 1941); C. Favez, *La consolation latine chrétienne* (Paris, 1937); R. C. Gregg, *Consolation Philosophy: Greek and Christian Paideia in Basil and the Two Gregories*, Patristic Monograph Series, no. 3 (Cambridge, Mass., 1975); Sister Mary Beyenka, *Consolation in Saint Augustine* (Washington, D.C., 1950); P. von Moos, *Consolatio: Studien zur mittellateinischen Trostliteratur über den Tod und zum Problem der christlichen Trauer*, 4 vols., Münstersche Mittelalter-Schriften, no. 3, pts. 1–4 (Munich, 1971–72). For a bibliography of sources in the consolatory tradition see von Moos, *Consolatio*, 4:19–39; for a comprehensive list of scholarly studies, see 4:40–68. Also, on ancient and medieval sources see those surveys in Auer, *Dambach*; Langston, "Tudor Books"; and Diekstra, "Introduction."

6. See Gorgias' *Encomnium of Helen* 14 (trans. in K. Freeman, *Ancilla to the Pre-Socratic Philosophers* [Oxford, 1948], p. 133). The account of the psychological clinic of Antiphon (presumably, but perhaps not certainly, this Antiphon is the famous contemporary of Gorgias) is in Ps.-Plutarch's *Antiphon* in the *Vitae decem oratorum* 833c–d: ". . . he invented a method of curing distress, just as physicians have a treatment for those who are ill; and at Corinth, fitting up a room near the market-place, he wrote on the door that he could cure by words those who were in distress; and by asking questions and finding out the causes of their condition he consoled those in trouble" (*Plutarch's Moralia*, vol. 10, trans. H. N. Fowler [1936 Loeb ed.], p. 351). On Gorgias and Antiphon, see P. Laín Entralgo, *The Therapy of the Word in Classical Antiquity*, trans. L. J. Rather and J. M. Sharp (New Haven, Conn., 1970), pp. 93, 97–98; also W.K.C. Guthrie, *The Sophists* (Cambridge, England, 1971; orig. vol. 3 of his *History of Greek Philosophy*, 1969), pp. 168, 290–91.

7. Cicero, *Tusculan Disputations*, trans. J. E. King (1971 Loeb ed. [rept. of 1945 second ed.]), p. 323; Buresch, *Consolationum historia critica*, p. 77; Langston, "Tudor Books," p. 35.

8. Renaissance writers would also resurrect the Ps.-Platonic *Axiochus* (or *On Death*), in which Socrates consoles an ailing man concerning his imminent death (on this dialogue see Buresch, *Consolationum historia critica*, pp. 8–20).

9. On Plato's somewhat inconsistent theories of the structure of the mind (as noncomposite [*Phaedo* 78c ff.], or as split into two [*Republic* 10.603e ff.] or three parts [*Timaeus* 69–70; *Republic* 4.439d ff.]) see Gregg, *Consolation Philosophy*, pp. 88–93; B. Simon, *Mind and Madness in Ancient Greece: The Classical Roots of Modern Psychiatry* (Ithaca, N.Y., 1978), pp. 160–66; Laín Entralgo, *Therapy of the Word*, pp. 122–38. In the *Republic* 10.603e ff., he discusses parental bereavement, advocating a moderate sorrow and discussing the opposition between rational and irrational forces in the mind (Gregg, *Consolation Philosophy*, pp. 88–93). As for his most explicit attempt at psychiatric, even psychosomatic healing, see his treatment of Charmides and the doctrine of *sophrosyne* (temperance) in the *Charmides* (Laín Entralgo, *Therapy of the Word*, pp. 114–26).

10. Other schools included the Cynic and the Megaric. For a general discussion of these schools, particularly as they filtered to Trecento and Quattrocento writers, see Cicero's *De finibus bonorum et malorum* and especially the *Tusc.* (and see "Introductions" of H. Rackham and J. E. King to the respective Loeb eds. [1914 and 1971] of these works); also E. Zeller, *The Stoics, Epicureans and Sceptics*, trans. O. J.

Reichel (New York, 1962), pp. 243 ff. and 472 ff; also Zeller, *Aristotle and the Earlier Peripatetics* (from Zeller, *Philosophy of the Greeks*), trans. B.F.C. Costelloe and J. H. Muirhead (New York, 1962), pp. 136 ff., 402–9.

11. See *Tusc.* 3.6.12; *Cons. ad Apol.* (*Moralia* 102d–e); see Gregg (who ties Crantor's notion of moderate grief to Plato's discussion in *Republic* 10.603e ff. [cf. n. 9 above]), *Consolation Philosophy*, pp. 11–14, 81–94; Moran, *Consolations of Death*, p. 8; Beyenka, *Consolation in Augustine*, pp. 3–5; Buresch, *Consolationum historia critica*, pp. 38–41.

12. *Tusc.*, King's trans., pp. 315–16.

13. On the *Tusc.* as a consolatory work see Langston, "Tudor Books," pp. 35 ff.; McNeill, *Cure of Souls*, pp. 26–30.

14. There is a marked Platonic strain in this dialogue: at 1.22.53 ff., he cites Plato's proof of immortality in *Phaedrus* 245c ff.

15. *Tusc.* 3.1.1.

16. Concentrating on bereavement, Cicero urges the consoler to minister his solace at the proper time, and he advances this tripartite approach: "Erit igitur in consolationibus prima medicina docere aut nullum malum esse aut admodum parvum; altera et de communi condicione vitae et proprie, si quid se de ipsius, qui maereat, disputandum, tertia summam esse stultitiam frustra confici maerore, cum intelligas nihil posse profici" (*Tusc.* 3.32.77).

17. *Tusc.* 2.4.11; trans. King at *Tusc.*, p. 157.; cf. Chap. 3, at n. 6 below.

18. For consolatory letters see *Ad familiares* 5.16 and *Ad Brutum* 1.9. Cicero also wrote a reply (*Ad fam.* 4.6) to Servius Sulpicius' famous *consolatoria* to him (*Ad fam.* 4.5) on the death of Tullia. Cicero thus wrote in several consolatory genres: the letter (and the reply to the *consolatoria*), the *Consolatio*, and the dialogue (which, in the case of the *Tusc.*, was partly a type of "manual"). Also, some of his other moral dialogues are partly consolatory in nature: he treats the fear of death in *De senectute* 19 ff.; the *De amicitia* is framed in the context of Laelius' reaction to the death of his friend Scipio Aemilianus.

19. See Samuel Dill, *Roman Society from Nero to Marcus Aurelius* (London, 1920), pp. 298–302.

20. Cf. Diekstra, "Introduction," p. 48n.

21. On Seneca and the tradition of the resident or personal philosopher, see Dill's chapter "The Philosophic Director," in Dill, *Roman Society*, pp. 289–333. In the *Cons. ad Marciam* 4 ff. Seneca refers to one such philosopher, Areus, attached to the imperial household, to whom Livia turned for consolation following the death of her son Drusus; Seneca identifies Areus as Augustus' "philosophus" (4.2) and "adsiduus comes" (4.3) (Dill, *Roman Society*, p. 294). Also cf. Martha, *Études morales*, pp. 145–46.

22. For *consolatoriae* on bereavement see *Ad Luc.* 63, 93, 98; for letters on a properly brave attitude toward meeting death itself see 4, 24, 26, 30, 36, 44, 61, 70, 82.

Seneca gained a particularly strong reputation among Christian writers, as was evidenced and prompted by the apocryphal tradition that he exchanged letters with Paul (Dill, *Roman Society*, p. 295; P. O. Kristeller, "Lay Religious Traditions and Florentine Platonism," in his *Studies*, pp. 99–122, at 107).

23. On Seneca's *Consolationes* see Fern, *Latin Consolatio*, pp. 53–82. Seneca also wrote various treatises concerning moral and emotional equanimity, for example, the *De tranquillitate animi*, *De brevitate vitae*, *De ira*, and *De sapientis constantia*. The most explicitly therapeutic of these works is the *De tran. animi*, in which he responds to the malady of dejection and *taedium vitae* of an acquaintance Serenus (and in which he includes some discussion of the fear of death [11.3 ff.]) (on this treatise see R. Kuhn, *The Demon of Noontide: Ennui in Western Literature* [Princeton, 1976], pp. 28–30).

Plutarch was a true successor to Seneca. His *Moralia* includes such treatises as *De tranquillitate animi*, *De capienda ex inimicis utilitate*, *De cohibenda ira*, *De exilio*, and a *Consolatio ad uxorem* on the death of his daughter. As for the *Consolatio* proper, however, Ps.-Plutarch had a more pervasive influence in the Renaissance. The *Cons. ad Apol.*, a major treatise, was a work reflecting the Academic school, not only citing Plato's writings on the immortality of the soul, but also Crantor's anti-Stoic notion that moderate grief is acceptable (see n. 11 above).

24. For a text see R. G. Palmer, *Seneca's "De remediis fortuitorum" and the Elizabethans* (Chicago, 1953), and his comment (p. 20n) that the dialogue is possibly only the abridgment of a larger work. On the controversy of its authorship, see Diekstra, "Introduction," pp. 35–36; T. Sundby discusses the sixth-century cleric Martin of Braga (or Dumio) as the author (*Della vita e delle opere di Brunetto Latini* [Florence, 1884], p. 177).

25. The interplay between amatory and other types of emotional experience ran in both directions, as is illustrated in *De rem. am.* 123–34, where Ovid discusses the issue of administering solace at the proper time by citing as an example the situation of comforting a mother bereaved of a son.

For a pseudonymous Ovidian verse consolation, see the *Consolatio ad Liviam* concerning the death of Drusus.

26. Urged on by the Muses, the sorrowful Boethius opens the *Cons. phil.* with a verse lament. Such (Ovidian?) attendants, the *poeticae Musae*, were immediately dismissed by Lady Philosophy, who insists that the healing of Boethius will be handled by her (philosophical) Muses: "Sed abite potius Sirenes usque in exitium dulces meisque eum Musis curandum sanandumque relinquite" (1.pr. 1.39–41). In addition to such poetic, medical, and philosophical images, also see 2.pr. 1.21–25 for references to rhetoric and music.

27. See P. Courcelle (*La "Consolation de Philosophie" dans la tradition littéraire: Antécédents et postérité de Boèce* [Paris, 1967]), who argues that Boethius' sources, vocabulary, and argument essentially reflect a classical framework. On Boethius' philosophy, the theological tractates attributed to him, and the *Cons. phil.* also see H. Chadwick, *Boethius: The Consolations of Music, Logic, Theology, and Philosophy* (Oxford, 1981). On Boethius' influence also see H. R. Patch, *The Tradition of Boethius* (New York, 1935).

28. See, for example, Isidore of Seville's chapters "De flagellis Dei," "De infirmitate carnis," and "De tribulatione justorum" in his *Liber sententiarum* 3 (chaps. 1, 3, 58; *PL* 83:653ff) or later, in the twelfth century, Peter of Blois' *De duodecim utilitatibus tribulationis* (*PL* 207:989–1006).

29. Christian theologians and preachers readily turned to Job as the cardinal *exemplum* for patience; see, for example, Gregory's *Moralia*, a twelve-book exposi-

tion on Job (*Moralia in Job*, ed. M Adriaen, Corpus Christianorum, Series Latina, no. 143 [Turnhout, 1979]).

30. On Paul's paradigm see S. Wenzel, *The Sin of Sloth: Acedia in Medieval Thought and Literature* (Chapel Hill, 1967), pp. 25–26.

31. Pauline perspectives were explicitly applied to bereavement in two sermons *De consolatione mortis*, works of dubious origin attributed both to Chrysostom and Augustine. (Texts of these sermons are found in the collections of both figures [see *PG* 56:293–306; *PL* 40:1159–68]; Beyenka convincingly argues that the works more closely resemble Chrysostom's writings than Augustine's.) The first sermon, framed as a highly "clinical" treatment of mourners, cites Paul's paradigm of sorrow thusly: "Beatus Paulus apostolus, fidelium doctor, medicus salutaris, duas esse dixit tristitias: unam bonam, et alteram malam; unam utilem, et alteram inutilem; unam quae salvat, et alteram quae perdit" (*PG* 56:295). The sermon explains why *tristitia saeculi* is dangerous: "Quare autem mortem operatur [as Paul warned]? Quia solet nimia tristitia aut ad dubitationem, aut ad perniciosam perducere blasphemiam" (p. 296). Excessive sorrow is thus not only senseless but also—and more importantly—potentially impious. The author argues that Old Testament figures might justifiably have wept but Christians may not, for such sadness is precluded by the hope of resurrection, the prospect of future beatitude, and the release from worldly trials. The second sermon urges the cultivation, instead, of that divine penitential sorrow (see discussion of these sermons by Beyenka, *Consolation in Augustine*, pp. 81–87). These sermons illustrate the somewhat dismissive Christian attitude toward bereavement and grief. Sorrow, which was inappropriate for the Stoic sage in the classical world, has become impious for all believers in the Christian era. Moreover, as the piety of mundane grief was discounted, so was the sanctity of contritional grief promoted.

32. Gregg, *Consolation Philosophy*, pp. 153–56.

33. Thus he continues: "For since we believe that Jesus died and rose again, even so, through Jesus, God will bring with him those who have fallen asleep" (1 Thes. 4:14).

34. Such travails, though mortal, were not, however, "secular," as they resulted not from the psychological cares of the world but from the spiritual dangers facing the early Church.

35. On funeral orations in Gregory of Nyssa, Gregory Nazianzen, and Ambrose, see Favez, *La consolation latine chrétienne*, pp. 18–23; Gregg, *Consolation Philosophy*; M. McGuire, "The Christian Funeral Oration," in *Funeral Orations by Saint Gregory Nazianzen and Saint Ambrose*, trans. L. McCauley, J. Sullivan, M. McGuire, and R. Deferrari (New York, 1953), pp. vii–xxi. On consolatory letters and on sermons and treatises on death, resurrection, and patience in writers such as Basil, Tertullian, Cyprian, Chrysostom, Jerome, Ambrose, and Augustine, see Favez, *La consolation latine chrétienne*; Beyenka, *Consolation in Augustine*; Gregg, *Consolation Philosophy*.

Probably the most prolific and versatile consoler among the patristic figures was Chrysostom. Besides his *consolatoriae* on bereavement and his longer *Consolatio*, the *Ad viduam juniorem* (*PG* 48:599–610), certain of his letters to Olympias offer consolations for misfortune, despair, and tribulation (see, for example, nos. 2 and 3 in *PG* 52). Most remarkable is his three-book consolation of a despondent monk, the *On Providence* (or *Oratio adhortatoria ad Stagirium ascetam a daemone vexatum*, as titled in the unattributed Latin translation in *PG* 47:423 ff.). Perhaps the most extensive treatment of despair in patristic literature, this work discusses the problem of tribulation and divine providence (for a discussion see Kuhn, *Demon of Noontide*, pp. 46–49). Chrysostom was also a congregational consoler, as evidenced by his homilies *On the Statues* to the people of Antioch, which console the flock for adversity, tribulation, and the fear of death. In these pastoral consolations, Chrysostom was undoubtedly following the lead of Paul, whom in his treatise *De sacerdotio* he praised as the exemplar of the eloquent pastor (see *PG* 48:668–72). He may also have been the author of the two sermons *De consolatione mortis* (see n. 31 above).

36. For other consolations for bereavement see his letters to Marcella (23), Paula (39), Pammachius (66), Theodora (75), Oceanus (77), Salvina (79), Eustochium (108: the *Epitaphium Paulae matris*), Julianus (118), and Principia (127) (Favez, *La consolation latine chrétienne*, pp. 23–32).

Jerome's influence in the Renaissance and early modern period would rest also on letters included among his dubious works; among these are a *consolatoria* to Tyrasius (no. 40 in *PL* 30) and letters addressing problems such as adversity, exile, and illness: the *Exhortatio ad Marcellam ut adversa toleret*, the *Consolatio ad virginem in exsilium missam*, two letters *Ad amicum aegrotum*, and the *Ad Oceanum de ferendis opprobriis hortatoria* (nos. 3–6, 41 in *PL* 30).

37. "Quid igitur faciam? Iungam tecum lacrimis? Sed *apostolus prohibet* Christianorum mortuos dormientes vocans. . . . Sed invito et repugnanti per genas lacrimae fluunt et inter praecepta virtutum resurrectionisque spem credulam mentem desiderii frangit affectus" (*Select Letters of St. Jerome*, trans. F. A. Wright [Loeb ed., 1933], p. 266; emphasis mine).

38. Ibid. (trans. Wright), p. 273.

39. In the consolation of bereavement, the most prominent Christian *topos* was that of resurrection, a theme sometimes linked to the related Platonic notion of immortality (on the relation between these two themes in patristic thought see Gregg, *Consolation Philosophy*, pp. 197–214). An influential example is found in the second of Ambrose's funeral orations *De excessu fratris sui Satyri*, a work sometimes titled *De fide resurrectionis*. Here, Ambrose remarks at one point on the wheat and chaff of classical consolation, and he emphasizes the Christian imperative to explore the theme on which his oration focuses: "Gentiles plerumque se consolantur viri, vel de communitate aerumnae, vel de jure naturae, vel immortalitate animae. Quibus utinam sermo constaret, ac non miseram animam in varia portentorum ludibria formasque transfunderent! Quid igitur nos facere oportet, quorum stipendium resurrectio est?" (*PL* 16:1328; J. Sullivan, "Introduction" to his translation in *Funeral Orations by Saint Gregory Nazianzen and Saint Ambrose*, pp. 159–60). For an Eastern dialogue on this *topos*, see Gregory of Nyssa's *De anima et resurrectione seu Macrinia* (*PG* 46:11–160), a treatise (after the *Phaedo*) portraying a conversation between Gregory (mourning the death of Basil) and his dying sister Macrinia, who discusses with him the notion of immortality and resurrection (Beyenka, *Consolation in Augustine*, pp. 19–20; Gregg, *Consolation Philosophy*, pp. 155, 171, 248–51). In general, on the adaptation of classical themes and on the development of Christian themes in patristic consolation see Gregg, *Consolation Philosophy*; Favez, *La consolation latine chrétienne*.

40. A work such as Isidore of Seville's *Synonyma* or *De lamentatione animae peccatricis* (*PL* 83:825–68) illustrates how distinctly new Christian themes (e.g., redemptive suffering) could be blended with classical concerns of adversity and misfortune in one psychological handbook (on this work, see Chap. 6 below).

41. Delighting in his grief ("Solus fletus erat dulcis" [*Conf.* 4.4]), he experienced a type of *voluptas dolendi* similar to that described in Ovid's *Tristia* 4.3.37 and similar to those maudlin excesses of the stage Augustine condemns in *Conf.* 3.2 (also cf. his comments on classical literature in 1.13; see discussion of Augustine's pre- and postconversion bereavements in Beyenka, *Consolation in Augustine*, pp. 31–40).

42. On the deaths (and beatific afterlives) of Verecundus and Nebridius see *Conf.* 9.3; on Adeodatus see 9.6; on Monica, 9.12 (Beyenka, *Consolation in Augustine*, pp. 34–37).

43. "Et quia mihi vehementer displicebat tantum in me posse haec humana, quae ordine et sorte conditionis nostrae accidere necesse est, alio dolore dolebam dolorem meum et duplici tristitia macerabar" (*Conf.* 9.12; trans. W. Watts, [Loeb ed., 1912], 2:61). Augustine still yielded to sorrow, which is, he recognized, part of man's flawed emotional state since the Fall. (As became clear in the psychological discussions in the *De civ. Dei*, Augustine opposed the Stoic notion of *apatheia*, favoring a Platonic and Peripatetic acceptance of emotional states. See *De civ. Dei* 9.4–5, 14.8 ff.; on the historical Augustine's psychological stance see K. Heitmann, "L'insegnamento agostiniano nel 'Secretum' del Petrarca," *Studi Petrarcheschi*, vol. 7, ed. U. Bosco, Accademia Petrarca di lettere, arti, e scienze di Arezzo [Bologna, 1961], pp. 187–93.) It should be noted that his necessary concession to nature in his grief over Monica was confined to one day and a night, his weeping to one hour. Thus his sadness was shorn of that secular, indulgent quality. Most importantly, as a Christian, Augustine felt a sense of displeasure, shame, and grief for his sorrow.

44. As for Augustine's notice of Paul's paradigm, see his citation and discussion of 2 Cor. 7:10 in *De civ. Dei* 14.8.

45. The title of this chapter offers a succinct view of the Christian perspectives on human misery: "De miseriis ac malis quibus humanum genus merito primae praevaricationis obnoxium est et a quibus nemo nisi per Christi gratiam liberatur."

46. *De civ. Dei* 22.22; trans. (rev.) W. M. Green (Loeb ed., 1972), 7:313–15.

47. He continues this passage by discussing the classical notion that philosophy can be a fount of consolation. Because, however, such "vera philosophia" is, according to Cicero, bestowed by the gods only on a few, misery must rightfully be the deserved lot of mankind: "Porro si paucis divinitus datum est verae philosophiae contra miserias huius vitae unicum auxilium, satis et hinc apparet humanum genus ad luendas miseriarum poenas esse damnatum" (*De civ. Dei* 22.22).

48. Cf. Fern's comment, *Latin 'Consolatio*,' p. 210. It should be noted, however, that Augustine did compose a few consolatory letters (on which see Beyenka, *Consolation in Augustine*, pp. 94–104).

49. For texts of these respective works see *PL* 16:23–184; *PG* 48:623–92; *PL* 77:13–128; *PL* 83:737–826.

50. I follow the Latin translation by B. de Montfaucon at *PG* 48:685.

51. Cf. James J. Murphy, *Rhetoric in the Middle Ages: A History of Rhetorical Theory from St. Augustine to the Renaissance* (Berkeley and Los Angeles, 1974), pp. 292–97.

52. For general surveys of pastoral care, see W. B. Clebsch and C. R. Jaekle, *Pastoral Care in Historical Perspective: An Essay with Exhibits* (New York, 1964), for here, esp. pp. 23–26; also see McNeill, *Cure of Souls*. On confession and penance see H. C. Lea, *A History of Auricular Confession and Indulgences in the Latin Church*, 3 vols. (Philadelphia, 1896); J. T. McNeill, *The Celtic Penitentials and Their Influence on Continental Christianity* (Paris, 1923); Thomas N. Tentler, *Sin and Confession on the Eve of the Reformation* (Princeton, 1977). On last rites see C. Ruch, "Extrême onction du Ier au IXe siècle," in *Dictionnaire de théologie catholique*, vol. 5 (Paris, 1913), 1927–85; and on the institutionalization of extreme unction as a sacrament, see L. Godefroy, "L'extrême onction chez les scolastiques," in *Dictionnaire de théologie catholique*, pp. 1985–97; on medieval liturgical practices surrounding death see, for example, P. Ariès, *The Hour of Our Death*, trans. H. Weaver (New York, 1982), pp. 143 ff.

53. See S. Wenzel's study of the complicated history of *accidia* in his *The Sin of Sloth: Acedia in Medieval Thought and Literature* (Chapel Hill, 1967); also Chap. 1 below; for a discussion of Paul's two types of *tristitia*, *accidia*, and medieval psychological theory, see S. Snyder's "The Paradox of Despair: Studies of the Despair Theme in Medieval and Renaissance Literature," (Ph.D. Diss., Columbia Univ., 1963), pp. 1–73.

For an early penitential treatment of sorrow see the seventh-century *Poenitentiale Cummeani*, which, in its catalogue of eight deadly sins, distinguished between *tristitia* and *accidia* (treated as sloth). For the former, the treatment is highly corrective, as it recommends that sorrow must be starved out. The remedies for *tristitia* run thus:

1. He who long harbors bitterness in his heart shall be healed by a joyful countenance and a glad heart.

2. But if he does not quickly lay this aside, he shall correct himself by fasting according to the decisions of a priest.

3. But if he returns to it, he shall be sent away until, on bread and water, he willingly and gladly acknowledges his fault.

(Cited in *Medieval Handbooks of Penance: A Translation of the Principal "Libri poenitentiales" and Selections from Related Documents*, J. T. McNeill, and H. M. Gamer [New York, 1938; rept. New York, 1965], p. 108 and introductory comments at pp. 98–99.) As for bereavement, the penitentials also took care to proscribe certain pagan or self-destructive mourning rituals; for example, see the penance imposed for female dirges ("keening") in the Irish penitentials (*Medieval Handbooks of Penance*, pp. 121, 154); also see the provision in the ninth-century *Poenitentiale Hubertense*: "If anyone lacerates himself over his dead with a sword or nails, or pulls his hair, or rends his garments, he shall do penance for forty days" (*Medieval Handbook of Penance*, p. 294). For further discussion of *accidia* see Chap. 1 below.

54. Obviously, this is not to say there was not a tradition of postpatristic medieval consolatory literature, as such writings can be found (e.g., Bernard's *Sermones*

super Cantica Canticorum 26 on the death of his brother Gerard [in *S. Bernardi Opera*, vol. 1, ed. J. Leclercq, C. H. Talbot, and H. M. Rochais (Rome, 1957), pp. 169–81] or Vincent of Beauvais' *Tractatus consolatorius ad Ludovicum IX regem de obitu filii* [see n. 59 below]; on these and other medieval writings see von Moos); however, it is fair to say that the preponderance of medieval spiritual and pastoral literature focused much more on those spiritual consolations concerned with reconciliation for sin and the preparation for the future life, rather than on those temporal consolations for worldly sorrow.

55. See Clebsch and Jaekle, *Pastoral Care*, pp. 23–25, who cite, as illustrative of larger currents in medieval pastoral perspectives and goals, the alternate title, *Corrector et medicus*, which Burchard of Worms gave to his eleventh-century manual *De poenitentia* (*PL* 140:949–1014) (Book 19 of his *Decretorum libri*); Burchard explained thusly: "Liber hic Corrector vocatur et Medicus, quia correctiones corporum et animarum medicinas plene continet, et docet unumquemque sacerdotem, etiam simplicem, quomodo unicuique succurrere valeat, ordinato vel sine ordine, pauperi, diviti, puero, juveni, seni, decrepito, sano, infirmo, in omni aetate et in utroque sexu" (p. 949). His corporeal "corrections" and spiritual medicines obviously are penitential, detailing specific penances for specific acts (for example, murder, robbery, adultery, magic). More abstractly moral and psychological conditions are given far less attention. Citing an earlier catalogue of the eight deadly sins (pp. 976–77), Burchard offers as counterpoise to these vices very brief remedies of appropriate virtues (for example, concerning *tristitia*: "Si tristitia te superat, patientiam et longanimitatem meditare" [p. 977]); later, he includes a chapter *De illis qui se affligunt de obitu charorum* (pp. 1008–9) which quotes from a letter of Pope Anastasius I warning against excessive grief and citing Paul's 1 Thes. 4:13. For an excerpted translation of Burchard's *Corrector et medicus*, see McNeill and Gamer, *Medieval Handbooks of Penance*, pp. 321–45. To Burchard's concept of spiritual "medicine" and the pastoral "medicus" cf. Cicero's view of therapeutic philosophy (at n. 17 above) and Chrysostom's interest in consolatory care (at n. 35).

For Burchard's manual for the treatment of the sick, see Book 18 of the *Decretorum*, the *De visitatione infirmorum* (*PL* 140:933–44).

56. Cf. T. Tentler's characterization of the confessional goal of offering "consolation" for "anxiety" or contritional sorrow (*Sin and Confession*, pp. 12–15, 347–49).

57. For a Latin and English text of this immensely popular work (extant in 672 mss) see *De miseria condicionis humane*, ed. R. E. Lewis (Athens, Ga., 1978); also see his comment in his "Introduction," p. 3; on the genre from the eleventh to the sixteenth centuries, see D. Howard, "Renaissance World-Alienation," in *The Darker Vision of the Renaissance: Beyond the Fields of Reason*, ed. R. S. Kinsman (Berkeley and Los Angeles, 1974), pp. 47–76, at 55–57.

58. Two works that (reflecting humanist currents) did, however, offer psychological comforts in the "classical" tradition were Vincent of Beauvais' *Tractatus consolatorius* to Louis IX (see following note) and Johannes von Dambach's *Consolatio theologiae* (1366) (see Auer, *Dambach*; Conclusion below).

59. His *Carmina miscellanea tam sacra quam moralia* (*PL* 171:1381–1442) includes several epitaphs as well as verse on his exile and misfortune (on Hildebert's verse see Charles H. Haskins' classic, *The Renaissance of the Twelfth Century* [Cam-

bridge, Mass., 1927; rept. Meridian, 1970], pp. 163–66; Patch, *Tradition of Boethius*, pp. 98–99).

As for the *Liber di quer. et conflictu* . . . (*PL* 171:989–1004), this work in prose and verse (titled *De dissensione interioris et exterioris hominis* in one ms) depicts a dialogue between an "interior man" and the "exterior man" on the problem of external calamities and the human psychological condition, much of the work dealing with the conflict between the flesh and the spirit (on the work and on its Boethian, self-consolatory character see introductory comments of editor[s] at *PL* 171:989–90).

As for the letters, see the *consolatoria* to King Henry I for the loss of two sons, which incorporates into its theological message some classical borrowings (*Epistolae* 1.12 [*PL* 171:172–78]). For consolations on adversity and other matters, see 1.17–19. Also, for a somewhat consolatory exhortation to a newly appointed abbot who laments his loss of contemplative repose, see 1.22, in which Hildebert makes some comments in defense of the active life, urging his addressee to mix the contemplative and active lives (cf. Salutati's letters on the active [secular] life to Andrea Giusti da Volterra and Pellegrino Zambeccari in the 1390s [see Chap. 4 below]).

Also from the twelfth century, see the British Benedictine Lawrence of Durham's *Consolatio de morte amici*, a self-consolatory dialogue on the death of a friend (for ed., see U. Kindermann, *Laurentius von Durham, Consolatio de morte amici: Untersuchungen und kritischer Text* [Breslau, 1969]). Like Hildebert's *Liber*, which Lawrence knew (Kindermann, pp. 75ff.), the *Consolatio* follows the Boethian prose-meter format. In their studies of the work, von Moos and Kindermann show that Lawrence's *Cons.* drew from Boethius' *Consolatio* (most heavily), Seneca's *Ad Luc.* (e.g., nos. 9, 63, 74) and Cicero's *De amicitia* (see von Moos, *Consolatio*, 1:427–45; 2:247–73; Kinderman's notes and sources references in his ed., pp. 137–89).

From the thirteenth century, a major northern consolation can be found in Vincent of Beauvais' *Tractatus consolatorius ad Ludovicum IX regem de obitu filii*. This lengthy work (66 folio pages in Amerbach's 1481 Basel ed. [*Opuscula*, sigg. N1–Q9v]) was addressed to Louis for the death of his eldest son. Joining classical and Christian sources in a *summa* of Christian consolation, the treatise includes chapters on grief, the nature of death, the soul's afterlife, purgatory, eternal beatitude. In his use of classical sources, Vincent shows a considerable humanist bent, as he draws widely on Roman moralists (for example, Cicero and Seneca) and poets (Ovid, Vergil, Statius). Among the patristic writers, Ambrose's *De excessu* is often cited. In his chapter "De morte non timenda," Vincent cites Cyprian's *De mortalitate* (*PL* 4:603–24) and Ambrose's *De bono mortis* (*PL* 14:539–68). Medieval writers such as Hugh of St. Victor, Bernard of Clairvaux, and Anselm are also cited. Before Dambach's *Consolatio theologiae*, Vincent's treatise was perhaps the most comprehensive medieval consolatory writing. To traditional arguments concerning consolation he joined a wealth of theological considerations concerning the human condition.

60. After his early studies in Paris in the 1140s (under John of Salisbury?), Peter pursued the law in Bologna for a time, after which he returned to Paris in the 1150s

to study theology. His tastes running more to the literary, he never obtained a degree in either law or theology. He worked for various secular and clerical figures (presumably chiefly in a secretarial capacity) and in 1182 became archdeacon of Bath. For these details on Peter's life and his letter-collection, see R. W. Southern, "Peter of Blois: A Twelfth-Century Humanist?" in his *Medieval Humanism and Other Studies* (Oxford, 1970), pp. 105–32; also Murphy, *Rhetoric in the Middle Ages*, p. 229.

61. This is Southern's point, "Peter of Blois," p. 114; as for this medieval French tradition of letter-writing see Salutati's comments on these figures in his *Epist.*, ed. F. Novati, 3:83–84 (see Chap. 4 below). On Abelard's collection (*PL* 178:113ff), which was probably originally compiled by Heloise, and which includes the well-known self-consolatory/consolatory *Historia calamitatum* (ed. J. Monfrin, 3rd ed. [Paris, 1967]) as well as Heloise's request that he likewise console her, see Southern, "The Letters of Abelard and Heloise," in Southern, *Medieval Humanism*, pp. 86–103.

62. In *PL* 207 see nos. 2, 12, 169, 170–71, 174, 177–78, 180–82, 201, 207; von Moos, *Consolatio*, 4:96–97. Finally, Peter also wrote or compiled a *Libellus de arte dictandi* (fragment only at *PL* 207:1127–28), which contained a section devoted to consolation (Murphy, *Rhetoric*, p. 229; von Moos, *Consolatio*, 2:22). His writing of such a handbook was perhaps inspired by his studies in Bologna in the 1150s, for it was in Italy that the *ars dictaminis* first arose (see discussion in text below).

63. See ibid., nos. 12, 22, 214, 227, 241.

64. For example, see comments in his consolation in *PL* 207:548–49.

65. For editions of Peter's two-part treatise see *PL* 207:871–958 (where the second part is titled *De charitate Dei et proximi*) and M.-M. Davy, *Un traité de l'amour du XIIᵉ siècle, Pierre de Blois* (Paris, 1932); for Aelred's *Spec. car.* and *De amic. spir.* see *PL* 195:503–620, 659–702. On his plagiarism of Aelred's *De amic. spir.* in his *De amic. christ.*, see P. Delhaye, "Deux adaptations du 'De amicitia' de Cicéron au XIIᵉ siècle," *Recherches de théologie ancienne et médiévale* 15 (1948), 304–31; also Southern, "Peter of Blois," pp. 123–24.

66. See Delhaye, "Deux adaptations du 'De amicitia' "; on friendship in medieval letters, also see J. Leclercq, "L'amitié dans les lettres du moyen âge: Autour d'un manuscrit de la bibliothèque de Pétrarque," *Revue du moyen âge* 1 (1945), 391–410; also G. Constable, *Letters and Letter-Collections* (Turnhout, 1976), pp. 16, 32.

67. Cf. Aelred of Riveaulx's commemoration of the death of a friend (*Epitaphium Simonis*) in his *Speculum caritatis* 1.34 (on this work see von Moos, *Consolatio*, 1:340–97; 2:191–216).

68. See Chap. 4 below.

69. For this work, which opens with a citation from Seneca, see *PL* 207:989–1066.

70. For this treatise, titled *Compendium in Job*, see *PL* 207:795–826; Southern, "Peter of Blois," p. 112.

71. On this thesis see Kristeller's "Humanism and Scholasticism in the Italian Renaissance," in his *Renaissance Thought and Its Sources*, ed. M. Mooney (New

York, 1979), pp. 85–105; also see his discussion of rhetoric in "Philosophy and Rhetoric from Antiquity to the Renaissance: The Middle Ages," also in his *Renaissance Thought*, pp. 228–42; also see his "Matteo de' Libri, Bolognese Notary of the Thirteenth Century, and his *Artes dictaminis*," in *Miscellanea Giovanni Galbiati*, vol. 2 (Milan, 1951), pp. 283–320; also his "Un'*ars dictaminis* di Giovanni del Virgilio," *IMU* 4 (1961), 181–200. Other scholars have continued to explore this problem: J. Seigel, in his *Rhetoric and Philosophy in Renaissance Humanism: The Union of Eloquence and Wisdom, Petrarch to Valla* (Princeton, 1968), pp. 200–25; and now particularly Ronald Witt, "Medieval 'Ars dictaminis' and the Beginnings of Humanism: A New Construction of the Problem," *RQ* 35 (1982), 1–35; Witt's "Boncompagno and the Defense of Rhetoric," *JMRS* 16 (1986), 1–31; also Witt and Benjamin G. Kohl, "General Introduction," in their *The Earthly Republic: Italian Humanists on Government and Society* (Philadelphia, 1978), pp. 3–22. Kristeller argues succinctly "that the humanist movement seems to have originated from a fusion between the novel interest in classical studies imported from France toward the end of the thirteenth century and the much earlier traditions of medieval Italian rhetoric" ("Humanism and Scholasticism," p. 97), and he suggests that the Italian humanists enriched and transformed the dictaminal tradition with classical interests. Witt further discusses the grammatical origins of protohumanist interests, interests pursued by both *dictatores* as well as others ("Medieval 'Ars dictaminis' "). In general, then, dictaminal, grammatical, and other moral and literary currents of the twelfth, thirteenth, and early fourteenth century fostered the cultural climate for the truer classicism and the richer rhetorical and literary pursuits of early humanism. This applied more narrowly to consolatory interests, as I shall illustrate immediately below.

72. See Murphy, *Rhetoric in the Middle Ages*, pp. 194–268 (also studies cited in preceding note). For editions of dictaminal writings of Alberico, Hugo of Bologna, Boncompagno, Guido Faba, and others, see L. Rockinger, *Briefsteller und Formelbücher des eilften bis vierzehnten Jahrhunderts*, Quellen und Erörterungen zur bayerischen und deutschen Geschichte, no. 9, pts. 1–2 (Munich, 1863; rept. New York, 1961). Although Italy was the principal center of this tradition, it was not the only one; on northern developments (e.g., especially in Orléans) see Murphy, *Rhetoric in the Middle Ages*, pp. 226 ff.; Witt, "Boncompagno."

73. On consolatory material in the manuals of the above-named writers, see Kristeller, "Francesco Bandini," *Studies*, p. 418n; also his "Matteo de' Libri," pp. 288, 312; also see James R. Banker, "Mourning a Son: Childhood and Paternal Love in the *Consolatoria* of Giannozzo Manetti," *History of Childhood Quarterly: The Journal of Psychohistory* 3 (1976), 351–62 at 352, 360–61. Also, on Boncompagno, Thomas of Capua, and Pietro della Vigna, see von Moos, *Consolatio*, 1:401–14; 2:224–238. As for Pietro della Vigna, chancellor of Frederick II, also see A. Huillard-Bréholles, *Vie et correspondance de Pierre de la Vigne* (Paris, 1864), including the eulogistic and consolatory letters contained among the *Documents* therein.

74. There is no complete edition of the *Rhet. ant.* (or *Boncompagnus*); as for the chapter "On Consolation," excerpts can be found in Rockinger, *Briefsteller*, pp. 140–41; also in von Moos, *Consolatio*, 2:224–26; 3:217. The work appeared in 1215 and again in 1226/27, the latter edition serving, it is argued, as the source of

extant mss (see V. Pini's entry in *DBI* 11:720–25; Witt, "Boncompagno," p. 3). For a ms of the chapter *De cons.* see that in BAV, MS, Archivio di S. Pietro, H 13, ff. 34v–43vA; hereafter referred to as "V¹."

75. For example, in sections titled "Littere generales super consolationibus defunctorum," "Littere consolationis ad patrem vel matrem pro morte filii," "Littere consolationis pro morte filii ad illum qui est in senecta et senio constitutus." Here and below I cite the section titles edited in von Moos (*Consolatio*, 2:224–25), with occasional emendations to follow titles as found in V¹, ff. 35vA–36A and/or at sections themselves as found at V¹, f. 36A ff.; for these three sections see V¹, ff. 36B–37A, 37vA.

76. "Quod non est tristibus in acerbitate doloris consolationis remedium exhibendum" (von Moos, *Consolatio*, 2:224; V¹, ff. 40A–B).

77. See sections "Quod immoderatam effusionem lacrimarum incipiant oculi caligare" (where he comments, "Lacrime quidem esse dicuntur melancolie superfluitates"), "Quod duplex afflictio proveniat illis qui lacrimari non possunt"; "Quod nimium lacrimantibus et non valentibus lacrimari afflictio spiritus dominetur; Quot modis lacrime proveniant" (in which he discusses how weeping can be caused by grief, joy, and childbirth, among other things) (von Moos, Consolatio, 2:224; 3:217; V¹, ff. 40rB–vB, 41vA–B); on restrained and excessive grief see below.

78. In the sections "Quod multi sancti viri super morte carorum flevisse leguntur et habuisse modum in fletu" (in which he cites biblical figures, including Christ as he wept for Lazarus) and "De temperantia sapientium super morte carorum" (von Moos, *Consolatio*, 2:224, 226; V¹, ff. 40B, 40vB–41A).

79. Here, Boncompagno displays a realism that borders on the cynical when he enumerates those situations in which death is a source of gain for others, as, for example, when a teacher's death means a potential job opportunity for an ambitious student: ". . . discipuli, qui aspirant ad magisterium, de morte doctorum gaudium concipiunt, non dolorem" (von Moos, *Consolatio*, 2:225; V¹, f. 41vA).

80. On Boncompagno's chapter "De cons." in general see von Moos, *Consolatio*, 1:403–7; 2:224–26.

81. "Stultum est ergo pro morte carorum ultra modum tristari, quia per immoderatum dolorem fiunt multi odibiles Deo, perditur sensualitas, et humana corpora desiccantur" (V¹, f. 40vA–B; cf. von Moos, *Consolatio*, 3:217).

82. ". . . cum lacrime interius retinentur anima pondere inenarrabili oneratur eiusque actiones tenebrescunt, unde uterque homo consuevit facile deperire" (V¹, f. 40vA; cf. von Moos, *Consolatio*, 3:217).

83. Like the Greek Sophist Antiphon, the medieval *dictator* as rhetorician could claim the psychological realm as part of his territory. Furthermore, Boncompagno also encroached on the domain of the anthropologist, as the two following chapters of the *Rhet. ant.* survey mourning and funerary practices (V¹, ff. 43vA–46A; the first of these chapters, "De consuetudinibus plangentium," is edited in Rockinger, *Briefsteller*, pp. 141–43; M. Barasch, *Gestures of Despair in Medieval and Early Renaissance Art* [New York, 1976], p. 88).

84. Aside from a reference to Cato (cf. Cicero's *De senectute* 23.84 and *De amicitia* 2.9) in the section "On the Temperance of the Wise in the Death of Loved Ones" (V¹, f. 40Bv), no other classical examples nor explicitly identified classical *loci*

are to be found. Religious perspectives or examples, however, are much in evidence; see, for example, those very brief sections (or *loci*) "Quod iacture et miserie saepe proveniunt occulto iudicio dei," "Quod deus frequenter punit, ut probet," and "Quod tyranni frequenter puniuntur homines permissione Dei" (von Moos, *Consolatio*, 2:225, and his comment at p. 226; V^1, ff. 42vB–43A); also see the section on "General Letters on Consolations for Death" in which Boncompagno discusses the Fall and man's descent "in hanc miserie vallem" and invokes the notion that the departed has migrated "ad celestis regni gloriam" (V^1, f. 36rB–vB); also see the spiritual consolations to be offered to him ". . . qui filium suum prius obtulerat ecclesie" (von Moos, *Consolatio*, 2:224), a section that Boncompagno opens, "Vapori stipule similatur omnis gloria terrenorum. Vita mortalium velut umbra lunatica evanescat, et humana conditio protoplasti rubigine denigrata subiacet vanitati. Unde universa vanitas est omnis homo vivens" (V^1, ff. 37vA–B); also see the biblical *exempla* of figures who wept moderately (see n. 78 above); also see religious passages and examples cited in von Moos (*Consolatio*, 1:407) and in Kristeller, "Francesco Bandini," p. 418n.

85. Boncompagno's interest in Cicero's moral thought is evidenced by his writing two treatises meant to rival (and, in content, partly to challenge) the *De amicitia* and *De senectute*. In contrast to Cicero's more sanguine praise of friendship, Boncompagno's *Amicitia* (c. 1204) is a considerably cynical and doleful catalogue of the many types of false friendship that far outnumber the genuine types and that decidedly dominate the social order (for an ed. see S. Nathan, *"Amicitia" di Maestro Boncompagno da Signa*, Miscellanea di letteratura del medio evo, no. 3 [1909]). In contrast to Cicero's eulogy of old age, Boncompagno's *De malo senectutis et senii* (c. 1240) is a lamentation on aging (for an ed. see "Il De *malo senectutis et senii* di Boncompagno da Signa," *Rendiconti della R. Accademia dei Lincei*, classe id scienze morali, series 5, no. 1 [1892], 49–67). The *De malo sen.* perhaps had both self-consolatory and consolatory purposes: Boncompagno suggests that he wrote the work "postquam cepi senectutis oneribus aggravari" (p. 51), and that it was meant to offer "consolationis refocilatio" to those in similar circumstances, the assumption being that misery loves company (on these works, see V. Pini's entry, *DBI* 11:722–23; also Witt, "Boncompagno," pp. 26–29). In the latter Witt argues that Boncompagno does not integrate Cicero's moral thought into his rhetorical theory; considering the case of the chapter "De cons.," I certainly agree that explicit classical references are virtually nonexistent, though Boncompagno's reference to Cato as a consolatory *exemplum* is likely drawn from Cicero (see preceding note). Furthermore, we should ask whether Cicero's notion of friendship (with its concept of mutual obligation and emotional ties) does not partly underlie Boncompagno's vision of psychological epistolary duty or exchange (for example, he devoted one section to "Littere quibus leprosus miseriam suam alicui suo amico revelat" [von Moos, *Consolatio*, 2:224]). As for the *De senectute*, its influence was perhaps indirectly at work in that section of the "De consolationibus" in which Boncompagno addressed the problem of writing *consolatoriae* for those "qui in senecta et senio constitutus" (von Moos, *Consolatio*, 2:224). Boncompagno's interest in Cicero's moral thought is not surprising given the influence of Cicero's *De inventione* and the Ps.-Ciceronian *Rhetorica ad Herennium* on medieval rhetoricians

and theorists both in France and Italy (on which see Murphy, *Rhetoric in the Middle Ages* and works cited in n. 71). In his writing of these two Ciceronian works, Boncompagno thus illustrates how the *dictatores* anticipated the humanists in beginning to explore and emulate ancient moral thought.

86. Other than the rhetoric manual, the moral treatise was another source of preceptive consolatory literature in the Duecento. In the first half of the century, the Lombard jurist Albertano da Brescia composed three treatises meant to instruct his sons in the proper conduct of life: for one he wrote the *De amore et dilectione Dei et proximi et aliarum rerum de forma vitae*; for another, the *De arte loquendi et tacendi*; for a third, the *Liber consolationis et consilii* (see Thor Sundby, "Introduction," in his ed. *Albertani Brixiensis Liber consolationis et consilii* [London, 1873], pp. xi–xii). Such works, from the pen of a jurist, reveal the interpenetration of legal, moral, rhetorical, and consolatory interests. The *Book of Consolation and Counsel*, addressed to his son the surgeon, was intended to complement the latter's medical knowledge with moral learning concerning the administering of *consilium, consolatio*, and *juvamen*. The work presents the story of Melibeus and Prudentia, which later made its way into the *Canterbury Tales*. The daughter of Melibeus is severely attacked—almost killed—by three neighbors, and the ensuing dialogue portrays the consolation and (principally) moral advice given Melibeus by his wife Prudentia concerning the matter. In a chapter titled "De consolatione," Prudentia, following Ovid's advice (*De rem. am.* 127–30) that words can be administered only after some natural grief has been expressed, presents her consolation. Her sources are both classical (including citations from several of Seneca's letters *Ad Luc.*) and Christian (including various biblical passages concerning sadness, such as Paul's 2 Cor. 7:10) (*Liber cons.*, pp. 3–6). The bulk of the treatise then proceeds to cover the areas of prudence and the giving, receiving, avoiding, and judging of counsels. There are also chapters on such problems as the will of God, fortune, vengeance, and clemency. In the end, Melibeus is reconciled with his enemies and shows great clemency toward them. An interesting work for a jurist to write, the treatise reveals how a criminal and legal matter can be handled in the loftier context of consolatory and moral thought. It also shows how consolatory interests, in concert with broader moral and social issues, were gaining some presence in literary discourse in the Duecento (it should also be noted that Albertano's *Liber cons.* and the other two above-mentioned treatises were translated into Italian twice in the second half of the century [Sundby, "Introduction," p. xii]).

87. The published work appeared under various titles, for which see A. Marigo, "Praefatio," in his ed., *Henrici Septimellensis: Elegia, sive de miseria* (Padua, 1926), p. 14.

88. One manuscript of the *Elegia* describes him as "optime peritus in arte grammatice ac in ditatoria facultate" (cited in Marigo, "Praefatio," p. 24). In his brief biography of Arrigo in his *De origine civitatis Florentiae et eiusdem famosis civibus*, Filippo Villani describes Arrigo's early education in "liberalibus artibus et studio poesis," his clerical vocation, and an unfortunate conflict that led to his impoverishment and to the writing of the *Elegia*: "Henricus, in causis in longum protractis consumpto patrimonio, liti ingruente vi, atque pauperie coactus est cedere, et pauperrime, relicto Beneficio, mendicare. Cumque is multis obsessus infortuniis

inquietam et miseram duceret vitam, opusculum suum edidit, invehens in For-
tunam,. . ." (*Liber de origine civitatis Florentiae et eiusdem famosis civibus*, ed. G. C.
Galletti [Florence, 1847], p. 31). On Arrigo and the *Elegia* see, besides Marigo
("Praefatio," here, esp. pp. 24–25), also A. Monteverdi's entry, *DBI* 4:315–16; D.
M. Manni's introductory letter "All' illustriss. . . Sig. Marchese Bartolommeo
Corsini," in his ed. of the vernacular version of the work, *Arrighetto ovvero Trattado
contro all'avversità della fortuna di Arrigo da Settimello* (Florence, 1730); on Arrigo's
sources in the *Elegia* see G. Spagnola, "La cultura letteraria di Arrigo da Settimello," *GSLI* 93 (1929), 1–68.

89. See *Elegia*, ed. Marigo, p. 46. Arrigo's consoler (the "mulier" referred to as
"Fronesis" and vera sophya" [see pp. 45, 47, 73]) tenders a *contemptus* of the variability of fortune, solace for the circumstances of poverty, and a general enchiridion
for virtuous living.

90. "Hic libellus, cui titulus Henriguethus est, primam discentibus artem ap-
tissimus, per scholas Italiae continuo frequentatur" (*De orig. civ. Flor.* . . , p. 31;
Marigo, "Praefatio," p. 25). On the dating of Villani's treatise and on Salutati's
emendation of it, see F. Novati, Salutati's *Epist.* 2:47n; B. L. Ullman, "Filippo
Villani's Copy of his History of Florence," in his *Studies in the Italian Renaissance*
(1955; rev. and exp., Rome, 1973), pp. 239–45.

91. Monteverdi, pp. 315–16; Manni's introductory comments to his ed. of the
Arrighetto ovvero Trattado contro all'avversità della fortuna.

92. On the citation of the *Elegia* in the *volgare* version of one of Albertano da
Brescia's moral treatises (appearing under the title *Trattado della forma della vita*)
see Manni, who also gives some evidence that Petrarch may have borrowed from
the vernacular version of the *Elegia* in his *Canzonieri* (Manni, "All'illustriss . . .
Corsini," pp. xxii–xxiii, xxv–xxvi). The certain impact of the *Elegia* on at least one
Renaissance consolatory treatise can be seen in the Spanish work, *Tratado de la
consolación* (1424), of Enrique de Villena. (On the influence of Arrigo's *Elegia* [as
well as that of Petrarch's *De vita solitaria, Bucolicum carmen*, and *Africa*] on this
work, see D. Carr, "Prologo," in his ed. of the *Tratado* [Madrid, 1976], pp. lxxxv–
lxxxvi).

CHAPTER 1

PETRARCH AS SELF-CONSOLER: THE *SECRETUM*

1. For a discussion of Petrarch's interests in rhetorical counsel and therapy, his
psychological concerns in the *Secretum* and the *De remediis*, and the relation of his
thought to medical and pastoral thought, see Charles Trinkaus, *The Poet as Philosopher: Petrarch and the Formation of Renaissance Consciousness* (New Haven, Conn.,
and London, 1979), passim. The scholarship on the vernacular and the Latin
Petrarch is voluminous. For selected studies on the three principal concerns of my
discussion—the *Secretum*, the *Epistolae*, and the *De remediis*—see nn. 4, 17, and 39,
and Chaps. 2 and 3 below.

2. For a biography of Petrarch see Ernest H. Wilkins, *Life of Petrarch* (Chicago
and London, 1961); also his *Studies in the Life and Works of Petrarch* (Cambridge,
Mass., 1955); his *Petrarch's Eight Years in Milan* (Cambridge, Mass., 1958); his

Petrarch's Later Years (Cambridge, Mass., 1959); also B. G. Kohl, "Introduction" to his translation of *Sen.* 14.1 in *The Earthly Republic: Italian Humanists on Government and Society*, ed. B. G. Kohl and R. G. Witt (Philadelphia, 1978), pp. 25–32. On Petrarch's clerical positions and aspirations see Wilkins, *Studies*, pp. 4–32, 63–80. In particular see Petrarch's revealing comments in *Variae* 15 concerning his reluctance to assume full priestly duties: "Praelaturam itaque nullam volo, nec volui quidem unquam; similiter nec beneficium curatum quodcunque, quamvis opulentissimum; satis est mihi unius animae meae cura: atque utinam illi uni sufficiam!" (cited in Wilkins, *Studies*, p. 31; *Epistolae: De rebus familiaribus et Variae*, ed. G. Fracassetti, 3 vols. [Florence, 1859–63], 3:336). Cf. n. 5 below. Thus, though he was *professionally* the beneficiary of ecclesiastical benefices, he was not *vocationally* a priest; because he did not serve as nor perceive himself as a priest, I shall generally refer to Petrarch as a "lay" consoler.

3. On the insecurity of the humanist life, cf. Charles Trinkaus, *Adversity's Noblemen: The Italian Humanists on Happiness* (New York, 1940).

4. On the dating of *Fam.* 1.9 and other fictitious letters in the *Familiares* see A. Bernardo, "Introduction," in *Francesco Petrarca: Rerum familiarum libri I–VIII*, trans. A. Bernardo (Albany, N.Y., 1975) pp. xx–xxvii; also G. Billanovich, *Petrarca letterato*, vol. 1, *Lo scrittoio del Petrarca* (Rome, 1947), pp. 3–55; E. H. Wilkins, *Petrarch's Correspondence* (Padua, 1960), pp. 49–50. Hereafter, unless indicated otherwise, all dates assigned to Petrarch's letters will be drawn from Wilkins' *Petrarch's Correspondence*, which catalogues the datings of G. Fracassetti and other scholars. With the understanding that there is sometimes uncertainty and disagreement concerning the dating of Petrarch's letters, I follow Fracassetti's dates, except when Wilkins disagrees, in which case I follow Wilkins.

5. *Le Familiari*, ed. V. Rossi (vol. 1–3) and U. Bosco (vol. 4)(Florence, 1933–42), 1:45 (hereafter, this edition cited as Rossi); A. Bernardo's translation in his *Rerum familiarum libri I–VIII*, p. 47. Hereafter, when his translation is indicated, I either quote or follow Bernardo's rendering. Given Petrarch's reluctance to accept a pastoral *cura animarum* (see n. 2), it is interesting to note his wording in this passage: "Animi cura philosophum querit, eruditio lingue oratoris est propria; neutra nobis negligenda, si nos ut aiunt, humo tollere et per ora virum volitare propositum est" (Rossi, 1:45). As a moral philosopher and rhetorician Petrarch perhaps saw his province of the *cura animi* as parallel to but distinct from the *cura animae*.

6. Rossi, 1:47–48; Bernardo, *Fam. I–VIII*, pp. 49–50.

7. Writing to his wife from exile, Ovid would urge her to weep, offering the larger truth that "est quaedam flere voluptas; / expletur lacrimis egeriturque dolor" (*Tristia* 4.3.37–38). On Ovid and Petrarch see R. Durling, "Introduction," in *Petrarch's Lyric Poems: The "Rime sparse" and Other Lyrics*, trans. and ed. R. Durling (Cambridge, Mass., and London, 1976), pp. 1–33; also F. Rico, *Vida u obra de Petrarca*, vol. 1, *Lectura del "Secretum"* (Padua, 1974), p. 204.

8. Petrarch's *Rime* (in the *Canzoniere*) are replete with the language of sweet grief. For instance, in those verses dealing with Laura "*in vita*" see "se ria, ond'è sì dolce ogni tormento" (132, 4); "Pascomi di dolor, piangendo rido" (134, 12; cf. *Opere latine di Francesco Petrarca*, ed. A. Bufano, 2 vols. [Turin, 1975], 1:141,

n.69); "dolce pianto" (155, 9); "dolci sospiri" (171, 14). Such sweet longing, of course, continues to be found in those verses on Laura *"in morte"* (*Rime* 267 ff.): e.g., "il dolce acerbo e 'l bel piacer molesto" (331, 19). For a guide to Petrarch's use of such language in the *Rime* see *Concordanza delle rime di Francesco Petrarca*, ed. K. McKenzie (Oxford, 1912). On sensibilities of mutability and death in Petrarch, see U. Bosco, *Francesco Petrarca* (Turin, 1946; rept. Bari, 1973), pp. 50–76.

9. For discussions on Petrarch's interest in *voluptas dolendi* see n. 15 below.

10. For a Latin verse on Laura, the *Laurus amena* (or *Elegia ritmica*), to which Petrarch would allude in the *Secretum* Bk. 3, see E. H. Wilkins, *The Making of the "Canzoniere" and Other Petrarchan Studies* (Rome, 1951), pp. 302–4 (esp. lines 7–8 for the theme of sweet grief). For a comment concerning Laura's death which Petrarch wrote in his copy of Vergil see Wilkins, *Life of Petrarch*, p. 77. For verse on Laura *in morte* see, besides *Rime* 267 ff., the *Triumph of Death*. On Petrarch's *Rime* and the loss of Laura see Wilkins, *The Making of the "Canzoniere,"* pp. 190–93; Durling, "Introduction," in *Petrarch's Lyric Poems*, pp. 1–33. Also, see the doleful metrical letter *Ad seipsum: Ep. met.* 1.14 in Petrarca, *Rime, Trionfi, e poesie latine*, ed. F. Neri, G. Martellotti, E. Bianchi, and N. Sapegno, La letteratura italiana, storia e testi, no. 6 (Milan and Naples, 1951), pp. 750–59 (Wilkins, *Life of Petrarch*, pp. 79–80; for dating see H. Baron, *Petrarch's "Secretum": Its Making and Its Meaning* [Cambridge, Mass., 1985], p. 240, n. 68). For a study of Petrarch's attitudes toward grief and death, as seen in various self-consolatory writings in prose and verse (particularly the *Triumphs*), following his losses in 1348 and 1361, see R. Watkins, "Petrarch and the Black Death: From Fear to Monuments," *SR* 19 (1972), 196–223. As for Petrarch's funerary verse in general, see, on his mother's death (c. 1318–19), the *Panegyricum in funere matris* in *Latin Writings of the Italian Humanists*, ed. F. Gragg (New Rochelle, N.Y., 1981), pp. 43–44.

11. *Rime, Trionfi, e poesie latine*, ed. F. Neri, *et al.*, p. 826.

12. See Rossi, 1:176. In contemplating this genre, Petrarch cited Cicero's similar endeavor concerning his daughter (the *Consolatio*) and Ambrose's concerning his brother (the *De excessu fratris sui Satyri*). Petrarch never wrote this particular work, though *Sen.* 10.4 approaches this genre (see Chap. 2 below).

13. Rossi, 2:121; Bernardo, *Fam. I–VIII*, p. 364. This tension between emotion and reason will continue to preoccupy Petrarch. It will become almost a psychological *"conflictus,"* an analogue to the spiritual *"conflictus"* of the *Secretum*. See discussion in text below and Chap. 2.

14. Rossi, 2:122; Bernardo, *Fam. I–VIII*, p. 366.

15. See *Fam.* 4.10 (at Rossi, 1:179), and from the plague years of 1348–49 see the mournful *Fam.* 8.7 and 9 (in the latter, Petrarch admitting to "Socrates" that "weeping also has a certain kind of sadness with which I have unhappily nourished myself in these days . . ." [Rossi, 2:182; Bernardo, *Fam. I–VIII*, p. 423]; on both letters see Chap. 2 below). Also see comments later in *Sen.* 3.1 to Boccaccio: "ego vero malis meis pascor, voluptate quadam effera, et qui fuerunt gemitus cibi sunt, impletumque est in me seu Davidicum illud, 'Fuerunt mihi lachrymae meae panes die ac nocte' [Ps. 42:3], sive illud Ovidianum, 'Cura dolorque animi, lachrymaeque alimenta fuere' [*Met.* 10.75]" (*Opera omnia* [Basel, 1554], p. 847). On weeping also see *Var.* 58 (discussed in Chap. 2 below). On *voluptas dolendi* in

the writings of figures such as Ovid, Seneca, Statius, Pliny the Younger, Ambrose, and Augustine, and on Petrarch's interest in this sensibility see von Moos, *Consolatio*, 3:55–56; Rico, *Lectura del "Secretum,"* pp. 202–6 (esp. p. 204n for several further instances of indulgent sorrow in Petrarch's writings on death); A. Bobbio, "Seneca e la formazione spirituale e culturale del Petrarca," *Bibliofilia* 43 (1941), 224–91, at p. 247; R. Kuhn, *The Demon of Noontide: Ennui in Western Literature* (Princeton, 1976), pp. 68–75; H. Cochin, *Le frère de Pétrarque et le livre "Du repos des religieux"* (Paris, 1903), pp. 205–21; also see nn. 54–55 below.

16. Petrarch also wrote penitential verse that resembled and possibly anticipated the ascetic, confessional tone of the *Secretum*. These penitential psalms, like those of David, are reflections on his own spiritual state and on the grandeur of God, and invocations of divine aid and mercy (see notes in Petrarca, *Rime, Trionfi, e Poesie latine*, ed. F. Neri, *et al.*, pp. 836–45; Wilkins, *Life of Petrarch*, pp. 37–38). It is uncertain whether these *Psalmi* preceded the start of the *Secretum*. Previously thought to be of 1342–43, they are now considered to be of 1347–49 (Baron, *Petrarch's "Secretum,"* p. 4; also his "Petrarch's *Secretum*: Was It Revised—and Why?" in his *From Petrarch to Leonardo Bruni: Studies in Humanistic and Political Literature* [Chicago and London, 1968], pp. 51–101 at 57, 90).

Another work that reflects Petrarch's sense of spiritual conflict and that scholars have compared to the *Secretum* is *Rime* 264 ("I'vo pensando") of 1347–48 (see Baron, *Petrarch's "Secretum,"* pp. 47–57).

17. Much has been written on the famous dialogue, Francisco Rico's *Lectura del "Secretum"* providing the most exhaustive study of sources and traditions. Among the more important other studies are F. Tateo, *Dialogo interiore e polemica ideologica nel "Secretum" del Petrarca* (Florence, 1965); Baron, *Petrarch's "Secretum,"*; C. Trinkaus, *In Our Image and Likeness: Humanity and Divinity in Italian Humanist Thought*, 2 vols. (Chicago and London, 1970), 1:3–50; also his *The Poet as Philosopher*, esp. pp. 52–89. For studies focusing on the section concerning *accidia-aegritudo* in Book 2, see n. 39 below.

18. Despite continuing scholarly disagreement over the principal dates of composition and/or revision, there is some consensus that the work was written or revised in stages. Allusions in the text that would date the dialogue to 1342–43 should perhaps be viewed in the same light as those fictitious letters that Petrarch also predated (see Baron's discussion [*Petrarch's "Secretum,"* pp. 4–5] of Rico's thesis that the tendency toward predating that Billanovich [*Petrarca letterato*] found in the *Familiares* should be applied to the *Secretum*). A key piece of evidence concerning the composition of the *Secretum* is a notation at the end of the transcript of Petrarch's autograph: "Modo 3. 1353. 1349. 1347." (see Baron, *Petrarch's "Secretum,"* passim, esp. p. 78; Baron, "Petrarch's *Secretum*: Was It Revised—and Why?"; Rico, *Lectura del "Secretum,"* passim). Rico and Baron agree with earlier scholars that these dates could refer to stages of composition or revision, but they differ significantly on the details. Rico argues that 1353 is the date of a major rewriting of earlier versions of the dialogue composed in 1347 and 1349; though drawing on the earlier drafts, the 1353 version nonetheless represents the true date of composition of the dialogue (*Lectura del "Secretum,"* esp. 1–16). Baron counters Rico's thesis, contending that the principal portion of the dialogue was com-

posed in 1347 and revised in 1349 and 1353 with sections reflecting changes in Petrarch's life and thought. He argues that the revisions of 1349 and 1353 reflect Petrarch's later move toward Stoic thought; for instance, he cites Stoic aspects of parts of the section on *acedia-aegritudo* (*Petrarch's "Secretum,"* passim, esp. pp. 72–183.) I have no intention here of entering the debate on dating. Suffice it to say that several factors point to 1347–53 (rather than 1342–43) as the period of composition: besides Petrarch's above-mentioned manuscript notation and besides other arguments advanced by Baron (in *Petrarch's "Secretum,"* pp. 3–6), one must consider other writings of the period 1347 ff. that reflect spiritual sensibilities similar to those in the *Secretum.* Such writings as the *De otio rel.*, the *Psalmi pen.*, and *Fam.* 10.3 and 5 (to his brother Gherardo) were, like the *Secretum*, possibly piqued in large measure by Gherardo's entering the Carthusian monastery in 1343 (on these and similar works see Baron, *Petrarch's "Secretum,"* pp. 4–6 and passim; also the following note).

19. The *De otio religioso* is a spiritual exhortation to Gherardo and his fellow Carthusians. In a similar vein is *Fam.* 10.3 (1348) to Gherardo, where again Petrarch urges on his brother in his monastic life and reflects on his own weakness and misery in the *saeculum* (Rossi, *Le Familiari*, 2:286–300). Cf. Petrarch's invocations to divine mercy in this letter to those in the *De otio* (*Opere*, 1:658) and the *Psalmi pen.* (see n. 16 above). *Fam.* 10.5 (1352) to Gherardo also discusses the contrasts between Gherardo's and Petrarch's spiritual lives; in it Petrarch says that he has adopted his brother's recommended spiritual regimen of offering confession, singing praises to God, and staying away from women. *Fam.* 4.1, the famous "Ascent of Mt. Ventoux" (1352–53), is an allegory on his brother's straighter climb to God (Bernardo, "Introduction," in *Fam. I–VIII*, p. xxix; Billanovich's dating in *Petrarca letterato*, pp. 193–98). On the *De vita solitaria* see n. 57 below.

In a word, Gherardo's monastic vocation seems to have provoked in Petrarch a heightened spiritual awareness and sense of insecurity concerning his secular way of life. Such religious doubts almost certainly fostered the interest in spiritual reflection and healing found in the *Secretum.* Baron discusses and rejects the thesis (for example, in A. Foresti, *Aneddoti della vita di Francesco Petrarca* [Brescia, 1928], pp. 98–131) that Petrarch experienced a particular spiritual crisis, which affected his perspectives and writings. He suggests that Foresti, who argued that Gherardo's taking the cowl was the catalyst for such a spiritual crisis, mistakenly believed the "I'vo pensando" to have been written in 1343 after Gherardo's retreat, citing this searching *canzone* as illustrative of Petrarch's new sensibility. Baron counters that the "I'vo pensando" and the *Secretum* came in 1347, some significant time after 1343, and that Gherardo was not the cause of concerns expressed in the writings of 1347 (Baron, *Petrarch's "Secretum,"* pp. 4–6, 47–52, 202–8, 218–20, and passim). I disagree, for I think it plausible that Petrarch's reaction to Gherardo's decision could well have taken some years to germinate. It eventually may have become a focus for his own doubts about his spiritual status. Writings of 1346–48 (the *De vita sol.*, the *De otio rel.*, the *Psalmi pen.*, the *Secretum*, *Fam.* 10.3) all reflect spiritual concerns that perhaps were piqued by Gherardo's new life.

20. Trinkaus, *Adversity's Noblemen*, p. 42n; Rico, *Lectura del "Secretum,"* p. 34n. In the 1554 Basel *Opera* it is titled *De contemptu mundi, colloquiorum liber, quem Secretum suum inscripsit* (*Opera*, p. 374).

21. This tension could have been due partly to the differing stages of composition (on Baron's thesis concerning which see n. 18 above), though in some measure Boethius' *Cons. phil.* (Bks. 2 and 3) does perhaps contain the germ (though in more classical terms) of such a tension: here Lady Philosophy consoles Boethius for his particular misfortunes (in the comparative light of the fortunes of others [2. pr. 4]) and then discusses the futility of the desire for fame and the insufficiency and irrelevance of worldly blandishments in the attainment of human happiness.

22. On the term *conflictus* and the genre of the *Secretum*, see Rico, *Lectura del "Secretum,"* pp. 16–38, esp. p. 34.

23. For Hildebert's treatise see *PL* 171:989–1004. The importance of French influences on early Italian humanism needs further study. I think Petrarch could have been influenced not only by Hildebert's *De querimonia et conflictu*, but also by Abelard's famous *Ad amicum suum consolatoria* ("*Historia calamitatum*"), which is also a self-consolatory lament (*Historia calamitatum*, ed. J. Monfrin, 3rd ed. [Paris, 1967]; on Petrarch's possession of a manuscript containing this [and other] of Abelard's letters see Monfrin, *Historia calamitatum*, p. 18–19; on this manuscript also see Leclercq, "L'amitié dans les lettres au moyen age"). Cf. Abelard's language ". . . de calamitatum mearum hystoria . . ." to Petrarch's phrasing in the *Secretum* Bk. 1, when Franciscus suggests that in his reading of Augustine's *Confessions*: ". . . legere me arbitrer non alienam sed propriam mee peregrinationis historiam." *Opere latine di Francesco Petrarca*, ed. A. Bufano, 2 vols. (Turin, 1975), 1:68 (on this ed. see n. 25 below). Also cf. Petrarch's comment in *Fam.* 8.7: ". . . historias virorum illustrium sperabamus, unam cernimus proprii doloris historiam . . ." (Rossi, 2:175.)

24. See Rico, *Lectura del "Secretum,"* pp. 16–38. For a study tying the *Soliloquies* to the *Cons. phil.*, see E. T. Silk, "Boethius's *Consolatio Philosophiae* as a Sequel to Augustine's Dialogues and *Soliloquia*," *Harvard Theological Review* 32 (1939), 19–39. As for the influence of Augustine on Petrarch's thought in general, see, besides Rico (*Lectura del "Secretum"*), Tateo, *Dialogo interiore*; Bobbio, "Seneca e Petrarca"; P. O. Kristeller, "Augustine and the Early Renaissance," in his *Studies*, pp. 355–72; K. Heitmann, *Fortuna und Virtus: Eine Studie zu Petrarcas Lebensweisheit* (Cologne and Graz, 1958); Heitmann, "L'insegnamento agostiniano nel 'Secretum' del Petrarca," in *Studi Petrarcheschi*, Accademia Petrarca di lettere arti e scienze di Arezzo, vol. 7 (Bologna, 1961), 187–93; P. Courcelle, "Pétrarque entre Saint Augustin et les Augustins du XIVᵉ siècle," in *Studi Petrarcheschi*, pp. 51–71; Courcelle, *Les "Confessions" de saint Augustin dans la tradition littéraire: Antécédents et postérité* (Paris, 1963), pp. 329–51; P. Gerosa, *Umanesimo cristiano del Petrarca: Influenza agostiniana, attinenze medievali* (Turin, 1966); Trinkaus, *Image and Likeness*, 1:3–50; Trinkaus, *Poet as Philosopher*, pp. 52–89; W. Bouwsma, "The Two Faces of Humanism: Stoicism and Augustinianism in Renaissance Thought," in *Itinerarium Italicum*, ed. H. Oberman with T. Brady, Jr. (Leiden, 1975), pp. 3–60; Rico, "Petrarca y el *De vera religione*," *IMU* 17 (1974), 313–64.

As for the influence of Boethius on Petrarch, see, besides Rico's *Lectura del "Secretum,"* E. Carrara, "Petrarca," *Enciclopedia Italiana di scienze, lettere ed arte* (Rome, 1935), 27:14; Patch, *Tradition of Boethius*, pp. 103, 166; Diekstra, "Introduction," esp. pp. 37–43. In his major study, *La "Consolation de Philosophie,"* P. Courcelle fails to discuss the influence of Boethius on Petrarch's *Secretum* and *De remediis*. One of the principal goals of my discussion of the *Secretum* is to stress the importance and meaning of the Boethian features of the dialogue.

For more general studies on Petrarch's interest in and collection of classical and Christian sources see P. de Nolhac, *Pétrarque et l'humanisme*, 2nd ed., 2 vols. (Paris, 1907); also B. L. Ullman, "Petrarch's Favorite Books," in his *Studies in the Italian Renaissance* (Rome, 1955), pp. 117–37.

25. ". . . passionum expertarum curator optime." *Opere*, ed. A. Bufano, 1:48. This edition essentially follows the text found in the Ricciardi edition by E. Carrara (Francesco Petrarca, *Prose*, ed. G. Martellotti and P. G. Ricci with E. Carrara and E. Bianchi, La letteratura italiana, storia e testi, no. 7 [Milan and Naples, 1955]), including Carrara's source identifications. It also includes an Italian translation and additional notes by A. Bufano. I will quote or follow (with minor alterations) the translation of W. H. Draper in his *Petrarch's Secret or the Soul's Conflict with Passion* (London, 1911); here, Draper, *Petrarch's Secret*, p. 4. I will also draw on Bufano's Italian translation in *Opere*.

26. On the non-Augustinian (particularly Stoicizing) aspects of Augustinus' position in the *Secretum* see Heitmann, "L'insegnamento agostiniano nel 'Secretum'"; Trinkaus, *Image and Likeness*, 1:4–17; Trinkaus, *Poet as Philosopher*, pp. 27–29, 58; Bouwsma, "Two Faces of Humanism," esp. pp. 19, 28–31, 34–35.

27. Augustine's drama of the will was central to Petrarch's view of his own moral condition (*Opere*, 1:66; cf. Augustine's *Conf.* 8.8; Trinkaus, *Image and Likeness*, 1:9).

28. On Franciscus as Everyman and on Franciscus as Petrarch, see Trinkaus, *Image and Likeness*, 1:29, 325–26, n. 5; also his *Poet as Philosopher*, p. 58. The figure of Franciscus does perhaps unite the medieval literary allegorical tradition with autobiographical experience. Baron (*Petrarch's "Secretum,"* pp. 174–75) rightly cautions those scholars who overemphasize the role of the former at the expense of the latter in their appraisals of Franciscus. I agree. The autobiographical quality of Franciscus is not only substantive but also central to understanding the historical importance of the *Secretum*.

29. But also cf. the *contemptus* theme in Book 2, in the discussion of avarice and ambition. *Opere*, 1:124–26.

30. On the "Platonic" influence of Cicero's *Tusc.* Bk. 1 and the *Dream of Scipio*, see discussion in text below; on that of Augustine's *De vera religione*, see n. 37 below.

31. For a discussion of classical and medieval influences in Petrarch's conception of the meditation on death, see Rico, *Lectura del "Secretum,"* pp. 81–122. The literary, oral, and visual image of death gained an increasingly commanding presence in high and late medieval and early modern culture. In art, for instance, the motif of the meeting between three living and three dead figures emerged in the first quarter of the thirteenth century in Italy. The intensification of a necromania

following the 1348 plague can be seen, of course, in the *danse macabre* which proliferated in the north in the fifteenth century and thereafter, Holbein's *Pictures of Death* and Pieter Brueghel's *Triumph of Death* being two well-known sixteenth-century examples. See A. Tenenti, *Il senso della morte e l'amore della vita nel Rinascimento* (Turin, 1957), esp. pp. 462–63, 475, and plates 45, 52–56; L. White, "Death and the Devil," in *The Darker Vision of the Renaissance: Beyond the Fields of Reason*, ed. R. Kinsman (Berkeley and Los Angeles, 1974), pp. 25–46, esp. at 30–31; J. Huizinga's chapter "The Vision of Death" in his *The Waning of the Middle Ages* (New York, 1954), pp. 138–51; N. Beaty, *The Craft of Dying: A Study in the Literary Tradition of the "Ars moriendi" in England* (New Haven, Conn., 1979), pp. 36–53, esp. at 43–45; Aries, *Hour of Our Death*, pp. 110–39.

On the influence of Petrarch's *Triumph of Death* on the analogous artistic motif see Tenenti, *Il senso della morte*, pp. 468–77 and plates 32, 41–43; also D. D. Carnicelli, "The Trionfi and Renaissance Iconography," in "Introduction," in *Lord Morley's "Triumphes of Fraunces Petrarke": The First English Translation of the "Trionfi,"* ed. Carnicelli (Cambridge, Mass., 1971), pp. 38–46. Petrarch's *Triumph*, however, cannot be considered the origin or sole source of such artistic representations: an artistic *Trionfo della Morte* preceding Petrarch's poetic *Triumph* could be found in the Camposanto of Pisa (Carnicelli, "Trionfi," p. 180, n. 2). On Petrarch's *Triumph of Death*, also see Watkins, "Petrarch and the Black Death."

32. *Opere*, 1:82; Draper, *Petrarch's Secret*, pp. 32–33. The macabre picture of death is also found in Petrarch's *De otio rel.* Bk. 2, where he presents an ascetic *ubi sunt* concerning the transformation of the famous into putrid corpses, posing it as a counterpoint to more sanguine classical attitudes that would view the dead as a source of secular inspiration (*Opere*, 1:708–12; text of G. Rotondi, with an Italian translation and notes by B. Aracri, and classical source identifications drawn from the Rotondi ed.).

33. *Opere*, 1:84; Draper, *Petrarch's Secret*, p. 35. Cf. *De otio rel.* Bk. 2: *Opere*, 1:717.

34. *Opere*, 1:60.

35. *Opere*, 1:82; Draper, *Petrarch's Secret*, p. 33.

36. See *Opere*, 1:238–56 and Carrara's note at 238. Petrarch follows Boethius (*Cons. phil.* 2. pr. 7) in drawing upon the *Dream of Scipio* (from the *De republica* Bk. 6, but extant to both authors only as a fragment *via* Macrobius) as a cure for the desire for fame. The *Somnium* depicts the deceased Scipio Africanus the Elder returning to counsel his grandson Scipio the Younger on the mutability and insignificance of human fame in the expanse of time and space.

The reflection on death and worldly mutability was a consistent concern both in Petrarch's verse and in much of his moral thought. His sense of temporality perhaps reflects a fusion of "secular" and "sacred" attitudes toward time. As the *Secretum* shows, the classical, philosophical sensibility and the medieval, theological sensibility concerning the brevity of life share a common assumption: a sense of temporality inspires mortals to be aware of their true nature. But whereas ancient notions often reflect a lament and resignation concerning the loss of time, medieval ones contemn life's shortness together with every aspect of mortal, mundane existence. Tenenti's thesis (*Il senso della morte*) that part of the Renaissance concern with death is a heightened attachment to life is certainly borne out by this secular aspect of Petrarch's thought. Petrarch is an important transitional figure in the passage from sacred to secular attitudes toward time. To the medieval ascetic's sacred contempt of the temporal, he adds an ancient and "modern" secular lament. In doing so he mirrors that larger psychological phenomenon of the "modern" literary and artistic contemplation on death and skulls. Though grounded in ascetic practices, this contemplation—e.g., Hamlet's meditation on Yorick's skull—becomes the quintessential secular lament. See B. G. Lyons, *Voices of Melancholy: Studies in Literary Treatments of Melancholy in Renaissance England* (New York, 1975), p. 104; cf. U. Bosco's chapter "Il senso della labilità" in his *Petrarca*, pp. 50–62.

37. See Diekstra, "Introduction," pp. 42–46. Citing the *Aen.* 6.730–34, Augustinus refers to the four affects in a highly Platonic context as corporeal contagions—in this, Petrarch is drawing on Augustine's characterization of Vergil's passage as "Platonic" (in *De civ. Dei* 14.3), a characterization Petrarch commented upon in a marginal notation of his copy of the *Aen.* (Heitmann, "Le'insegnamento agostiniano nel 'Secretum,'" esp. at pp. 188–89; Heitmann, *Fortuna und Virtus*, pp. 89–92, 127). In pursuing this subject, Franciscus refers to Augustine's discussion of the notion of corporeal distresses in the *De vera religione*, a work that Augustinus here characterizes as being not only "*catholica*" in doctrine but also "*platonica ac socratica*" (*Opere*, 1:92–94).

38. Cf. Dante's allusions to his own spiritual state in the *Purgatorio*: on pride see *Purg.* 13.136–38; on anger, 15.115–32.

39. *Opere*, 1:140; Draper, *Petrarch's Secret*, p. 84. Petrarch's "confessional" requires little time for the treatment of envy, gluttony, and anger; ambition is not part of the canon of seven deadly sins and is linked with avarice. For discussions of the *Secretum* Bk. 2 and its treatment of the deadly sins, and, in particular, of *accidia*, see *Opere*, ed. Bufano, 1:102n, 114n, 133n; also Tateo, *Dialogo interiore*, pp. 39–54; S. Wenzel, "Petrarch's *Accidia*," *SR* 8 (1961), 36–48; Wenzel, *Sin of Sloth*, pp. 155–63; E. H. Wilkins, "On Petrarch's *Accidia* and His Adamantine Chains," *Speculum* 37 (1962), 589–94; Baron, *Petrarch's "Secretum,"* pp. 23ff.; Trinkaus, *Poet as Philosopher*, pp. 65–69; R. Kuhn, *Demon of Noontide*, pp. 68–75.

40. On Petrarch's fusing the medieval sin and the Stoic affect, and on earlier precedents for such a fusion, see Wenzel, "Petrarch's *Accidia*" and Wenzel, *Sin of Sloth*, pp. 156–63; Trinkaus, *Image and Likeness*, 1:334–35 n. 62.

41. Wenzel, *Sin of Sloth*, p. 162.

42. For a history of the term see Wenzel, *Sin of Sloth*. In his Appendix A, "*Acedia* and the Humors*," Wenzel cites numerous high and late medieval texts that connect *accidia* and melancholy, including some that offer guidelines for the office of confession recommending that the priest consider the humoral nature of the penitent (pp. 191–94; also see pp. 59–60). On *accidia* also see R. Kuhn, who argues that nothing analogous in antiquity—at least not *taedium vitae* or *horror loci*—could match the intensity of this psychic malady (*Demon of Noontide*, pp. 15–64, esp. at 64).

43. This is a summary of Wenzel (*Sin of Sloth*), who argues that Aquinas concentrated his discussion of *accidia* on its more sublime aspect as a "sadness concerning the divine good" rather than on its secular dimension, considered harmful because

it might impede spiritual happiness and duty (*Sin of Sloth*, pp. 47–67). To illustrate the conjunction of differing medieval perceptions of *accidia*, Wenzel cites the thirteenth-century Franciscan David of Augsburg's definition of the sin: "The vice of *accidia* has three kinds. The first is a certain bitterness of the mind which cannot be pleased by anything cheerful or wholesome. It feeds upon disquiet and loathes human intercourse. This is what the Apostle calls the sorrow of the world that worketh death. It inclines to despair, diffidence, and suspicions, and sometimes drives its victim to suicide when he is oppressed by unreasonable grief. Such sorrow arises sometimes from previous impatience, sometimes from the fact that one's desire for some object has been delayed or frustrated, and sometimes from the abundance of melancholic humors, in which case it behooves the physician rather than the priest to prescribe a remedy" (*Sin of Sloth*, p. 160). The second type of *accidia* is a laziness; the third a torpor concerning spiritual things (the vice essentially developed in early Egyptian monastic thought) (*Sin of Sloth*, pp. 160, 180). Referring to the *Secretum* Bk. 2, Wenzel rightly argues: "Of these three kinds, it is the first with which Petrarch's *acedia* agrees neatly and in detail" (*Sin of Sloth*, p. 160).

44. *Opere*, 1:142; Draper, *Petrarch's Secret*, pp. 84–85.

45. *Opere*, 1:196; see Bufano's observation of this textual similarity at *Opere*, p. 142 n. 69; on Petrarch's interest in *voluptas dolendi*, see n. 15 above. Cf. the probable influence here of Boethius' *Cons. phil.* 2. pr. 39–41.

46. On Burton and other writings on melancholy see Chap. 7 and Conclusion.

47. Petrarch mentions Cicero's sarcastic comment (in *Tusc.* 1.33.80) on [Ps.–] Aristotle's notion of the melancholy of the gifted (in *Problems* 30.1) in *Fam.* 20.14 (Rossi *Le Familiari*, 4:44–45; R. Klibansky, E. Panofsky, and F. Saxl, *Saturn and Melancholy: Studies in the History of Natural Philosophy, Religion, and Art* [New York, 1964], 249n). Petrarch undoubtedly was also influenced by Cicero's more serious critique of the term in *Tusc.* 3.5.11 (cf. Lyons, *Voices of Melancholy*, p. 5). Also, cf. Augustine's rejection of *aegritudo* and *dolor* in favor of *tristitia* for similar reasons in *De civ. Dei* 14.7 (Wenzel, *Sin of Sloth*, p. 162).

48. L. Babb suggests that it is in the Renaissance that lovesickness came to be classed as a type of melancholy disease (*The Elizabethan Malady: A Study of Melancholia in English Literature from 1580 to 1642* [East Lansing, Mich., 1951]).

49. Franciscus' sufferings at the hands of Fortuna and his subsequent consolation by Augustinus parallel the structure of Boethius' work considerably. Seneca's *De tran. animi*, which Augustinus cites as a source of solace for this disease, also mentions the various assaults of fortune. The Ps.-Senecan *De remediis fortuitorum*, of course, also treats this theme. But in comparison to these classical precedents Petrarch seems most fully to define a specific *malady of despair* in terms of the woes of misfortune. In this respect, his truest model among the ancient works is probably Boethius' *Cons. phil.*, which uses the language of sickness, mental disquiet, and sadness ("*aeger*," "*mentis perturbatio*," "*tristitia*"). On *tristitia*, see *Cons. phil.* 1. pr. 3.

50. *Opere*, 1:142, 144; see Wenzel, *Sin of Sloth*, p. 157; Kuhn, *Demon of Noontide*, p. 72.

51. Wenzel, *Sin of Sloth*, p. 162. Wenzel cites various theological and other definitions of the deadly sin on which Petrarch could have drawn (p. 246, n. 67).

And though a "worldly" dimension of *accidia* had been defined prior to Petrarch (as seen in n. 43 above), still, as Wenzel argues, Petrarch provides a remarkably detailed, autobiographical development of that secular dimension, concentrating not on the potential spiritual dangers (e.g., the neglect of piety) of such a sorrow but on the psychological causes and cures. He also ponders the explanation for Petrarch's replacement of *accidia* with *torpor animi* in the *De remediis'* treatment of the seven deadly sins. Even more important to my discussion is the fact that the malady that was *accidia-aegritudo* in the *Secretum* became *miseria-tristitia* in the *De rem.* Wenzel cites Petrarch's use of the term *accidia* also in the *De otio rel.*, where, like all the maladies discussed in this section of the work, it is given a Scriptural remedy: "Dicitur accidiosis ac etiam tristibus: '[Ecclus. 30:21–24]' " (*Opere*, 1:594; Wenzel, *Sin of Sloth*, pp. 161, 246). Wenzel makes an important observation concerning the absence of *accidia* in the *De rem.*: "I cannot tell what reason lies behind the change: whether Petrarch learned of the aspect of physical torpor implied in *acedia* later, or—which seems more likely—whether he discarded the name "*accidia*" with its strong theological flavor because, in contrast to the *De otio religioso*, the later *De remediis* was conceived of as a compendium of prudential ethics, of moral philosophy" (Wenzel, *Sin of Sloth*, p. 161). I wholly agree that the latter explanation is more plausible. In the more ascetic settings of the *De otio rel.* and the *Secretum*, Petrarch used the religious terminology of despair; in the laic setting of the *De rem.*, he pursued a more laic vocabulary.

52. Wenzel, *Sin of Sloth*, pp. 157–58; E. H. Wilkins, "On Petrarch's *Accidia*"; Kuhn, *Demon of Noontide*, pp. 72–73.

53. See Wenzel, *Sin of Sloth*, pp. 162–63.

54. Though *accidia* is theoretically a "sin," Petrarch clearly develops it here as a condition requiring solace more than repentance.

55. Franciscus' complaint concerning his relative station in life and his lament over not achieving "that tranquility and serenity of mind" (*Opere*, 1:150) recall a similar theme in Seneca's *De tran. animi* 2.10–11. His complaint concerning his dependency on others (*Opere*, 1:152) reflects the insecurities of Petrarch's scholarly life (on which theme see Trinkaus, *Adversity's Noblemen*, esp. pp. 42, 84–86).

56. See *Opere*, 1:148 (where he cites Seneca's *Ad Luc.* 15.10–11 for this consolation [on the general influence of Seneca in Petrarch's cure for *accidia-aegritudo*, see Bobbio, "Seneca e Petrarca," pp. 250–54]) and 162; cf. *Cons. phil.* 2. pr. 4.

57. See Petrarch's *De vita solitaria* of 1346 (*Opere*, 1:262 ff. [Ricciardi ed. of G. Martellotti with additional notes and Italian trans. by A. Bufano; on dating see *Opere*, p. 262n]). For a discussion of Petrarch's contemplative ideal see J. Zeitlin's "Introduction" in *The Life of Solitude by Francis Petrarch*, trans. Zeitlin (Urbana, Ill., 1924). Drawing on the monastic model of retreat and the philosophical model of contemplation, Petrarch's vision of *otium* informs not only the *De vit. sol.* but also his *Rerum memorandum libri* and the *De otio rel.* (E. Carrara, "Petrarca," *Enc. Ital.* 27:14).

58. See Augustinus' earlier chiding of the careerist Franciscus for abandoning the safety of his solitude for the opportunities of the city (*Opere*, 1:120). Petrarch is simultaneously attracted to and repelled by city life. On the one hand, he complains about the disgusting features of the urban world. On the other, his greed for

fame and advancement inexorably draws him into that world. In the discussion of *accidia-aegritudo*, Augustinus also tells Franciscus that his remaining in the city is his own choice—a charge Franciscus denies (but not in any detail) (*Opere*, 1:162–64). Petrarch's implied position here in the *Secretum*, and perhaps his general predicament in his career, is that he is caught on the horns of a dilemma. He knows that urban life compromises his moral and psychological equanimity, but he feels that the insecurity, poverty, and dependency of the literary life necessitates such commerce with the urban world. How else could a poet and humanist ensure that literary vocation be sustained and sustaining as an adequate career? On the themes of ambition and urban life in the *Secretum*, see Baron, *Petrarch's "Secretum,"* passim, esp. pp. 155–83.

59. *Opere*, 1:156. Petrarch's phrasing here of "vite mee tedia" suggests that this aspect of his despair should be compared to the ancient malady *taedium vitae*; his disquiet also resembles classical descriptions of *horror loci* (for a brief discussion of these two maladies in classical thought see Kuhn, *Demon of Noontide*, pp. 24–36; also see Seneca's *Ad Luc.* 56 cited in the following note). Petrarch's reaction to the city should perhaps be seen not only in terms of the tradition of philosophical and monastic contempt of the world, but also in terms of his own specific experiences and reactions to fourteenth-century urban life. This is suggested by the extreme detail (here and elsewhere, for example, in the Preface to Book 1 of the *De rem.*) with which he probes the psychological morass of urban life.

60. *Opere*, 1:158. On the *De tran. animi* see Introduction, n. 23 above. *Ad. Luc.* 56 deals with the disquiet and restlessness of urban life.

61. *Opere*, 1:158 (see Chap. 3 below).

62. See *Opere*, 1:158, 160; also Wenzel, "Petrarch's *Accidia*," p. 39.

63. *Opere*, 1:162. Cf. Petrarch's elaboration of man's generic happiness and dignity in *De rem.* 2.93 (see Chap. 3 below).

64. See Bufano's observation (*Opere*, 1:165 n.109) that this is a "negative" consolation: Petrarch is simply less miserable than others. It is also for this reason a highly secular, relativistic perspective. Cf. *Cons. phil.* 2. pr. 4.59–61.

65. A general pessimism, of course, can be found in ancient thought: for example, see Homer's *Iliad* 17.446–47 and Plutarch's comment on this in his fragmentary *Animine an corporis affectiones sint peiores* (*Moralia* 500b); also Hesiod's *Works and Days* 100–105 (Kuhn, *Demon of Noontide*, pp. 34–35). Certain other classical sources of this nature Petrarch knew, as he cited them; in discussing the theme of the misery of the human condition in the *De otio rel.* Bk. 1 he cites Pliny the Elder's *Naturalis historia* Bk. 7 and Cicero's *Consolatio* (*Opere*, 1:658; Petrarch also cites Augustine's *De civ. Dei* 22.22 here). Petrarch would draw on Lactantius' critique (in *Divinae institutiones* 3.19 [*PL* 410–14]) of Cicero's pessimism in the *Consolatio* in *Sen.* 1.5 to Boccaccio (see Chap. 2 below). Though there are, then, classical sources dealing with human misery, nonetheless I believe that it is the Christian tradition—and particularly the *contemptus mundi*—that substantively developed the motif of misery. Cicero's despairing *Consolatio* was inspired by and presumably focused on bereavement rather than on a generalized "existential" pessimism. Likewise, other more general ancient consolatory works such as his *Tusc.* Bk. 3, Seneca's *De tran. animi*, or Boethius' *Cons. phil.* do not truly formulate a malady centered in

the human condition itself. Petrarch, however, hints at such a malady in the *accidia-aegritudo* discussion and develops it more fully in the *De rem.* 2.93 (see Chap. 3 below).

66. Augustinus, however, does not completely relinquish his "medieval" role as spiritual adviser: he chides Franciscus that his involvement in urban life is a freely chosen one. See n. 58 above.

67. Franciscus' ultimate lack of spiritual resolution takes on added meaning not only in the context of Augustine's conversion in the *Confessions*, but also in that of Dante's beatific ascent in the *Commedia*.

CHAPTER 2
PETRARCH AS PUBLIC CONSOLER: THE LETTERS

1. Besides the major collections of the *Familiares* and *Seniles*, Petrarch also compiled the *Epistolae metricae* and the *Sine nomine*. There were also an additional 77 prose letters, some of which appeared in the sixteenth-century editions as a collection of miscellaneous letters by Petrarch and others (Wilkins, *Petrarch's Correspondence* [Padua, 1960], p. 9; in the 1554 Basel *Opera* this miscellany was titled *Variarum epistolarum liber* [see *Opera*, pp. 1070–1141]): in the nineteenth century the majority of these letters were assembled as the *Variae*; the remainder in the twentieth as the *Miscellaneous Letters* (see Wilkins, *Life of Petrarch*, p. 265). For editions of the *Familiares* see Rossi (ed.), *Le Familiari*. There is no modern edition of the *Seniles*; I cite the collection as found in the Basel *Opera* of 1554, and I draw on the Italian translation by G. Fracassetti in his *Lettere Senili di Francesco Petrarca*, 2 vols. (Florence, 1869–70); I follow the numbering of the *Seniles* in Wilkins, *Petrarch's Correspondence*. For the *Metricae* see *Poëmata minora*, ed. D. Rossetti, 3 vols. (Milan, 1829–34), vols. 2–3; also those in *Rime, Trionfi, e poesie latine*, ed. F. Neri *et al.* (Milan and Naples, 1951). For the *Variae* see *Epistolae: De rebus familiaribus et Variae*, ed. G. Fracassetti, 3 vols. (Florence, 1859–63), vol. 3.

Petrarch first conceived the idea of making a letter-collection in 1345 when he found Cicero's *Ad Atticum* and *Ad Quintum fratrem*. The first resulting collection, the *Rerum familiarum libri*, was assembled between 1345 and 1366 (Bernardo, "Introduction," *Fam. I–VIII*, pp. xvii–xxii). Bernardo (p. xxiv) suggests that Petrarch first conceived of a collection of his later letters in 1356. The plan took clearer shape after the death of "Socrates" in 1361: that year Petrarch wrote the dedicatory *Sen.* 1.1 to Francesco Nelli ("Simonides"), launching his *Rerum senilium libri* (Wilkins, *Petrarch's Later Years*, pp. 16–18). Thus, 1361 may loosely be considered a general dividing line between the two collections, though there are exceptions in post–1361 *Familiares* and pre-1361 *Seniles* (see Wilkins, *Petrarch's Later Years*, pp. 17–18; also his *Petrarch's Correspondence*).

2. On Petrarch's revising, splitting, and inventing of letters see Billanovich, *Petrarco letterato*, pp. 3–55; Bernardo, "Introduction," pp. xxv–xxxi; his "Letter-Splitting in Petrarch's *Familiares*," *Speculum* 33 (1958), 236–41; Baron, "The Evolution of Petrarch's Thought: Reflections on the State of Petrarch Studies," in his *From Petrarch to Leonardo Bruni*, pp. 7–23.

3. This is Billanovich's thesis; he argues that all of the letters of Book 1 of the *Familiares*—except the first, dedicatory letter to van Kempen, and possibly a version of the sixth—are fictitious, later creations invented for this "earliest" book of his first collection (*Petrarca letterato*, pp. 47–55; Bernardo, "Introduction," pp. xxv–xxvii).

4. In his lists of favorite books which he made in the later 1330s, Petrarch included Seneca's *Ad Lucilium*. As for Cicero's letters, he obtained the *Ad Atticum* and *Ad Quintum fratrem* in 1345, but never possessed a copy of the *Ad familiares* (see B. L. Ullman, "Petrarch's Favorite Books," in *Studies in the Italian Renaissance* [1955; revised and expanded, Rome, 1973], pp. 118–20; also his "Coluccio Salutati ed i classici latini," in *Studies in the Italian Renaissance*, pp. 479–80; also Bernardo, "Introduction," p. xxii). In *Fam.* 1.1 he discusses the letters of Cicero and Seneca, saying that he himself follows Cicero in his personal style, even against Seneca's criticisms of it (see Rossi, 1:9–11).

5. As will be seen in Chap. 4, however, such a social foundation for epistolary consolation was much stronger in the letters of Coluccio Salutati.

6. See Wilkins, *Studies in the Life and Works of Petrarch*, pp. 5–6; his *Life of Petrarch*, pp. 9–10.

7. Rossi, 2:123; Bernardo, *Fam. I–VIII*, p. 367. Except where indicated, I cite or follow Bernardo's translation of the *Fam.*

8. "Venerunt ad manus meas epystole quedam, quas visitante nos sepius fortuna, per hos annos utroque stilo ad te miseram, . . ." (Rossi, 2:124). As for such letters extant, see the prose *Fam.* 4.12 and the metrical *consolatoria* in *Poëmata minora quae extant omnia*, ed. Rossetti, 2:352–79.

On the ancient Stoic "director," see S. Dill's chapter "The Philosophic Director" in his *Roman Society*, pp. 289–333, esp. 293–94; cf. Trinkaus, *Image and Likeness*, 1:329, n. 28.

9. Rossi, 1:54; Bernardo, *Fam. I–VIII*, p. 57. Sometimes Petrarch confesses his doubts that eloquence can cure grief. In *Fam.* 5.1 to Barbato da Sulmona he comments on his own inconsolable grief: "et qui solari alios interdum soleo, nunc qua me ipsum ratione vel oratione consoler, non invenio. Hinc ergo consolandi desperatio, hinc flendi pudor, hinc ad utrumlibet stili diffidentia, . . ." (Rossi, 2:4). Interestingly, in one case Petrarch suggests that when he had exhausted the possibilities of rhetorical solace he retreated to silence and to the final spiritual remedy of Christ. In *Fam.* 7.13 to Cardinal Colonna (cited above at nn. 7–8) he confesses that he was unable to find any comfort from previous consolations he had written, and unable to compose any suitable new ones: "His ego difficultatibus implicitus, silere firmaveram et presentem gemitum Cristo consolatori optimo solandum finiendumque committere" (Rossi, 2:124). He thus seems to oppose to the "rhetoric" of consolation the "quiet" of a Christological silence, implying a divergence between rhetorical and spiritual consolation. Such comments perhaps betray a lingering medieval attitude toward the possible vanity of worldly solace. But, as Petrarch immediately admits, "Hec pro excusatione silentii mei dixerim." The rhetorician in him prevailed, as he then proceeds with a *consolatoria* for Colonna.

10. For this letter see *Opera*, pp. 966–73; also discussion below. Also cf. *Fam.* 23.12.

11. For prose *consolatoriae* on bereavement, see *Fam.* 2.1; 7.13; 13.1; 14.3; *Sen.* 8.5; 10.4 and 5; 11.10 and 14; 13.1, 10 and 11; *Var.* 9, 16, and 18; one might also include here those letters that explicitly are personal laments over loss (but perhaps also are implicitly consolations for the addressee) and those that concern the loss of a mutual friend: e.g., *Fam.* 4.10 and 11; *Sen.* 13.2; *Var.* 19. For the notion of immortality see *Fam.* 2.1, where he cites Cicero's *De senectute*. For a discussion of the influence of Seneca and Cicero on Petrarch's consolatory treatment of death, see Bobbio, "Seneca e Petrarca," pp. 238–50.

12. Rossi, 2:175; Bernardo, *Fam. I–VIII*, p. 415. On this letter, revised in 1350, see Bernardo, "Letter-Splitting."

13. Rossi, 2:175; Bernardo, *Fam. I–VIII*, p. 416. His admission of defeat tendered, he then proclaims the urgency of his grief: "Sed quid agam? moriar nisi dolorem in fletum ac verba profudero" (Rossi, 2:176).

14. See Bernardo, "Letter-Splitting," pp. 236–41; Rossi, 2:174n.

15. Rossi, 2:182; Bernardo, *Fam. I–VIII*, p. 423. On the revision of this letter see Bernardo, "Letter-Splitting"; also Baron, *Petrarch's "Secretum,"* p. 217. Watkins suggests that the revision of the original letter of 1349 may have been made in 1350 ("Petrarch and the Black Death," pp. 201–2). The above passage is from the revised version, where Petrarch's remarks here concerning his uncontrollable, cathartic need to write and weep about this tragedy are an expansion of the corresponding passage in the earlier version (for which, see Rossi, 2:204). His added comments in the revised letter perhaps reflect a later interest in further explaining or excusing such doleful letters (see discussion in text below).

16. Rossi, 2:185–86 (cf. corresponding passage in the original version of the letter at 2:208); Bernardo, *Fam. I–VIII*, p. 427.

17. For example, see his comments on his emotional weakness in *Fam.* 8.7 and 9; also his sense of conflict between emotion and reason in *Fam.* 7.12.

18. Watkins, "Petrarch and the Black Death," pp. 200–1, 216–17.

19. Rossi, 1:12; Bernardo, *Fam. I–VIII*, p. 11. Cf. Seneca's repudiation of the instance of his own earlier grief (over the death of Annaeus Serenus) in *Ad Luc.* 63.14.

20. Rossi, 1:12; Bernardo, *Fam. I–VIII*, p. 12.

21. Rossi, 1:12; M. Bishop's translation in *Letters from Petrarch* (Bloomington, In., 1966), p. 21.

22. Rossi, 1:13–14; Bernardo, *Fam. I–VIII*, p. 14. Petrarch's new resolve was tested shortly after the writing of *Fam.* 1.1. In January of 1351 (in *Fam.* 11.2) he wrote to Boccaccio of the death of Jacopo da Carrara the Younger, discussing his newfound fortitude ("Vivendo didici vite bella tractare; iam fortune ictibus non lamenta non gemitus ut quondam, sed callum durati animi obicio et titubare solitus immobilis iam consisto") and claiming that he bravely rose to the fresh challenge posed by this loss (Rossi, 2:325–26).

23. *Opera*, p. 812; I follow M. Bishop's translation in his *Letters from Petrarch*, p. 223; cf. Watkins, "Petrarch and the Black Death," p. 216.

24. For example, letters on the loss of his son and "Socrates" (*Sen.* 1.3) and of his grandson (*Sen.* 10.4) are quite restrained (see Watkins, "Petrarch and the Black Death," pp. 216–17 and discussion below). In the former, he writes to his "Simonides" (Francesco Nelli) of his battle to resist emotion: "Dicerem, hei mihi ter et amplius, nisi quod luctum pellere est animus, possem simul utinam, et dolorem pellere, nitar equidem" (*Opera*, p. 815). Expressions of grief can still be found in the *Seniles*, but the emotional tenor generally seems moderated. A notable lapse into indulgent grief, however, can be found in *Sen.* 3.1 to Boccaccio. Written in 1363, this letter specifically laments Petrarch's loss of his "Laelius" and "Simonides" and generally reflects on the years of plague that have raged since 1348. It was to "Simonides" that Petrarch had promised (in *Sen.* 1.1) a braver front—with his death perhaps Petrarch feels not only yet another tragic loss but also temporary freedom from his promise. In any case, *Sen.* 3.1 shows some backsliding, as Petrarch reflects on his vulnerability to and struggle with indulgent sorrow (see *Opera*, pp. 847–48; see Chap. 1, n. 15 above). But, it must be remembered that this letter is written to a fellow love poet; moreover, in it Petrarch does discuss his intention to stand firm against the vicissitudes of fortune (see *Opera*, p. 848; cf. passages cited at Chap. 3, nn. 83–84 above). Also, on Petrarch's suppression of certain other letters that reveal his vulnerability to sorrow, see discussion in text below.

25. It should be noted that, despite this allowance for tears (at Rossi, 1:178), at the end of the letter Petrarch does call for an end to weeping. Though thus proscribing boundless grief, nonetheless the letter does seek to explain the importance of allowing a sufficient expression of emotion. Cf. Seneca's *Ad Luc.* 99 (e.g., at 16), which allows for a healthy, moderate grief while condemning excess.

26. Rossi, 2:127; Bernardo, *Fam. I–VIII*, p. 371. On this letter as an example of "professional" consolation, see discussion in text above.

27. Having heard of Gui's sorrow, Petrarch suggests (in *Fam.* 13.1) that he has intentionally waited to write, allowing him proper time to spend his innate, or even pleasant, grief—Petrarch sanctions "one night" of mourning, citing Augustine's one day of mourning for Monica (Rossi, 3:53–54, 56; on the delay in writing, cf. a letter Freud wrote to Rozsi von Freund on the death of her mother in 1926 which begins: "I have purposely allowed your first period of mourning to pass before sending you a few words of sympathy. I feel that someone who has suffered a great loss is entitled to be left in peace. In fact, I think this period of silence ought to be extended for a long time if the fear of appearing unsympathetic did not compel one to communicate. As it is, anything one can say must sound to the bereaved like so many empty words. The 'work of mourning' is an intimate process which cannot stand any interference" [*Letters of Sigmund Freud*, ed. Ernst L. Freud, trans. Tania and James Stern (New York, 1960), pp. 373–74]. I would like to thank Dr. John Frosch for bringing this letter to my attention). Though written after his first promise of personal equanimity in *Fam.* 1.1, Petrarch's *Fam.* 13.1 still reflects perspectives of the earlier years. We should bear in mind, however, that Petrarch's discussion and approval of weeping here could have chiefly been a response to the reports of Gui's grief that he mentions.

28. On this letter see discussion in text below. Also, cf. his comments in *Sen.* 1.3 (see n. 24 above) and his criticism of tears in the closing of *Sen.* 13.2 (see *Opera*, p. 1015).

29. Cf. Chap. 1, n. 13 above.

30. See G. Fracassetti's note in *Lettere di Francesco Petrarca: . . . Delle cose famiiliari—Lettere varie*, trans. and ed. Fracassetti, 5 vols. (Florence, 1863–67), 5:336–38; also see Wilkins, *Petrarch's Eight Years in Milan*, p. 93.

31. *De reb. fam. et Var.*, Fracassetti, 3:381–82. I follow Fracassetti's translation of the *Variae* in *Lettere delle cose fam.—Lettere var.*

32. *De reb. fam. et Var.*, 3:382.

33. Ibid., p. 383.

34. Presumably he is referring to *Fam.* 8.1. See discussion in text below and n. 43.

35. *De reb. fam. et Var.*, 3:384.

36. Ibid., p. 384.

37. Ibid., p. 392.

38. Ibid., p. 393. Cf. the Stoic language of this letter with that of the *De remediis*, possibly begun the following year in 1356, if not earlier (on dating of the *De rem.* see Chap. 3 below).

39. *Var.* 19 (1362), written to Moggio dei Moggi, is plangent ("En qui alios solari soleo qualiter me consolor, non veri inscius, sed dolori impar et angore obrutus ac moerore") and closes with a reference to the familiar "sweet grief" ("Certe quo possum nisu fraeno animum, sed me calcar fraeno potentius praecipitat ad amaram quamdam dulcedinem lacrimarum. Nec facile dixerim quam dulce mihi fuerit flere dum scriberem, . . . ")(*De reb. fam. et Var.*, 3:347–48).

40. *De reb. fam. et Var.*, 3:456. In this letter of 1363 Petrarch responded to Bartolomeo's concern over a comment Petrarch had recently made to him; as Petrarch described it: "Scripsi equidem me curis pluribus circumventum et miseriorem quam esse me noscerem" (p. 455).

41. Wilkins, *Petrarch's Later Years*, pp. 67–68.

42. *De reb. fam. et Var.*, 3:466.

43. On this letter, described in the superscription as "mixta lamentis consolatio super gravissimis fortune vulneribus" (Rossi, 2:147), see Wilkins, *Life of Petrarch*, pp. 78–79. Though there are constructive consolations in this letter, it is also a strikingly sad letter, recounting such a bitter history of family tragedy. Particularly poignant is Petrarch's recalling a conversation he had with Stefano during a stroll through Rome in 1337, when Stefano "foretold" that he would survive all of his sons, a premonition that tragically came true (Rossi, 2:153–54; Wilkins, *Life of Petrarch*, pp. 78–79). Toward the end of the letter Petrarch urges that, if Stefano may have been tearful at the plangent start of this letter, he should be composed by the calmer close, where Petrarch presents an exhortation to fortitude. Clearly, Petrarch hoped the letter would guide Stefano through stages of mourning. Strangely enough, he also cautions that Stefano remain strong "ne unquam forte . . . vetera memorando in novas miserias relabaris, ac nimis indulgens patrio dolori rescindas herentium iam vulnerum cicatrices" (Rossi, 2:156), a rather anomalous

comment, given that Petrarch's letter in fact has done exactly what he warns against—namely, it has "recalled" Stefano's many old "wounds."

44. *De reb. fam. et Var.*, 3:466.

45. Ibid., pp. 466–67. Cf. this resolution to remain calm "non si simul orbis totus succumberet" to similar ones Petrarch made in *Fam.* 1.1 and *Sen.* 10.4 (see nn. 22 and 57).

46. We cannot fully know how much this was truly Petrarch's original goal in the letter and how much it was a "retrospective goal," crystallized at a later time, perhaps after hearing of Stefano's reaction. Whichever the case, it is fair to characterize this letter as a particularly poignant, evocative one.

47. "Hoc remedii genere ipse mecum, cogente impia Fortuna, saepe postea usus sum" (*De reb. fam. et Var.*, 3:467).

48. In *Var.* 54 Petrarch had promised Bartolomeo some presence in the *Seniles* collection (ibid., p. 454), but the latter's death precluded such a correspondence and, thus, Petrarch planned to commemorate his name by including "*Var.*" 54 in the *Familiares* (see ibid, p. 467; Wilkins, *Petrarch's Later Years*, pp. 55, 67–68).

49. "[E]t quoniam delectabat ac proderat exonerare animum fletu, feci omnia quibus quam necessario flendum esset, semel flerem, et non saepius, quod fieri non poterat nisi abundantissime semel flessem. Quamobrem inter caetera fletus incitamenta, ad familiarem viri illius epistolam scripsi, ut artificio vacuam, sic refertam vivis affectibus, quam et scribens et relegens flevi, quantum desiderio leniendo, levandoque gemitui visum esset expediens; et valuit, ut post saepe suspirans nunquam fleverim, nunquamque deinceps, ut auguror et ipse tale aliquod fleturus exhausisse fontem mihi video lacrimarum" (*De reb. fam. et Var.*, 3:467–68).

50. Heitmann suggests Petrarch may have sent a draft of the *De remediis* (i.e., that portion, according to Heitmann, completed in 1356–57): "E' presumabile che almeno Azzo da Correggio ricevette il *De remediis* già nel 1357–58" (Heitmann, "La genesi del *De remediis*," p. 18).

51. *De reb. fam. et Var.*, 3:468.

52. See Wilkins, *Petrarch's Later Years*, p. 68, n. 11.

53. And in one, *Var.* 32 on Paolo, this failure is particularly ironic, given the letter's condemnation of Paolo's sorrow.

54. This letter probably followed all the excluded *Variae* discussed above. Certainly it came after *Var.* 32 (1356), 19 (1362), 54 (1363). It perhaps also followed *Var.* 58, though the latter's dating is disputed: P. de Nolhac suggests 1369 and F. Novati ca. 1372–73, but V. Rossi and C. Garibotto date it to 1363–65 (Wilkins, *Petrarch's Correspondence*, p. 117). Given the arguments in *Sen.* 10.4 (see below), I find the earlier period for *Var.* 58 more plausible.

55. *Opera*, p. 968. Cf. *Fam.* 23.12 at Rossi, 4:185–86.

56. For language recalling the *De remediis*, completed in 1366, see his comment: "Succurro ego tibi, et solor te amice . . . et me ipsum solum, quibus sunt cuncta communia, spes et metus, et gaudia et dolores; ideo ut dixi, vulnera nostra coniungo, ut medicamenta permisceam. Possem pro remedio Philosophorum et Poetarum omnium vireta percurrere, . . ." (*Opera*, p. 968). In some way, Petrarch's *Sen.* 10.4 fills a gap left by the *De remediis*. As we shall see in Chap. 3, Petrarch's

chapters on bereavement in the latter are perfunctory. His major Stoic statement on mourning comes in this later *consolatoria* to Donato.

57. *Opera*, p. 968. In particular cf. the *locus* here "in me unum totus orbis ut corruat" (derivative of Horace, *Carm*. 3.3.7–8) to that in *Fam*. 1.1 and 8.1 (see nn. 22 and 45 above). Also, cf. Seneca's *Ad Luc*. 63.14.

58. *Opera*, p. 968. Such a palpable monument is constructive in that it keeps alive the memory of the departed (cf. R. Watkins' thesis in "Petrarch and the Black Death: From Fear to Monuments"). Petrarch also suggests that besides the classical tribute of physical monuments for the dead, there is also the Christian duty of praying for their salvation.

59. *Opera*, p. 969. Cf. Seneca's attack on public weeping in *Ad Luc*. 99.16–17.

60. *Opera*, p. 969. The lessons of the suppressed *Var*. 32 were thus not lost on Petrarch's contemporary readers. In this way, Petrarch could make good Stoic use of Paolo's case, but without the embarrassingly excessive and harsh tone of *Var*. 32.

For the ancient *exempla*, Petrarch cites Octavia's grief (over Marcellus) and Nestor's (over Antilochus).

61. *Opera*, pp. 434–35 (in this edition, *Sen*. 14.1 appears separately as *De republica optime administranda liber*) and p. 123.

62. *Opera*, p. 972; emphasis mine.

63. Ibid., pp. 972–73. From the ancients, he compares to the excessive grief of Octavia and Nestor (see n. 60 above) the controlled grief of Cornelia (over the Gracchi) and Cato the Censor (over his son). From the Bible he cites the fortitude of Job (in Job 1:21) and David (over the loss of Bathsheba's first son to him) (in 2 Samuel 12:22–24).

64. On Stefano, he cites Stefano's loss of three sons and a grandson within three years, focusing on Stefano's brave response to the deaths of Stefano the Younger and his son in the noble uprising against Cola di Rienzo in 1347. (Not surprisingly, this is a strikingly different use of Stefano from that Petrarch makes of him in the suppressed *Var*. 58, in which he violently spends his grief while reading Petrarch's *Fam*. 8.1.) There follows a longer treatment of King Robert of Naples' reaction to the illness and death of his son Charles of Calabria. Petrarch compares Robert's bravery and public composure to that of Aemilius Paullus (for which see *Tusc*. 3.28.70; Valerius Maximus, *Factorum et dictorum memorabilium libri* 5.10.2; cf. Giannozzo Manetti, *Dialogus consolatorius*, ed. A. de Petris [Rome, 1983], p. 34).

65. *Opera*, p. 973. Petrarch also urges that Donato see his son as a potential divine intercessor for him. Cf. this theme in Manetti's *Dialogus consolatorius* (see Chap. 5 below).

66. *Opera*, p. 973; Wilkins, *Petrarch's Later Years*, pp. 154–55.

67. On the doleful *Fam*. 8.7 and 9 and on the warning about constrained grief to Cardinal Giovanni Colonna (*Fam*. 4.12 and 7.13) see discussion in text above.

68. Petrarch thus salvages some Stoic "wheat" from the emotional "chaff" of the repressed *Var*. 32. In *Sen*. 10.5, also addressed to Donato, Petrarch continued his warning concerning sorrow, urging his friend not to prolong his grief and again making reference to the case of Paolo Annibaldeschi (see *Opera*, pp. 973–74).

69. This addressee is not Petrarch's patron Cardinal Colonna, but a Dominican uncle of the latter's.

70. Similarly, in *Fam* 20.12 he presents a short consolation for his friend "Laelius" (Angelo or Lello di Pietro Stefano dei Tosetti), whose two recent letters showed him to be greatly disturbed (pergraviter turbatus). Petrarch responds with a brief remedy "contra omnes impetus fortune" and the "vite huius asperitates" (Rossi, 4:35).

71. *Fam.* 23.5 (*de senectute et morte non modo fortiter sed lete etiam obeundis*) is devoted entirely to the problem of sustaining and confirming an aging friend in his fearless attitude toward death. Petrarch's consolation draws on several of the traditional philosophical and Christian *topoi*: the shortness and evils of life, the inevitability of death, death's being bad for the evil and good for the virtuous. Among other things he cites (secondhand) Plotinus' argument (which he also cites in *De rem.* 2.119) that "misericordiam . . . Dei esse nos fecisse mortales" (Rossi, 4:170), a sentiment, Petrarch observes, echoed by such Christian thinkers as Cyprian and Augustine. The argument that death is "good for the virtuous" appears twice, the second time in the maxim found also in *De rem.* 2.117 (and later in the northern *Tractatus artis bene moriendi*): "Ut enim 'mors peccatorum pessima, . . . sic optima mors iustorum' " (Rossi, 4:170–71; on the *Ars moriendi* see Chap. 3 below).

72. On Petrarch and Salutati as lay consolers, counselors, and confessors, see Marvin Becker, "Individualism in the Early Italian Renaissance: Burden and Blessing," *SR* 19 (1972), 278–79. For this notion I also benefited from a reading of his unpublished "History in the Eye of Possibility."

73. For the story see Fracassetti, *Lettere Senili*, 1:51–52; Wilkins, *Petrarch's Later Years*, pp. 31–32; V. Branca, *Boccaccio: The Man and His Works*, trans. R. Monges and D. McAuliffe (New York, 1976), pp. 129–31.

74. For example, he cites Cicero's statement in *Tusc.* 1.31.75 and in the *De republica* Bk. 6 (*Somnium Scipionis*) that "haec nostra quae dicitur vita mors est," confirming it with a similar notion drawn from Gregory the Great's sermons (*Opera*, p. 820).

75. Ambrose's prominence as a patristic source in this area is underscored by the fact that his are the only extant funeral orations in ancient Latin Christian thought. Besides the *De excessu*, Ambrose also wrote funeral orations *De consolatione Valentiniani* and *De obitu Theodosii*. As for the *De excessu*, M. McGuire suggests that the first of the two orations is closer to the *laudatio funebris* and the second to the *consolatio* ("The Christian Funeral Oration," in *Funeral Orations*, pp. xvi–xix). Ambrose also wrote consolatory letters and a *De bono mortis*, which dealt with the positive face of death and offered arguments against the fear of death (see Beyenka, *Consolation in Saint Augustine*, p. 25).

76. Cf. *De rem.* 2.117–18, in which Petrarch follows a chapter on the fear of death with one on suicide.

77. He also returns to the *De excessu* to cite Ambrose's argument for the spiritual benefits of reflecting on death (*Opera*, pp. 820-21). Petrarch's interest in Ambrose may have been heightened by his stay in Milan (1353–61), where for some time he lived near Sant'Ambrogio (see his comment to this effect at p. 821; Wilkins, *Petrarch's Eight Years in Milan*, pp. 16–18).

True to his Senecan counsel to others, Petrarch's letters reveal his own steady resolve to die well. Responding to the threats of plague or old age, Petrarch in several instances evinces his readiness to accept a good, calm death: see, for example, *Sen.* 3.7 and particularly *Sen.* 8.1 to Boccaccio, written on Petrarch's sixty-third birthday, a traditionally superstitious year (see Chap. 3 below).

78. *Opera*, p. 822.
79. Ibid., p. 822.
80. Ibid., p. 823; Wilkins, *Petrarch's Later Years*, pp. 30–31.
81. On *Sen.* 3.1 as an exception to this, see n. 24 above.

CHAPTER 3
PETRARCH AS UNIVERSAL CONSOLER:
THE *DE REMEDIIS UTRIUSQUE FORTUNE*

1. There is no modern edition of the entire *De rem.* (though for an edition of six chapters see *Francesco Petrarca: Prose*, ed. G. Martellotti, P. G. Ricci, E. Carrara, and E. Bianchi, La letteratura italiana, storia e testi, no. 7 [Milan and Naples, 1955]; and for Chaps. 2.1–11 see F.N.M. Diekstra, *A Dialogue Between Reason and Adversity: A Late Middle English Version of Petrarch's 'De remediis'* [Assen, 1968]; also for an edition of both Prefaces and 13 chaps. see *Heilmittel gegen Glück und Unglück, De remediis utriusque fortunae: Lateinisch-deutsche Ausgabe in Auswahl*, trans. and comm. by R. Schottlaender [Munich, 1988]). I shall cite the edition found in the Basel *Opera* of 1554, pp. 1–256. The only major study of the treatise thus far is K. Heitmann, *Fortuna und Virtus: Eine Studie zu Petrarcas Lebensweisheit*, Studi italiani, no. 1 (Cologne and Graz, 1958). Also see Diekstra ("Introduction," in his *A Dialogue Between Reason and Adversity*, pp. 15–65) for a discussion of sources and genre; Auer, *Dambach*, at, for example, pp. 250–51, 256–59; Trinkaus, *The Poet as Philosopher*, pp. 119–128, for some discussion of the *De rem.* as a therapeutic manual and type of pastoral care; B. G. Kohl, "Introduction," in the facsimile reprint of Thomas Twyne's 1579 translation *Phisicke Against Fortune* (Delmar, N.Y., 1980), pp. v–xvii; R. Starn, "Petrarch's Consolation on Exile: A Humanist Use of Adversity," in *Essays Presented to Myron P. Gilmore*, ed. S. Bertelli and G. Ramakus, 2 vols. (Florence, 1978), 1:241–54.

2. On dating see comments of P. G. Ricci in Martellotti *et al.*, *Prose*, pp. 1169–70. It is uncertain when Petrarch began the work. As an approximate guide, scholars use *Sen.* 16.9, in which Petrarch claims he is at work on *De rem.* 2.93 (see below). The date of this letter, however, is disputed. A. Foresti (*Aneddoti della vita di Francesco Petrarca* [Brescia, 1928], pp. 312–15), P. G. Ricci (*Prose*, ed. Martellotti *et al.*, pp. 1169–70), and Wilkins (*Petrarch's Eight Years in Milan*, pp. 69–72) would date the letter to 1354. Heitmann ("La genesi del *De remediis utriusque fortune* del Petrarca," *Convivium*, N. S., 1 [1957], 9–30), however, assigns it to 1357, believing that Petrarch began the *De rem.* the previous year. Envisioning the treatise as having two stages of composition, Heitmann suggests the following chronology: "Il *De remediis utriusque fortune* fu concepito indubbiamente già prima del 1347 (forse si può risalire perfino al 1342–43 o anche piú in là) e venne redatto in due tappe. Il primo 85 per cento (molto probabilmente fino al cap. II 93 inclusivamente) fu scritto fra la fine del 1356 e la metà del 1357. L'opera giunse allora ad un pieno compimento e fu dedicata ad Azzo da Correggio. Alcuni anni dopo la

morte di Azzo, piú precisamente nell'autunno (settembre) del 1366 fu ampliata, con l'aggiunta dell'ultimo 15 per cento. Molti indizi ci fanno credere che allo stesso tempo l'umanista ritoccò lievemente anche quello che aveva scritto nel 1356–57. Il compimento definitivo del testo data finalmente del 4 ottobre 1366. Immediatamente dopo l'opera fu pubblicata" (p. 25).

It is not crucial to my treatment of the *De rem.* to try to settle the question of when (1354 or 1356–57) Petrarch began the treatise, but a couple of points concerning the possible stages and the process of composition do bear mentioning. Though Petrarch seems to have completed a version of the treatise at least by 1360, when he referred to the work in *Fam.* 23.12, and though he dedicated the work to Azzo (who may have even received an early version [Heitmann, "La genesi," p. 18]) before the latter died in 1362, Petrarch was still at work on the treatise in 1366. On Sept. 1 of that year he mentions in *Sen.* 5.4 to Donato Albanzani that he is writing the chapter "De auditu perdito" (Heitmann, "La genesi," p. 17). This chapter (and perhaps those on similar topics—"On Blindness" (96), "On Dumbness" (104)—and even other chapters on physical ills in this section of the *De rem.* 2.94–114) may have been prompted by the recent letter from Donato that he is losing his hearing (cf. Wilkins, *Petrarch's Later Years*, pp. 106–7). Though I concur with Wilkins in his questioning Heitmann's assumption that the dialogues were necessarily all written in order, I agree with Heitmann that Chap. 97, along with part or all of the remainder of Book 2, was probably written in 1366. I believe that, like Chap. 97, no. 114 and possibly all or part of nos. 117–32 were written in a second phase. The first (pre-1360) draft of the treatise may well have ended with Chap. 93 on misery, a dialogue which, however, might in fact have been, as Wilkins suggests, the first dialogue written (*Petrarch's Eight Years in Milan*, p. 66; also see nn. 87 and 91 below).

3. See Chap. 1, n. 37.

4. *Opere*, 1:158; I follow Bufano's Italian translation in *Opere*, 1:159. Cf. Trinkaus, *Poet as Philosopher*, p. 94.

5. "Haec est enim vera Philosophia, non quae fallacibus allis attolitur, et sterilium disputationum ventosa iactantia per inane circumvolvitur, sed quae certis et modestis gradibus compendio ad salutem pergit" (*Opera*, p. 2; Heitmann, *Fortuna und Virtus*, p. 113). Here, as elsewhere, I follow the translation of the *De rem.* in Thomas Twyne's rendering, *Phisicke Against Fortune* (London, 1579).

6. Rossi, 3:19; Bernardo, *Fam. IX–XVI*, p. 142; Heitmann, *Fortuna und Virtus*, pp. 113–14.

7. *Opera*, pp. 2–3.

8. For the Stoic metaphor of "arma" cf., for example, *Tusc.* 2.22.51 and nn. 72 and 77 below.

9. For example, on gout cf. discussions in *Fam.* 3.13 and 6.3 to that found in *De rem.* 2.84; also cf. the treatment of aging in *Fam.* 6.3 to that found in *De rem.* 2.83; also cf. the counsels on high office in *Fam.* 14.1 to the chapter on papal office in *De rem.* 1.106.

10. See Rossi, 4:183–94. He was gratified to learn, however, that Guido did possess (and find useful) an earlier *consolatoria* for gout (*Fam.* 6.3) Petrarch had written to Friar Giovanni Colonna. This fact prompted Petrarch to reflect on the

unexpected and enduring benefits one's efforts may bestow. If a single *consolatoria* could have such a longer life, Guido's report must have sparked ever greater expectations in Petrarch concerning the potential usefulness of his *De rem.*

11. Heitmann does point out a reference Petrarch made in the *De otio* concerning a future work on misery. Having presented a type of *contemptus mundi* Petrarch says: "Multa nunc possem talia referre vel publica vel privata, sed et satis ista sufficiunt satisque perturbant, et si de omnibus loqui velim, non unius libri angulus, sed multa michi sunt implenda volumina, quod alio quodam libro michi videor pro ingenii viribus et facultate otii prestiturus" (*Opere*, 1:654; Heitmann, "La genesi," pp. 10–11). Heitmann here compares this passage (from the revised version of 1356–57) to that found in the first version of 1347, in which he voiced some doubts about his ability to tackle such a project. The more confident comment in the revised passage of 1356–57 would thus have come either after Petrarch had already begun the *De rem.* (assuming a *terminus a quo* of 1354) or around the time he began it (assuming one of 1356–57).

I believe, however, that the influence of the *De otio* could run much deeper than this. The above-mentioned passage from the *De otio* follows a section enumerating a list of human ills (see esp. *Opere*, 1:652–54) that, on the one hand, mirrors Innocent III's *De miseria humanae conditionis* and, on the other, reflects the therapeutic interest of the *De remediis*. As I shall discuss below, Petrarch provides a theocentric "remedy" for this human misery in the *De otio*, just as he will provide an anthropocentric one in the *De rem.* 2.93. In both discussions of human misery the influence of Augustine's *De civ. Dei* Bk. 22 is clearly at work. Also, much of the *De otio* Bk. 2 discusses the blandishments, temptations, and vanities of the world, seeking remedies in, among other things, the contemplation of death ("nulla tamen utilior quam proprie mortis cogitatio; neque enim de nichilo dictum est: 'Memorare novissima tua et in eternum non peccabis' [Ecclus. 7:36]. His et similibus contra carnis incendia remediis instructum assidue et armatum habere animum atque in excubiis semper intentum tenere profuerit: ..." [*Opere*, 1:744–46]). In general, then, the *De otio* Bk. 1, with its consolations for misery, and the *De otio* Bk. 2, with its remedies for vanity (remedies of divine *misericordia* and hope) foreshadow the similar concerns of the *De rem.* Bks. 1 and 2. Revising the *De otio* in 1356–57 may thus have greatly inspired or informed the writing of the *De rem.*

12. Cf. Salutati's *De seculo et religione* (see Chap. 4 below). I am indebted to Professor Marvin Becker for this notion.

13. Cf. Petrarch's recently completed *De vita solitaria* (1346).

14. See *Opere*, 1:572; Trinkaus, *Image and Likeness*, 1:43. Petrarch cites Augustine's gloss on the passage in the *De vera rel.* 35.65, which drew upon a Latin translation that antedated Jerome's rendering of "Vacate" in the Vulgate. Petrarch will thus develop a notion of spiritual *otium*, as Augustine does briefly in the above. On Petrarch's annotated manuscript of the *De vera rel.* see n. 21 below.

15. On the *De otio* and its relation to Augustine's *De vera rel.* and on its place in Petrarch's thought, see Baron, *Petrarch's "Secretum,"* pp. 5–6, 31–32, 246–47.

16. Augustine presents scriptural cures for the greedy, lustful, proud, wrathful, discordant, superstitious, curious, and mankind as a whole (*Augustine: Earlier*

Writings, trans. J. Burleigh [Philadelphia, 1953], p. 228.). Petrarch quotes this set of eight remedies (*Opere*, 1:588–90) and then adds to them.

17. *Opere*, 1:590; I follow B. Aracri's Italian translation accompanying this edition of the *De otio*. Cf. *Sen*. 10.1 (1367–68), in which Petrarch similarly exhorts a Cistercian, Sagremor de Pommiers, in his monastic life. Like the *De otio*, this letter is a *contemptus mundi*, and offers various therapeutic *loci* for human misery in general and for several specific conditions such as temptation, worldly vicissitudes, illness, blindness, and deafness (see *Opera*, pp. 956–57). Though briefer, this section represents a type of monastic remedy collection such as that found in the *De otio*.

18. *Opere*, 1:590–98. Whereas the problems that Augustine treated were exclusively moral, Petrarch's compilation extended also to other areas: for example, he cites biblical remedies to be said "pauperibus," "lugentibus," "fatigatis et oppressis," "paralitico," "leproso," "ceco," "penitenti," and "accidiosis et etiam tristibus" (on which see Wenzel, *Sin of Sloth*, p. 161). In another, "mediocritate non contentis," he seems to anticipate his treatment of his avarice and his *accidia-aegritudo* concerning his not even attaining "mediocritas" in the *Secretum* Bk. 2 (cf. *Opere*, 1:114 ff.; 150 ff.). In treating both worldly vanities (e.g., "longas spes vita habentibus" or "temporali elatione tumentibus et humane conditionis oblitis") and worldly woes, Petrarch's 38 remedies resemble the similar categories of the *De rem*. Bks. 1 and 2 (where, as in the *Secretum*, Petrarch will later treat some of these same ills in fuller detail, using other than scriptural remedies). He ends this section by saying: "Sed quid ago? at quis usquam est Scripturarum angulus qui non utilibus minis ac monitis, qui non *consolationibus ac remediis anime* plenus sit? Vacate itaque, fratres, ab occultis pestibus, quarum vos supra premonui et de quibus plura dicturus sum, . . ." (*Opere* 1:598; emphasis mine).

19. Cf. M. O'Rourke Boyle, "Erasmus' Prescription for Henry VIII: Logotherapy," *RQ* 31 (1978), 161–72.

20. Cf. the two passages in the *De otio* (*Opere*, 1:590 and 598) cited above to his comments concerning the "diseases of minds" (*animorum morbi*) in the preface to Book 1 of the *De remediis* (*Opera*, p. 6) and the reference to philosophers as "*animorum medici*" in the *De rem*. 2.117 (cited at n. 97 below). This is not to say, however, that Petrarch exclusively uses the terminology of "anima" in the *De otio* and that of "animus" in the *De rem*. I am arguing that there is a noteworthy contrast in the use of the different terms in the two texts.

21. See Rico's analysis of the ms (Paris lat. 2201), "Petrarca y el *De vera religione*," *IMU* 17 (1974), 313–64, esp. 317–318; also, Baron, *Petrarch's "Secretum,"* pp. 5–6, 31–37, 202–8. This is not to suggest that Petrarch's marginal comments were unusual in this section, as they occur throughout the manuscript (see Rico, "Petrarca").

The influence of the *De vera rel*. is found not only in the *De otio* but also in the *Secretum* Bk. 1, where Franciscus cites the work in discussing his notion of the plague of sensual distractions (*Opere*, 1:94; Baron, *Petrarch's "Secretum,"* pp. 31–32).

22. For discussions of Petrarch's conflict with the doctors, see Seigel, *Rhetoric and Philosophy*, pp. 37–42; Trinkaus, *Poet as Philosopher*, pp. 90–113.

23. Rossi, 2:44; Bernardo, *Fam. I–VIII*, p. 279.

24. Ibid.

25. On Bosco's dating of the *Contra medicum,* see *Opere,* 2:820, 848–49.

26. Authors of such works include Salutati (his *De nobilitate legum et medicine*), Poggio, and the physicians Giovanni Baldi, Giovanni d'Arezzo, and Antonio de Ferrariis (Galateo) (see Garin, *La disputa delle arti nel Quattrocento* [Florence, 1947]; also his "La polemica sulla dignità delle leggi," in his edition of *Salutati: De nobilitate legum et medicinae—De verecundia* [Florence, 1947], pp. xlv–lviii; also L. Thorndike, "Medicine versus Law at Florence," in his *Science and Thought in the Fifteenth Century* [New York, 1929], pp. 24–58).

27. Seigel, *Rhetoric and Philosophy,* pp. 39–41; Trinkaus, *Poet as Philosopher,* pp. 90–113; Kristeller, "Petrarch's 'Averroists': A Note on the History of Aristotelianism in Venice, Padua, and Bologna," in his *Studies in Renaissance Thought and Letters II* (Rome, 1985), pp. 209–16; also his "Il Petrarca, l'Umanesimo e la scholastica a Venezia," in *Studies II,* pp. 217–38. One of Petrarch's four disputants in the *De ignorantia* is identified (in a notation in a Venetian manuscript of the work) as the doctor Guido da Bagnola (Kristeller, "Petrarch's 'Averroists,' " pp. 212–16); he is apparently the one of the group whom Petrarch ridicules as learned in natural philosophy. For Ricci's edition of the *De ignorantia* (with additional notes and Italian trans. by C. Kraus Reggiani) see *Opere,* 2:1025–1151, esp. 1036–40; for an English translation of it and other of Petrarch's criticisms of dialectic (in *Fam.* 1.7), of Averroists (in *Sen.* 5.2 and 15.6), and of Arabian thought generally (in *Sen.* 12.2) see *The Renaissance Philosophy of Man,* ed. E. Cassirer, P. O. Kristeller, and J. H. Randall, Jr. (Chicago, 1948), pp. 47–143.

28. See edition of P. G. Ricci (with C. Kraus Reggiani's Italian trans.) in *Opere,* 2:938.

29. *Opere,* 2:934.

30. *Opera,* p. 861.

31. *Opera,* p. 861; see Seigel, *Rhetoric and Philosophy,* p. 39; cf. the certain influence of Seneca's *Ad Luc.* 75.6–7 in this letter.

It is difficult to pin down the exact nature of this medical speaking that Petrarch assailed. He referred to it variously as argumentative, as syllogistic, as dialectical (see, for example, *Cont. med.* at *Opere,* 2:938; also comments in *Sen.* 5.3; 13.9; 16.3 [at *Opera,* pp. 884, 1019, 1053]). In one case, he even described it as a (failed) attempt at consolation; writing to the physician Giovanni Dondi in *Sen.* 12.2, he complained that in his experience with doctors he has received "promissiones, et verba solantia, quasi mihi consolatore moralique Philosopho, non Medico opus esset, . . ."(*Opera,* p. 1002). Finally, a most telling description of medical discourse is found in those letters in which he characterized his medical acquaintances and their speech as humanistic and literary (see, for example, his comment to Boccaccio in *Sen.* 5.3, concerning his four surviving medical friends who spout "much Aristotle, much Cicero, much Seneca, and what will amaze you, much Vergil" [*Opera,* p. 883]; also see comments at *Opera,* pp. 887, 1001, 1053; *Opere,* 2:938). See A. Chiappelli, *Studii sull'esercizio della medicina in Italia negli ultimi tre secoli del medio evo* (Milan, 1885), pp. 62–64.

32. For various criticisms concerning medical incompetence and inaccuracy see *Sen.* 12.1 and 2; 13.9; 15.14. On their audacity, pomposity, and greed see *Sen.* 5.3 to Boccaccio.

33. See Seigel, *Rhetoric and Philosophy*, p. 39; Kristeller, "Il Petrarca, l'Umanesimo e la scholastica," pp. 228–32; Chiappelli, *Studii sull'esercizio della medicina*, pp. 65–68; and n. 27 above. On the place of scholastic logic and Aristotelian natural philosophy in medieval and Renaissance medical thought and curricula, see also Kristeller, "The School of Salerno: Its Development and Its Contribution to the History of Learning," in his *Studies*, pp. 495–551; N. Siraisi, *Taddeo Alderotti and His Pupils: Two Generations of Italian Medical Learning* (Princeton, 1981), pp. 96 ff.

Petrarch's doctor friend Giovanni Dondi held university posts not only in medicine but also in astronomy, astrology, logic, and philosophy. Another medical acquaintance, Francesco da Siena, also taught logic and philosophy. On these two figures, see. F. Maddison, Giovanni Dondi, *Dictionary of Scientific Biography*, ed. C. C. Gillispie (New York, 1971), 4:164; V. Bellemo, *Jacopo e Giovanni de' Dondi dall'Orologio* (Chioggia, 1894); I. Ettore, "Francesco Petrarca e i medici: La polemica con Giovanni Dondi" and "Petrarca e i medici: I medici amici," in *Il giardino di Esculapio* 3 (Milan, 1930).

34. He describes them as mechanics in *Sen.* 5.3.

35. For a discussion of various medical, cultural, and social motivations for medical eloquence, and for a profile of some of Petrarch's doctor friends, see my "Healing Eloquence: Petrarch, Salutati, and the Physicians," *JMRS* 15 (1985), 317–46 at 328–330.

36. See passage cited at n. 97; also see n. 102 below; also cf. the comments concerning "*animi morbi*" in *Sen.* 10.4 (*Opera*, p. 967).

37. See the Preface to Book 2 (*Opera*, p. 125); Diekstra, "Introduction," pp. 18–19. On Petrarch and the tradition of Fortuna, see Heitmann, *Fortuna und Virtus*, passim, esp. p. 55.

38. W. Fiske, *Francis Petrarch's 'De remediis utriusque fortunae': Texts and Versions*, Bibliographical Notices no. 3 (Florence, 1888); Nicholas Mann, "The Manuscripts of Petrarch's 'De remediis': A Checklist," *IMU* 14 (1971), 57–90 at pp. 57–59; Diekstra, pp. 18–19, 23n.

39. See his "Introduction" in *Phisicke Against Fortune*, pp. x–xi.

40. For his classical references here see Schottlaender edition (cited in n. 1 above) at pp. 50, 248. In this position Petrarch was presumably influenced by Boethius' *Cons. phil.* 2. pr. 8.

41. As Diekstra rightly argues, Petrarch's overall scheme in the *De rem.* loosely, though not expressly, draws on the Peripatetic framework of the "goods of the body, the mind, and external things." On the ancient (e.g., *Nic. Ethics* 1.8.2.1098b ff.; *Tusc.* 5.40) and medieval tradition of such discussions and on the occasionally related treatments of the deadly sins, see Diekstra, "Introduction," pp. 51–53. On the structure of the *De rem.* also see Trinkaus, *Poet as Philosopher*, pp. 121–24.

42. As for strains of the *contemptus*, cf. Ratio's occasionally graphic images in Chaps. 1.2 and 20; 2.94.

43. Trinkaus has suggested that the *De rem.* is a type of lay *summa confessorum* (*Poet as Philosopher*, p. 125). Certainly its very scope (including the treatment of worldly blandishments in Bk. 1) supports such a view. Of course, the framework is nonetheless secular, a lay "Ratio" replacing the pastoral "Augustinus" of the *Secretum*, the scheme of the four Stoic affects fully dominating that of the deadly sins (which, by contrast, had dominated in the *Secretum*). And though the chapters on

the seven deadly sins (2. 105–11) are preceded by a somewhat pastoral Chapter (104) "De virtutis inopia" (which not only draws from "*terrena philosophia*" the notion that virtue is perfected by habit [*Nic. Ethics*] but also hails "*coelestis sapientia*" as a guide to virtue and cites the notion of a divine grace enabling a receptive, actively striving will [*Opera*, p. 222]), still these chapters on the priestly canon of sins are rather perfunctory. In general, the *De rem.* basically aims to treat the *cura animorum*, filling in the psychological gaps left by the pastoral *cura animarum*.

44. For this point, and generally in this section, I am indebted to Diekstra's "Introduction," pp. 17–22, 42–43, 51–53.

45. As for Petrarch's notion of the passions, he cited Vergil's comment concerning the four emotions (*Aen.* 6.730–34) in the *Secretum* Bk. 1 and he referred to this passage in the Preface to the second book of the *De rem.*, in the latter alluding to Augustine's commentary on the passage. In that commentary (*De civ. Dei* 14.3), as Petrarch observed in notations he made in his copy of the *Aen.*, Augustine suggested that Vergil's view in this verse is Platonic in nature (cf. Chap. 1, n. 37 above). The formal scheme of the four affects, however, was formulated by the Stoics (cf. *Tusc.* Bks. 3 and 4; also cf. Augustine's critique of Stoic theory in *De civ. Dei* 14.8). See the comments concerning the passions in the translator's prologue to the second French translation of the *De remediis*, made for Louis XII in 1503 by an unknown author; the translator cites Boethius' reference to the four emotions at *Cons. phil.* 1. m. 7. 25–28 and Augustine's discussion in *De civ. Dei* Bk. 14 (L. Delisle, "Anciennes traductions français du traité de Pétrarque *Sur les Remèdes de l'une et l'autre fortune*," *Notices et extraits des manuscrits de la Bibliothèque Nationale et autres bibliothèques*, no. 34 [Paris, 1891], 273–304 at 297). On Petrarch and the tradition of the affects, see Heitmann, *Fortuna und Virtus*, pp. 89–150; Diekstra, "Introduction," pp. 42–43.

Because the four passions (which serve as the framework of the treatise) were associated with the Stoics, and because Petrarch suggests in his Preface to Book 1 that his work will remedy false "opiniones" (a Stoic concept), and because Petrarch is expressly imitating a Ps.-Senecan genre, the *De rem.* can generally be classified as a "Stoic" work (on Stoic sentiments in Petrarch see Heitmann, *Fortuna und Virtus*, e.g., pp. 98–109, 181–82, 220). It should be noted, however, that Petrarch could, like Cicero, be critical of Stoic positions (see nn. 72 and 78 below for discussion of Peripatetic sentiments in Chap. 2.114 and *Fam.* 23.12; in the latter he describes his overall plan in the *De rem.* in an equivocating manner that accommodates both Stoic and Peripatetic terminology [see Rossi, 4:187]). And, in general, it should also be noted that Ratio's speeches in the treatise are eclectic, revealing variously Stoic, Peripatetic, Platonic, and Christian strains (on which see Heitmann, *Fortuna und Virtus*, passim, and discussion in text below).

46. Cf. *Tusc.* 4.6.

47. Diekstra, "Introduction," p. 18; cf. M. Françon, "Petrarch, Disciple of Heraclitus," *Speculum* 11 (1936), 265–71; also Trinkaus, *Image and Likeness*, 1:49.

48. *Opera*, pp. 124–25.

49. Diekstra, "Introduction," pp. 16, 21–22.

50. *Opera*, p. 6. Cf. the notion of "*medicamenta verborum*" in *Fam.* 10.4 addressed to his brother (Rossi, 2:313).

51. If in an immediate sense monitory, Book 1 is, however, perhaps also consolatory: disparaging worldly blandishments is itself a consolation for those readers not possessing them.

52. Wenzel, *Sin of Sloth*, p. 161.

53. At the end of Chap. 93 Ratio suggests to Dolor that his complaint about fortune, one of the general laments the latter utters, is addressed generally in the second book of the manual as a whole.

54. *Opera*, p. 211. Dolor also complains: "Moestum me originis vilitas, et naturae fragilitas nuditasque et inopia, et fortunae asperitas, et vitae brevitas et finis incertus facit" (*Opera*, p. 212).

55. *Opera*, p. 211.

56. Cf. Wenzel (*Sin of Sloth*, pp. 25–26, 159–60), who points out that Petrarch also made this distinction between *tristitia secundum Deum* and *tristitia saeculi* in the *Secretum* Bk. 2 (*Opere*, 1:162).

57. See Wilkins, *Petrarch's Eight Years in Milan*, p. 67. On Innocent's popular work and other medieval works in the *contemptus* tradition see D. Howard, "Renaissance World-Alienation," in *The Darker Vision of the Renaissance: Beyond the Fields of Reason*, ed. R. Kinsman [Berkeley and Los Angeles, 1974], pp. 47–76 at 55–57). The genre continues into the Renaissance and beyond. Besides those strong traces of the *contemptus* in Petrarch's *Secretum* and *De otio*, see Salutati's *De seculo et religione*, Poggio Bracciolini's *De miseria humanae conditionis*, Giovanni Garzoni's *De miseria humana*, and Erasmus' *De contemptu mundi* (see Trinkaus, *Image and Likeness*, 1:173 ff.; Howard, "Renaissance World-Alienation," pp. 56–57). Petrarch's linking misery with the clinical malady of *tristitia* has important ramifications: man's unfortunate condition of "medieval" *miseria* is now substantively viewed in a psychological, consolatory context. As Augustine's discussions of *miseria* and *tristitia* in the *De civ. Dei* would foreshadow, such a connection between these two terms was perhaps generally not made in religious thought. However, one can find a blending of various "secular" and "sacred" psychological categories in a work such as *Della miseria dell'uomo* of the thirteenth-century *dictator* Bono Giamboni (*Della miseria dell'uomo, Giardino di Consolazione, Introduzione alle virtù di Bono Giamboni*, ed. F. Tassi [Florence, 1836]). Even so, perhaps Petrarch's special contribution is his connecting *miseria* so explicitly and "clinically" to a specific malady, with a specific pathology (viz. sweet grief) and a specific cure (viz. human dignity and happiness).

58. Trinkaus, *Image and Likeness*, 1:173–96. For "*aegritudo animi*" Ratio also suggests Cicero's *Tusc.* Bk. 3 and Seneca's *De tran. animi* (*Opera*, p. 213), as he did in the *Secretum* Bk. 2.

59. In the 1554 Basel *Opera* (p. 213) the phrase reads "praesertim philosophice partim catholice," but more likely is "partim philosophice, partim catholice" as found in the 1536 Venice edition (Bernadinus Stagninus) at f. 356v and as cited in Heitmann, *Fortuna und Virtus*, p. 210.

60. For Petrarch's sources and precedents see Heitmann, *Fortuna und Virtus*, pp. 209–12; Trinkaus, *Image and Likeness*, 1:179–99. In *De civ. Dei* 22.22 Augustine discusses the miseries of life that resulted from man's sin. On the other side of the coin, in 22.24 he presents the positive aspects of human life that exist even

in this basically wretched existence. Petrarch also balances the scale which, in late medieval thought, had been tipped toward the negative portrayal of human existence. Under the influence perhaps largely of Cicero's *De nat. deo.* Bk. 2, Petrarch's work has considerably more anthropological detail than does Augustine's. Also Petrarch marshals as consolation the fact of man's immortality, hope of resurrection, and his dignity *via* the Incarnation.

61. See *Opere*, 1:658. On the relation between the discussion of misery in the *De otio* and the *De rem.* see Heitmann, "La genesi," pp. 10–11.

62. "Horror stuporque ferit animum nostram simul et humilitatem et illius altitudinem contemplantis—illud quod ne contemplari quidem ad plenum possumus ex quo factum est, quis antequam fieret cogitasset?—quo scilicet, quam potenti et quam misericordi remedio huic tante miserie sit consultum" (*Opere*, 1:658). As in the *De rem.*, Petrarch poses here the consoling fact of the Incarnation, but there is a telling contrast in the tones of the two discussions. In the *De otio*, the Incarnation is presented as the remarkable feat bridging the tremendous chasm between lowly man and an omnipotent God. In the *De rem.* it is framed more in terms of man's special dignity.

63. On Petrarch's varying perspectives in the *De otio* and *De rem.* see Wenzel, *Sin of Sloth*, p. 161. On the idea of the rhetorically "apppropriate" see Trinkaus, *Image and Likeness*, 1:27–28; idem, *Poet as Philosopher*, p. 127; also cf. Seigel, *Rhetoric and Philosophy*, passim.

64. *Opera*, p. 1064; cf. Trinkaus's trans., *Image and Likeness*, 1:179–80; also see his discussion of Innocent's treatise and Petrarch's Chap. 93 at 1:174, 179–80; on Petrarch's notion of curing with "contraries" (in the *De rem.* 2.93 as well as in 1.69 and *Fam.* 7.9 and 17 and *Sen.* 12.2) see Heitmann, *Fortuna und Virtus*, p. 208.

65. Cf. his claim in *Sen.* 5.4 of being at work on *De rem.* 2.97, "De auditu perdito" when he received Donato Albanzani's letter complaining of hearing loss (Wilkins, *Later Years*, pp. 106–7). Also cf. his account in *Fam.* 4.4 of receiving offers of laurel crowns at Rome and Paris on the same day (Wilkins, *Life of Petrarch*, p. 25).

66. Ratio is aware of the nobler *tristitia secundum Deum* (see discussion in text above and n. 56), but rather than contemning and dismissing its counterpart, he offers remedies for it.

67. As Trinkaus argues, though there were medieval discussions of human dignity, the humanists gave this topic relatively more attention and a greater prominence (*Image and Likeness*, 1:173–321). Also see Kristeller, "The Dignity of Man," in *Renaissance Thought and Its Sources*, pp. 169–81.

68. In both of these chapters Petrarch presents a manifesto on the need for a moral philosophy that can be useful in these problems of illness and death—a type of wisdom he contrasts to the meaningless kinds of philosophy he finds in contemporary culture. In Chap. 114 he argues the worthlessness of knowing matters of astrology and natural philosophy compared to knowing the nature of the mind (see passage in text below cited at n. 73). Because he generally identifies doctors with those interests, it is clear that Chap. 114 is his counterstatement to medical learning. In Chap. 117 he complains of the uselessness of present-day philosophy. Perhaps it is partly because of the inherent importance of death and illness, and per-

haps because these two concerns are so prominent in the *Tusc.*, that Petrarch uses these chapters to defend the legitimacy of his philosophical and rhetorical craft. Nonetheless, his imbroglio with the doctors must also have inspired his comments in Chap. 114.

69. See Diekstra's comment ("Introduction," p. 43) that Dolor has a marked role in this chapter.

70. Whether begun in 1354 or 1356, the writing of the *De rem.* followed the warning to Clement VI and the *Cont. med.* (Petrarch having asked in the latter: "Quid enim ergo longa oratione opus est, cui fere verbum omne molestum est . . . ?" [*Opere*, 2:934]). If, in fact, Chapter 114 was written in a second stage of composition in 1366 (postulated by Heitmann, see n. 2 above), which I think likely, then it may have also followed Petrarch's principal letter on medical eloquence, *Sen.* 3.8 to Guglielmo da Ravenna (dated by Wilkins to "1363 or somewhat later" [*Later Years*, p. 138]). It would then also have followed *Sen.* 5.3 to Boccaccio (1365?; see Wilkins, *Later Years*, pp. 88–89) and *Sen.* 5.4 to Donato Albanzani (1366), which also issue attacks on the doctors. In the latter, Petrarch indicates that he is at work on Chap. 97, "On the loss of hearing" (perhaps this and other chapters on physical ills in this section of Book 2 [see n. 2 above] were prompted by Donato's recent letter to Petrarch indicating that he was losing his hearing). I believe that *Sen.* 5.4 on physical infirmity, particularly with its indictment of doctors, may well have led to Petrarch's major treatment of illness and pain in Chap. 114.

71. *Opera*, pp. 227–28. Cf. Job's reply to his "comforters" (Job 19:2).

72. Ratio draws not only on Stoic thought but also on other classical schools and Judeo-Christian perspectives. Ratio opens with the Stoic argument that only vice—not pain—is evil, but later yields to Dolor's protestations and concedes the (Peripatetic) perspective that pain could in fact be called an evil (following Cicero's position in *Tusc.* Bk. 2) and develops Cicero's arguments (in *Tusc.* Bk. 2) concerning the power of patience and mental "arms" to overcome physical suffering. Ratio also cites Christian notions of divine deliverance, a deliverance that comes, however, not to the languid but to those striving in their will (cf. 2.104).

73. *Opera*, p. 229. Cf. Seneca's *Ad Luc.* 88.14.

74. Ibid., p. 231.

75. Ibid., p. 231.

76. Cf. the attempt of "Socrates" to engender a *sophrosyne* in the mind of an afflicted "Charmides" in *Charmides* 157a. As, of course, Petrarch did not know the *Charmides*, his theory is all the more interesting as a Renaissance notion of healing eloquence.

77. Besides this general notion of healing eloquence, there can be found in Chap. 114 another more specific theory of therapeutic rhetoric. Once Dolor admits his readiness to be instructed in the mental weapons with which to combat pain, Ratio responds with an extrapolation of *Tusc.* 2.22.51, in which Cicero named three techniques for fortifying the mind: "contentio," "confirmatio," and "sermo intimus." Petrarch seeks to distinguish and discuss all these terms. In developing the notion of "sermo intimus" he not only adds an expressly religious dimension unknown to Cicero (citing, for example, the case of Job), but also frames it in

highly rhetorical terms, discussing a modern-day example of a torture victim who seemed to calm himself with the power of self-directed speech (on this section and particularly on Petrarch's comments on the potential of an interior, silent rhetoric [and on such notions elsewhere in his thought], see my "Healing Eloquence," pp. 336-39). Of course, for Petrarch himself or for a reader who ails, the counsels of Chap. 114, as well as those found elsewhere in the *De rem.*, themselves potentially represent the content of "inward speeches" that can be read, memorized, and silently recited.

78. In *Fam.* 23.12 one can see Petrarch's actual practice of such a verbal therapy for pain. In 1360 he wrote to his good friend Guido Sette urging him to endure gout patiently. As in Chap. 114, so also in this letter one finds a discussion of the theory of the efficacy of healing eloquence. Petrarch acknowledges the doubts concerning verbal ministrations to the sick, and advances his claim for eloquence: "pain is removed by poultices not by words, although it is mitigated and diminished by words. Often a friendly chiding or virile exhortation thus arms the mind with shame and ardour, so that it does not feel the pain inflicted upon its body" (Rossi, 4:185). Petrarch's solace in *Fam.* 23.12 is both classical and Christian, discussing the Stoic position (that evil is found not in *dolor* but only in *vitium*) but inclining toward Peripatetic revisionism of that rigid position (claiming here that "et ad summam sic me invenio, ut sepe ratio stoica, sensus michi perypatheticus semper sit" [Rossi, 4:186]) and presenting scriptural passages dealing with divine mercy, hope, and comfort.

If it is true that Chap. 114 was part of the "last 15 per cent" (Heitmann, "La genesi," p. 25) of the *De rem.* that Petrarch wrote in 1366, as it might well have been, then this letter of 1360 to Guido Sette came earlier. In fact, this letter may have been in part the "testing ground" for the consolation in Chap. 114. As was seen in Chap. 2 above, Petrarch had earlier in his life (1342) written a consolatory letter (*Fam.* 6.3) to Friar Giovanni Colonna on old age, poverty, and gout. Comparing Petrarch's consolations for gout in this earlier letter and in the later *Fam.* 23.12, it seems that Petrarch felt a greater need to defend and argue the potential benefit of verbal ministrations. Evidently, his bout with the papal doctor had made him more sensitive to the problems of trying to comfort the ailing with words.

79. Cited in n. 31 above. If Chap. 114 was composed after *Sen.* 3.8 (see n. 70 above), then it may well have been partially intended to show exactly how the humanist, the "true philosopher and orator," might attempt to move and cure the mind of one who is in pain.

80. It is not surprising that these are such prominent subjects in the remedy-book, because, besides their innate importance, they are also discussed at length in the first three books of the *Tusc.*, one of Petrarch's chief sources.

81. Cf. this theme also in *De rem.* 2.94.

82. See *Opera*, p. 847 (see Chap. 2, n. 24 above).

83. *Opera*, p. 847, emphasis mine.

84. "[M]ihi quocunque consuetudo antiqua [indulgent grief], linguam aut calamum impulerit propositum recens est, fixumque animo, quod dixi, multo quidem nisu fateor, sed et multo rerum turbine stabilitum, ex aequo despicere spes, metusque gaudia et dolores" (*Opera*, p. 848).

85. *Opera*, p. 848.

86. Cf. Wilkins, *Later Years*, pp. 61–62.

87. Specifically, were these chapters part of a second stage of writing in 1366? This question cannot be answered with any certainty. On the one hand, it would seem more likely that some or all of the death chapters appeared in the pre-1360 version; certainly, chapters on death figured prominently in the Ps.-Senecan *De remediis* and the problem of death was the subject of the beloved *Tusc.* Bk. 1. On the other hand, Petrarch could have thought it an unwelcome reminder, even a jinx, to include these chapters in the original version dedicated to the long-suffering Azzo. Or, possibly, he did include some treatment of death in the original version and expanded it in 1366. As I explain below in n. 91, there is some logic to the possibility that all or part of Chaps. 117–32 were added in the 1366 phase of composition.

88. (On Boccaccio's scare, see discussion of *Sen.* 1.5 in Chap. 2 above.) Clearly, he thought the subject of *Sen.* 8.1 could disturb the somewhat delicate Boccaccio, as he delayed his dispatch of the letter. Also, it is perhaps some measure of Petrarch's attitude toward the unlucky year that, on his sixty-fourth birthday, he again wrote Boccaccio (*Sen.* 8.8) announcing his survival (see Fracassetti, *Lettere Senili*, 1:496n; Wilkins, *Later Years*, pp. 103–4).

89. *Opera*, pp. 915–18. For other letters (besides *Sen.* 8.1 and 8) in which Petrarch reflects on death see *Fam.* 8.4, written during the 1348 plague, and *Fam.* 22.12; *Sen.* 3.7; 8.2; 13.8 and 9.

90. See Heitmann, "La genesi," p. 17.

91. Heitmann believes a second phase of the *De rem.* began probably with Chap. 94 and continued through Chap. 132. I agree that certain of these chapters did come in a second period, though not necessarily *all* of them, for I do not accept Heitmann's general assumption that all the dialogues of the *De rem.* were written sequentially (see n. 2 above). He suggests Chap. 93 as a natural ending for the first phase, the second phase beginning with the abruptly less sublime chapters on physical ills, including Chap. 97, which he convincingly dates to 1366 ("La genesi," p. 24). As the major, culminating, theoretical chapter on physical ills, Chap. 114 could thus well have been written in this same period. Finally, there is one piece of evidence that might, in turn, tie Chaps. 114 and 117 ("On the Fear of Death") to the same period. Petrarch chooses both of these chapters to present his strongest defenses of philosophical remedies. Of all Petrarch's efforts to be a moral and rhetorical *medicus* in the *De rem.*, they both seem to reflect the most determined attitude. Perhaps, then, they are products of the same period. Finally, it should be noted that, even if the death chapters were part of the pre-1360 version of the *De rem.*, they still, I believe, in part reflect Petrarch's attempt to deal with the prospect of his own death.

92. Like Ps.-Seneca, Petrarch has chapters on death in general, on violent death, on dying in a foreign land, on dying young, on dying without burial (cf. Diekstra, "Introduction," p. 35). The Ps.-Senecan dialogue opens with a treatment of death, owing to its prominence (see comment in edition reproduced in *Seneca's "De remediis fortuitorum" and the Elizabethans*, by R. G. Palmer [Chicago, 1953], at p. 28). For a discussion of the relationship between the Ps.-Seneca's and Petrarch's rem-

edy-books, and of Petrarch's use of Seneca's thought in the *De rem.*, see Bobbio, *Seneca e Petrarca*, pp. 270–79.

93. The concern with sudden death and incomplete projects can be found in *Secretum* Bk. 3—as can the concern with fame after death.

94. I.e., last rites. As mentioned above, Petrarch does, however, include a chapter "On Dying in Sin."

95. An earlier medieval work that rivals Petrarch's discussion of death is Vincent of Beauvais' *Tractatus consolatorius ad Ludovicum IX regem de obitu filii*, a philosophical and theological *consolatio* for bereavement dealing somewhat with the fear of death (see his *Opuscula* [Basel, 1481]).

96. *Opera*, p. 233. Cf. *Cons. phil.* 2. pr. 3.4–9; also cf. comment in *Secretum* Bk. 2 (at *Opere*, 1:158).

97. *Opera*, p. 233.

98. On Seneca's similar criticism of the dialectical, useless philosophy of his day (e.g., in *Ad Luc.* 49, 71, 88, and 117), and on Petrarch's attacks as perhaps drawing on and certainly paralleling such criticism, see Dill, *Roman Society*, pp. 299–301; Bobbio, *Seneca e Petrarca*, pp. 236–37.

99. *Opera*, p. 233.

100. Ibid., pp. 233–34.

101. See n. 92 above. Though I argue that all or part of the death chapters could have been written in 1366 (see n. 91), I acknowledge that Petrarch could have written them in the first phase (1356–57), even in the early stages of that phase, and that for this reason could have included his defense of eloquence here.

102. The centrality of this chapter is underscored by Petrarch's definition here of philosophers as *medici animorum* (cited at n. 97 above), a term also found at the end of the important Chap. 93 "On Misery and Sadness" (*Opera*, p. 213).

103. Petrarch criticizes Seneca's praise of Cato's action, and cites Cicero's discussion in the sixth book of *De republica* (*Somnium Scipionis*), in which Scipio Africanus the Younger, who expresses his desire to enjoy the rewards of death, is chided by his father to live out his appointed time. In general, however, as I think Petrarch knew from *Ad Luc.* 82, Seneca also advised against both the fear of and lust for death.

104. For the theme of "dying well" see, for example, Cicero's *De senectute* 19 ff. and Seneca's *Ad Luc.* 61, *De brevitate vitae* 7.4 and 15.1, and *De tran. animi* 11.4 ff. (see Beaty, *Craft of Dying*, p. 88n; also see n. 111 below).

105. *Opera*, p. 235.

106. Ibid., p. 234.

107. Ibid., p. 239.

108. Ibid., p. 240.

109. On these two late medieval cultural currents surrounding death and on the *ars moriendi* see Beaty, *Craft of Dying*, pp. 36–53.

110. Cf. Tenenti's discussion of Petrarch's writings on death in relation to general currents and to the *ars moriendi* in his *Il senso della morte*, pp. 48–117, 143–45, 468–75; cf. Trinkaus, *Image and Likeness*, 1:330, n. 36.

111. See Savonarola's *Predica dell'arte del ben morire*, a recorded sermon of 1496; Barozzi's *De modo bene moriendi* (pub. 1531); Bellarmino's *De arte bene moriendi* (pub. 1620); Erasmus' *De praeparatione ad mortem* (pub. 1534); Lupset's *The*

Waye of Dyenge Well (pub. 1534); Becon's *The Sycke Mans Salve* (pub. 1561); Taylor's *The Excercises of Holy Dying* (pub. 1651). For discussions of the text of the *Tractatus*, its sources, and the development of the genre, see Beaty, *Craft of Dying*; also M. C. O'Connor, *The Art of Dying Well: The Development of the "Ars Moriendi,"* (New York, 1942); Tenenti, *Il senso della morte*, pp. 80–138. In my discussion of the *ars moriendi*, I shall concentrate on the longer *Tractatus* rather than the abridged block-book, which, drawing only on Chap. 2 of the *Tractatus*, illustrated the temptations of the deathbed (Beaty, *Craft of Dying*, p. 3). For tables charting the editions both of the *Tractatus* and the illustrated *Ars moriendi* from 1465 to 1500, see Tenenti, *La vie et la mort à travers l'art du xve siècle*, Cahiers des Annales, no. 8 (Paris, 1952), Appendix B (pp. 92–95). As for the term "art (or) science of dying," Tenenti claims: "L'espressione di *scientia* o *doctrina moriendi* non s'incontra prima di Suso . . ." (*Il senso della morte*, p. 83), though in Seneca's *De brevitate vitae* 19.2 see the phrase "vivendi ac moriendi scientia."

As for Gerson's seminal *De scientia mortis*, a Latin edition can be found in his [*Opera*], 4 vols. in 3 (Paris, 1521), 2:176v–177; an edition of the original French work (*La médicine de l'ame*) can be found in *Oeuvres complètes*, ed. P. Glorieux, 10 vols. (Paris, 1960–73), 10:404–07. Though Gerson was interested in the consolatory genre (writing, for example, a *Traité de consolation sur la mort de ses amis* [*Oeuvres*, 7. pt. 1:312–26] and a *De consolatione theologiae* [*Oeuvres*, 9:185–245]; see Auer, *Dambach*, p. 294) and though he cites or draws upon various of Petrarch's works (he makes reference to the *De viris illustribus* and the *De vita solitaria* [*Oeuvres*, 5:237 and 7. pt. 2:784, respectively] and he draws upon the *De rem.* Bk. 1 [*Oeuvres*, 7. pt. 2:974; see N. Mann, "La fortune de Pétrarque en France: Recherches sur le 'De Remediis,' " *Studi Francesi* 13 (1969), 1–15]), I find no evidence that his *De scientia mortis* was influenced by Petrarch's *De rem.* 2.117–32. Gerson's work is a brief set of "exhortations, interrogations, prayers, and observations" that generally reflect a sacramental approach, as opposed to the more rhetorical, philosophical, consolatory approach that prevails in Petrarch's chapters on death. Nonetheless, we should perhaps not exclude the possibility that Petrarch's treatment of death could have generally influenced Gerson's interest in, if not his treatment of, the art of dying.

112. Cf. Erasmus' treatment of despair in his *"ars," De praeparatione ad mortem* (for an edition see n. 116 below; for a study of Erasmus' treatise see Thomas Tentler, "Forgiveness and Consolation in the Religious Thought of Erasmus," *SR* 12 [1965], 110–33).

113. O'Connor, *Art of Dying Well* (p. 4) suggests that the sole vestige of the *danse macabre* mentality in the *Tractatus* is the notion that death strikes everyone. On the *Tractatus*' author's knowledge of Innocent III's *De contemptu mundi*, see O'Connor, *Art of Dying Well*, pp. 5, 25 (n. 78), 29. Beaty argues that the *Tractatus* can be seen as a rational counterpart to the irrational climate of death characterized by the *danse macabre* and by religious preaching and sensibility. Drawing on Huizinga's thesis, she also argues Huizinga's point that the *Ars* was a manifestation of the late medieval penchant for the formalization of emotion (pp. 7–10, 37–53; cf. J. Huizinga, *The Waning of the Middle Ages*, passim).

The impact of the *Ars*, however, was not completely without its threatening side, as the illustrations in the block-book version depict the presence of demonic figures (in contention with divine ones) (Ariès, *Hour of Our Death*, pp. 108–9; A. Tenenti, *La vie et la mort*, pp. 52–54). For an edition of an *Ars moriendi*, see the latter, pp. 97–120.

114. Edition of the *Tractatus* found in C. Horstmann, *Yorkshire Writers: Richard Rolle of Hampole and His Followers*, 2 vols. (London, 1895–96), 2:406–20.

115. See her *Craft of Dying*, pp. 54–107; O'Connor, *Art of Dying Well*, pp. 187–88; Tenenti, *Il senso della morte*, pp. 127–29. On Lupset, who held various benefices and taught in the humanities at Oxford, see J. A. Gee, *The Life and Works of Thomas Lupset* (New Haven, 1928).

116. This is in notable contrast to his fellow humanists Thomas More (in *De quatuor novissimis*) and Erasmus (in *De praeparatione ad mortem*), who deal with dying in the more spiritual medieval fashion (O'Connor, *Art of Dying Well*, pp. 187–88; Beaty, *Craft of Dying*, pp. 55–56). Though it cites the "rational" Platonic maxim (*Phaedo* 67e) that philosophy is "the meditation or exercise of death," More's work, with its description of the portrayal of the *danse macabre* in the old St. Paul's, employs the emotional tenor of the *memento mori* (Beaty, *Craft of Dying*, p. 55, n. 3; for a facsimile of the 1557 London edition and for a modern edition of More's *The Four Last Things*, see *The English Works of Sir Thomas More*, ed. W. Campbell and A. Reed, vol. 1 [London, 1931], for here, esp. pp. 467–68 in the modern edition). Erasmus' *De praeparatione* contains only scattered classical citations (for example, like More, Erasmus cites the famous *Phaedo* maxim), in contrast to the highly humanistic tenor of his *Declamatio de morte* (cited in Conclusion below); clearly, he meant this to be a more conventional, spiritual work. For an edition of the *De praeparatione* see that by A. van Heck in *Opera omnia Desiderii Erasmi Roterodami*, 5. pt. 1 (Amsterdam, 1977), 337–92.

117. For an edition see Gee, *Life and Works of Thomas Lupset*; also see O'Connor, *Art of Dying Well*, p. 188; Beaty, *Craft of Dying*, pp. 57–107.

118. See, for example, Josse Clichtove's *De doctrina moriendi* (on which and other such works see Conclusion, n. 36 below).

119. On Drelincourt's work, see McNeill, *Cure of Souls*, pp. 212–13; also Conclusion, n. 40 below.

120. Cf. the *Tractatus artis bene moriendi*, which condemned an excessive concern with temporal things in its section on the temptations to avarice, yet commended one's making a will and providing for one's household.

121. In a seventeenth-century French translation (or paraphrasing) of portions of the *De rem.*, the death section was given some measure of autonomy. In the second edition of this trans., *La sage resolu contre la fortune, et contre la mort* (1661), one of the three books of the second volume deals with the sage "contre la mort" and consists of 14 chapters drawn from the death section (2.117–32) (see Fiske, *Petrarch's "De rem.": Texts and Versions*, pp. 28–29).

122. *Cure of Souls*, pp. 157–62.

123. Cf. Trinkaus, *Poet as Philosopher*, p. 120.

124. See Wenzel, *Sin of Sloth*, pp. 158–59; Kuhn, *Demon of Noontide*, pp. 68–74 and passim; but also cf. Baron, *Petrarch's "Secretum,"* pp. 215–18.

125. See Chap. 7 and Conclusion below.

126. *Opera*, p. 77. This chapter is one of the longest in Book 1.

127. *Opera*, p. 78.

128. In discussing and culling remedies for love, Petrarch cites Ovid (for whom, however, here he also has some critical comments) and Cicero, who both wrote on this problem (*Opera*, p. 78). As for the remedy involving the will, cf. discussions of the will in the *Secretum* and *De remediis* 2.104.

129. On Johannes von Dambach's manual, see Conclusion below.

130. Cf. n. 43 above.

CHAPTER 4
CONSOLATION AND COMMUNITY: COLUCCIO SALUTATI AS FRIEND AND COMFORTER

1. E. Garin includes this letter in his edition of Salutati's *Tractatus quod medici eloquentie studeant et de verecundia, an sit virtus aut vitium*, in *De nobilitate legum et medicinae—De verecundia* (Florence, 1947), p. 277. On the dating of this exchange between Baruffaldi and Salutati to 1390, see Garin, *De verecundia*, p. xxxiv; Francesco Novati, *Epistolario di Coluccio Salutati*, 4 vols., Fonti per la storia d'Italia, vols. 15–18 (Rome, 1891–1911), 3:182n. Garin suggests that Baruffaldi's reference is to *Sen.* 3.8, and I think he is correct. Though there were other letters to doctors in the *Seniles* chastising them about their eloquence, this letter presented the most substantive discussion on this topic (see Chap. 3 above).

2. Seigel, *Rhetoric and Philosophy*, p. 67. Though disagreeing with Petrarch here, Salutati did, however, rank law over medicine in his *De nobilitate legum et medicine* (Garin, *Italian Humanism*, pp. 31–33).

3. *Tractatus*, ed. Garin, pp. 282–84.

4. "Non enim credam, si quando vehementior tristitia morbum contraxerit, non nihil disertum medicum oratione facunda non posse, cum legamus musicam tum gravioribus tum concitatioribus modulis furorem iracundie non solum mitigasse sed extinxisse" (ibid., p. 286). For a fuller discussion of Salutati's argument, see my "Healing Eloquence," pp. 340–44.

5. For a thorough and careful study of Salutati's life and thought see Ronald G. Witt, *Hercules at the Crossroads: The Life, Works, and Thought of Coluccio Salutati*, Duke Monographs in Medieval and Renaissance Studies, no. 6 (Durham, N.C., 1983). I was able to see this study only after originally completing my work on Salutati in my "The Renaissance Vision of Solace and Tranquility: Consolation and Therapeutic Wisdom in Italian Humanist Thought," Ph.D. diss. (University of Michigan, 1981). Where our studies have overlapped— particularly in the analysis of Salutati's letters to Zabarella on the loss of his son Piero, which I present in Chap. 5—I find our appraisals to concur. Also on Salutati's thought see B. L. Ullman, *The Humanism of Coluccio Salutati* (Padua, 1963). For a Quattrocento account of Salutati's literary contributions see Giannozzo Manetti's comments in his *De illustribus longaevis*, cited by L. Mehus, in *Ambrosii Travesarii . . . latinae epistolae* [ed. P. Canneti]. . . . *Adcedit eiusdem Ambrosii vita in qua*

historia litteraria florentina ab anno MCXCII usque MCCCCXL . . . deducta est [L. Mehus] (Florence, 1759; rept. Bologna, 1968; hereafter *Vita Ambrosii Traversarii*), p. 288.

6. For edition see *Epistolario*, ed. Novati, whose dating of the letters I follow. On Salutati's role as lay consoler and counselor I am indebted to Marvin Becker (see Chap. 2, n. 75).

7. On his training under the *dictator* Pietro da Moglio, his career as a rhetorician (working, among other places, in the Lucchese chancery and serving as chancellor of Florence from 1375–1406), and the influence of such figures as Pietro della Vigna and Geri d'Arezzo, see Witt, *Hercules*, pp. 9 ff. and Seigel, *Rhetoric and Philosophy*, pp. 64–65. On the notarial and dictaminal tradition to which Salutati fell heir, see F. Novati, *La giovinezza di Coluccio Salutati* (Turin, 1888), pp. 66 ff; also Kristeller, "Humanism and Scholasticism," in his *Renaissance Thought and Its Sources*, p. 93. On Salutati's official letters see Ronald Witt, *Coluccio Salutati and His Public Letters* (Geneva, 1976). As for the private letters, Witt makes the point that, unlike Petrarch, who went back to revise his letters, Salutati left his in their original form, thus giving us a truer picture of his progression from the dictaminal style to a freer, more individual one (*Hercules*, pp. 60–61, 418).

8. On Salutati's acceptance of medieval Latin writers see Witt, *Hercules*, pp. 254–56; R. Donovan, "Salutati's Opinion of Non-Italian Latin Writers of the Middle Ages," *SR* 14 (1967), 182–201. As for scholastic influences on Salutati, see Witt, *Hercules*, pp. 293–99, 331–32, 424–25. As for the religious tenor in Salutati's letters, Witt suggests that this would be found in the mature rather than early phase of Salutati's letter-writing. He argues that the early letters (those of the 1360s), influenced by the *dictatores*, were more secular (*Hercules*, pp. 11–13, 64, 417), and he suggests that Salutati had a "conversion" to Christianity in the late 1360s (pp. 62–66). My own study would support this argument of an intensification of religious concerns in the letters, as the major religious discussions that I cite date from the 1370s or later. I would, however, also suggest that, compared to Petrarch's letters, Salutati's collection as a whole is generally more traditionally religious in tone and that such strains might have been informed partly by the dictaminal tradition (for examples of religious themes or references in the chapter "De consolationibus" in Boncompagno's *Rhetorica antiqua*, and in the consolatory writings of Pietro della Vigna, see von Moos, *Consolatio*, 1:406–7, 410–14; 2:224–26, 234–38; 3:334–35; also Introduction above). Witt (*Hercules*, p. 71) suggests that the development of more spiritual interests in Salutati's thought could be due partly to the influence of Petrarch's thought. And while this may be true (and while Petrarch's writings reveal many spiritual currents), I find that some of Salutati's *consolatoriae* are still much more conventionally or predominantly religious than Petrarch's. Perhaps one explanation for the greater spiritual tone in Salutati's letters lies in his conscious or unconscious attempt to blend more fully the classical and medieval traditions of letter-writing. An excellent source for understanding his perception of the history of Latin eloquence is his letter 9.9 (*Epist.* 3:76–91) to Bartolomeo Oliari, the Paduan Cardinal. Oliari had written Salutati, praising his reputation as an epistolographer and recommending that he collect his

letters. Salutati responds with a survey of Latin eloquence from the ancients (such as Cicero, Seneca, Valerius Maximus, Livy, Tacitus) to late ancient and early Christian figures (such as Martianus Capella, Macrobius, Cyprian, Lactantius, Ambrose, Jerome, Augustine, Boethius, Cassiodorus) to the twelfth and thirteenth centuries, when there were but a few "fairly good" writers (Ivo of Chartres, Hildebert of Lavardin, Abelard, Bernard of Clairvaux, John of Salisbury, Peter of Blois, and Richard of Pofi), to the modern age, which showed renewed interest in eloquence in the figures of Mussato, Geri d'Arezzo, and Petrarch and a flourishing of vernacular eloquence in Dante, Petrarch, and Boccaccio. At one point he discusses the theory of letter-collecting and cites many famous letter-writers, thus giving us a good idea of his view of the epistolary tradition: he cites Cicero, Seneca, Ausonius, Symmachus, Ennodius, Cassiodorus, Augustine, Jerome, Ambrose, Peter Damian, Gregory, and, in the modern era, Geri d'Arezzo and Petrarch (cf. Witt, *Hercules*, pp. 254–56; Ullman, *Humanism of Salutati*, p. 95). As for Salutati's knowledge of Seneca's and Cicero's letters, he read the former's *Ad Lucilium* in the 1350s and obtained the latter's *Ad Atticum* and *Ad familiares* only in the 1390s (see Ullman, *Humanism of Salutati*, p. 45 and idem, *Studies in the Italian Renaissance* [Rome, 1973 ed.], pp. 220–21.) As for Christian writers, Salutati cited letters of Jerome's and Gregory's. Though there is no evidence of his having a copy, he twice tried to gain possession of Abelard's letters (Donovan, "Salutati's Opinion," p. 194). For Salutati's knowledge, possession, or use of these and other classical and Christian letter-writers see Ullman, *Humanism of Salutati*, pp. 129–259. Perhaps the *ars praedicandi* also influenced Salutati's letters. A letter such as 5.14 (discussed in text below) almost has the tone of a homily. On Salutati's citing one of Gregory's homilies see Ullman, *Humanism of Salutati*, p. 230.

9. It is difficult to ascertain which patristic letters Salutati knew. It would be particularly interesting to determine if he knew Jerome's *consolatoriae*. In the extant manuscripts that belonged to Salutati, Ullman finds Jerome's letters 5, 22, and 78 (*Humanism of Salutati*, p. 231). In his letters, one can find Salutati directly citing Jerome's letter 53. It is uncertain whether or not he knew any of the consolatory letters such as 23, 39, or 60— I find no citation of these particular letters. In 9.4 he does reveal a considerable knowledge of Jerome's female correspondents, whom he defends as worthy women (*Epist.* 3:42–43). In this same letter he also refers to Peter of Blois' correspondence with women (p. 43). On Peter also see n. 11 below.

10. See G. Constable, *Letters and Letter-Collections* (Turnhout, 1976), pp. 16 and 32. On Peter of Blois' debt to Aelred of Riveaulx in his discussion of friendship, see Introduction above.

11. For references to Peter see *Epist.* 3:43, 83. See Donovan, "Salutati's Opinion," p. 194. Also on Peter and the popularity of his letter-collection see Southern, "Peter of Blois," pp. 105–32.

12. Though basically a lament concerning the failures of typical "worldly" friendships, Boncompagno's *Amicitia* also contained some comments concerning the "celestial" ideal of friendship (see Sarina's edition, esp. at pp. 52–54; cf. Introduction, n. 85 above). On Salutati's interest in friendship cf. Witt, *Hercules*, pp. 70, 344–45, 417; also Ullman, *Humanism of Salutati*, pp. 73 and 88.

13. See letter 3.12 (*Epist.* 1:212). Also, cf. letter 6.11 at *Epist.* 2:175.

14. In consoling Malatesta di Pandolfo Malatesta (11.1) on the death of his sister, he refers to his duty "amicably to console" (*Epist.* 3:331).

15. For instance, in consoling Filippo di ser Landino in 3.11 for a loss he argues: "Non enim aliud amicicie nostre munus potuit quam in tuis lacrimis lacrimare inque tuis agitationibus agitare. Caritatis enim perfectissime signum est felicium infeliciumque rerum communicatio et in rebus iocundis letum, in adversis mestum in anxium se prebere" (*Epist.* 1:162). Also to Pietro Turchi in 12.1: "Non possum, dilectissime fili, tuis in doloribus non dolere. Hoc enim vere caritatis munus est flere cum flentibus et cum gaudentibus iocundari" (*Epist.* 3:435). This problem will be further discussed in text below.

16. See *Epist.* 3:365.

17. Salutati also recognizes consolatory letters written to him as fulfilling the office of friendship and affection. For instance, he characterizes Rosello de' Roselli's letter of condolence this way: "In quibus pro dilectionis et amicicie, que rara reperitur, officio et condolendi solatium et consolandi debitum persolvisti: de quo quidem ingratum esset gratias non referre" (*Epist.* 3:134). Also see similar comments in the following two letters to Jacopo Manni and Pellegrino Zambeccari at *Epist.* 3:135, 142.

18. These are the sources he cites. Witt (*Hercules*, pp. 299 n. 10; 358) suggests that Salutati began substantively drawing on the *Nicomachean Ethics* only after 1390. Another work that may have been influential is the *De amicitia*, an apocryphal work of Cassiodorus which he cites in 9.9 (*Epist.* 3:79). And, again, Peter of Blois' and Boncompagno's treatises on friendship could have been influential. Also, the (twelfth-century?) consolatory dialogue *Altividus de immortalitate animae*, which Salutati knew, discusses friendship to some extent (see E. Garin, "Una fonte ermetica poco nota: contributi alla storia del pensiero umanistico," *La Rinascita* 3 [1940], 202–32 at 214–15; see BML, MS. Laur. 84, 24, ff. 204v–234, esp. at 205v–206; on this work further see note 53 below; also Chap. 5).

19. "For—as I speak more truly concerning this—I believe that, since friendship is nothing but love and since we believe love to be God himself, it ought to be embraced most highly" (*Epist.* 1:246–47).

20. *Epist.* 1:247.

21. In letter 14.5: "Sed nondum de celo descenderat vera caritas, in qua legimus: multitudinis autem credentium erat cor unum et anima una. Qua fit, ut verissimum sit aureum verbum illud Hieronymi: vera enim illa necessitudo est et Christi glutino copulata, quam non utilitas rei familiaris, non presentia tantum corporum, non subdola et palpans adulatio, sed Dei timor et divinarum Scripturarum studia conciliant" (*Epist.* 4:20). He cites from Jerome's *Epist.* 53, *Ad Paulinum* (PL 22:540).

22. *Epist.* 4:20.

23. *Epist.* 4:23.

24. *Epist.* 1:211–12.

25. On composition and dating of the *De seculo* see Witt, *Hercules*, pp. 195–96.

26. Salutati, *De seculo et religione*, ed. B. L. Ullman (Florence, 1957), pp. 1–2.

27. (*Epist.* 2:318–19). Novati speculates on the dating on this letter at p. 318 n. 2.

28. In his 1377 praise of *caritas* to Alberto degli Albizzi he lauds the love that "binds together (conglutinat) all of mankind"; in the *De seculo* he refers to the "glue (gluten) of the Christian religion" (see passages cited at nn. 20 and 26); as seen in n. 21, he cites Jerome's reference (in the latter's *Epist.* 53) to the "Christi gluten" (cf. Peter of Blois' use of the term "gluten charitatis" in his *De amic. christ. et de dil. Dei et prox.* [Davy's ed., *Un traité de l'amour*, p. 482]); in a praise of friendship to Roberto Rossi, Salutati stresses the worth of seeking an "amicum, qui tali tecum glutino copuletur, . . ." (*Epist.* 2:175); see comment on natural social bonds at *Epist.* 1:117; discussing friendship and social theory in a letter to Antonio Baruffaldi (the doctor to whom he addressed his *Quod medici studeant eloquentie* and *De verecundia*), Salutati argued that unity and association are natural impulses and that "not only is it useful and pleasant but also necesssary for the good to be glued into true friendships (in veras amicicias glutinari)." (*Epist.* 3:186).

29. See Trinkaus, *Image and Likeness*, 1:55. Salutati mentions the work in letter 3.9 to Boccaccio. It is indicative of the contrast between their thought that Petrarch would write a *De vita solitaria* and that Salutati would undertake a *De vita associabili.* But also see Witt's comments in *Hercules*, pp. 207–8.

30. "Summum ergo vinculum amicicie est, summum proculdubio gaudium, summa iocunditas, summe etiam res cara" (*Epist.* 1:117–18). He praises friendship as unique from and superior to other human relationships.

31. *Epist.* 1:118.

32. "Si igitur desideras alterius ope leniri tibi hanc molestiam, nichil est quod minus ex me possis expectare, nisi illud est efficax in erumna et afflictione solamen habere socium qui tecum mereat, tanquam in ponderibus levius affligat divisum onus in plures vel, quod philosophis placet, minuatur egritudo animi, dum sui misericordia commotum cernit amicum, cuius in affectu non gaudere non potest" (for Zabarella's letter see Salutati's *Epist.* 4:347–49 at p. 348). Zabarella is presumably drawing on *Nicomachean Ethics* 9.11.1171 (see n. 35 below).

33. *Epist.* 3:412.

34. "Proprie quidem consolator est, qui se solatur et alium; qui vero lenire nititur alterius egritudinem, cum tamen ipse non doleat, consolator vel, ut dicatur expressius, adsolator potest, non solator, si recte loqui voluerimus, appellari" (*Epist.* 3:412).

35. Zabarella's and Salutati's notion of the fellowship of grievers and Salutati's following argument concerning the comfort of silent co-sufferers are perhaps generally inspired by Aristotle's *Nicomachean Ethics* 9.11.1171.

36. *Epist.* 3:412.

37. For a discussion of the language of shared grief see Buresch, *Consolationum historia critica*, p. 119. Also see von Moos, *Consolatio*, 3:31–33.

38. For the former argument and for his citations from Boethius' *Cons. phil.* see *Epist.* 1:8–9, 22–23. For the latter argument see *Epist.* 1:248. On Salutati's concern with the problem of fortune vs. virtue in the early letters see Witt, *Hercules*, pp. 62–63.

39. He opens his letter by dealing with the essentially humoral character of melancholy, classing it with corporeal conditions of phlegmatic, choleric, and sanguine humors. Because humors are corporeal, however, they need not affect the

"vigor mentis" (*Epist.* 1:298). Salutati emphasizes the dichotomy between corporeal emotions and mental tranquility: "Considera te, sicut corpore mortalem et fluidum, sic animo fore non corruptibilem, sed eternum" (*Epist.* 1:299). As for 4.17, much of Salutati's consolation consists of a refutation of Juvenal's negative portrait of aging in the *Satires* 10. After discussing the fact that virtue is greater in old age, he speculates as to why God did not merely place men in old bodies from the start. For Salutati, man's life history of transgression, the conflict of the flesh against the spirit, assures that there is a meaningful role for divine *misericordia*: a divine mercy that forgives where divine justice would have seen fit to damn. In old age one should accept this divine scheme of human life and strive to correct the faults of younger years (see *Epist.* 1:314–20).

40. In the former, he cites *Tusculans* 2.25.61 and condemns those who are querulous and cowardly in pain (*Epist.* 1:168–70). In the latter (at *Epist.* 2:247), the notion that sickness helps make people aware of the nature of the human condition (cf. Petrarch's *De rem.* 1.3) would seem to be a traditional and common one.

41. See Witt's argument that the spiritual content of the letters emerges only after the late 1360s (see n. 8 above).

42. The bulk of these discussions starts in 1383. However, there is a letter of 1374 (*Epist.* 1:167–72) that first deals with the issue of leaving Florence and the question of divine will.

43. See Garin, *Italian Humanism*, p. 28; C. Bec, *Les marchands écrivains: affaires et humanisme à Florence, 1375–1434* (Paris, 1967), pp. 372–76.

44. See Witt, *Hercules*, pp. 280–81.

45. *Epist.* 2:93.

46. See letters 5.17 and 20; 6.23, 24, 25 (*Epist.* 2:83–98, 104–9; 221–44); from Augustine, Salutati cites, for example, the *De genesi ad litteram* Bk. 6 (in letters 6.23 and 24); in letter 6.25 he also cites Aquinas' *Exposition on Job*.

47. See *Epist.* 2:105–9.

48. See *Epist.* 2:125–27.

49. One of those who fled, Antonio di ser Chelli, responded to Salutati with the argument that divine providence called for his fleeing the city. Perhaps this particularly contributed to Salutati's discussion at this time concerning the question of human free will and divine will.

50. He discusses the problem of divine will and the human domain in a letter of 1371 to Francesco Bruni, a papal secretary. Here Salutati considers the role of divine will in the apostolic succession—specifically in terms of the recent elevation of Gregory XI. In this letter one finds much of the language of divine omnipotence seen in the later "plague" letters and consolatory letters (see *Epist.* 1:143–44). This intellectual and theological problem, then, concerned Salutati before his reflections on the plague. However, it seems fair to argue that the plague issue sparked and intensified his sustained and profound interest in this problem—an interest manifested in Salutati's writing of the *De fato* and in his language in the later consolations.

51. C. Trinkaus discusses the connection between the pestilence letters and the *De fato* and presents an analysis of the latter; he mentions the personal context of

Salutati's position concerning the plague and the larger issues of providence and human choice (*Image and Likeness*, 1:76–102).

52. Another important consolation for the fear of death (and for bereavement) is found in 11.24 (*Epist.* 3:422–33), written in 1400 to Pietro di ser Mino di ser Domenico da Montevarchi (see discussion in Chap. 5, n.27 below).

53. In addition to such *consolatoriae* proper, Salutati also composed letters in the slightly different, but related, genre of the epistolary eulogy: in 1374 he wrote one upon the death of his famous predecessor Petrarch (*Epist.* 1:176–87); and in the following year, one concerning Boccaccio's death (*Epist.* 1:223–28). The former letter, addressed to Count Roberto da Battifolle, is a praise of Petrarch's character and a review of his various literary and philosophical accomplishments. It is written in a genre that resembles the ancient funeral oration and presages, in epistolary form, the later humanist flowering of that genre (on which see Kristeller, "Francesco Bandini," *Studies*, p. 418; and now, McManamon, *Funeral Oratory*). And not only the form but also the content of Salutati's letter reveals a classicizing spirit. That is, it reflects the Renaissance interest in reviving the themes of individual fame and secular immortality (cf. Kristeller, "Francesco Bandini," *Studies*, p. 419). Salutati taunts "death" with the fact that Petrarch triumphed over it by achieving fame and an "eternal name." In the last section of the letter he presents various arguments concerning Petrarch's fortunate passage from the temporal to the eternal, citing the case of the dying Hermes Trismegistus, who speaks to his friends about anticipating his death. If the pagan Hermes joyfully accepts death, he argues, imagine how surely the Christian Petrarch did likewise. Salutati's source, as Novati points out, is the (probably twelfth-century) *Altividus de immortalitate animae* (also known as the *Liber Alcidi* and referred to by Salutati, in the *De verecundia*, as the "dialogi fraterne consolationis" [*De verecundia*, p. 294]) (see Novati, *Epist.* 1:186n, who suggests that Salutati loosely cites here from the *Altividus*; cf. BML, MS. Laur. 84, 24, f. 214v; on this work see E. Garin, "Una fonte ermetica," and idem, "Per la storia della tradizione platonica medioevale," *Giornale critico della filosofia italiana*, 3rd series, no. 3 [1949], 125–50; also see Chap. 5 below.) What is important here is that Salutati draws on this Hermetic dialogue for the notion of the dying man consoling his surviving friends. This same motif, of course, can be found in the Platonic tradition (see Chap. 7 below; also see the comments of the *Altividus* author himself, who compares to Hermes the case of Socrates [Laur. 84, 24, f. 215]). Thus Salutati's letter on Petrarch represents various dimensions of the Renaissance interest in the rhetorical and philosophical treatment of death. He draws on the genres of the prose eulogy and the consolatory dialogue of the sage. In both cases he presages aspects of the greater flowering of fifteenth-century Italian humanist literature on death.

54. *Epist.* 2:75.

55. *Epist.* 2:248–49. As for the earlier discussion of sickness in this letter see n. 40 above.

56. One could compare earlier consolatory letters to Luigi de' Gianfigliazzi (*Epist.* 1:15–20), Ugolino Orsini (*Epist.* 1:103–14), Tomasso Orlandi (*Epist.* 1:172–75) (although the latter already [1374] does exhort "tunc enim te Deo

placiturum puta, cum et que numine sue dispositionis intulerit et que per alium referri permiserit, patienter duxeris supportanda" [p. 175]), or Donato Albanzani (*Epist.* 2:68–76) to those of the late 1380s and 1390s—such as those to Bernardo da Moglio (*Epist.* 2:180–83), Antonio da Cortona (*Epist.* 2:245–50) cited earlier, Francesco d'Ugolino Grifoni (*Epist.* 3:192–96), Malatesta di Pandolfo Malatesta (*Epist.* 3:331–35), or Zaccaria Trevisan (*Epist.* 3:349–59). The new preoccupation with divine providence is sometimes very marked. In the letter to Malatesta: "O si daretur nos posse supra carnis sarcinam nos erigere videreque simul omnia sicut sunt, preterita presentibus iungere et presentia futuris alligare cernereque in omnibus, que videremus, Dei iusticiam, Dei sapientiam misericordiamque et miserationem eius essentie, que, cum summa bonitas sit, bene sine dubio cuncta facit . . . pudeatque non guadere summaque cum complacentia non amplecti quicquid erga nos divina sapientia divinaque bonitas ordinavit" (*Epist.* 3:335). The letter to Grifoni was the first consolation written after Salutati's description of his own highly theological consolation concerning the death of his wife Piera (note the language of divine providence in letters to Jacopo Folchi [*Epist.* 3:126–28] and to Pellegrino Zambeccari [*Epist.* 3:138–42]). Perhaps as a result, this letter too is strongly theological. He opens with references to the notion of divine providence ruling all things, he praises God's goodness and wisdom, and he closes with a citation of Augustine's *Contra academicos* 1.1 that "si divina providentia portenditur usque ad nos, quod minime dubitandum est, sic tecum agi oportet, ut agitur" (*Epist.* 3:196). This Augustinian citation also appears later in his discussion of his own divine consolation at the death of his son Piero in a letter to Zabarella (see *Epist.* 3:419 and Chap. 5 below). Also see his consolatory use of notions of divine providence and goodness at *Epist.* 3:132 and *Epist.* 3:384–88.

57. The notion of the consolation of "time" vs. the consolation of "reason" can be found in Servius Sulpicius' letter to Cicero (*Ad fam.* 4.5). Cicero mentions the notion of the proper time for giving solace in *Tusc.* 3.31.76. Also, in his chapter on consolation in his *Rhetorica antiqua* Boncompagno has a section dealing with the therapeutic power of time (see von Moos, *Consolatio*, 2:224). In one of his letters to Salutati, Francesco Zabarella cites Terence's notion of healing time in *Heautontimorumenos* 3.1.422 (see Salutati, *Epist.* 4. pt. 2:358). On the *topos* of time see von Moos, *Consolatio*, 3:17–19, 228–33.

58. See *Epist.* 3:133–42 and Chap. 5 below.

59. See *Epist.* 3:411–22; 456–478; and Chap. 5. On the notion of time see *Epist.* 3:477–78.

60. *Epist.* 3:333.

61. Salutati also discusses "time" in a letter (1390) to Antonio da Cortona (where also he mentions the loss of some of his own sons) (*Epist.* 2:249–50); also see *Epist.* 3:367. In a letter to Niccolò da Tuderano, Salutati presents a consolation of "reason" (using as part of it the argument of divine will and goodness), and suggests that if *ratio* is insufficient, one can add the solace of *exempla*; if the solace of exempla is insufficient, one can add the solace of *tempus* (*Epist.* 3:386–87).

62. For a discussion of Salutati's consolatory advice to Giusti in these letters see A. Tenenti, *Il senso della morte*, pp. 55 and 70; and now also Witt, *Hercules*, pp. 347–48. Novati presents biographical information on Giusti in *Epist.* 2:439n.

63. *Epist.* 2:442.

64. See text above and n. 25 above.

65. See *De seculo*, ed. Ullman, p. 165. In the second book of this treatise he suggests that these hundredfold rewards for piety are given to monks, those who have relinquished worldly ties. He ranks the other vocations on a similar scale: those who lead a lay life will be rewarded thirtyfold for their deeds; those leading a clerical life, sixtyfold. Thus, in the *De seculo*, monastic retreat is seen as guaranteeing the greatest spiritual rewards and safety (*De seculo*, pp. 92, 111, 163–67; cf. Witt, *Hercules*, pp. 201–3).

66. "[L]icite lucrari, ut pauperibus subvenias, et honeste santeque versari, ut pluribus prosis" (*Epist.* 2:444).

67. "[S]icut tu ipse testaris, sic velis quod factum est, quod non factum esse non velis" (*Epist.* 2:445). Also: "Miror autem hac optima stante sententia sepius repetenda, quod sic videlicet id quod luges velis factum, quod non factum esse non velis, quomodo possit caro contra spiritum concupiscere" (p. 446).

68. *Epist.* 2:448.

69. As will be seen below, Salutati will make the distinction between the life of penance and the life of alms, which perhaps also suggests that the issue here is that of monastic vs. secular life. Also, in the third letter there is another statement that seems to indicate Andrea's seeking monastic life (see passage cited at n. 86 below).

70. After warning Andrea not to "cling to God" for the wrong reasons Salutati continues: "Et ut ab his ad unum, in quo nescio quid titubare videris, accedam, noli querere honores, sed nec velis etiam obvios recusare; noli de lucrando sollicitus esse, sed si honestum lucrum obvenerit, non declines. Non contigit omnibus penitentia peccata tollere, sed eleemosynis datur multis illa delere" (*Epist.* 2:448–49).

71. "Queris mutare vitam et solitudinem desideras, ut merori possis indulgere tuo. Noli te sepelire cum vivis; vive, dum fata sinunt. Nec ob merorem et tristiciam filiorum renuncies illi, qui defertur, honori" (*Epist.* 2:449).

72. "Sperabam te vera scripsisse; sed, ut video, michi, imo tibi, vera dedisti. Constantissime quidem affirmaveras te sic velle quod tecum factum est, quod non factum esse non velles. Nunc autem, quasi verbo tuo captus, exitum querens et interpretari cupiens que dixisti, inquis: sat michi est quod ratio subsistat, ita quod a sententia mea non discrepem quam scripsi. Et si non est, cogor eam iure esse posse; et si sic esse non potest, fingo posse esse quod non velim non esse factum quod actum est" (*Epist.* 2:450). That Andrea again wrote to Salutati suggests that this laic dialogue concerning his grief is important: he seems to be interested in communicating the stumbling blocks and stages of his mourning.

73. On the notion of lay piety see Marvin Becker, *Florence in Transition*, 2 vols. (Baltimore, 1967–68), 2:47.

74. Again it is difficult to know to what extent Andrea's refusal to accept the job is motivated by his grief. The discussion here could derive merely from his reactions to Salutati's position on accepting public offices and honor. (According to Salutati he says: "Sed subdis de non recusandis honoribus consilium damnans meum: O me Coluci, miror, quod tu, vates cum sis, facis te ipsum vulgarem hominem, cum dicis me delatis non debere renunciare honoribus" [*Epist.* 2:454]). What is interesting to

us, however, is that Salutati connects Andrea's general desire for fleeing the active life, his refusing the office, and his grief over family deaths.

75. *Epist.* 2:453. The Jerome source is *Epist.* 53, *Ad Paulinum* (PL 22:542). See Witt, *Hercules*, pp. 347–48.

76. *Epist.* 2:454. Salutati's attitude toward his own life of pious service is found in a later letter (*Epist.* 3:539–43) to Fra Giovanni da Sanminiato, a figure whom he had convinced to enter monastic life and who, incidentally, made the first Italian translation of Petrarch's *De remediis* (on Giovanni and his contact with Salutati see B. L. Ullman, *Humanism of Salutati*, pp. 59–63). At one point in the letter—in which Salutati is defending secular studies against Giovanni's attacks—Salutati portrays the contrasting nature of his own secular literary/social endeavors and Giovanni's *sancta rusticitas* (*Epist.* 3:542–43; cf. Trinkaus, *Image and Likeness*, 1:54).

77. *Epist.* 2:455.

78. See, for example, his comment in the fifth chapter: "O finis speculationis verus, sublimis, nobilis atque clarus! Vos finem humane speculationis et felicitatis vultis verum invenisse; nos invento vero frui solummodo, sed operari ut homo bonus fiat, ut conservetur civitas, et humani generis societas atque communitas non turbetur" (*De nobilitate*, p. 36); on the related issue of the supremacy of the "volitional" over the "intellectual," see the twenty-third chapter, titled "Quod voluntas est nobilior intellectu, et activa vita sit speculativa preferenda" (*De nobilitate*, pp. 182–96). On Salutati as an advocate of the active life and on the *De nobilitate*, see Garin, *Italian Humanism*, pp. 27–55; H. Baron, *The Crisis of the Early Italian Renaissance* (Princeton, 1966 ed. [orig. pub. 1955]), pp. 104–20; Seigel, *Rhetoric and Philosophy*, p. 71; Witt, *Hercules*, pp. 331–54; L. Thorndike, "Medicine versus Law at Florence," pp. 24–58 at 44–45; Bec (*Les marchands écrivains*, pp. 372–78), who, in discussing Salutati's social theory, cites his defense of marriage (*Epist.* 2:365–74) against Petrarch's attacks. As Bec would argue, marriage is, along with friendship and the city, another one of the units of society that Salutati is interested in defending or lauding. Thus, in another way Salutati defends the social, active life, and the contrast between his bias toward an active "ideal" and Petrarch's bias toward a contemplative one is sharpened.

79. Garin, *Italian Humanism*, pp. 27–28. The humanist defense of the active life is not completely original to Salutati. As Garin points out, Petrarch in *Fam.* 3.12 reassures someone's doubts concerning the active life (*Italian Humanism*, p. 20): the addressee (Marco Genovese) appears to be one who, perhaps once planning monastic life, now is about to enter princely service. Petrarch's letter, however, lacks the moral urgency and the social, religious, and personal conviction that animates Salutati's efforts actively to dissuade Andrea and Pellegrino from their plans for religious retreat.

80. *Epist.* 3:295). There is now an English translation of this letter to Zambeccari by R. Witt in *The Earthly Republic: Italian Humanists on Government and Society*, ed. B. Kohl and R. Witt (Philadelphia, 1978), pp. 93–114. Also included in this collection is a letter Salutati wrote to a Caterina di messer Vieri di Donatino d'Arezzo, who broke her vows as a nun and returned to the world to marry and have a family. Salutati condemns her breaking of her vows and exhorts her to return

to religious life. It is a good companion piece to the Zambeccari letter. Salutati's ability to minister varying counsels is affirmed: Caterina should return to the cloister; Andrea and Pellegrino should remain in secular life. In all three cases Salutati argues against people's foolishly forsaking their chosen station in life. Also see the discussion of the *De seculo* above.

81. In letter 9.2 Salutati chides Pellegrino for paying his Giovanna higher distinction even than that given to the Virgin: "sed, amo unam, inquis, ex honestissimis dominabus. . . . nec eam ambitiosiore digneris vocabulo, quam salutifere nostre Virgini attributum sit, quam celestis ille nuncius beatam in mulieribus dixit; . . ." (*Epist.* 3:11). Salutati's letters to Pellegrino show his range as a moral and spiritual counselor. He warns him first (in 9.2) of the perils of an over-zealous secular love and later (in 10.16) of the dangers of an over-zealous or misdirected divine love.

82. "Te statuit Deus multorum patrem et multis propter multa refugium et amicum; deditque quod in republica tua possis plus quam communiter quivis alius operari. Se hec reliqueris, nonne ea Deus exiget de manu tua? Talentum hoc accepisti; ne defodias illud, exerce, labora, fac te servum utilem reddas in his que tibi tradita sunt" (*Epist.* 3:301–2).

83. See *Epist.* 3:304, where he cites this passage from Augustine's *Enarratio in Psalmum 51* 6 (*PL* 36:604).

84. *Epist.* 3:304–5. Witt's trans. in *Earthly Republic*, p. 110. Salutati even makes the point that no active life can be without contemplation and no contemplative life can be without action. Man is by definition social; he has a religious obligation to help his neighbor and a natural inclination to care and grieve for him. Like Jesus, even the contemplative must be moved by grief and compassion for his fellow man; not to be so moved would prove a man to be more wood or stone than human: "Qui profecto talis foret et in hac conversatione mortalium se talem exhiberet, non homo reputandus esset, sed truncus et inutile lignum, lapidea rupes et durissimum saxum, nec foret, quod consumate perfectionis est, mediatoris Dei et hominum imitator" (*Epist.* 3:306–7). Salutati will use this same sentiment later in justifying his own emotion at the loss of his son Piero in a letter to Francesco Zabarella: "Quod sentiens ac probans Cicero dixit: quid enim interest, motu animi sublato, non dico inter pecudem et hominem, sed inter hominem et truncum aut saxum aut quodvis generis eiusdem?" (*Epist.* 3:468). (Just as Cicero's *De amicitia* 13.48 was Salutati's source here in the Zabarella letter, so also perhaps was it an influence in the Zambeccari letter.) As we shall see in Chap. 5, Salutati strongly rebels against the idea of Stoic indifference in discussing his own experience of mourning. For himself, even as for the "contemplative" monk, grief is an inevitable part of everyone's "active" participation in the human community.

85. *Epist.* 3:51.

86. *Epist.* 2:453–54. As for Andrea's fate, after a hiatus of Sienese documentation concerning him (between 1389 and 1394), subsequent records reveal that he reassumed a position as a public notary he had held there earlier (see Novati, *Epist.* 2:439 ff., n. 1).

87. Again, it is unknown whether he actually saw the letters of Abelard or Peter.

Nonetheless, he knew their collections existed, trying to obtain Abelard's and making mention of Peter's (see nn. 8 and 11 above).

88. See Ullman, *Humanism of Salutati*, pp. 39–40; also see nn. 7–9 above.

CHAPTER 5
THE ART OF MOURNING: AUTOBIOGRAPHICAL WRITINGS
ON THE LOSS OF A SON

1. See esp. the discussions of *Fam.* 1.1; *Sen.* 1.1; *Var.* 58; *Sen.* 10.4 in Chap. 2 above.

2. As for the general literary tradition concerning the loss of a son, see Quintilian's discussion of the death of his son in the *Prooemium* to Book 6 of his *Institutiones oratoriae*. In the thirteenth century Vincent of Beauvais wrote a lengthy *Tractatus consolatorius ad Ludovicum IX regem de obitu filii* (see Introduction, n. 59 above). The loss of children was treated in several categories in Boncompagno's "De consolationibus" in Book 1 of his *Rhetorica antiqua* (see, for example, sections listed in Introduction, n. 75 above). In addition to consolatory letters, there are also dialogues on the theme. Besides those by Giovanni Conversini and Manetti, there is one (probably early Quattrocento) by the doctor Giovanni Baldi entitled *Tractatus quo ratione concluditur non possibile hominem filium habuisse et si potest haberi quod non possit amicti et si possit amicti quod non sit illius morte dolere* (BML, MS. Plut. 19, cod. 30, ff. 32–39v; on this work see L. Thorndike, "Medicine Versus Law at Florence," pp. 25–28). Also from the fifteenth century see the dialogue by Tommaso di Rieti, *Ad Ioannem Cardinalem Rothomagensem S. R. E. Vice Cancellarium Thomae Reatini in consolationem in obitu filii: Dialogus* (in J. Gaddi, *De scriptoribus non ecclesiaticis, Graecis, Latinis, Italicis, . . .*, 2 vols. [Lyons, 1648–49], 2:219–41). On Renaissance writings on the loss of sons, and on the tradition in general see J. Banker, "Mourning a Son: Childhood and Paternal Love in the *Consolatoria* of Giannozzo Manetti," *History of Childhood Quarterly: The Journal of Psychohistory* 3 (1976), 351–62; A. De Petris, "Il *Dialogus consolatorius* di G. Manetti e le sue fonte," *GSLI* 154 (1977), 76–106; idem, "Giannozzo Manetti and his *Consolatoria*," *BHR* 45 (1979), 493–525; and now his edition of the *Dialogus* (see n. 35 below).

3. See Chap. 2 above.

4. Petrarch's comments on the loss of his son are relatively brief and are joined with those concerning van Kempen, his friend of 33 years, "quem mihi orbe alio genitum" (see *Opera*, pp. 814–17 at p. 814). While it lacks the intensity and depth of Salutati's letter to Zabarella on the death of Piero, this letter could have had a partial influence on Salutati—though *Sen.* 10.4 probably had a greater impact.

5. For this letter see *Opera*, pp. 966–73, and Chap. 2 above. As for the likely influence of Petrarch's letter on this fifteenth-century tradition, it seems reasonable to speculate that the Stoicism found in this, Petrarch's lengthiest *consolatoria*, could have served, along with Zabarella's letter to Salutati, as a foil for Salutati's anti-Stoic stance. Also, Filelfo implicitly uses the same rhetorical device in his *Oratio* as Petrarch did here—namely, the assumption that the consolation of one similarly afflicted is the most effective. As for textual similarities, the *locus* recalling or citing

Tobit 10.4 (see n. 71 below) found in the respective works of Petrarch, Salutati, Manetti, and Filelfo is too common in such literature to confirm connections among these writings, but also cf. Petrarch's variation of the sentiment in Terence's *Andria* 309 (*Opera*, p. 968) with Salutati's quotation of that passage (*Epist.* 3:411) and Manetti's (*Dialogus*, p. 12).

6. Like Cicero and Petrarch, Salutati thus used the reply to the *consolatoria* as a forum to discuss personal grief. For Cicero's letters in this vein, see his *Ad fam.* 4.6, a response to Servius Sulpicius' letter (*Ad fam.* 4.5) to him on the death of Tullia; also see *Ad Atticum* 12.14, 18, 20, 28, and 40. As Salutati acquired the *Ad Atticum* and the *Ad familiares* in the 1390s, he may well have been partly inspired by Cicero to write such letters on his own (on his acquisition of Cicero's letters, see Chap. 4, n. 8). Cicero's discussions, however, were not as long or detailed as those Salutati would address to Zabarella; as for Petrarch's letter in this vein (*Sen.* 1.3), see n. 4 above.

7. The bulk of these discussions began in 1383. See, for example, letters 5.17, 20, and 22; 6.23–25.

8. *Epist.* 3:135.

9. *Epist.* 3:138.

10. Novati, *Epist.* 3:139 n.2. For a discussion of the *De fato et fortuna*, see Trinkaus, *Image and Likeness*, 1:76–102. On the loss of Piera and on the *De fato*, see R. Witt, *Coluccio Salutati and His Public Letters* (Geneva, 1976), p. 83; also, now idem, *Hercules at the Crossroads*, pp. 313–30.

11. *Epist.* 3:141.

12. Piero died in one of the recurring waves of epidemic which, ironically, Salutati had counseled his Florentine friends to brave rather than flee (see *Epist.* 3:396–97 and Novati's notes there; also Chap. 4 above). Novati places Andrea's death between mid-July and early August (*Epist.* 3:406n). On Salutati's letters to Zabarella concerning the loss of Piero and on his views on consolation, see now Witt, *Hercules*, pp. 355–67.

13. In the first of these letters (*Epist.* 3:392–96) Salutati tells Ugolino Caccini: "Illum siccis oculis infirmum vidi; sibi paternam benedictionem humiliter postulanti sine lacrimis benedixi; eum orans et Deo commendans immotis affectibus aspexi dulcem animam expirantem; eumque funerandum sine fletu et sine gemitu sociavi" (pp. 393–95). He then declares that he believes God does all for the best and that "me dispositione divine voluntatis, quicquid statuat, adherere" (p. 396). On the loss of Piero and Andrea also see letters 11.18, 21, and 22 as well as 11.19 and 23 and 12.4 discussed immediately below in text.

14. *Epist.* 3:400–403.

15. For the letter see Salutati's *Epist.* 4:347–49. Zabarella refers to consolatory and moral works Salutati had written. Citing some Stoic *loci* he says: "Quid enim est horum, quod non milies ad amicos consolandos dixeris et scripseris; munus tibi frequentissimum ob humanitatem tuam singularem tum et eloquentiam, que in te uno spes atque opes hac etate collocavit?" (p. 348). He also refers to Salutati's *De seculo et religione* as a work giving counsel on the harshness of fortune (p. 349). Zabarella thus attempts to recall and summarize Salutati's Stoic and ascetic advice concerning the vicissitudes of the world.

16. Before taking the offensive, Salutati does have the tact first to present a praise of Zabarella. He then quotes a considerable part of Zabarella's letter in his reply, presumably for the benefit largely of a wider audience which he apparently anticipates: with its Stoic tone and praise of his composure, Zabarella's letter provides a background for (and a foil to?) Salutati's intense, lengthy attack on Stoicism. Clearly, Salutati intends his letter to be much more than merely a private response to a *consolatoria*.

There was one Peripatetic theme in Zabarella's letter that Salutati developed with great interest—namely, the idea of shared grief among friends (see discussion in Chap. 4 above).

17. See *Epist.* 3:413–16.

18. "Cum enim Petrus meus, spes mea, delicie mee, sublevator meus atque laborum, gloria mea, senectutis instantis baculus, domus et familie columen, in quem iam hec celeberrima civitas oculos cum amore quodam incredibili coniecerat suos, egrotare cepit, mens presaga mali mox vidit quod futurum erat seque in merore et anxietate, qualem imminentis mali magnitudo secum afferrebat, prostravit coram in Domino in amaritudine, qualem hactenus nunquam sensi; devoteque supplicans petii, ut transiret ille calix a me" (*Epist.* 3:416).

19. Cf. the *loci* Zabarella briefly cited to Salutati: "Illo autem pervulgato sermone frustra te quisquam admonuerit nichil accidisse novi, quod mortale mortem oppetierit; talem esse legem nature vitam ut precario tribuat, repetat cum vult, humanum id fuisse tibique ferendum modice quod nec inopinatum esse debuit" (*Epist.* 4:348; cf. *Epist.* 3:412–13).

20. For discussions of Salutati's letters to Zabarella concerning his grief see A. Tenenti, *Il senso della morte*, pp. 56–58; J. Seigel, *Rhetoric and Philosophy*, pp. 71–73; and now R. Witt, *Hercules*, pp. 355–67. For an earlier attack on Stoicism see Salutati's letter of 1382 to Lombardo della Seta (*Epist.* 2:55).

21. *Epist.* 3:419–20.

22. Ibid., p. 420. Cf. Salutati's exchange with Andrea Giusti (see Chap. 4, nn. 67 and 72).

23. *Epist.* 3:421.

24. See n. 84 below.

25. See *Epist.* 4:354–55.

26. Ibid., p. 360.

27. It is important to point out, as does J. Seigel, the puzzling fact that in the interim between the writing of these letters to Zabarella, Salutati composed another letter that contradicted much of the spirit and the letter of his arguments concerning the nature of death. In September 1400, he wrote to Pietro di ser Mino di ser Domenico da Montevarchi to console him for the loss of family members and for his own fear of death (*Epist.* 3:422–33). One of his principal arguments was that death is not evil. He presented the essentially Christian view that death is bad only for the evil, and he draws on the positive consolations for death found in Cicero's *Tusc.* Bk. 1 (p. 427; could Zabarella's second letter have been partially a spur in his turning here to the first book of the *Tusc.*?). Yet in the second letter to Zabarella (Feb. 1401) Salutati resumed his attack on the Stoic view of death, forcefully returning to his earlier position. Though he argued in this letter that the

premeditation on death is consoling, he also said that in some cases it can worsen grief. On the disparity among these letters see Seigel, *Rhetoric and Philosophy*, pp. 71–73 and now Witt, *Hercules*, p. 365n. As for some explanation of this discrepancy in Salutati's thought, possibly he felt that his personal construction of the emotional realities of mourning (namely, his poignant recognition of the tragedy and evil of loss, and his rejection of rational consolation) would be bitter medicine, particularly for someone who was not only bereaved but also fearful of his own death. In terms of personal conviction as a mourner and in terms of theory, Salutati may thus have come to espouse one position, but in terms of his practice as a consoler (at least in this case) he could voice another, perhaps feeling compelled to minister to Piero more traditional Stoic comforts. True to rhetorical practice, Salutati followed a situational approach. Perhaps he was taking Zabarella's advice, offering to Pietro the mundane "lower" level of Stoic consolation.

28. *Epist.* 3:460–61; to affirm that maxim "optimum esse non nasci proximumque quam primum mori" (*Tusc.* 1.48.114) is to deny the goodness of God's plan in creating man, granting him immortality in Eden, bestowing a regained "immortal beatitude" after resurrection. Cf. Salutati's comments in the first letter that both human and divine law view death as a punishment (p. 418).

29. Letter 12.4 (*Epist.* 3:463). Witt argues that Salutati began to draw substantively on Peripatetic thought only in the 1390s. Though he sees earlier scattered citations from Aristotle's *Nicomachean Ethics* in Salutati's writings, he suggests that Salutati's significant interest in the work came in this later period (*Hercules*, pp. 299, 358). If in the first letter to Zabarella the specific textual influence of the *Ethics* is minimal (see *Epist.* 3:418 and Novati's note there), it is considerable in the second (see the many citations, esp. at pp. 462–64).

30. *Epist.* 3:463.

31. For example, he cites the case of Christ's agony concerning his imminent death (ibid., pp. 464–65).

32. *Epist.* 3:475; cf. 419.

33. See *Epist.* 3:333. Salutati also discussed "time" in letter 7.1 (1390) to Antonio da Cortona and in 11.8 (1399) to Bernardo da Moglio. For Cicero's comment on the consideration of time in the administering of solace see *Tusc.* 3.31.75.

34. *Epist.* 3:477.

35. For discussions of the *Dialogus* and its sources, see Banker, "Mourning a Son"; de Petris, "Il *Dialogus*"; idem, "Manetti and his *Consolatoria*." Originally, for my study I used BNC, Magl. 21.18, ff. 1–45v. There has since appeared de Petris' ed. (*Dialogus de Antonini, sui filii, morte consolatorius*, Edizioni di storia e letteratura [Rome, 1983]), which lists seven extant manuscripts of the Latin version (judging BAV, Pal. Lat. 1601 to be the most authoritative) and seven of the Italian (pp. liii–ci). Citations are to De Petris' edition.

36. His tastes running to the Peripatetic, Manetti also translated the *Eudemian Ethics*, the *Magna Moralia*, and the *De memoria et reminiscentia*. On these and other of Manetti's endeavors see Vespasiano, *Vite di uomini illustri del secolo XV*, ed. P. d' Ancona and E. Aeschlimann (Milan, 1951), pp. 259–91 (including comments on Manetti's views on the death of children at p. 262 [for which reference I thank Arthur Field]); Cosenza, *Biographical and Bibliographical Dictionary*, 3:2111–15;

Trinkaus, *Image and Likeness*, 1:230–58; Garin, *Italian Humanism*, pp. 56–60; E. Leonard, "Introduction," in her edition *Ianotii Manetti de dignitate et excellentia hominis* (Padua, 1975); on the *De illustribus long.* see discussion in text below.

37. See A. della Torre, *Storia dell'Accademia Platonica di Firenze* (Florence, 1902), pp. 233–34. For discussions of the *Dialogus* other than those major ones cited above, see della Torre, pp. 234–37; also Garin, *Italian Humanism*, pp. 57–58.

38. See Novati, *Epist.* 3:421n. In discussing Salutati's character, Manetti cites the first letter to Zabarella (11.23): "Fuit staturae plusquam mediocris, . . . mirabilisque constantiae, quod, ut alia omittam, in morte duorum adolescentium filiorum Petri, et Andreae manifestissime demonstravit. Nam in funeribus eorum ita modeste se gessit, ut non modo lacrymas non emitteret, sed etiam domesticos flentes egregie consolaretur, idque precipue in obitu Petri, qui unica spes sua esse videbatur, fecisse dicitur. Ab eius namque latere toto aegrotationis suae tempore numquam discedebat, ut extremum filii spiritum forte hauriret, quem ut toto pector accepit, illico supinum cadaver statuit, palpebras oculorum propriis manibus composuit, labia clausit, manus insuper, et bracchia in crucem constituit. Ad extremum quum vultum eius etiam, atque etiam intueretur, nullum mestitiae signum, mirabile dictu, exinde discedens prae se tulit, atque haec omnia ipse in epistola quadam, in qua acerba huius filii sui morte ad amicum consolantem rescribit, sese fecisse testatur" (see L. Mehus, *Vita Ambrosii Traversarii*, 1:289). Though it is possible that Manetti took note of Salutati's letters after the writing of the *Dialogus*, it is far more likely that he knew them before: as will be shown, the textual and thematic similarities are striking.

39. See de Petris, "Manetti and his *Consolatoria*," p. 499.

40. The conversation begins: " 'Dic mihi,' inquit, 'amice, quonam modo dolorem ob repentinam filii tui mortem nuper tolerasti.' At ego, quamquam acerbam filii mei mortem mihi molestiorem fuisse significarem quam ullo unquam tempore antea putassem, me tamen et patienti et equo animo tulisse laturumque esse aperte respondere non dubitavi." Angelo then says that he notes in Giannozzo's words and expression signs of grief (*Dialogus*, p. 8).

41. Ibid., p. 8.

42. Ibid., p. 12; Cf. Garin, *Italian Humanism*, p. 57.

43. *Dialogus*, pp. 12–44. On Angelo's Senecan sources and on these five arguments (which Manetti will address), see de Petris, "Il *Dialogus*," pp. 81–89 and his "Manetti and his *Consolatoria*," pp. 502–6. Before turning to the *exempla*, Angelo also cites other *loci* from Seneca's *Ad Marciam*: i.e., the universality of tragedy, man's corporeal fragility and the inevitability of death, the importance of tranquility in all things; the inability of tears to bring back the dead.

44. *Dialogus*, p. 46. There is a misprinted line in the final sentence of this passage in the edition. The sentence should read: "Ego autem peripateticorum opinionem utpote humane vite magis consentaneam et sequor et probo" (see de Petris, "Il *Dialogus*," p. 93 and BNC, Magl. 21.18, f. 10). On this passage also cf. Garin, *Italian Humanism*, pp. 57–58.

45. Particularly close (almost verbatim) in both works is the linking of two passages concerning the legitimacy of emotion (from Julius Capitolinus' *Antoninus*

Pius 10.5 [in *Scriptores historiae augustae*] and from Cicero's *De amicitia* 13.48) (see *Dialogus*, p. 58 and Salutati's *Epist.* 3:468).

46. *Dialogus*, p. 88. Cicero had approved this maxim of Crantor's in *Tusc.* 3.6.12. And this condemnation of Stoic insensibility was also found in Ps.-Plutarch's *Cons. ad Apol.* 102c-e. Carlo Marsuppini's *Consolatoria oratio* of 1433 (to Lorenzo di Giovanni and Cosimo de' Medici), which drew on the *Ad Apol.*, also cited this Crantorian sentiment (see P. G. Ricci, "Una consolatoria inedita del Marsuppini," *La Rinascita* 3 [1940], 363–433; also Chap. 7 below). I think it likely Manetti was influenced by Marsuppini as well as by Salutati in his position.

47. Like Salutati, Niccolò presents the argument that not only divine but also human law prescribes death as grave punishment for the worst crimes (*Dialogus*, pp. 142, 144; cf. Salutati, *Epist.* 3:418, 461). On Niccolò's role as an arbiter see della Torre, pp. 236–37. D. Marsh suggests that the use of a "neo-Augustinian" arbiter who renders a religious judgment is a technique found in various fifteenth-century dialogues (on this convention in Poggio Bracciolini and Valla see his *The Quattrocento Dialogue: Classical Tradition and Humanist Innovation* [Cambridge, Mass., 1980], pp. 138–77; in Manetti, see his "Boccaccio in the Quattrocento: Manetti's *Dialogus in symposio*," *RQ* 33 [1980], 337–50).

48. For an identification and discussion of these and some other religious sources that Manetti draws on in this section, see de Petris, "Il *Dialogus*," pp. 101–4.

49. *Dialogus*, pp. 204–6; thus runs the Latin version; for added religious comments in the corresponding Italian version of this passage, see p. 207.

50. *Dialogus*, pp. 210–12. At this point Niccolò now praises the virtue of emotional moderation and fortitude, saying that God rewards those who suffer "modeste" the bitter loss of children, as the case of Job illustrates. Thus besides acknowledging the naturalness of grief, Manetti's treatise also invokes the Judeo-Christian concept of redemptive suffering and fortitude: Manetti's regimen thus calls for a Peripatetic balance between Stoic impassivity and emotional excess.

51. Ibid., p. 214.

52. In the first letter to Zabarella, Salutati presented an address to God; in the second, a discussion of divine omnipotence and goodness that developed some of the same themes found in the address. I think Manetti draws on both of Salutati's letters in his address to God (for example, cf. *Dialogus*, pp. 214–16 and Salutati's *Epist.* 3:478).

53. Manetti does not cite Plato a single time in the *Dialogus*. On the Platonic revival see Chap. 7 below.

54. On Manetti's hope to reach a more popular audience through the *volgare* version, see M. Langdale, "A Bilingual Work of the Fifteenth Century: Giannozzo Manetti's *Dialogus consolatorius*," *Italian Studies* 31 (1976), 1–16, at 2–3.

55. From the *Proemio* to Mariotto Banchi (see *Dialogus*, pp. 3–4; Langdale, "Bilingual Work," p. 3).

56. See the prologue to the third book of his *De familia* (*Opere volgari*, ed. C. Grayson, 3 vols. [Bari, 1960–73], 1:153–56; trans. in R. Watkins, *The Family in Renaissance Florence* [Columbia, S.C., 1969]) and the dedicatory letter to his self-

consolatory dialogue *Theogenius* (*Opere*, 2:55–56). See J. Gadol, *Leon Battista Alberti: Universal Man of the Early Renaissance* (Chicago, 1969), pp. 218–19.

57. "Però che mi pare in questo nostro *Dialogo*, intra l'altre cose, sie per ragioni naturali e ancora per auttorità de' gentili e similmente per la testimonianzia de' santi, avere assai apertamente mostrato quanto sia l'afezione paterna e la carità de' padri verso de' proprii figiuoli: la quale, in verità, è tanta e tale che niuna in questo mondo ne può essere o immaginarsi maggiore di cosa mortale e caduca. E benché questo amore paterno sia sì grande che quaggiù tra noi non si possa trovare maggiore, niente di meno io mi sono pure ingegnato di chiarire in che modo e con che animo si debba, sanza offensione di Dio e sanza fare forza alla natura, sopportare la molestia che comunemente suole intervenire a' padri per la perdita de' loro cari figliuoli, . . ." (*Dialogus*, p. 4; emphasis mine).

58. See comments of "Angelo" at pp. 22, 24 (see discussion in text above) in which he questioned Manetti's Christian sensibilities: as his Antonino certainly enjoys a happier existence now, Manetti's sorrow must center on his own sense of misfortune, a posture that could appear ungrateful to God. In his response "Giannozzo" affirms his religiosity by agreeing that he laments his own situation rather than that of his son ("Christiana nanque religione ita imbutus sum, . . ."); but he also goes on to defend the legitimacy of his sense of loss, having naturally anticipated enjoying further "voluptates" from his son (p. 58; see Banker, "Mourning a Son," pp. 354–55).

59. Kristeller, "Francesco Bandini," p. 421n; R. Sabbadini, *Giovanni da Ravenna, insigne figura d'umanista (1343–1408)* (Como, 1924), pp. 87–88. The dialogue remains unedited, save for brief excerpts in Sabbadini, pp. 174–76. I am using the ms in Oxford, Balliol College 288, ff. 51vB–71vA (on mss of Conversini's works see Sabbadini, pp. 121–24; R. Weiss, "Il codice oxoniense e altri codice delle opere di Giovanni da Ravenna," *GSLI* 125 [1948], 133–48; also, B. G. Kohl, "The Works of Giovanni di Conversino da Ravenna: A Catalogue of Manuscripts and Editions," *Traditio* 31 [1975], 349–67, esp. 356). For a lengthy consolatory letter to Donato Albanzani (the recipient of Petrarch's *Sen.* 10.4) concerning Petrarch's death, see the ed. by B. G. Kohl and J. Day, "Giovanni Conversini's *Consolatio ad Donatum* on the Death of Petrarch," *SR* 21 (1974), 9–18. For his *Dragmalogia de eligibili vite genere* see ed. and trans. by H. L. Eaker, with introduction and notes by B. G. Kohl (Bucknell, Pa., and London, 1980).

60. Sabbadini, *Giovanni da Ravenna*, pp. 3–4. On Conversini's life and career see Sabbadini and the recent entry by B. G. Kohl, "Giovanni Conversini da Ravenna," *DBI* 28:574–78.

61. On Conversini's letters to Salutati, see Salutati's *Epist.* 4:305–30 and Sabbadini, *Giovanni da Ravenna*, pp. 74–75, 218–19. On his residence in Padua and his acquaintance with Zabarella see Sabbadini, *Giovanni da Ravenna*, pp. 227, 236. There are some similarities between Salutati's letters (to Zabarella) and Conversini's dialogue. Although their citations were worded differently, they both used the Antoninus Pius story (cf. Balliol, 288, f. 54A and Salutati's *Epist.* 3:468). And, in general, Conversini treated some of the same issues that Salutati did—the legitimacy of grief, the irreparability and untimeliness of the loss, the question of whether death is evil or good, the notion of divine will. These textual similarities—

in addition to Conversini's personal connections with both Salutati and Zabarella—strongly suggest the influence of Salutati's letters on him.

62. For dating of the *Oratio* see n. 64 below. L. A. Sheppard convincingly
argues that this work was probably published in Milan by Filippo di Lavagna in the
latter half of 1475. A c. 1484 ed. of Filelfo's *Opuscula* includes the *Oratio consolatoria* and mentions the errors of the Milanese text (see Sheppard, "A Fifteenth-Century Humanist, Francesco Filelfo," *Transactions of the Bibliographical Society*, 4th
series, no. 16 [1935], 1–26, at 7–10). A Basel edition of Filelfo's writings (*Orationes cum quibusdam aliis eiusdem operibus*, Amerbach, not after 1498) also mentions the errors of an earlier Milanese edition. I assume that the c. 1484 edition of
the *Opuscula* and the Basel edition of the *Orationes* offer identical or similar texts.
I will cite the Basel edition. There were a number of other edns. of Filelfo's orations, and, thus, the *Oratio* to Marcello was published at least six times in the course
of the fifteenth century (see L.F.T. Hain, *Repertorium bibliographicum*, 2 vols.
[Stuttgart and Paris, 1826–38], 2.2:97–98). I have learned, first through Professor
Kristeller and now Margaret King, that Filelfo's *consolatio* was part of a collection
dealing with the death of Valerio Marcello (in the University Library in Glasgow
[Hunterian Museum MS 210 (U. 1. 5)]). Besides Filelfo's work, this collection
contains *consolatoriae* from other prominent humanists: e.g., Battista Guarino and
George of Trebizond (the latter edited in J. Monfasani, *Collectanea Trapezuntiana:
Texts, Documents, and Bibliographies of George of Trebizond* [Binghamton, N.Y.,
1983], pp. 235–48) (on Marcello and this collection see Margaret King, "An Inconsolable Father and His Humanist Consolers: Jacopo Antonio Marcello, Venetian Nobleman, Patron, and Man of Letters," in *Supplementum Festivum: Essays in
Honor of Paul Oskar Kristeller* [Binghamton, N.Y., 1987], pp. 221–46; also R.
Fabbri, "Le *Consolationes de obitu Valerii Marcelli* ed il Filelfo," in *Miscellanea di studi
in onore di Vittore Branca*, 5 vols., Biblioteca dell' "Archivum Romanicum," Series
1, nos. 178–82 [Florence, 1983], 3. pt. 1:227–50). On Filelfo, in general, see C.
de' Rosmini, *Vita di Francesco Filelfo da Tolentino*, 3 vols. (Milan, 1808); D. Robin,
"A Reassessment of the Character of Francesco Filelfo (1398–1481)," *RQ* 36
(1983), 202–24; idem, "Unknown Greek Poems of Francesco Filelfo," *RQ* 37
(1984), 173–206.

63. As Fabbri ("Le *Consolationes*," p. 234) and King ("Inconsolable Father," p.
234n) argue, a letter that Filelfo wrote Marcello in late June indicates the work was
apparently undertaken at Marcello's request. The evidence is very persuasive:
"Marchesius Varisinus, et mihi familiaris et nominis tui observantissimus, id a me
petiit, verbis tuis, quod tuli equidem, ut par fuit, egerrime. Quippe qui in re laeta
maluissem quam in lugubri et permolesta meam erga te benevolentiam experireris.
Sed quoniam ea lege nati sumus, ut naturae parendum sit, feramus aequo animo
necessitatem. . . . Ego propediem quod cupis effectum dabo" (*Epistolarum familiarium libri xxxvii* [Venice, 1502], p. 116 *bis* [sig. q4]). Marcello did later bestow a
present upon Filelfo (King, "Inconsolable Father," p. 234; de' Rosmini, *Vita*,
2:127).

64. See de' Rosmini, *Vita*, 2:123. Sheppard suggests that Filelfo's printing
of the work in 1475 closely followed the deaths of two other sons ("Fifteenth-
Century Humanist," pp. 8–9). Filelfo's Olimpio died in early March 1461

(*Orationes*, sig. E2); Marcello's Valerio, just over two months earlier, on Jan. 1. Filelfo dates his *Oratio* Dec. 25, 1461 and twice comments in the treatise that Marcello has had a year to mourn (see n. 117 below; King, "Inconsolable Father," p. 228n).

65. Besides the beginning of the treatise (*Orationes*, sigg. E2–E3) there are various references to Olimpio or to Filelfo's own situation (sigg. F1v; H7r–v; I7v–I8). Filelfo attempts to make their situations very analogous—more so, even, than they actually were. For example, in one passage (sig. F6v) he points out that their sons were born in the same year (1453) and month, that neither reached the age of eight, and that he and Marcello are both entering their sixty-fourth year. Filelfo, however, was wrong in saying that Valerio, like Olimpio, was born in 1453—he was born in 1452, failing to reach his ninth birthday (Monfasani, *Collectanea Trapezuntiana*, pp. 235, 237; King, "Inconsolable Father," p. 228n).

66. In the idea both of the co-suffering consoler and of the mutually consoling discourse, *Sen.* 10.4 may well have been an important influence on Filelfo's *Oratio*.

67. It is, of course, difficult to assign motive in such a case. Nonetheless, whatever Filelfo's motivation, he infused into this *Oratio* a more than passing autobiographical tone, which likely drew upon the earlier such tradition we have examined in this chapter. For letters (one of which was to Piero de' Medici) in which Filelfo spoke of Olimpio's death, see his *Epist. fam. xxxvii* (Venice, 1502), pp. 121r–v *bis* (sig. q2r–v).

68. In the letter to Senofonte he comments: "Pudet me fateri mollicam animi mei, qui alios plaerosque, in huiusmodi naturae casibus, saepe ad constantiam gravitatemque, adhortatus me a gemitu, ac lachrymis, continere nequiverim. Magna est profecto naturae vis, cui adversari qui potest, supra hominem est ducendus" (*Epist. fam.*, p. 229r; de' Rosmini [*Vita*, 3:124–26] discusses this letter and Filelfo's other comments on the loss of children). For editions of letters dealing with the loss of his two young sons (in 1475) and third wife Laura (in 1476) see *Vita*, 2:398–403, 430–34; 3:173–74. It is interesting to note that, not long after Filelfo wrote the *Oratio*, a family death would prompt him to make reference to the work: in 1462 he recommended the treatise to his son Senofonte as a consolation for the death of the latter's baby son (see *Epist. fam.*, p. 124r; de' Rosmini, *Vita*, 3:121).

69. *Orationes*, sig. E2r–v. Cf., for example, Manetti's comment on the "naturalis humanae fragilitatis impetus" (*Dialogus*, p. 214), though, however, this does not of course prove that Manetti was Filelfo's source for such a comment, as this vocabulary can be found in other consolatory writings. Manetti's *Dialogus* may also be influential in those sections of Filelfo's *Oratio* that deal with the inevitability of grief and the naturalness of parental mourning (see *Orationes*, sigg. E8, F2r–v, F3, F4).

70. On the *Commentationes* (written in the 1440s) see C. Errera, "Le 'Commentationes Florentinae de exilio' di Francesco Filelfo," *Archivio storico italiano*, series 5, no. 5 (1890), 193–227.

71. Both describe their thoughts and laments at the time of their children's deaths (cf. *Orationes*, sig. E2r–v and Salutati's *Epist.* 3:416 [see n. 18 above]). Like Salutati, and Petrarch before him in *Sen* 10.4 (*Opera*, p. 969), Filelfo also lamented the loss of his "senectutis . . . baculus," although this common locution does not

prove any textual influence (for Manetti's use of the term in his citation of Tobit 10.4, see *Dialogus*, p. 174).

72. Cf. Ps.-Plutarch's *Cons. ad Apol.* 103c–d; and Marsuppini's *Consolatio* to Lorenzo and Cosimo de' Medici (Ricci, "Una consolatoria inedita," p. 407).

73. *Orationes*, sig. E3. On the *locus* "amisi-praemisi," also invoked by Salutati in a *Epist.* 3:401, see von Moos, *Consolatio*, 3:320–22.

74. Balliol, 288, f. 52A–52B. Among other things, Conversini argues that "amplius amamus ampliore dolore torquemur" (f. 53A); he also contends that the natural and Christian emotion he feels for others in a time of tragedy, he may also feel for himself (f. 54A–54B). When citing this ms, I have, for the sake of clarity, converted "u"s to "v"s where appropriate.

75. "Ita meror animum quo tegitur, eo infestius imbullit, ubi vero percunta animi claustru effunditur residet quiescit sensimque dilabitur. Sine itaque lamentari, plangere, lacrimari, suspirari iusto dolore tumentem. Habet quippe levamen et voluptatem suam meror. Quemadmodum enim quies intermissa laborem, ita permisso lacrimarum et comploracio eiulatusque mesticiam comminuit et temperat sistitque animum fluctuantem" (f. 58vA–58vB).

76. Cf. Garin, *Italian Humanism*, pp. 27–59.

77. Discussed in Chap. 4 above.

78. *Epist.* 3:285–308 at 306–7, trans. found in B. G. Kohl and R. G. Witt, *The Earthly Republic: Italian Humanists on Government and Society* (Philadelphia, 1978), p. 112. Cf. Conversini's adaptation of Christian social emotion to the realm of private feeling (see n. 74 above).

79. For the comparison of an unfeeling man to wood or stone, Salutati here is probably drawing on (other than, as Novati observes, Horace's *Sat.* 1.8.1) Cicero's *De amicitia* 13.48, which he quotes in the second Zabarella letter (*Epist.* 3:468); for the example of Christ's tears for Lazarus, cf. both letters to Zabarella (at *Epist.* 3:413, 465).

80. See Garin, *Italian Humanism*, pp. 41–59.

81. *Dialogus*, p. 48. In his anthropological perspective here, Manetti would seem to anticipate his major study *De dignitate et excellentia hominis*.

82. *Dialogus*, p. 52.

83. Garin discusses the development of anti-Stoic thought in Cosma Raimondi da Cremona and in Valla, and discusses various aspects of humanist psychological theory, including a comparison of Manetti's attack on Stoicism (in the *Dialogus*) with an anti-Stoic sentiment voiced by Guarino Veronese (*Italian Humanism*, pp. 47–59). On Valla's critique of Stoic consolation in the *De vero bono*, see Trinkaus, *Image and Likeness*, 1:121.

84. See, for example, the chapter "Quod voluntas est nobilior intellectu, et activa vita sit speculativa preferenda" (*De nob.*, ed. Garin, pp. 182–96). On Salutati's valuation of the will over the intellect, and for discussions of the *De nobilitate*, see Garin, "La polemica sulla dignità delle leggi," in his edition of the *De nobilitate*, pp. xlv–lviii; his *Italian Humanism*, pp. 27–33; Trinkaus, *Image and Likeness*, 1:51–102; Witt, *Hercules*, pp. 331–54; however, also see Seigel's point (*Rhetoric and Philosophy*, pp. 73–74) that Salutati was not entirely consistent in esteeming the will over the intellect. Cf. Chap. 4, n. 78.

85. See his *De sui ipsius et multorum ignorantia*, *Opere*, 2:1110; trans. by H. Nachod in *The Renaissance Philosophy of Man*, ed. E. Cassirer *et al.*, p. 105. Also, on the role of the will in attaining spiritual and psychological health, cf. the *Secretum*.

86. Filelfo perhaps saw it as one of the goals of his *Consolatio* to make accessible (latinize) for such as Marcello a wealth of Greek consolatory lore (cf. his comment concerning his copious use of Greek material [*Orationes*, sig. G1v]).

87. Ficino's work fed the sixteenth-century controversy over immortality involving such figures as Pomponazzi, Contarini, and Nifo (see Kristeller, "The Immortality of the Soul," in his *Renaissance Thought and Its Sources*, ed. M. Mooney [New York, 1979], pp. 181–96).

88. G. di Napoli, *L'immortalità dell'anima del Rinascimento* (Turin, 1963), pp. 86–97; Kristeller, "The Dignity of Man" and "The Immortality of the Soul" in his *Renaissance Thought*, pp. 169–96; also, his "Pier Candido Decembrio and His Unpublished Treatise on the Immortality of the Soul," in *Studies II*, pp. 281–300; orig. in *The Classical Tradition: Literary and Historical Studies in Honor of Harry Caplan*, ed. L. Wallach (Ithaca, N.Y., 1966), pp. 536–58; Trinkaus, *Image and Likeness*, 1:200–58. Both Fazio (*De hominis excellentia*) and Manetti, like Petrarch, discuss the notion of man as the image and likeness of God. They also deal with various philosophical positions concerning immortality.

89. On the immortality theme in Petrarch's letters see, for example, *Fam.* 2.1; on Salutati's discussions of immortality and on Zabarella's treatment of the theme in a treatise (1400) entitled *De felicitate*, see di Napoli, *L'immortalità dell'anima*, pp. 69–72, 74–75; on Marsuppini, see the same, p. 75 and Ricci, "Una consolatoria inedita," pp. 388, 419–20; on this theme in its particularly Platonic context see Chap. 7 below.

90. Ricci, "Una consolatoria inedita," p. 421; di Napoli, *L'immortalità dell'anima*, p. 75.

91. On the struggles of the 1430s, see Zippel, *Carlo Marsuppini d'Arezzo*, pp. 12–13; idem, "Il Filelfo a Firenze (1429–1434)," in his *Storia e cultura del Rinascimento* (Padua, 1979; orig. Rome, 1899), pp. 215–53 at 222 ff.; G. Holmes, *Florentine Enlightenment*, pp. 98–99. On Filelfo's belittling of Marsuppini, see Ricci, "Una consolatoria inedita," pp. 384–86.

92. The argument from "nature" adduces funerary customs and notions of immortality from various sources secular (a most extensive one being from Euripides' *Hecuba*) and religious. The argument from "divine justice" cites the theological notion that souls must survive to fulfill the scheme of divine justice in which rewards are given to the virtuous, punishments to the evil.

93. Ficino's major treatment of this theme came in a formal philosophical treatise (the *Theologia Platonica*), not in a *consolatio*; his development of the theme in his consolatory letters, though, as we shall see, it could be quite vivid, never aspired to lengthy rhetorical or philosophical argumentation. As for Filelfo's *Oratio*, besides those Renaissance writings mentioned above (n. 89), there were various philosophical precedents or possible influences concerning the theme of immortality and death. On the *Phaedo* and the Ps.-Platonic *Axiochus*, see Kristeller, "Francesco Bandini," pp. 417, 421–24. As for the tradition of the *Consolatio* proper, Cicero's

lost *Consolatio* seems to have discussed the problem of the mind (as can be inferred from the *Tusc.* Bk. 1), and Ps.-Plutarch's *Ad Apol.* presents some discussion of immortality. However, the other principal extant *Consolationes* (Seneca's *Ad Marciam* and *Ad Polybium* and Plutarch's *Ad uxorem*) do not substantively address this topic. In terms of ancient sources, I believe that Cicero's discussion in *Tusc.* Bk. 1 was probably an important model for Filelfo. I do not know if Filelfo knew the (twelfth-century?) dialogue *Altividus de immortalitate animae* (or *Liber Alcidi*), a work that substantively linked the theme of immortality to the problem of consolation. Garin discusses this work's similarity to the Calcidius' commentary on the *Timaeus*, Macrobius' commentary on the *Dream of Scipio*, and Boethius' *Cons. phil.* Associating it with the Platonic interests at Chartres, he reasonably dates the work to the twelfth century. The treatise portrays the vision of an "Alcidus," who, having lost his brother, receives two levels of consolation from visitors in his dream: a superficial solace represents the consolation of the "exterior man"; a more sublime one, that of the "interior man." The solace tendered by the latter group (among whom an "Altividus" is the principal speaker) deals with the notion of the soul's immortality and divine similitude. Besides examining various philosophical theories concerning the nature of the soul (including those, for example, of Democritus, Zeno, Epicurus, Plato, and Aristotle), part of "Altividus" ' discussion here consists of an account of the dying Hermes Trismegistus' consolation of his surviving friends—an account cited by Salutati in a letter on the death of Petrarch (cf. Chap. 4 above) and included by Ficino in his translation of the *Pimander* (for this discussion of the work, see E. Garin, "Una fonte ermetica"; also his "Per la storia della tradizione platonica mediovale"; on Ficino's inclusion of it in his Pimander trans. see Kristeller, *Supplementum Ficinianum*, 1:cxxix–xxxii; for a ms see BML, Laur. 84, 24, ff. 204v–234). Besides Salutati and Ficino, figures such as Bruni and Agostino Nifo also knew the work. It apparently had a considerable Florentine currency: Garin points out that, in addition to a (probably) twelfth-century ms that Salutati presumably knew or possibly owned, four (the majority) of the extant mss emerged "dall'ambiente fiorentino" of the fifteenth and/or sixteenth centuries (Garin, "Per la storia," pp. 127–28; "Una fonte ermetica," pp. 202–10).

94. For this section, which includes considerable discussion of Plato and Aristotle, see *Orationes*, sigg. G8–H7v.

95. *Orationes*, sig. H7v. Six years later, in an *Oratio parentalis de divi Francisci Sphortiae Mediolanensis ducis foelicitate*, Filelfo again developed the theme of immortality, citing numerous thinkers and religious notions of divine similitude and resurrection (*Orationes*, sigg. C2–C4).

96. Kristeller, "The Immortality of the Soul," pp. 181–84.

97. On Filelfo's aspirations and reputation as an orator, see de' Rosmini, *Vita*, 3:45–72.

98. In the dedicatory epistle in the 1481 edition of the *Opuscula* (also included in Amerbach's Basel edition of the *Orationes*), he singled out his treatment of immortality: "Nam siquis hasce tris orationes diligentius lectitarit, cum pleraque inveniet non inutilia (ut mea fert opinio), tum vero quae ad animorum immortalitatem pertinent; animadvertet non inepte a me esse pro tempore et discussa et disputata" (*Orationes*, sig. A1v; de' Rosmini, *Vita*, 2:125–27). The discussion of

immortality in the *Oratio* to Marcello apparently had some impact: de' Rosmini (*Vita*, 2:124–25) suggests it is the work (on immortality by Filelfo) referred to by one of his discussants in Matteo Bosso's fifteenth-century dialogue *De veris ac salutaribus animi gaudiis*; it is cited by the sixteenth-century Flemish cleric Josse Clichtove in the consolatory section of his *De doctrina moriendi* (Clichtove, *De doctrina moriendi* [Paris, 1520], f. 85v).

99. *Orationes*, sig. E7. See Banker's thoughtful comments on the notion of immortality through children and cf. his treatment of Manetti's discussion of paternal bonds in "Mourning a Son," pp. 355–58.

100. See Balliol 288, ff. 56vB–57vB.

101. "Sane quia nulla res sive edificatio sive opus sive fama unicuique proprior atque immediator quam ex se edita proles extat nec sic autorem effigiat ac refert. Summa caritas liberorum est. Quippe in ore filii et patris imago in moribus virtus in studiis elucet gloria. Singula queque mortalium opera ab arte prodeunt et imagine mortua visuntur. Filius autem nature munus viva imagine genitorem exprimit ut filio conspecto similitudine tua effigieque conpereas videaris cognoscaris memoreris" (f. 57B–57vA). Solator also later says: "In quo utique vera mei imago, impressa, mores, affectus, et studia radiabunt. . . . Cum illum igitur intuerer me velud in speculo contemplabar recognoscebam ac tamquam ipse proficerem illius virtute gratabar. Impresenciarum sublato speculo nec sencio nec cerno nec me me recognosco. Leta michi omnia secundaque cum illo tumulavi quorum loco adversa ac tristitia successere et regnant" (f. 57vB). Parents' identification with and joy in children generates powerful bonds: "Propter hoc vehementissimus animi nexus commiseracio consuetudoque ita exaggerant dilectionem affectusque conglutinant, ut haud secus ac te te imo interdum plus quam te ipsum prolem studeas procures diligas . . ." (f. 57vA). On parental love, cf. Aristotle's *Nicomachean Ethics* 8.12.2.1161b and Manetti's *Dialogus cons.*, pp. 64–68.

102. The likelihood of such a connection would perhaps be greater in humanists later in the fifteenth century (e.g., Filelfo) than in Conversini, as the Renaissance development of the "dignity of man" theme began to be substantively explored only in the mid-Quattrocento (e.g., Manetti's *De dignitate*; see above and n. 88). Petrarch, however, did deal with this theme in the mid-Trecento in his *De remediis* 2.93.

103. On Conversini and this elder son, see B. G. Kohl, "Introduction," *Dragmalogia* (cited in n. 59 above), and idem, "Conversini," *DBI* 28, 574–78.

104. "Imo impresenciarum mori potissimum metuo, eo sublato qui rerum nominis et siqua fuit virtus heres futurus suo apud posteros fulgore radiasse; ve michi soli cuinam tantorum divine humaneque sapiencie thesaurum voluminum congressi (*lege*: congessi?)? Quis possidebit, quis fruetur?" (Balliol 288, f. 66vA–66vB; Sabbadini, *Giovanni da Ravenna*, p. 176).

105. "Diuturniorem splendioremque calamus, quem operosum laudabiliter habuisti quam filius prestabit. Ex filiis nanque laus mortalis brevique peritura, monimentis litterarum eterna manet" (Balliol 288, f. 67B).

106. For an interesting discussion of the "types" of immortality to which people turn, see R. J. Lifton, "The Sense of Immortality: On Death and the Continuity of Life," in *Explorations in Psychohistory: The Welfleet Papers*, ed. R. J. Lifton with E.

Olson (New York, 1974), pp. 271–87. As for Conversini, I believe that it is possible that some of the discussions of death in his dialogue might have been motivated not merely by his son's death but also by the prospect of his own.

107. As for precedents other than Cicero, on Quintilian see n. 3 above. Plutarch's *Ad uxorem* on the death of his daughter was perhaps a type of mutual consolation for himself and his wife, but I have found no evidence of the influence of this work on the humanists discussed in this chapter. This work could not have been known to Petrarch (on Plutarch's arrival in Italy see R. Sabbadini, *Le scoperte dei codici latini e greci ne'secoli XIV e XV*, 2 vols. [Florence, 1905–14], 1:44–49); and although Filelfo cites from the *Cons. ad Apol.* (*Orationes*, sig. G6) in his *Oratio* to Marcello, he does not cite the *Ad ux.*

108. Cosenza, *Dictionary of Humanists*, 3:2724; de' Rosmini, *Vita*, 3:126.

109. In his *Sen.* 10.4 Petrarch was perhaps trying not only to identify with his addressee but also truly, as he indicates, to console himself. In his *Oratio* to Marcello, Filelfo was perhaps also moved by these twin aims, though he does not state the latter goal; and even if his work was commissioned, we should not rule out an attendant self-consolatory function.

110. See his *Familiares* 7.12 (Rossi, 2:122; Bernardo's trans. *Fam. I–VIII*, p. 366) discussed in Chap. 1 above.

111. For a text of Morelli's comments on the death of the child and his longer account of the anniversary ritual, see Giovanni di Pagolo Morelli: *Ricordi*, ed. V. Branca (Florence, 1969), pp. 455–59, 475–516. For discussions of Morelli and some comments on the bereavement account see C. Bec, *Les marchands écrivains*, pp. 53–75 and passim; also, Branca's "Prefazione" in *Ricordi*, ed. V. Branca. R. Trexler translates and analyzes the bereavement account in his "In Search of Father: The Experience of Abandonment in the Recollections of Giovanni di Pagolo Morelli," *History of Childhood Quarterly: The Journal of Psychohistory* 3 (1975), 225–52; also see his fuller treatment in his *Public Life in Renaissance Florence* (New York, 1980), pp. 159–86. Trexler rightly views Morelli's account in terms of ritual.

112. On the entire Marcello collection and its circumstances, see Margaret King's "An Inconsolable Father" (cf. n. 62 above). As Professor King indicates her intention to do a larger study of the Marcello collection, I shall not exhaustively examine this treatise here, but I shall make a few comments on the relevance of the *Excusatio* to the larger tradition I have examined in this chapter. As to the origins of the *Excusatio*, King would seem inclined to consider the work to have been commissioned or instigated by Marcello (King, "Inconsolable Father," pp. 231–32; also, see Fabbri, "Le *Consolationes*," p. 232n). This cannot be ascertained for a certainty, however, from Bevilacqua's prefatory letter (for the *Excusatio*) to Marcello, preserved in Verona, Biblioteca Civica, 1472 (B. Lett. 82.4), ff. 3(misnumbered 4)–6. In this letter Bevilacqua would seem to suggest that the idea for the *Excusatio* originated with himself, out of a desire to explain the "justice of [Marcello's] tears" (f. 4 *bis*; cf. King, "Inconsolable Father," p. 232), though of course such a prefatory letter would be bound to obfuscate such a matter as a commission. Whether it was Marcello or Bevilacqua who initiated the project, it seems very likely that Marcello would have known of the work from the start: it was written in his voice; it was a major project (at 166 folios about three times longer than

Manetti's *Dialogus cons.*); it called for the compilation and sending of the Valerio *consolatoriae* to a third party. Finally, once the work was completed, Marcello presumably authorized the preparation of the compilation of the fourteen consolations and the *Excusatio*, which comprise the anthology preserved in the Hunterian cod. 201 (King, "Inconsolable Father," pp. 233–34). On Bevilacqua see Cosenza, *Dictionary of Humanists*, 1:610–11.

113. I am using the ms found in Verona, Biblioteca Civica di Verona (1472 [B. Lett. 82.4], ff. 7–173), hereafter "Ve"; on this ms and on Bevilacqua's authorship, see R. Sabbadini, *Epistolario di Guarino Veronese*, 3 vols. (Venice, 1915–19), 3:140–41; Fabbri, "Le *Consolationes*," p. 232n; King, "Inconsolable Father," p. 224n.

114. Descriptions or protestations of grief abound in the treatise. For example, near the beginning of the work "Marcello" says: "Verum me tantus moeror afflixit. In tanto floetus langore fui consternatus ut id minime facere potuerim et semper inter angustias et afflictiones oppraesus nunquam dolores nunquam gemitus excutere phas fuerit" (Ve, f. 7r–v). Also see comments, for example, at f. 68v and at the account of Valerio's death at f. 158r–v.

115. Notable in this is Valerio's intellectual interests, to which Marcello appealed in his presenting Valerio a history of Venice (presented in Ve, ff. 69v–96). But this history also spoke to the secular dimensions of the *Excusatio*: the "consolations of philosophy" failing, Bevilacqua turns to a "consolation of history" (see n. 126 below).

116. As for "his" replying to particular arguments presented by his consolers (e.g., that his grief does not comport with his dignity and reputation [Ve, ff. 128 ff.]), I find no direct reply to Filelfo's monumental discussion on immortality, although at the end of the work Bevilacqua does refer to Plato's work "on the immortality of the soul" (*Phaedo*) and the issue of attitudes toward life and death. In this section, in which "Marcello" discusses reasons why he does not commit suicide to escape his great sorrow, he cites the examples of Cato the Younger and Theobrotus, whose suicides were preceded by a reading of the *Phaedo* (Ve, ff. 164, 167). But he also says that Plato himself, though writing on immortality, did not urge suicide (f. 167v), and he goes on to oppose the idea that death should be welcomed and not feared: e.g., "Nam mortem contemnere et hanc vitam odisse ritum belluarum semper existimavi (f. 169v–170), and later, "Ego vero mortem laudavi nunquam" (f. 170). In this, as in other ways, the *Excusatio* is truly a celebration of the secular realm.

117. On Marcello's presumably sustained grief and on the train of *consolatoriae* that came to him over the course of a period of almost two years after Valerio's death, see King, "Inconsolable Father," pp. 229 ff. Despite the allowances for grief in certain of these works, "Marcello" clearly focused chiefly on the cautions (King, "Inconsolable Father," pp. 242–46); Filelfo, for one, twice cautioned Marcello that a year of mourning was sufficient: "Quid quod iam annum prope agis in luctu? Hic est natalis christianus. Ad proximum Kalendas Ianuaris Valerius tuus reliquit membra mortalia. Satis naturae affectu, satis consuetudine datum est" (*Orationes*, sig. I6v); also: "Sed ecce annus iam tibi praeterit: satis naturae imbecillitati, satis opinioni, satis officio tributum est" (sig. I8). "Marcello" must explain his sorrow to

such consolers who would recommend an impassivity that truly would warrant a greater censure than his sorrow (see Ve, f. 10v). Also, much later he comments: "Adduxerunt mihi rationes et exempla ut me a lachrymis abducerent ac nolim me diurturniori moerore torquere" (f. 104).

118. See Ve, f. 42.

119. "Tot summi oratores ad me super obitu filii scripsere. Atque suis eloquentissimis non epistolis non orationibus modo sed libellis delere mihi lachrymas et consolari enixe me conati sunt. Qui nec dum me permovere atque incitare potuerunt ut aliqua ex parte me a floetu revocarent" (Ve, f. 99v).

120. Scc Vc, f. 145r.

121. For this section see Ve, ff. 122–24v. In his Christian evidence supporting the compatibility of sadness and virtue, Bevilacqua cites Paul's approval of a "*tristitia secundum Deum*" (f. 123), though, of course, he omits his accompanying warning concerning a "*tristitia saeculi*." Also see, preceding this section, the general discussion of the "affects" (ff. 117 ff.).

122. See Ve, ff. 124v ff.; cf., above, Conversini's comments on weeping. Bevilacqua addresses the paradox of whether an effect (weeping) can be the remedy of its cause (sadness). One of the benefits of weeping is external release: "in interiore corpore occlusum magis affligat, quia magis circa ipsum intentio animi multiplicatur. Ubi vero ad exteriora distendatur, tunc ad exteriora intentio animi quodam modo disgregatur" (f. 125). He also mentions the pleasure of behaving in accordance with one's mood, characterizing tears and sighs as "contristanti se aut dolenti convenientes," citing here the example of Augustine's indulgent behavior following the death of a friend in *Conf.* Bk. 4 (see f. 125v; also cf. Bevilacqua's comments in his prefatory letter at f. 5r–v). Cf. these arguments to similar ones listed a couple of years later in Nicolaus of Modruš' chapter on weeping in his *De consolatione* (see Chap. 6 below).

123. See Ve, ff. 127v–128. Also, cf. his rejection of Stoicism earlier: "Nunquam praeterea stoicorum sententias ego probavi" (f. 118) and cf. Manetti's *Dialogus cons.*, p. 46 and n. 44 above.

124. See Ve, ff. 145v ff.

125. René was to be the judge, so appointed by "Marcello": "Atque hac epistola mea te inter me et eiusmodi repraehensores [the consolers] censorem arbitrumque constituam" (Ve, f. 8v; King, "Inconsolable Father," p. 232). The debate on grief was thus potentially (the collection not sent) becoming increasingly public and increasingly structured in the course of the century. Salutati's exchange with Zabarella lacked an arbiter; Manetti's encounter with Acciaiuoli was adjudicated by "Niccolò da Cortona"; Marcello's dispute with his consolers was to be judged at the bar of international opinion at René's court.

126. Marcello will thus be "glorious" in his grief—an ambition ironically opposed to the charge leveled by his consolers that his grief does not befit his glory (a charge "Marcello" characterized thusly: "Nam ex ipsorum argumentationibus pro dignitate mea et rerum mearum me gerere iure meo non videor, qui tot honores, tot laudes, tantum gloriae in rebus tam bellicis quam domesticis, tam foris quam domi habitis fuerim consecutus, nunc languere videar" [Ve, f. 128]). Bevilacqua clearly sought to link the fame of the child, the fame of Marcello's grief, and the

fame of Venice (see King, "Inconsolable Father," pp. 240–41). Cf. the efforts of the earlier humanists discussed in this chapter, who perhaps also sought to immortalize their grief and to "replace" their children with literary works.

CHAPTER 6
THE SCIENCE OF CONSOLING: A LITTLE-KNOWN
CLERICAL MANUAL OF CONSOLATION

1. There was, of course, in general a wide interest in humanist studies on the part of Renaissance clerics, both secular and regular. In this chapter I am interested in the specific blending of humanist perspectives with traditional religious assumptions and roles. That is, how did certain clerical figures endeavor to develop consolatory themes from vantage points that reflect particular religious or pastoral interests and backgrounds? Matteo Bosso and Nicolaus of Modruš are two striking examples of the interplay between new humanist currents and established religious tradition. Not surprisingly, the interest in patristic sources was an essential feature of this clerical humanism.

2. On Giovanni Dominici's *Lucula noctis* and Salutati's reply (*Epist.*, ed. Novati, 4:205–40) see E. Emerton, *Humanism and Tyranny* (Cambridge, Mass., 1925), pp. 341–77. On Archbishop Antonino's later criticism of humanist currents, and on the decidedly religious (as opposed to classical) consolation sent by his former secretary Francesco da Castiglione to Cosimo de' Medici in 1463, see Chap. 7 below.

3. On Traversari, see Mehus, *Vita Ambrosii Traversarii*; C. Stinger, *Humanism and the Church Fathers: Ambrogio Traversari (1386–1439) and Christian Antiquity in the Italian Renaissance* (Albany, N.Y., 1977).

4. See Stinger, *Humanism and Church Fathers*, pp. 130–31. In a dedicatory letter Traversari comments on the consolatory nature of the work: "Quo in opere vir ille eximius vires omnes ingenii exerit, ut consoletur Stargirium [*sic*] monachum, . . . amicus ille [Stagirius] sub divino judicio permissus est a demone corripi, atque post plurimos in Dei opere exactos annos, qua ex re cum fere in desperationem precipitaretur, Joannes noster [Chrysostom], ut dixi, ita illum consolatur, tam multis rationibus nititur ut constantissime perferre spurcum illum impurum infestumque vexatorem persuaserit" (G. Battelli, "Una dedica inedita di Ambrogio Traversari all'Infante Don Pedro di Portogallo, Duca di Coimbra," *La Rinascita* 2 [1939], 613–16, at 615–16; this same dedicatory letter appears in two versions, one sent to Don Pedro di Portogallo, Duke of Coimbra [Batelli, "Una dedica inedita," pp. 613–16] and another to King René, Duke of Anjou [Canneti, 2:964–65]; the latter, to René, is thought by some not to be from Traversari [but perhaps from Jacopo Antonio Marcello (Stinger, *Humanism and Church Fathers*, pp. 269–71)]). On Chrysostom's consolation to Stagirius (in *PG* 47:423–94) see Kuhn, *Demon of Noontide*, pp. 46–49, and Introduction, n. 35 above.

Among Traversari's translations of other works of Chrysostom that might have had a consolatory appeal were three of the letters to Olympias (for the 17 letters to her see *PG* 52:549–623) and the first of the 21 homilies to the people of Antioch *On the Statues*, which treats the theme of suffering (Stinger, *Humanism and Church*

Fathers, p. 133; for this sermon, a reflection on 1 Timothy 5:23, see *PG* 49:15–34). Also he probably translated the *On the Priesthood*, which contains a section on the importance of pastoral eloquence (*PG* 48:665–66; Stinger, *Humanism and Church Fathers*, pp. 130–33, 278; Mehus, *Vita*, 1:401; A. Sottili, "Autografi e traduzioni di Ambrogio Traversari," *Rinascimento*, 2nd series, no. 5 [1965], 3–15). As for other of Chrysostom's writings which might have struck a consolatory chord, later in the century his *Sermones on the Patience of Job* were translated by Lilius Tifernas (Stinger, *Humanism and Church Fathers*, p. 157).

5. Canneti, 2:957–58; here, as in the passage cited in the following note, I follow Stinger's translation (*Humanism and Church Fathers*, p. 149); see his discussion of this dedication at pp. 148–50.

6. Canneti, 2:958; Stinger, *Humanism and Church Fathers*, pp. 149–50.

7. Traversari's translation of 1436 was, however, apparently never copied or never sent to the addressee, Alonzo da Cartagena (Stinger, *Humanism and Church Fathers*, pp. 147–48).

As for other consolatory writings known to Traversari, see his comment in the *Hodoeporicon* concerning an unidentified *Consolatio* given to him in 1432 by a fellow religious in Perugia: "Invenimus illic Opusculum de Consolatione, Auctoris ignoti quidem, sed bene eruditi" (edition of *Hod.* in A. Dini-Traversari, *Ambrogio Traversari e i suoi tempi* [Florence, 1912], p. 31).

8. For letters lamenting or commenting on Girolamo's death see his collection, Books 2.31, 32; 12.10; 17.13; 19.16, 17 [Canneti, 2:102–3, 579–80, 779–80, 868–70]); for replies to letters written to him concerning this loss, see 7.15, a reply to Lorenzo di Giovanni de' Medici; 9.3; 19.18 (Canneti, 2:343–44, 428–29, 871).

The discussion in the *Hodoeporicon* includes an account of Girolamo's sickness and death, Traversari's attempt to repress and to hide his grief, a *laudatio* of his brother, and a lamentation concerning the loss (*Hodoeporicon*, pp. 91–94). Especially striking are Traversari's comments on his struggle to curb and disguise his sorrow: "Coeterum nos, et juniorum dolori prospicere cupientes, ne ex nostris lachrymis acrius ingemiscerent, et fidei nostrae atque dignitatis habentes rationem, merorem insitum, quo transfixa erant praecordia nostra, tegere ac premere magna intentione curavimus; ita ut et sepulturae traderemus, et iremus atque rediremus absque lachrymis" (p. 91). But this account of public restraint is later followed by a plangent lament; e.g., he bemoans: "In quo mihi post te, Hieronyme dulcissime, requies? Quem jam in ambiguis consulam? Cui in adversis confidam? Quis portabit onera nostra? Ad quem aspiciam ultra, destitutus te, dulci solatio et unico meae vitae praesidio? Ad quem scribam et effundam aestus omnes cordis mei? Quis me jam consolatibur merentem? Heu miser! Nec jam expectabo literas tuas; jam fraterni amori indicia referam nulla. Sed alius lamentationi servetur locus" (p. 94; cf. Bernard's *Serm. sup. Cantica Cantoricum 26*, in *Opera*, ed. J. Leclercq *et al.*, vol 1 [Rome, 1957], at pp. 173–74). Following this lament he relates that he sent consolatory letters to his sister. Could Traversari's discussion here of his bereavement have influenced Manetti's *Dialogus cons.* written just a few years hence?

As for consolatory comments elsewhere to others concerning death, tribulation, or illness, see, for example, letters 14.21–22; 15.23; 18.20; 22.1 (Canneti, 2:665–

66, 693–95, 837–38, 931–32). For an account of his consolation (in person) of the imprisoned Cosimo in 1433, see *Hodoeporicon*, pp. 87–88; Stinger, *Humanism and Church Fathers*, pp. 31–32.

9. Cf. Stinger, *Humanism and Church Fathers*, pp. 131 ff.

10. On Bosso see C. Mutini's entry, "Matteo Bosso," in *DBI*, 13:341–44; also G. Soranzo, *L'umanista canonico regolare lateranense Matteo Bosso di Verona (1427–1502)* (Padua, 1965); on Pierleoni da Rimini see Cosenza, *Biographical and Bibliographical Dictionary*, 3:2667. As for the influence of Filelfo on Bosso, in the dialogue *De veris ac salutaribus animi gaudiis* one of Bosso's discussants remarks: "[N]uper quidem Franciscus Philelphus, vir summo ingenio eximiaque doctrina Mediolani libri edidit, in quo ea omnia quae dici posse de immortalitate animorum visa sunt, est eleganter et copiose complexus, quem eundem et te vidisse paucis ante diebus reor, cum ibi esses" ([*Opera*], [Strasbourg, 1509], sig. A7v). As de' Rosmini suggests (*Vita*, 2:124–25), this must refer to Filelfo's *Oratio consolatoria* to Marcello.

11. On Maffei see Cosenza, *Dictionary of Humanists*, 3:2065–66; on Maffei's praise of Traversari (in his treatise *In sanct. rust. lit. imp.*) as one of Italy's "eruditissimi viri" (in the company of such as Bruni, Gasparino Barzizza, Vittorino da Feltre, Poggio, and Francesco Barbaro), see Mehus, *Vita*, 1:395. On Bosso and Maffei (to whom Bosso dedicated the *De veris . . . gaudiis*), see Soranzo, *L'umanista*, p. 11 and passim.

12. N. Widlöcher, *Enciclopedia Italiana*, 7:558; as for Bosso's ties with Poliziano, see the latter's prefatory letter to Bosso's *De veris . . . gaudiis*, addressed to Lorenzo de' Medici ([*Opera*], sig. A1v; Soranzo, *L'umanista*, pp. 46–47). For a discussion of the dialogue, written (as was the *De tolerandis adversis* [discussed immediately below in text]) in the first half of the 1460s, see Soranzo, *L'umanista*, pp. 45–51. Among Bosso's other writings were the *De gerendo magistratu iustitiaque colenda*, the *De instituendo sapientia animo*, and three volumes of letters, the first of which was published in 1492 and again in 1493, the second in 1498, and the third in 1502 (Mutini, "Bosso," *DBI*, 13:341–44).

13. This volume, titled *Recuperationes faesulanae*, was published three times in the 1490s (Mutini, "Bosso," p. 342; Soranzo, *L'umanista*, pp. 92–93; Hain, *Repertorium bibliographicum*, 1. pt. 1:505). On the dating of the *De tol. adv.* see Soranzo, *L'umanista*, pp. 30, 52. For a treatment of the work, see Soranzo, *L'umanista*, pp. 52–53; Trinkaus, *Adversity's Noblemen*, pp. 104–8.

14. [*Opera*], sig. Q1.

15. Ibid., sig. Q1v.

16. Ibid., sig. Q2.

17. For other references to the pulpit, see [*Opera*], sigg. S4r–v, T1v. His mentor, Timeteo Maffei, after reading the *De tol. adv.*, compared it to Bosso's preaching. In a letter to Bosso he commented: "Accepi et libellum 'de perferendis adversis,' quem ad Johannem Philippum fratrem et eleganter et christiane scripsisti, in quo mihi visum est, non te quidem legere, sed concionantem audire ea suavitate atque vehementia qua soles ad populum loqui" (cited in Soranzo, *L'umanista*, p. 52n; also p. 77).

18. See Petrarch, *Opera* (Basel, 1554), pp. 233–34; Chapt. 3 above.

19. [*Opera*], sig. Q2.

20. This influence is also evident in his *On the true and salutary joys of the mind*, the third book of which contains a digression on eloquence in which Bosso asserts, among other things: "Etenim cum non sim nescius, fortius se immittere auribus, atque influere in animos disertam, et ornatam veritatem, quam rusticam et simplicem, tantasque vires habere eloquentiam, ut nihil sit tam incredibile quod non dicendo fiat probabile . . ." ([*Opera*], sig. F3v; on Bosso's orations and oratorical theory see Soranzo, *L'umanista*, pp. 61–90).

21. [*Opera*], sigg. Q2v–Q3.

22. "Constare satis omni sapienti, qui dignitatis humanae rationem tenet equidem arbitror, Deum ab initio hominem condidisse. . . . Altior fuit fingendi hominis ratio, altius consilium, sacramentumque divinius, ut qui plane esset viva, et constans, et certa quaedam divinitatis effigies, non terrena sed coelesti virtute omnino praeditus" (ibid., sig. Q4). From the ancients, Cicero's influence is evidenced by his comment that "Consequens itaque est, si coelestis, si divinus, si sapiens, si et immortalis, et formis formosior humanus est animus, et delibatus, ut pythagoraeos dicere memorat Cicero e menta ipsa divina . . ." (ibid., sig. Q4; also see the allusion to the Delphic "Nosce te" at sig. Q4v; cf. Cicero, *Tusc.* 1.16 ff.; 5.25.70. For discussions of immortality, divine similitude, and the trinitarian qualities of the human mind (i.e., discussions also reflecting contemporary humanist interests), cf. Bosso's *De veris . . . gaudiis*, esp. at [*Opera*], sigg. A7v–B3v, G2–G3v; Soranzo, *L'umanista*, pp. 48–50.

23. [*Opera*], sigg. Q8v–R1.

24. Ibid.; cf. (from *De tol. adv.*) sigg. S5r ff. and (from *De veris . . . gaudiis*) sigg. K3 ff.

25. [*Opera*], sig. S6v.

26. For his use of the term "divinae consolationis genus" see ibid., sig. S3v.

27. It is difficult to know exactly which sources of these writers Bosso knew or turned to as consolatory sources. As for Chrysostom, there were some medieval translations of his writings (Stinger, *Humanism and Church Fathers*, pp. 85–93). Did Bosso know some of Traversari's translations (such as the *On Providence*) or others that followed? It would seem quite possible, for in the *De veris . . . gaudiis* he refers to other of Traversari's translations (namely, those of Diogenes Laertius' *Lives of the Philosophers* and Aeneas of Gaza's *Theophrastus* or *De animorum immortalitate* [(*Opera*), sigg. A6v, A7v]). As for Jerome's letters, beyond the established authentic canon, did he know the dubious *Ad amicum aegrotum* (in dialogue form) or *Ad Oceanum de ferendis opprobriis hortatoria* (*PL* 30, letters 5 and 41), the latter of which was cited by Nicolaus of Modruš (see nn. 45 and 70 below)? As for Cyprian, pertinent writings might include his *De mortalitate*, addressed to the Carthaginians concerning their persecutions and bereavements (*PL* 4:603–24), or the *De bono patientiae* (*PL* 4:645–62), or those of his letters dealing with persecution (Favez, *La consolation latine chrétienne*, pp. 16–17; Beyenka, *Consolation in Augustine*, pp. 17, 69). Also cf. Ps.-Basil's *De consolatione in adversis* (*PG* 31:1687–1704); also, from the twelfth century, Peter of Blois' *De duodecim utilitatibus tribulationis*. It is perhaps revealing that Bosso opens his treatise by saying that in his endeavor he will draw "de beatis atque uberrimis fontibus christianae *philosophiae*"

([*Opera*], sig. Q1; emphasis mine). It is the early Christian rhetoric and philosophy of the Fathers that will guide him here, not scholastic theology.

28. See the comments at the opening of Book 2, in which a doctor who has been attending "Mattheus" praises this "dialogue" in contradistinction to the rhetorical formats found in the "schools" or the "pulpits": "Interea medicus hoc dicendi genus me delectat magnopere inquit, in quo et assensio, et confutatio, et interpellatio conceditur libera. Nam et scholae et sacra pulpita vestra, quae iubent auditorem assentiri tacitum, et si acrius movere quidem animos possunt, et impellere quocumque voluerint, et pectora lachrymasque ciere, attamen non profecto docent ita fide, neque tam explent eruditos cupidosque sciendi" ([*Opera*], sig. T1v).

29. Bosso's interest in consolation can also be seen in his letter-collections, which contain several *consolatoriae* (see descriptions of letters in Soranzo, *L'umanista*, pp. 230, 242, 273, 279, 280, 288, 292; in a letter of 1498, adddressed to an ailing woman, he promises to forward a copy of his *De tol. adv.* [Soranzo, *L'umanista*, p. 292]).

30. The similarities between the *De rem.* and Nicolaus' work were remarked upon by E. Leone in a letter edited in C. Frati, "Evasio Leone e le sue ricerche intorno a Niccolò vescovo Modrussiense," *La Bibliofilia* 18 (1916), 1–35, 81–98, at p. 5.

I would like to thank Professors James Hankins and John Monfasani for their editorial suggestions, revisions, and corrections in the following study of Nicolaus, an earlier version of which appeared in *Supplementum Festivum: Essays in Honor of Paul Oskar Kristeller*, ed. J. Hankins, J. Monfasani, and F. Purnell, Jr. (Binghamton, N.Y., 1987), pp. 247–77.

31. For these and other details of Nicolaus' life, see Frati, "Evasio Leone"; G. Mercati, "Notizie varie sopra Niccolò Modrussiense," in Mercati, *Opere minori*, vol. 4, Studi e Testi, no. 79 (Vatican, 1937), pp. 205–67. As for Nicolaus' name, he referred to himself as Nicolaus de Catharo before his appointment to the bishopric of Modruš in 1461, after which time he identifies himself with this position—e.g., in the *De consolatione*, as in the *De mortalium foelicitate* and the *Oratio in funere Petri*, he uses the name "Nicolaus episcopus Modrusiensis" (Mercati, "Notizie," p. 212; also see Dražen Budiša, "Humanism in Croatia," in *Renaissance Humanism: Foundations, Forms, and Legacy*, ed. A. Rabil, Jr., 3 vols. [Philadelphia, 1988], 2:265–92, at 282).

32. On Nicolaus' works, see Mercati, "Notizie," pp. 205–42; F. Lepori, "La scuola di Rialto dalla fondazione alla metà del Cinquecento," in *Storia della cultura Veneta*, vol. 3, pt. 2 (Vicenza, 1980), pp. 559–70. Other than a single letter (written in Croatian, concerning the Church's approval of slavic liturgy), the *Oratio in funere Petri* was the only work of his published before this century, when some other of his letters have been published in addition to translations of Isocrates' *Ad Nicoclem* (with an accompanying dedication) and (the dubious) *Ad Demonicum* possibly attributable to him (Mercati, "Notizie," pp. 231–32, 236; L. Gualdo Rosa, *La fede nella "paideia": Aspetti della fortuna europea di Isocrate nei secoli XV e XVI*, Studi storici dell' Istituto storico italiano per il Medio Evo, 140–42 [Rome, 1984], pp. 43–47, 192–94; as for the Isocrates translations, they were found in an autograph codex of Nicolaus' works, but in a different hand).

33. See Frati, "Evasio Leone," pp. 84–90.

34. Mercati, "Notizie," pp. 209–11.

35. For this work (alternately titled *De foelicitate humana*), which Mercati dates to ca. 1461–62, see Biblioteca Casanatense, MS. 276 (B IV 13), ff. 2–21; P. O. Kristeller, *Iter Italicum*, 3 vols. to date (London and Leiden, 1963–83), 2:97; Mercati, "Notizie," pp. 220–21; Lepori, *La scuola di Rialto*. The dialogue portrays an encounter between Nicolaus (a silent participant), his erstwhile teacher Paolo della Pergola, and two other figures. The discussion focuses on the issue of man's contemplation of the divine, for "our beatitude" or happiness rests in a "clear contemplation of divine substance" (Casanatense 276, f. 4; Lepori, *La scuola di Rialto*, p. 561). The debate considers the question of whether man can perceive his divine nature and "finis" through natural reason or only through Revelation—i.e., can man plumb God's truth and plan? A Scotist critique of rationalism is pitted against a defense of natural reason (Nicolaus' position) (the preceding is Lepori's analysis in *La scuola di Rialto*, pp. 559–70). And though thus highly scholastic in content, heavily citing Aristotle (*Nicomachean Ethics* and the *Metaphysics*), Averroës, and Scotus, the work also contains humanistic currents, with its citations of Augustine's *De civ. Dei* and references to various classical schools, figures, and works (for example, Plato's *Phaedo* and Cicero's *Dream of Scipio* are cited at f. 18v). Moreover, it is humanistic in its very genre as a dialogue (on the humanist tradition of writings on happiness [by such figures as Francesco Zabarella, Maffeo Vegio, and Filippo Beroaldo] see Trinkaus, *Adversity's Noblemen*, passim).

36. Frati ("Evasio Leone," p. 28) dates the treatise from the colophon in BAV, MS. Vat. lat. 5139, f. 123v: "In arce Viterbiensis secundo Pauli editum scriptumque vestro nomine, Reverendissime Pater et Domine." In the early nineteenth century, the Carmelite scholar Evasio Leone planned an edition, but the project was never completed (Mercati, "Notizie," pp. 222–23). Nicolaus' treatise survives in at least two manuscripts, both found in the Vatican collection: MS. Vat. lat. 5139 and Vat. lat. 8764. A third ms (Casale Monferrato, Seminario Vescovile, MS I a 8) is a nineteenth-century copy made by Evasio Leone for his planned edition (for these listings see Kristeller, *Iter*, 1:40; 2:331, 345). In my study I shall cite MS. Vat. lat. 8764 (hereafter "V²"), a manuscript (running to 135 folios) written by the scribe Stephanus Sabinus that contains emendations that appear to be in the hand of the author (based on a comparison to photographs in Mercati, "Notizie," pp. 262, 264, 266) and that in their substance would suggest the prerogative of the author (cf. citations below).

To my knowledge there is no evidence whether or not Nicolaus' treatise influenced other major consolatory writings of the last half of the fifteenth century, such as Platina's *De falso et vero bono* or Aurelio Brandolini's *Dialogus de humanae vitae conditione et toleranda corporis aegritudine*. Platina wrote his self-consolatory dialogue in the late 1460s or early 1470s (see Conclusion, n. 10), before Nicolaus' manuscripts had passed to the Papal library, of which he was librarian from 1475 to his death (many of Nicolaus' manuscripts came into the Vatican collection in 1480 after his death, but the *De consolatione* passed to the library later with Marco Barbo's [d. 1491] collections [Mercati, "Notizie," pp. 205–11; E. Lee, *Sixtus IV and Men of Letters* (Rome, 1978), pp. 114–15]). Mercati ("Notizie," p. 223) cites one reference to the work: in 1474, Nicolaus' Perugian friend, the poet and humanist Francesco Maturanzio, wrote Nicolaus saying that he wished he had Nicolaus' treatise at hand to ease his grief following recent news of his mother's death.

37. "Conatus sum igitur hoc in opere consolandi rationem explicare non quidem secundum exactam philosophiae legem—nunc enim non de rerum natura disputamus aut de illis tenuioribus [et *canc.*] magis[que *add.*] minutis rebus de quibus a turba secrete cum sapientibus disserendum—sed secundum pinguirorem crassioremque rationem quae etiam in populo non ignava [aut ociosa *canc.*] possit versari. Est enim propositum nostrum praecepta tradere quibus, ut caeteris perturbationibus, ita et consolatione, quando res postulabit, auditoris animum afficere possimus ac laborantibus succurrere eorumque aegritudinem quam comodissime levare. Nec mihi vanum hunc laborem assumpsisse puto, tametsi multa a peritissimis viris egregia monumenta extent in hanc rationem [*add. supra*; rem *canc.*] conscripta, ut sunt pene⟨s⟩ omnes illi et praeclari quidem Boetii *De consolatione* libri, et Senece, tam ille *De consolatione* codex insignis quam alter quem *De remediis fortuitorum* appellavit, Isidorique *Sinonimorum* clarissima gemmula; Ciceronis vero, si extaret opus quod de hac ipsa ratione conscripsit, forsan et nos et omnes alios hoc labore emisset [et nobis et omnibus aliis hunc laborem ademisset *canc.*]. Extant tamen plereque eius consolatoriae dignae epistolae. Quales etiam sunt nonnullae Cypriani, Hieronymi, Basilii Magni, aliorumque complurium doctissimorum virorum tam latinorum quam graecorum. Scripserunt enim hac ipsa de re et graecorum complures: Plato, Cleantes, Crato, Diogenes, Epicurus, Dicaearchus, Possidonius, Carneades, Crysippus, et Crantor quem Cicero [illo in opere quod meminimus *canc.*] secutus est" (V^2, ff. 1v–2v). The Senecan "De consolatione codex" could refer to any or all of Seneca's three treatises *De consolatione ad Marciam*, *Ad Polybium*, or *Ad Helviam*. As for the patristic authors, Augustine is included among this group in Vat. lat. 5139 (f. 2v). The series of Greek writers included at the end of passage (but omitted in Vat. lat. 5139) resembles the list made by Jerome in *Epist.* 60 (*PL* 22:592); also cf. Cicero's discussion of Greek figures in *Tusc.* Bks. 1 and 3.

As for Nicolaus' disclaimer concerning the nonphilosophical quality of his treatise, cf. his comments at "V^2," f. 73v, where he again explains that it would be inappropriate in such a work as this "subtiliori dialethica ratione de earum differentis aut generibus disputare." Nicolaus' intention to write on a broader, exoteric level was perhaps in conscious contrast to his goals in the more philosophical *De mortalium foelicitate*, written a few years before the *De consolatione* (see n. 35 above). Both deal with the problem of the human psychological condition, though the *De mort. fel.* does so in a highly philosophical manner, the *De cons.* in a fully rhetorical manner. The thematic overlap between the two works can be seen, for example, by comparing the "Locus a cogitatione finis humani" in the *De cons.* to the major question as to how "mortales certam sui finis rationem coniicere possent" (Casanatense 276, f. 2; Lepori, *La scuola di Rialto*, p. 560) examined in the *De mort. fel.*

38. For an edition see *PL* 83:825–68. On the dialogue see Diekstra, "Introduction," p. 41.

39. "Verum hi omnes consolandi perfuncti sunt et quidem dignissime sapientissimeque. Caeterum quo pacto idem munus et alii [as- *canc.*]sequi possent? Pauci admodum praecipere voluerunt et hi quidem [*add. supra*; nimirum *canc.*] pro ad-

mirabili ingenii eorum acumine fortasse satis copiose, se pro illorum desiderio [aut exigentia *canc.*] qui nondum in philosophia [aliisque liberalibus disciplinis *canc.*] admodum exercitatos habent sensus, meo iudicio et pressius et parcius. Neque id eos peccati ignoratione admisisse certo scio. Quid enim divina illa ingenia ignorarunt? a quibus nobis altissimi ita ferente providentia, quicquid luminis est, illuxit. Quin potius negligentia aut incuria quadam et ipsius rei prae facilitate contemptu. . ." (V², f. 2v).

40. "Nec pudori esse debet infantibus lac praebere pro quibus Christus mori ⟨non⟩ erubuit, praecipue cum sit ipse dominus non solos philosophos aut eos dumtaxat qui habiti sunt sapientiores, verum omnes omnino homines interrogaturus si se in carceribus et in tribulatione positum visitaverint aut consolati fuerint. Unde videre licet quanta necessitate mortales cogantur consolandi munus [sedulo *canc.*] obire, cuius se dominus tam severum exactorem comminatur [*add. supra*; promittit futurum *canc.*]. Itaque et nos universis prodesse cupientes eisque viam ostendere ad id consequendum quod divino pariter ac humano iure ab his exquiritur [et desideratur *canc.*], praecepta consolandi ex ordine digessimus, illius ope adiuti qui solus est cunctorum miserorum optimus consolator" (V², ff, 2v–3).

41. On the consolatory and funerary material in the *Rhet. ant.* see Introduction above.

42. The rhetorical nature of Nicolaus' manual is evident, as it is composed almost entirely of *loci* (including some pertaining to the funeral oration) and draws to a large extent on the tradition of the *epistola consolatoria* for its principles.

43. For a study of the confessor's *summa* and the pastoral handbook, see Thomas N. Tentler, *Sin and Confession on the Eve of the Reformation* (Princeton, 1977).

44. It is uncertain whether the citations from Greek writers were firsthand, secondhand (*via*, for example, Cicero) or both. Marginal notations in one of his autograph manuscripts indicates that he knew Greek (Gualdo Rosa, *La fede nella "paideia,"* p. 45n; and cf. Mercati, "Notizie," p. 232), and he may have translated two of Isocrates' orations (see n. 32 above). However, that either his fluency or his interest in or access to Greek sources was limited is suggested by the fact that he did not cite such writings as Plutarch's *Consolatio ad uxorem* or, particularly, Ps.-Plutarch's *Cons. ad Apol.*

He describes well the encyclopedic range of his sources when he characterizes his method (in his "prima ratio consolandi") as a "culling of philosophers, theologians, satirists, historians," drawing "arguments from some, examples from others" (V², f. 54v).

45. He uses such letters as Servius Sulpicius' famous letter to Cicero on the death of Tullia (*Familiares* 4.5) and Cicero's letters in which he discusses that loss (*Fam.* 4.6 and 5.13); Cicero's consolations to Titius (*Fam.* 5.16) and to Brutus (*Ad Brut.* 1.9); Seneca's letter to Lucilius on the death of Flaccus (*Ad Luc.* 63); Jerome's *consolatoriae* to Heliodorus (*Epist.* 60), Pammachius (66), Theodora (75), Oceanus (77), and the doubtfully authentic letter to Tyrasius (no. 40 in the collection of Jerome's dubious letters in *PL* 30). Besides these letters on bereavement, Nicolaus also draws on other types of consolatory letters, such as Cicero's consolation to Ligarius concerning his political difficulties (*Fam.* 6.13), a *consolatoria* for illness by Seneca, and Jerome's dubious *Ad virginem in exilium missam* and *Ad Oceanum de ferendis opprobriis hortatoria* (nos. 4 and 41 in *PL* 30). Also cited is

Jerome's *Epist*. 38 to Marcella, in which he discusses the illness of Blesilla. This list
is not meant to be exhaustive, as the treatise may well draw on other sources.

46. "Qua in re [*add. supra*; nobis ergo *canc.*], quando curandorum animorum
artem professi sumus nobis [*add. supra*] veluti corporum medicis faciendum statui
generales quasdam ac praecipuas medendi rationes tradere, particulares vero et
quae sedulo accidere possunt, prudentiae medici relinquere, . . ." (V², f. 3v). As for
the medical analogy, also see his chapter "Quomodo et quibus rationibus sit consolandum," in which he presents the body-soul analogy concerning healing (V²,
f. 22r–v); cf. Cicero's *Tusc*. 4.10 ff.

47. "Consolatori optimo tria cognoscere expedit: primum qualiter affecti sint
qui consolatione indigent; deinde a quibus personis illam precipue expetunt; tertio
loco [*add supra*; vero *canc.*] qua ratione consolandi officium sit suscipiendum et
quibus exequendum rebus" (V², f. 3v). At ff. 3v–4 Nicolaus presents his definition
of consolation: "Proinde primum quid ipsa sit consolatio videamus: est igitur consolatio (quatenus ad propositum negotium spectat) amicis dictis vel factis [vel
prudenti secum reputatione *canc.*] moerentis animi refocillatio quaedam."

48. Below is a list of section and chapter headings in the *De consolatione* as found
in V² (the "ae" diphthong is inconsistently indicated; here, as elsewhere, the text is
recorded as is). BOOK I: —Qualiter affecti sunt qui consolatione egent—Que nocu-
menta afferat egritudo—Quibus incommodis aegritudo afficiat animum—Qui fa-
cilius et qui minus facile consolationem admittunt—Quae propria sunt antidota
harum aegritudinum singularium: Antidotum senum et pusillanimorum; Antidotum illorum qui rebus terrenis nimium sunt dediti; Antidotum irreligiosorum—
Qui homines consolandis aliis sint idonei—BOOK II: —Quomodo et quibus rationibus sit consolandum—De tempore consolandi—Quomodo aggrediende sunt grav-
iores egritudines—Egritudo quibus medicaminibus funditus tollitur: Primus locus
a munere naturae; Secundus locus ab universitate; Tertius locus a damno, De miseria vitae humanae; Quartus locus a nocumento; Quintus locus ab utili vel com-
modo, De bono mortis; Sextus locus a iudicio sapientum; Septimus locus a contrario et de incommodis vitae: Quam mors sic bona; Contra avaritiam et de paupertate; Contra tyrannidem; Contra cupidos laudis; Unde haberi possunt rationes
quibus vera bona a falsis discernuntur—BOOK III: DE SECVNDA CONSOLANDI RATI-
ONE —Primus locus a iusto—Secundus locus a voluntate divina—Tertius ⟨locus⟩ a
voluntate maiorum—Quartus ⟨locus⟩ a varietate et lege fortunae—Quintus locus a
conditione humana—Sextus locus a societate—Septimus locus a necessitate—Oc-
tavus locus a diligentia—Nonus locus ab honesto—Decimus locus ab utili—DE
TERTIA CONSOLANDI RATIONE —Primus locus a tempore debito—Secundus locus a
brevitate temporis—Tertius locus ab inevitabilitate—Quartus locus a compara-
tione alterius mali gravioris—Quintus locus a non impuni—Sextus locus a com-
memoratione peiorum—De sex locis funebribus: Primus locus a re morientis; Secundus locus ab operibus defuncti; Tertius locus a genere mortis; Quartus locus a
causa mortis; Quintus locus a ratione funeris; Sextus locus a loco mortis—De
multis aliis locis ex quibus mali opinio minuitur: Quomodo ex collatione boni mali
opinio minuitur; Secundus locus a discrimine—BOOK IV: DE QVARTA CONSOLANDI
RATIONE—Primus locus a pudore—Secundus locus ab exemplo—Tertius locus a
virtute—Quartus locus a metu—Quintus locus a ratione inimici—QVINTVS RATIO
CONSOLANDI—Primus locus a compassione—Secundus locus a lamentatione—

Tertius locus a laudatione—De propriis locis huius quintae rationis, quorum primus est a studio: Secundus locus a faceto dicto et facto; Tertius locus a spe futuri boni; Quartus locus a munere; Quintus locus ab eventu—De tribus locis qui a persona accipiuntur inimici, quorum primus a vindicta est: Secundus locus a criminatione adversarii; Tertius locus a frustratione—De tribus locis sapientum quorum primus est a recordatione dominicae passionis: Secundus locus a cogitatione finis humani; Tertius locus a recordatione mortis.

49. Cf. Cicero's *Tusc.* Bk. 3, which, dealing exclusively with the treatment of *aegritudo*, is perhaps the single greatest influence on Nicolaus' treatise in general.

50. See V^2, ff. 4v–5.

51. "Neque enim omnes aequaliter hac aegritudine afficiuntur, sed pro varietate aetatum personarum temporum ac malorum, et alii quidem levantur celerius, alii tardius, alii vero numquam. Eorum autem animi precipue refocillantur miseriaque levantur qui sunt ad laetitiam voluptatemque proniores. Quales imprimis sunt iuvenes . . ." (V^2, f. 9).

52. For example, concerning the irreligious, on the one hand, and the pious, on the other, Nicolaus suggests: "Viri quoque irreligiosi et qui de providentia iustitiaque dei non recte sentiunt et truces nimium ac melancolici solatium accipere nesciunt, quoniam illi quidem iniuste se afflictos putant. . . . At vero homines pii et deum metuentes, quoniam ea quibus premuntur [incommodis *canc.*] omnipotentis iudicio destinata recte arbitrantur, ut Job, Thobias et alii sanctorum, plerique aequo animo ferunt et consolationem lubentes amplectuntur" (V^2, f. 11).

This section on the varying receptivity of people to solace and on the cure of difficult cases perhaps particularly reflects the influence of the confessional. This is hard to establish for a certainty, because ancient rhetorical theory also addressed itself to similar problems concerning situational variables or "circumstances." In some ways, it is difficult to separate completely the rhetorical and confessional traditions, as ancient theories of "circumstance" perhaps had some impact on the notion of the "circumstances of the sinner and the sin" in the confessional (see D. W. Robertson, "A Note on the Classical Origin of 'Circumstance' in the Medieval Confessional," *Studies in Philology* 43 (1946), 6–14; T. Tentler, *Sin and Confession*, pp. 116–18). In Nicolaus' manual the interplay between classical rhetoric and the medieval confessional is perhaps thus extended and refined, the rhetorical framework clearly ascendant. As for the pastoral treatment of pusillanimity, cf., for example, Jean Gerson's *De remediis contra pusillanimitatem*, in *Oeuvres complètes*, ed. P. Glorieux, 10 vols. (Paris, 1960–73), 10:374–86.

53. "Quod optime intelligens, Servius Sulpitius scribit ad Ciceronem oportere eos per quos consolationis munus obeundum sit propinquos esse ac familiares" (V^2, f. 20; see Sulpicius' letter to Cicero [*Fam.* 4.5.1]).

54. "Valent ergo ad consolandum amici, parentes, filii, aut alia quavis necessitudine coniuncti, inter quos consolatio filiorum est precipua, et presertim adulescentium vel parvulorum, si quando contingit ut quipiam aptius proferant aut genitori collacriment, quorum altero parentes maxime delectantur, altero post delectationem ob pietatem paternam stringuntur, seseque cohibent ne filiis quos tenere diligunt dolorem iniciant aut eos cruciari cernant. Eadem hac ratione et uxoris amicaeque nimium dilectae consolatio egregie valet" (V^2, f. 20r–v).

55. V^2, f. 20v.

56. For example, in consoling prudent men: "In consolandis gravioribus ac prudentioribus viris ut et nostri pudoris et eorum auctoritatis curamus [*lege*: curemus] rationem habere, et non illis nos praeceptores aut doctores exhibeamus, ne nostrum consilium sapientiae eorum preferre videamur, verum quicquid vel dicere vel facere voluerimus verecundius agere ac ipsorum dignitatem in omnibus conservare. Ita fiet ut et impudentiae notam pulchre effugiamus et apud eos non minus oratione quam benivolentia valeamus" (V^2, f. 12v).

57. See V^2, ff. 24–25.

58. Readily blending classical and Christian sources, Nicolaus' approach is truly that of a Christian humanist. For instance, the chapter "De bono mortis" draws on Plato and cites biblical figures and church martyrs. The "Locus a contrario et de incommodis vitae" contains a long citation from Augustine's lamentation on the human condition in the *De civ. Dei* 22.22 (the same vision of human misery Petrarch refers to in his *De otio rel.* [see *Opere*, 1:685]), and it also refers to the ancient Cyrenaic philosopher Hegesias' lamentation on earthly life, reputed to have incited some to suicide (see *Tusc.* 1.34.83–84).

59. It is in this section that Nicolaus expands his perspectives from the problem of death to other matters. That is, as he had done for death in the "Locus a contrario et de incommodis vitae," he offers consolation for the concerns of poverty, power, and fame "a contrario": by discounting the life of wealth, power, fame.

60. See V^2, ff. 99v–102; cf. *Tusc.* Bk. 3. As for the classical schools in general, in the chapter "Quomodo et quibus rationibus sit consolandum" Nicolaus discusses Cicero's panorama of the consolatory theory of the Stoic, Epicurean, Peripatetic, and Cyrenaic schools presented in *Tusc.* Bk. 3 (V^2, ff. 21v–22).

61. Both of these chapters include passages from Jerome, cited as the "divus orator" (at V^2, f. 72) and clearly a favorite of Nicolaus'. In the "Locus ab utili," besides the lengthy passage (ff. 69–72) from the *Ad virginem in exilium missam*, there is also a brief quotation (at f. 72r–v) from Jerome's *Epist.* 38, which discusses adversity in the context of Blesilla's illness.

62. See *Oratio in funere . . . Petri* (Rome, 1481–87), 6 ff. unnumbered. For the letter to Francesco Maturanzio containing the possible allusion to Riario, see Mercati, who speculates that Nicolaus' lament on his corrupt surroundings and the comment that "C. Calligula [sic] imperium obtinet" probably refer to Riario (Mercati, "Notizie," pp. 227–29; Gualdo Rosa, *La fede nella "paideia*," pp. 44–45; Lee, *Sixtus IV*, pp. 33–38, 195).

In the *Oratio* Nicolaus presents a *laudatio* on the life, learning, and virtue (!) of Riario (cf., thus, from the *De cons.*, the "Locus ab operibus defuncti"). He also presents a portrait of his "good" death, describing his tranquility and piety at his end (*Oratio*, ff. 5v–6v; cf., from the *De cons.*, the "Locus a re morientis," where Nicolaus cites Jerome's account [*Epist.* 60.13] of Nepotian's composure at his death [V^2, f. 85v]).

63. In the "Locus a virtute" Nicolaus makes an interesting use of the *Tusc.* Bk. 2, by adapting one of Cicero's arguments concerning physical *dolor* to the problem of mental grief.

64. V^2, f. 109. See n. 48 for the "Quinta ratio consolandi."

65. Cf. *Tusc.* 3.15 ff.

66. "[C]um maeror duplicem habeat sedem, unam in corpore et in animo alteram, in corpore melancoliae humorem, qui ut phisici docent precipuus in cerebro est, in animo vero fantasiam aut opinionem malorum quibus se oppressum cernit" (V², f. 112).

67. Not only is this section bracketed, but also the marginal notations, which appear to be in Nicolaus' hand, number the arguments.

68. [As for the fact that] "lamentationibus et querelis opinionem malorum opido extenuari: cuius multiplex causa est, sed precipua quoniam in lamentatione pergit homo enumerando praeterita bona, quorum sicut possessio fuit iocunda, ita et recordatio. Quo fit ut omnis lamentatio veluti et ira admixtam habeat cum dolore voluptatem. Hinc venit ut homo, si vel solus apud se ipsum queratur, levetur miseria, sed multo melius si apud alium fuerit lamentatus, illa de causa quam superius assignavimus. Levant quoque questus dolorem et ista ratione, quia animus dum continet intra se mali spetiem, totus circa illam occupatur et eam [*add. supra*; illam *canc.*] intuendo diutius, vehementius affligitur et cruciatur. Cum vero plorat aut querelas fundit, animus ad exteriora expanditur et ab illa urente cura quodammodo se non parva ex parte avertit. Et rursum lamentationibus mitigatur aegritudo, quoniam omnis lamentatio cum voluptate est ex eo, quod homo malis honeratus lachrimando et querendo putat convenientia sibi obire munera. Omni vero eo quod quis⟨que⟩ sibi conveniens ducit oblectari necesse est [ununquenque *canc.*]. Unde aliquos maerentes delectant solitudines, ut apud Homerum Bellorophontem, apud Virgilium vero Latini uxorem; alii se sponte cruciatibus vel doloribus deputant, ut ille Terentianus Demea; alii nec [nullis *canc.*] voluptatibus nec ullis ornamentis uti volunt, quoniam illa in tantis malis putant sibi minime convenire . . ." (V², ff. 112–13). And later: "Ovidius quoque ait, 'Flebilis ut noster status est, ita flebile carmen/ Materiae scripto conveniente suae [suo *ms.*]' [*Tristia* 5.1.5–6]" (V², f. 113v). Cf. Nicolaus's last two points here to Bevilacqua's arguments in the *Excusatio* (Verona, MS 1472, f. 125r–v; see Chap. 5, n. 122 above).

69. In discussing the "pleasant" features of sorrow (see his use of the term "*voluptas*" in passage in the preceding note), Nicolaus seems to provide a fairly well-developed explanation of the Epicurean conception of sorrow (on *voluptuosa* sorrow cf. Chap. 1, esp. at n. 15).

70. "Harum atque similium rerum pia reputatio, credite mihi, ita animum nostrum omnibus levat angoribus ut loco tristitiae mirificam inducat suavitatem totumque recreet ac confirmet" (V², f. 130). Though it is not identified as a source, some of this chapter seems to be drawn from Jerome's dubious *Ad Oceanum de ferendis opprobriis hortatoria*.

71. Cf. the discussion in Nicolaus' dialogue *De mortalium foelicitate* (see n. 35 above).

72. See n. 48 for the "De tribus locis qui a persona accipiuntur inimici."

73. See Introduction above. The truest clerical antecedent to Nicolaus' work was perhaps Dambach's *Consolatio theologiae* (see Conclusion below).

74. In his *De tol. adv.* Bosso invoked a reflection on the otherworldly joys of the afterlife; also cf. the Epicurean character of his treatise *De veris ac salutaribus animi gaudiis*. Nicolaus recommended worldly distractions in his "Quinta ratio con-

solandi." In an earlier section of his treatise Nicolaus, perhaps sensing the potential controversy in his "Epicurean" approach, felt compelled to defend himself from any charges of Epicureanism. At the end of his "Argument from Utility," he acknowledged that his discussion here and an earlier one "Ab Honesto" would seem to suggest that "tanta est laudis utilitatisque apud homines voluptas" (V², f. 73). He then explains that, for those who would see this as Epicurean, any appeal to delight whatsoever would thus fall into the Epicurean camp. Clearly, Nicolaus feels that such a perspective is unduly inhibiting, and he wants to justify the legitimacy of his approach without having to accept the unfortunate label "Epicurean."

75. Cf. Chap. 7, n. 23, and Conclusion.

CHAPTER 7
GRIEF AND MELANCHOLY IN MEDICEAN FLORENCE:
MARSILIO FICINO AND THE PLATONIC REGIMEN

1. On Ficino's life and thought see Paul Oskar Kristeller, *Supplementum Ficinianum*, 2 vols. (Florence, 1937), and *The Philosophy of Marsilio Ficino*, trans. V. Conant (New York, 1943) (here, pp. 16–19); also, among numerous articles, "Per la biografia di Marsilio Ficino," *Studies*, pp. 191–211; "The Scholastic Background of Marsilio Ficino," *Studies*, pp. 35–97; "Lay Religious Traditions and Florentine Platonism," *Studies*, pp. 99–122. Also see E. Garin, *Italian Humanism*, pp. 88–100; M.J.B. Allen, *The Platonism of Marsilio Ficino: A Study of His "Phaedrus" Commentary, Its Sources and Genesis* (Berkeley and Los Angeles, 1984); "Introduction," *The Letters of Marsilio Ficino*, Fellowship of the School of Economic Science, London, 3 vols. (London, 1975–81), 1:19–24. On the Platonic Academy see Della Torre, *Storia*.

Although primarily a philosopher, Ficino is generally classed in my study as a humanist because many of his interests and endeavors emerge within the humanistic context of studying and reclaiming ancient thought and texts. On Ficino's humanism see Trinkaus, *Image and Likeness*, 1:461; Kristeller, "Scholastic Background of Ficino," *Studies*, pp. 37–38.

2. Kristeller, *Philosophy of Ficino*, p. 28; Garin, *Italian Humanism*, pp. 88–100.

3. Della Torre, *Storia*, passim.

4. On Petrarch's limited exposure to and knowledge of Greek learning and on Boccaccio's study of Greek, see Kristeller, "Italian Humanism and Byzantium," *Renaissance Thought and Its Sources*, ed. M. Mooney (New York, 1979), p. 142. Prior to Chrysoloras' appearance, Leontius Pilatus taught at the Studio in the 1360s (Kristeller, "Byzantine and Western Platonism in the Fifteenth Century," *Renaissance Thought and Its Sources*, p. 302, n. 22). On Salutati's role in bringing Chrysoloras to Florence, see G. Cammelli, *I dotti bizantini e le origini del umanesimo*, 3 vols. (Florence, 1941–54), 1:46n.

5. Kristeller, "Italian Humanism and Byzantium," pp. 137–50. One of Chrysoloras' most notable apprentices, Leonardo Bruni, translated various Platonic dialogues and others works by Aristotle and other Greek classical or patristic authors (see J. Hankins, "General Introduction," *The Humanism of Leonardo Bruni: Selected Texts*, ed. G. Griffiths, J. Hankins, D. Thompson [Binghamton, N.Y., 1987], pp. 9–15). In the early decades of the Quattrocento, Florentine Greek

studies were also advanced by the Camuldensian monk Ambrogio Traversari (see Chap. 6 above).

6. On Plethon's influence on Cosimo, which Kristeller suggests may have been exaggerated, see Kristeller, "Byzantine and Western Platonism," p. 161.

7. As we have seen above, the Greek revival had also, for example, sparked a revival of Peripatetic consolation in Florence (in Salutati and Manetti) and in Milan had inspired the eclectic compilation of Greek lore in Filelfo's *Oratio*.

8. See Kristeller, "Francesco Bandini," p. 419n. For a study of the collection as a depiction of Cosimo by his clients and admirers, see Alison Brown, "The Humanist Portrait of Cosimo de' Medici, Pater Patriae," *Journal of the Warburg and Courtauld Institutes* 24 (1961), 186–221; also her *Bartolomeo Scala, 1430–1497, Chancellor of Florence: The Humanist as Bureaucrat* (Princeton, 1979), pp. 40–41, 268–70. It is uncertain exactly when Scala compiled the anthology, though Brown argues for a date close upon the death of Cosimo (*Scala*, p. 41n). Though many of the writings in the *Collectiones* can be found in other manuscript sources, some are unique to this collection, which is preserved in BML, MS. Laur. 54, 10. Professor Brown informs me, for instance, that to her knowledge the anthology preserves the only copy of Scala's consolatory dialogue. Aside from the fortunes of the separate pieces within the codex, many of which have been published (Brown, "Humanist Portrait"), the *Collectiones* warrants study as a compilation itself, which, taken as a whole, has much to teach us about the history of consolatory genres, roles, and themes in the Quattrocento.

9. On Cosimo's exile see D. Kent, *The Rise of the Medici: Faction in Florence 1426–1434* (Oxford, 1978), pp. 1–2.

10. For example: "Quid loquar de studiis humanitatis, quae maxime esse adjumento solent ad levandas aegritudines animi, atque ad corroborandam mentem vel exemplis, vel sapientissimorum virorum auctoritate? Scis enim disputari ab eis extra omnem fortunam esse animum sapientis; qui cum liber sit nulla in eum vis externa discendit. Virtutem vero summum bonum esse, reliqua perinde haberi; atque ejus sit animus, qui illis utitur" (*Opera omnia*, ed. R. Fubini, 4 vols. [Turin, 1964], vol. 2 [rept. of *Epistolae*, ed. T. Tonelli, 3 vols. (Florence, 1832)], Tonelli, 2:37–46 at 41).

11. Tonelli, 2:43. Cf. discussion of Poggio's dialogue *De miseria humanae conditionis* in the text below.

The *Collectiones Cosmianae* also contains the letter Poggio wrote to Cosimo celebrating his recall to Florence (Tonelli, 2:64–71; Brown, "Humanist Portrait," pp. 188–89). Poggio also composed a funerary piece for the Medici: see his *Oratio in funere* upon the death of Lorenzo di Giovanni in 1440 (*Opera* 1 [rept. of 1538 Basel edition], 278–86); with its citations of authors such as Theocritus, this work reveals the advances in Greek studies.

12. In preparing his edition of the *Consolatio*, P. G. Ricci found twelve manuscripts of the work ("Una consolatoria inedita," pp. 363–69).

13. See A. Brown, *Scala*, p. 39; G. Zippel, *Carlo Marsuppini d'Arezzo: Notizie biografiche* (Trento, 1897), pp. 10–11.

14. On Marsuppini's indebtedness to the *Ad Apollonium* (which, in turn, was indebted to Crantor's *On Consolation*) and on his anti-Stoicism, see Ricci, "Una consolatoria inedita," pp. 372–74, 382. Though rejecting Stoic *apatheia* and advo-

cating an avoidance of excessive emotion (whether grief or happiness), Marsuppini nonetheless affirms in rather Stoic language, reminiscent of Petrarch's *De rem.*, the importance of avoiding "perturbationes" and "morbi" and controlling both "secunda fortuna et adversa" with the "remedia" of philosophy (Ricci, "Una consolatoria inedita," p. 400; Ricci's comments at p. 382).

15. Ibid., pp. 389–90; cf. Manetti, *Dialogus*, p. 88. In support of this notion Marsuppini also cites the case of the learned Niccolò Niccoli, who shed "pias lacrimas" at the funeral of Piccarda (Ricci, "Una consolatoria inedita," pp. 390–91; G. Holmes, *Florentine Enlightenment*, p. 107). He then goes on to argue that our "sensus humanitatis" requires grief at the loss of loved ones. Discussing the question of "nature" vs. "opinion" (cf. Manetti's *Dialogus*), he suggests that moderate grief is innate, but excessive grief is not (p. 392).

16. Ricci, "Una consolatoria inedita," pp. 419–22. He also cites the authority of Aristotle, Augustine, and other philosophers and Christian thinkers. Cf. Ricci's comments ("Una consolatoria inedita," p. 388); also G. di Napoli, *L'immortalità dell'anima*, p. 75. Cf. Ps.-Plutarch's *Cons. ad Apol.* (Plutarch 120d–121e).

17. As we have seen earlier in our study, Petrarch, Salutati, and Francesco Zabarella discussed the consolation of immortality to some extent. In the same period of Marsuppini's *Consolatio*, Leonardo Bruni cited this theme in a *consolatoria* of 1433–34 to Nicola di Vieri de' Medici, drawing on the *Apology*, which he had earlier translated on two different occasions (see his collection, Book 6.8 in *Epistolarum libri VIII*, ed. L. Mehus, 2 vols. in 1 [Florence, 1741], 2:53–57 at 55–56; trans. by J. Hankins, in *The Humanism of Leonardo Bruni*, pp. 337–39 at 338–39; see his nn. 17 and 18 at p. 392).

18. Ricci, "Una consolatoria inedita," p. 421; Di Napoli, *L'immortalità dell'anima*, p. 75.

19. On the Greek content of the *Oratio* and on the scope of Filelfo's discussion of immortality and on his bragging about it, see Chap. 5 above.

20. Kristeller, "Francesco Bandini," p. 421n. For Rinuccini's preface see *Lettere ed Orazioni*, ed. V. Giustiniani (Florence, 1953), pp. 59–63. (This letter was not included in the *Collectiones Cosmianae*.) Nine years later he sent his translation to Federico da Montefeltro also to console him for the loss of a son. In the longer version of a *consolatoria* for Federico, Rinuccini discusses the debate between the Stoics and the Peripatetics concerning the expression of grief, and he sends along a copy of *Cons. ad Apol.* For this letter (and the shorter version) see *Lettere ed Orazioni*, pp. 63–68.

21. For Pius II's brief letter, which warns Cosimo "Aetati tuae moeror non convenit, et valetudini contrarius est," see edition in W. Roscoe, *The Life of Lorenzo de' Medici, called the Magnificent* (London, 1862), p. 414; for Francesco da Castiglione's letter see BML, Laur. 54.10 (hereafter referred to as "L"), ff. 89v–96v; for Antonio Agli's, L, ff. 97–104. On Francesco, see Brown, "Humanist Portrait," p. 211; della Torre, *Storia*, pp. 348–51, 771; Kristeller, "Per la biografia di Ficino," pp. 198, 200. On Agli, who became bishop of Fiesole and Volterra in 1467 and 1470, respectively, see Brown, "Humanist Portrait," pp. 211–12; Della Torre, *Storia*, pp. 775–76. Also included in the *Collectiones* is a funeral oration for Giovanni by Andrea Alamanni (L, ff. 86–89).

22. In a letter to him, Ficino indicates that he has read Francesco's commentary on the Psalms (*Opera*, p. 616; for trans. see *The Letters of Marsilio Ficino*, 1:50).

23. "Cum enim lego ea que summi oratores ad consolandos amicorum animos conscripsere, levia profecto videntur nec tali ratione edita que possint tam gravibus medelam langoribus adhibere. Sic non recipit consolationem Cicero ex amicorum litteris in morte filie. Eadem forte Demosthenes unicam natam amittit et in tantam animi effractionem deicitur" (L, f. 90). By contrast, the *consolatoria* to Cosimo from Agli comfortably cites some classical *exempla* (L, ff. 98v–99) alongside the biblical ones. On Antonino's opposition to humanist learning see Brown, *Scala*, p. 269n; della Torre, *Storia*, pp. 261–65.

24. "Quid enim paraclitus nisi consolator, quid παρακαλ[εῖν] greco verbo nisi tum exortari tum consolari interpretamur? Nonne de illo canit in suis celebrationi-bus ecclesia consolator optime dulcis hospes animae dulcis hospes animae dulce refrigerium. In labore requies, in estu temperies, in fletu solatium, hic est spiritus patris ac filii deus omnipotens qui qua via ad hanc consolationem mestis animis inducendam accedat, quo primum pharmaco, quo curationis genere, ad mitigandos erigendosque afflictorum animos utatur audiamus" (L, f. 90).

Interestingly, Francesco apparently later wrote a work "quem ad Marsilium [Ficino] scripsi, ubi de immortalitate animorum agebatur," to which he refers in a *consolatoria* he composed for Sigismondo Stufa on the death in 1473 of his fiancée Albiera degli Albizzi (Kristeller, *Supp. Fic.*, 2:230; on a collection of such writings for Stufa in which this work was included see F. Patetta, "Una raccolta manoscritta di versi e prose in morte d'Albiera degli Albizzi," *Atti della R. Accademia delle Scienze di Torino* 53 (1917–18), 290–94, 310–28, at 321–22; see n. 96 below. Among Francesco's other *consolatoriae* to the Medici were letters to Lorenzo and Giuliano upon the death of Piero in 1469 (Brown, "Humanist Portrait," p. 211n; ed. in K. Müllner, *Reden und Briefe italienischer Humanisten* [Vienna, 1899], pp. 213–19) and to Lorenzo upon the death of his mother Lucrezia Tornabuoni in 1482 (Della Torre, *Storia*, p. 349n).

25. Alison Brown has prepared an edition of the *Dialogue* forthcoming in a collection of Scala's writings. Some years ago she was kind enough to send me a typescript of her edition (with its source identifications), from which I cite in the passages from the *Dialogue* below. She discusses the *Dialogue* in her "Humanist Portrait" (pp. 199–200) and her *Scala* (pp. 36–37, 268–69, 312).

26. On Scala's career and ties with the Medici see Brown, *Scala*, pp. vii, 3–60. As for Argyropoulos, it should be noted that his preface to his Latin translation of the *Nicomachean Ethics* can be found in the *Collectiones Cosmianae*, as can his prefaces to Aristotle's *Physics*, *On the Soul*, and *Posterior Analytics* (edition in Brown, "Humanist Portrait," pp. 214–21).

27. See the dedicatory letter to Lorenzo in L, f. 104. Alison Brown informs me that an alternate version of this letter (cited by her in her "Humanist Portrait," p. 199n) is dated Dec. 31, 1463.

28. Scala describes himself as one "qui ea audirem quae ab eo de rebus humanis arcanisque naturae dicerentur plane divinitus . . ." (L, f. 105v; I follow Alison Brown's forthcoming edition, with its duly noted standardizations of the text [e.g., the insertion of certain "ae" diphthongs]).

29. See L, f. 105v.

30. For the dialogue, dedicated to Sigismondo Malatesta, see Poggio, *Opera*, 1:86–131; for a discussion, on which I draw here, see Trinkaus, *Image and Likeness*, 1:258–70.

31. On Poggio's drawing on the historical world for his proclamation of human misery see Trinkaus, *Image and Likeness*, pp. 258–70. In this sense Poggio extended Petrarch's exploration of the misery of mankind from individual physical, moral, and psychological problems to broader issues of society (corruption of the religious) and history (decline of Rome and the barbarian invasions). Poggio thus continued the process, begun by Petrarch, of particularizing the vicissitudes of worldly experience. Like Petrarch he perhaps further shifted the theme of misery from the purely ascetic framework of the *contemptus mundi* to a more worldly framework of temporal chaos and unrest.

32. See esp. Cosimo's speeches at *Opera*, pp. 90–91, 130–31. Toward the beginning of the dialogue, when Palmieri cites Heraclitus' comments on the misery of man (cf. Petrarch's Preface to *De rem.* Bk. 2), Cosimo responds by acknowledging the existence of human misery, but also by arguing that nature has given man many "iucunditates" and "voluptates" with which to combat this misery. Moreover, God has given man the faculty of reason to keep him steady in the tumult of fortune: "Id tibi certe ratio praestabit, se ei obtemperaveris, ut firmo constantique sis animo adversus utranque fortunam, ut omnes casus aequo animo feras, . . ." (p. 90). Acknowledging the positive features of human life, Cosimo cautions that unhappiness stems from misusing or becoming prey to these goods in life. In this, his position is perhaps partly Peripatetic. Still, the tone of his comments clearly reveals the influence of the Stoic belief in reason to triumph over worldly vicissitude. On Poggio's relatively Stoic portrait of Cosimo see Trinkaus (*Image and Likeness*, pp. 261, 264), who rightly observes both the work's resemblance to and its divergence from Petrarch's *De rem.*

33. By contrast, in Petrarch's *De rem.* the figure of *Ratio* has the dominant speaking role. Poggio may have revealed his own true position early in the dialogue when he suggests that Cosimo's optimism perhaps stems from his assumption that all people are as blesssed as he with the virtue, constancy, and good fortune that aid in combatting the "vitae molestiae." After all, Cosimo, whose only misfortune is gout, is special (see p. 91).

34. See discussion in text above.

35. *Opera*, pp. 90–91, 130–31.

36. Poggio had much in common with Scala: both had close ties to Cosimo; both were prominent in Florentine intellectual and political life; both wrote psychological dialogues featuring Cosimo. Such similarities, I think, increase the likelihood that Scala would have known of Poggio's treatise. Moreover, Scala, in fact, may have partly drawn upon the pessimism of Poggio's dialogue, albeit changing Cosimo's position from a hearty Stoicism to a resigned Platonism.

37. L, f. 105v.

38. I do not know if Scala was familiar with Petrarch's discussion, but his knowledge of Manetti's treatise would seem likely. Like Scala (L, f. 106), Manetti had also cited *De legibus* 1.7.22 (*De dignitate et excellentia*, ed. E. R. Leonard

[Padua, 1975], p. 69) and like Scala (L, f. 108v) he cited Lactantius' *De opificio Dei* (for example, *De dign. et exc.*, pp. 12–22).

39. L, ff. 107v–108r; Brown, *Scala*, pp. 268–69. Brown argues that Scala's argument might reflect a concern not to offend conservative religious currents.

40. Brown, *Scala*, pp. 268–69, 312; as for Eusebius' *De prep. evang.*, a copy of George of Trebizond's translation, found in the Laurenziana, is dated 1462 (D. P. Walker, *The Ancient Theology: Studies in Christian Platonism from the Fifteenth to the Eighteenth Century* [Ithaca, N.Y., 1972], p. 28). Ficino translated the Hermetic *Pimander* in 1463, and thereafter began work on the Platonic corpus, completing ten dialogues by the time of Cosimo's death (see Kristeller, *Philosophy of Ficino*, p. 17; *Supp. Fic.*, 1:cxxix–cxxx; on the dialogues completed for Cosimo see *Supp. Fic.*, 2:103–5).

41. For example, Cosimo says: "Neque probare possum Stoicos tuos, quos aut nequaquam recte interpretantur, aut certe videntur praeter verum praeterque humanam sortem de dolore disputare" (L, f. 111); also: "Quod neque Crantor ille nobilissimus academicus dandum putat, qui illud nil dolere affirmat non sine magna mercede evenire immanitatis in animo et in stuporis corpore" (L, f. 112; for this *locus* from *Tusc.* 3.6.12, cf. Marsuppini [Ricci, "Una consolatoria inedita," p. 390; Brown, *Scala*, p. 268n] and Manetti [*Dialogus*, p. 88]). Cosimo also cites instances of Christ's sorrow and emotion (L, f. 112r–v); cf. Salutati (*Epist.* 3:464–65) and Manetti (*Dialogus*, pp. 184–85).

As for the possible influence of Manetti's treatise on Scala, it is interesting that Scala had ties with Donato Acciaiuoli and possibly with his cousin Angelo Acciaiuoli, the Stoic interlocutor in Manetti's dialogue (Brown, *Scala*, pp. 23–24). As Angelo played the Stoic foil in Manetti's treatise, so does Scala in his dialogue.

42. Brown, *Scala*, pp. 268–69. Cosimo argues that the Epicurean concern with *voluptas* could leave one inconsolable in the event of misfortune (L, f. 114). Cosimo thus coaxes Scala into breaking his allegiance to the Stoics and rejecting the doctrines of the Epicureans: "Illam enim ut ita dixerim stoicitatem, quam tu nunc primum fecisti ut non probem, etsi antea sum sectatus, magis me hercule Epicureos et voluptatem callidam quidem et blandam vita nostrae insidiatricem fugiens, quam quod [*lege*: quamquam?] illi mihi omnino satisfacerent, iam non possum non despicere. Eaque, quae soleo splendore ductus virtutis atque honestatis laude magnopere admirari, nunc demum, postea quam audivi te falsa etiam apparere occeperunt" (ff. 114v–115; Brown, *Scala*, p. 316n).

43. Having critiqued Stoic and Epicurean thought, Cosimo then argues that "I find nothing has as great a consolatory power as does a contemplation of human circumstances . . ." (L, 54.10, f. 119v). Here he suggests the dangers of wealth and its inability to remedy his gout, his former exile, or his present grief. A truer medicine is to be found "in contemplating our circumstances and in knowing in what condition we were born" (f. 116v). The ensuing contemplation reflects upon the goods of the body, mind, and external things; "Cosimo" does not identify this paradigm as Peripatetic, but its origin is Aristotle's *Nicomachean Ethics* 1.8.2.1098b (see Brown, *Scala*, p. 269).

44. L, f. 119r–v. In raising the question of mind Scala returns to the Stoics, as can be seen in the comment preceding this passage: "Veruntamen tertium quod-

dam bonorum genus, cui quidem Stoici omnia tribuenda censent, nunc restat, quod ego existimo propter excellentissimam mentem tuam non esse non etiam elaturum laudibus" (L, f. 119).

45. L, f. 119v.

46. Ibid., f. 119v. Cf. *Phaedo* 67e; *Tusculans* 1.30.74; Brown, *Scala*, p. 312n.

47. On this work (*PL* 22:239–82) see E. Rice, *Saint Jerome in the Renaissance* (Baltimore, 1985), pp. 49, 218–19. Rice dates the author to the late thirteenth or early fourteenth century.

As for religious sources that might have inspired otherworldy Platonic-Christian perspectives on death in the historical Cosimo, we should include one of Traversari's translations. Included in the *Collectiones Cosmianae* is Traversari's dedication to Cosimo of his translation of the *Sermons* of St. Ephraem (edition in Canneti, 2:965–67). Describing a metaphorical colloquy between himself and Ephraem, Traversari characterizes Ephraem's comments (i.e., the content of his sermons) thusly: "[O]mnis eius oratio de Deo est, rebusque divinis, de Poenitentia, de Iudicio futuro, de Aeterna vita, de Gaudio Iustorum, de Reproborum poenis, de acquirendis, consummandisque virtutibus, de evellendis radicitus vitiis. *Iam vero laudatissimam illam Platonis sententiam, qua summam philosophiam, meditationem mortis esse definivit, ita probasse deprehenditur, ut omnis ferme eius sermo in ea tuenda esse videatur*" (Canneti, 2:967; emphasis mine). Also, he described the consolatory quality of Ephraem's thought, saying "quid gaudii, quid solatii, quantumque emolumenti ex hospitis adeo insignis ore percepi . . ." (p. 966), and explains that he is translating the sermons "ut commodi tui, atque consolationis caussa latine quoque loqui disceret" (p. 966; see Stinger's discussion of this dedication, *Humanism and Church Fathers*, pp. 163–65). (As for Traversari's translations for Cosimo, also see his dedication to Cosimo of Diogenes Laertius' *Lives* [Canneti 2:967–69; also cf. the letter in the *Collectiones Cosmianae* (edition in Canneti, 2:330–31)].)

48. L, f. 120r–v.

49. Ibid., f. 121. Cosimo then presents a third quotation from this source, in which Jerome addresses "death" in blissful strains.

50. On the *Altividus* (BML, Laur., ff. 204v–234) see Garin, "Una fonte ermetica"; Kristeller, *Supp. Fic.*, 1:cxxix–cxxx; his "Renaissance Platonism," in *Renaissance Thought and Its Sources*, p. 56; also see Chap. 4 (n. 53) and Chap. 5 (n. 93) above.

51. L, f. 121v.

52. I qualify this by saying that there are perhaps Stoic strains in this Platonism: as was seen in n. 44 and in passages cited at nn. 45–46 above, Scala's discussion of the mind seems to blend Stoic with Platonic thought. As for Scala's interest in the various schools and his vacillation concerning Stoicism, see Brown, *Scala*, pp. 268–69, 310–26. Later in his life Scala engaged Poliziano in a dispute over Epictetus' *Manual*, which Poliziano translated for Lorenzo de' Medici and which Scala subsequently criticized, invoking Poliziano's rejoinder in 1479 *Pro Epicteto Stoico epistola* (R. Oliver, "Politian's Translation of the *Enchiridion*," *Transactions and Proceedings of the American Philological Association* 89 [1958], 185–217; for Poliziano's *Pro Epicteto Stoico* see *Prosatori latini del Quattrocento*, ed. E. Garin, La letteratura italiana, storia e testi, no. 13 [Milan, 1952], pp. 912–25; Brown, *Scala*, p. 316n). This

exchange illustrates the ongoing debate over Stoic psychology, which clearly continued to have appeal. After the appearance of Poliziano's translation, Scala argued that Epictetus' Stoicism is "superhuman" and that man is not just a spiritual being but instead has a corporeal essence that is indeed part of the human condition. Scala apparently cited an anti-Stoic sentiment from Juvenal's *Satires* 15.138–39 (*Pros. lat.*, p. 920) a passage that Marsuppini had also cited in his *Consolatio* (Ricci, "Una consolatoria inedita," p. 389). Not surprisingly (in Laurentian Florence), Poliziano's response to Scala relied chiefly on Plato. He endeavored to unite Platonic and Stoic thought, drawing on the *Alcibiades, Protagoras*, and, it would seem, the *Phaedrus*. (At some time prior to his Epictetus translation, Poliziano had also translated for Lorenzo the psychological *Charmides* [for the prefatory letter and a fragment of this translation see *Opera omnia* (Venice, 1498), sigg. t5v–t8v].)

53. L, f. 94; for an edition, see Roscoe, *Life of Lorenzo de' Medici*, pp. 414–15. Cf. Cicero's *De rep.* 6.14; also *Tusc.* 1.31.75; on Cicero's reliance on Plato's *Phaedrus* 245c in his *De rep.* Bk. 6, see *Tusc.* 1.22.53; Brown, *Scala*, p. 38.

54. Brown, *Scala*, pp. 38–39; for Rinuccini's comment, see the preface to his translation of *Cons. ad Apol.* (*Lettere*, ed. Giustiniani, p. 62). Furthermore, Brown argues that the influence of the *Dream* can also be seen in a deathbed speech to Piero, recorded in a *consolatoria* Scala wrote to Lorenzo and Giuliano for Piero's death in 1469. Professor Brown has loaned me the typescript of her edition of this letter (BNC, Magl. VIII, 1439, ff. 73–76v) forthcoming in her Scala collection. Scala's account of Cosimo's speech is very much in the Platonic tradition of such speeches, showing Cosimo's readiness to depart with such comments as "Quid enim est in morte mali? Quid in vita boni?" and the notion that "vitam humanam esse quandam quasi nebulam, quae minima quaque aurae motione citissime dissolvatur" (BNC, Magl. VIII, 1439, f. 75r–v). After his speech, Scala reports, Cosimo "totum se ad futurae cogitationem vitae convertit" (f. 76v).

55. For the former letter (L, f. 81r–v) see Kristeller, *Supp. Fic.*, 2:87–88); for the latter (L, ff. 79v–81r) see *Supp. Fic.*, 1:37–38.

56. See della Torre, *Storia*, pp. 560–61; Kristeller, *Supp. Fic.*, 1:cxxxvi–vii, and "Francesco Bandini," p. 421.

57. L, f. 79r–v; *Opera*, (Basel, 1576; rept. Turin, 1959), p. 1965.

58. On the fortunes of the *Phaedo* (Henricus Aristippus's twelfth-century translation [known to Petrarch] and Bruni's fifteenth-century one) and of the *Axiochus* (three Quattrocento translations) prior to Ficino's translations, see Kristeller, "Francesco Bandini," p. 421n, and *Supp. Fic.*, 1:cxxxvii; on a *consolatoria* Bruni wrote reflecting Platonic influence see n. 17 above. One of the three earlier translators of the *Axiochus* was Cencio de' Rustici, who also seems to have used it in a remedial or consolatory context. In the dedicatory letter to Cardinal Giordano Orsini, Cencio discusses the need for remedying the fear of death and suggests that in the *Axiochus* Plato "quasi diuino quodam pharmaco mortis metum abstergat . . ." (L. Bertalot, "Cincius Romanus und seine Briefe," in Bertalot, *Studien zum italienischen und deutschen Humanismus*, ed. P. O. Kristeller, 2 vols. [Rome, 1975], 2:131–80 at 134; also see Di Napoli, *L'immortalità dell'anima*, p. 75n). On the content and authorship of the *Axiochus*, see K. Buresch, *Consolationum historia critica*, pp. 8–20; also Introduction above.

59. L, f. 79v; *Opera*, p. 1965.

60. L, f. 79; *Opera*, p. 1965; della Torre, *Storia*, p. 561.

61. Cf. S. Dill's chapter "The Philosophic Director" in his *Roman Society*, pp. 289–333.

62. Finally, concerning Platonic views of Cosimo's death, one last piece of consolation literature from the *Collectiones* bears mentioning. In addition to his *consolatoria* to Cosimo for Giovanni's death, Antonio Agli also wrote one to Piero for Cosimo's death the following year (L, ff. 123v–134). Agli, who at some point wrote a treatise *De immortalitate animae*, had ties to Ficino's circle (Della Torre, *Storia*, p. 775–76; Kristeller, "Immortality of the Soul," p. 188): he is in attendance at part of the symposium described in Ficino's *De amore* (edition in R. Marcel, *Marsile Ficin, Commentaire sur le Banquet de Platon* [Paris, 1956], p. 136; trans. in S. Jayne, *Marsilio Ficino: Commentary on Plato's "Symposium" on Love* [Dallas, 1985], at. pp. 35–36; also see Jayne's "Introduction," p. 8); in 1474 Ficino wrote him a *consolatoria* (see n. 98 below). Agli only briefly cites the notion of immortality in the letter to Cosimo (for example, at L, f. 102); in the letter to Piero, however, he imaginatively develops this theme. In one section of the latter letter, Agli discusses Cosimo's tranquility in the face of death. Turning on the theme of the Platonic deathbed speech, he presents an imaginary speech that Cosimo, in his equanimity, "seemed" to be saying to his friends. Though Agli cites as an analogy here the example of St. Anthony, the content of part of Cosimo's "speech" is not unlike that found in the *Apology* 40e–41c, as Cosimo anticipates the opportunity to meet such people as Abraham, Constantine, Theodosius, Charlemagne, Dante, and his own father and brother (L, ff. 124v–125v). Agli also dicusses the idea of fame, presenting a *laudatio* of Cosimo (ff. 127v ff.), commenting at one point: "Itaque eum non ut mortuum lugeamus sed ut meliori vita hic apud nos fama in celo autem essentia viventi congaudeamus" (f. 128). In this *consolatoria* Agli thus perhaps bears out Kristeller's suggestion that philosophical and theological interests in the notion of immortality in the Renaissance were linked to cultural attitudes toward the importance of secular fame ("Immortality of the Soul," esp. at pp. 181–84); on this, also cf. discussion in Chap. 5; on the link between worldly and otherworldly immortality, cf. Cicero's *De senectute* 21–23.).

63. Ficino refers to Lorenzo's company in a letter to him, in which, urging him to emulate his remarkable grandfather, he recalls how Cosimo died a philosopher's death: "Denique Solonem Philosophum imitatus, quum per omnem vitam vel in summis negotiis egregie philosophatus esset, illis tamen diebus, quibus ex hac umbra migravit ad lucem, quam maxime philosophabatur. Itaque postquam Platonis librum de uno rerum principio, ac de summo bono legimus, sicut tu nosti, qui aderas, paulo post decessit, tanquam eo ipso bono, quod disputatione gustaverat, re ipsa abunde iam potiturus" (*Opera*, p. 649; *Letters*, 1:136; Della Torre, *Storia*, p. 561).

64. Cf. Della Torre, *Storia*, p. 562.

65. For this letter, titled *Medicina corpus, musica spiritum, theologia animum*, see *Opera* (Basel, 1576; rept. Turin, 1959), p. 609; *Letters*, 1:39–40. Ficino, like Petrarch, collected his letters for publication; the first edition appeared in 1495 (Kristeller, "Preface," *Letters*, 1:17–18).

As for other works that refer to various types or combinations of healing, see *Nobilitas, utilitas et usus medicinae* (*Opera*, pp. 645–46; *Letters*, 1:127–30); *De musica* (*Opera*, pp. 650–51; *Letters*, 1:141–44); *Apologia, in qua de medicina, astrologia, vita mundi, . . . de Magis . . . agitur* (*Opera*, pp. 572–74; English translation in *Marsilio Ficino: The Book of Life*, trans. C. Boer [Irving, Tex., 1980], pp. 184–89); also see his comments at the close of his *Quod necessaria sit ad vitam securitas et tranquillitas animi* (see n. 80 below).

66. In general, on Ficino's philosophical system and on the structure of his Platonic and Neoplatonic universe, see Kristeller (*Philosophy of Ficino*), who points out there were also non-Platonic influences (e.g., Aristotelian and Epicurean) on Ficino's thought, particularly in its early stage (*Philosophy of Ficino*, p. 17).

67. On earlier humanist writings on immortality see Chap. 5 above; Di Napoli, *L'immortalità dell'anima*, pp. 51–120; Kristeller, "Immortality of the Soul," pp. 187–88. In 1456 Ficino transcribed Traversari's translation of Aeneas of Gaza's work *Theophrastus* (*de animarum immortalitate*) (Kristeller, "Spigolature ficiniane," in his *Studies*, pp. 164–65; Stinger, *Humanism and Church Fathers*, pp. 77–79).

68. Garin, *Italian Humanism*, pp. 88–100.

69. For a description of the soul's ascent *via* moral philosophy, mathematics, and metaphysics, see *Opera*, pp. 669–70; trans. from *Letters*, 1:189 (hereafter when *Letters* [3 vols.] are cited, all quotations are from this translation). Kristeller cites and discusses this passage (from a letter titled *Laus philosophiae oratoria, moralis, dialectica, theologica*) in *Philosophy of Ficino*, pp. 222–23; at p. 303 he cites other instances of Ficino's discussion of the ladder of philosophy.

70. See, for example, the *Quinque questiones de mente* (*Opera*, pp. 675–82, trans. in *Renaissance Philosophy of Man*, ed. E. Cassirer, P. O. Kristeller, and J. H. Randall [Chicago, 1948], pp. 193–212); Kristeller, *Philosophy of Ficino*, pp. 171–230.

71. In this *De amore* (a commentary on the *Symposium*) Ficino says that frenzy (or madness) in general is discussed in the *Phaedrus*; the poetic and amatory frenzies, in the *Ion* and *Symposium*, respectively (see seventh speech, Chap. 14, *De amore*, ed. Marcel, p. 260).

72. For this letter, *De divino furore*, see *Opera*, pp. 612–15; *Letters*, 1:42–48; on its currency see Allen, *Platonism of Ficino*, p. 47. On the similar topic of forms of ecstatic "affects," "abstraction," and "alienation" see *Theologia Platonica* 13.2, in R. Marcel's edition *Théologie Platonicienne de l'immortalité des âmes*, 3 vols. (Paris, 1964–70), 2:201–22 (hereafter, the edition cited); Allen, *Platonism of Ficino*, pp. 42, 59).

73. On the primacy of the amatory frenzy, see the letter of Ficino and Giovanni Cavalcanti to Naldo Naldi titled *Quattuor divini furoris species sunt, amor omnium praestantissimus* (*Opera*, p. 830) and the *De amore*, Chap. 16; on Plato's and Ficino's views on madness, see Allen, *Platonism of Ficino*, pp. 41–67. As for its social adaptation by Ficino, see his comments in which he refers to his friendships as unions of divine love (see, for example, his letters 1.129 [*Opera*, pp. 672–73; *Letters*, 1:196–98] and 5.25 [*Opera*, p. 795]). As for its theological adaptation by Ficino, see his *Dialogus inter Deum et animam theologicus* (*Opera*, pp. 609–11; *Letters*, 1:35–39) and his *Oratio ad Deum theologica*, which describes his soul's frenzied experience with God (*Opera*, pp. 665–66; *Letters*, 1:178–81). Also, see

his fusion of Platonic and Pauline notions of love in his *De raptu Pauli* (Marcel, 3:346–67), a work that, interestingly, Ficino seems to have intended as a type of consolatory diversion (from the terrors of the plague) for his good friend Giovanni Cavalcanti.

74. Though the Muses are perhaps most closely associated with poetry, it seems that Ficino, like such figures as Pythagoras and Plato before him, fairly generally associated the literary, philosophical life also with the Muses (on the connections between the Muses, music, poetry, and philosophy in Greek culture, see G. Hanfmann and J. Pollard, "Muses," in *Oxford Classical Dictionary*, ed. N. Hammond and H. Scullard, 2nd ed. [Oxford, 1920], p. 704). Perhaps this is why Ficino's medical *De vita* for literati treats those who are devoted to the Muses. As we shall see in our treatment of the *De vita*, the contemplative rapture of the Platonic philosopher-mystic, like the frenzy of the Platonic poet, is fundamentally linked to the "heroic melancholy" that afflicts the intellectual.

75. On Ficino's musical interests and talents, see "Introduction," *Letters*, 1: 20; Della Torre, *Storia*, pp. 788–91.

76. For a discussion relating Ficino's moral, hortatory philosophical letters to Seneca's letters and to the tradition of the Christian spiritual letter, see Kristeller, "Lay Religious Traditions."

77. Consider, for instance, his discourses on happiness addressed to his Medici patrons Cosimo (1.2) and Lorenzo (1.115). For a longer (and, presumably, the original) version of the letter to Cosimo see n. 55 above; for the letter (*Quae sit ad foelicitatem via*) in the collection see *Opera*, p. 608; *Letters*, 1:32–34. For the much longer letter (*Quod est foelicitas, quod habet gradus, quod est aeterna*) to Lorenzo, written after the *De amore* and the *Theologia Platonica*, to which it refers Lorenzo, see *Opera*, pp. 662–65; *Letters*, 1:171–78. According to Ficino, this latter letter is his prose account of a recent discussion at Careggi with Lorenzo, a verse account (in the *L'Altercazione*) having been completed by Lorenzo (for an edition see Lorenzo, *Opere*, ed. A. Simioni, 2 vols. [Bari, 1913–14], 2:35–70). Essentially, this letter argues that true happiness lies in the action of the will rather than in that of the intellect. Corresponding to his interest in love and to his concept of "appetite," Ficino's argument counters Plato's thesis in the *Philebus* that the "highest good" pertains to the domain of the intellect rather than the will (see Kristeller, *Philosophy of Ficino*, Chaps. 10 ["*Appetitus Naturalis*"] and 13 ["Will and Love"], the latter esp. at pp. 271–76). On Lorenzo, see Kristeller, "Lorenzo de' Medici Platonico," in his *Studies*, pp. 213–19.

78. *Opera*, p. 633; *Letters*, 1:95; see Kristeller (*Philosophy of Ficino*, pp. 297–99), who also treats Ficino's letter *Della fortuna* to Giovanni Rucellai (edited by him in *Supp. Fic.*, 2:169–73). For other letters on worldly vicissitude and fortune see *Quod fallax sit humana prosperitas* (*Opera*, pp. 722–23; *Letters*, 2:5–8); *Malis quidem bona fortuna mala est, bonis autem mala fortuna bona* (*Opera*, pp. 748–49; *Letters*, 2:76–78); *Fortuna neque benefacere potest malis, neque malefacere bonis* (*Opera*, p. 778; *Letters*, 3:68).

79. For this letter, titled *Dolores omnes ex amore animi erga corpus nascuntur*, see *Opera*, p. 860. Also, for a "clinical" discussion of "worldly ills" and "divine remedies" see *Mundanorum medicina malorum est supermundani Dei cultus* (*Opera*, p. 753; *Letters*, 3:6–7). On the afflictions and blandishments that beset the soul (or

mind) in the corporeal and temporal state, also see the Lenten letter to Lorenzo (*Opera*, p. 749; see n. 82 below); *Ubi bonorum viget, ibi solum reperitur omnium medicina malorum* (*Opera*, p. 824) and *Anima in corpore dormit, somniat, delirat, aegrotat* (*Opera*, pp. 837–38).

80. *Opera*, pp. 659–60; *Letters*, 1:164, 166. For other letters of psychological advice, also see the *Exhortatio ad moralem et contemplativam religiosamque vitam* (*Supp. Fic.*, 1:64–65; also Chap. 26 of the *De vita* [*Opera*, pp. 508–9]; Kristeller, "Lay Religious Traditions," pp. 117–18; see discussion in text below); also the *Quod necessaria sit ad vitam securitas et tranquillitas animi* (*Opera*, pp. 574–75; trans. in Boer, *The Book of Life*, pp. 190–92); at the close of this letter Ficino comments on his roles as priest and doctor, characterizing his advice here as medical (presumably, in the "psychiatric" sense of the word): "Haec autem non tam ut sacerdos amici mando vobis, quam ut medicus. Nam absque hac una tanquam medicinarum omnium vita, medicinae omnes ad vitam producendam adhibitae moriuntur" (*Opera*, p. 575; Boer, pp. 191–92).

81. On Ficino's priestly status and cast and on his preaching, see Kristeller, "Lay Religious Traditions"; on his performing two exorcisms in 1493–94, see Kristeller, *Philosophy of Ficino*, p. 314.

82. Kristeller, "Lay Religious Traditions," esp. at pp. 116–18. For a Lenten "declamatiuncula" to Lorenzo de' Medici with the "Platonic" title *Animus mortalibus non impletur, quoniam aeterna requirit*, see *Opera*, p. 749; *Letters*, 2:79–80; Kristeller, "Lay Religious Traditions," p. 117n.

83. *Opera*, p. 636; *Letters*, 1:103.

84. Kristeller, "Lay Religious Traditions," p. 117.

85. See Kristeller, *Supp. Fic.*, 2:162–67; the letter is also identified under the title *De consolatione parentum in obitu filii* (*Opera*, p. 619; *Supp. Fic.*, 1:clx).

86. "Sogliono le ombre dell'anime che sono nell'altra vita passate, spesse volte in sogno occupare l'immaginatione di quegli che a loro con passione pensano. Ma questo dì ad me non dormendo né immaginando, anche vigilando in contemplatione tranquilla subito come fulgore, fulgido come radio mattutino el puro et felice spirito del nostro Anselmo per dono da Dio concesso s'è manifestato et con voce spirituale agli orecchi mentali venerando sermone offerse e le parole sue comandò che in scriptura notassi, accioicché il padre suo et madre, frategli et sirocchie fussino per la scriptura partecipi di tanto colloquio" (Kristeller, *Supp. Fic.*, 2:162).

As for contacts between the departed and the living, cf. Ficino's "transcript" of an oracle delivered by the deceased King Alfonso I of Naples to his son Ferrante. Ficino, who suggests that he was privy ("nescio quo spiritu raptus") to this mystical encounter, recorded it in a work titled *Oraculum Alfonsi Regis ad Regem Ferdinandum*, which he sent to Ferrante's son Cardinal Giovanni d'Aragona in 1479 (*Opera*, 1:816–820). Alfonso having been dead some 20 years, this work was not specifically consolatory but rather was framed as Alfonso's instruction of Ferrante in the mysteries and beatitude of the divine sphere and a prophecy concerning Ferrante's own eventual return to his *"coelestis patria."* I thank Professor Jerry Bentley for this reference.

87. Among the ancients: Lucian's *De luctu*, Cicero's *Somnium Scipionis* (in some sense), Seneca's *Ad Marciam* 26; among the Latin Fathers, Ambrose's *De excessu*; among the moderns, Laura's appearance to Petrarch in the *Triumph of Death*

(Moran, *Consolations of Death in Ancient Greek Literature*, p. 78). On this motif in the Quattrocento, also see Donato Acciaiuoli's consolatory letter to Lorenzo and Giuliano de' Medici concerning the death of Piero (in 1469). After presenting a *laudatio* of Piero and remarking on his tranquil exit, he simulates what "Piero" would say, if he could, to his survivors—namely, that a virtuous death brings a "supremo pulchritudo" greater than any conceivable in the earthly realm (see BNC, MS. Magl. XXVII, 115, f. 14–20v; Kristeller, *Iter Italicum*, 1:140).

88. As for prominent influences on Ficino other than the ancient Platonic corpus, we might consider the *Altividus de immortalitate animae*, the highly Platonic consolatory vision dealing also with the death of a brother (on this work and Ficino's knowledge of it, see n. 50 above).

89. Kristeller, *Supp. Fic.*, 2:162.

90. Ibid., p. 163.

91. Ibid., p. 165.

92. See n. 86 above.

93. Kristeller, *Supp. Fic.*, 2:164.

94. Kristeller, *Supp. Fic.*, 2:174; on this letter, the exact dating of which is uncertain, see *Supp. Fic.*, 1:clxi.

95. *Opera*, p. 654; *Letters*, 1:150.

96. As Kristeller has informed me, Ficino's letter was included in a collection of funerary literature on Albiera's death; among the other authors in this anthology were Francesco da Castiglione (see n. 24 above), Scala, Poliziano, Carlo Marsuppini the Younger, and Bartolomeo della Fonte (see Patetta, "Una raccolta manoscritta," p. 313; Kristeller, "Francesco Bandini," p. 419n).

97. *Opera*, p. 617; *Letters*, 1:54.

98. *Opera*, p. 617; *Letters*, 1:55. For two other Latin *consolatoriae* see *Opera*, p. 660 (*Letters*, 1:167–68) and *Opera*, p. 884 (Kristeller, "Francesco Bandini," p. 418n). The former of these, dated 1474, was addressed to Antonio Agli, then Bishop of Volterra. As seen above, in 1463–64 Antonio wrote consolatory letters to Cosimo and Piero de' Medici (contained in the *Collectiones Cosmianae*). In his letter proffering "consolatio divina" to the cleric, Ficino characterizes Antonio himself as a consoler and, urging that the "physician heal himself," he ends on a Platonic note: "Sed quid ego ineptus medicinas offero Hippocrati? Medici cura teipsum, imo te Deo committe curandum, nullum est enim, ut ipse optime nosti, remedium contra mortis terrenae venenum, nisi et coelestis, et super coelestis vitae fervens amor, et consideratio frequens" (*Opera*, p. 660). For a letter in which Ficino discusses the loss of a friend, see *Opera*, p. 894.

99. By contrast, see Filelfo's highly rhetorical eclectic *Oratio* for Marcello, which presents a lengthy philosophical discussion on immortality. A philosopher on this and other subjects elsewhere, Ficino does not philosophize in these *consolatoriae*.

100. On Bandini's life see Kristeller, "An Unpublished Description of Naples by Francesco Bandini," in his *Studies*, pp. 395–410; orig. pub. in *Romantic Review* 33 (1942), 290–306. For an edition of the *Dialogue* and for a discussion of its circumstances and themes, see his "Francesco Bandini and His Consolatory Dialogue," in his *Studies*, pp. 411–35. As for Bandini's place in Ficino's circle, Kris-

teller speculates that he might even have been the instigator of the Platonic *symposia* held at the Academy, such as that one commemorated by Ficino's *De amore*. For a letter from Ficino to Bandini, see *Opera*, p. 660; *Letters*, 1:166–67. Bandini continued to have contact with Ficino once he was in Hungary: for example, see Ficino's *De vita Platonis*, which he sent to Bandini (*Opera*, p. 763–70; *Letters*, 3:32–48); also see the dedicatory preface (1477–78) to Bandini (*Opera*, p. 782; *Letters*, 3:xi, 77–78, 98); also see the following letter in the collection (*Opera*, p. 782; *Letters*, 3:78–79, 98–99), which Ficino wrote to the Bishop of Vacz in 1479, responding to his and Bandini's invitation that he come to Hungary. Ficino sends his regrets and his *Secunda Platonicae sapientiae clavis* (edition in Marcel, 3:297–300). On Bandini, also see della Torre, *Storia*, pp. 768–69; *Letters*, 1:222.

101. Kristeller, "Francesco Bandini," pp. 414–15. In a letter to Salviati, Bandini recounts Gondi's composure after his last confession and communion: "Quem cum variis sermonibus cohortari studerem, excelso animo me vicissim mirabilibus argumentis admonuit, quibus non acerbam sibi videri asserebat mortem sed iocundissimam. Que omnia collegi et ostendere, ut susceptum dolorem aliquo modo levare valeant" ("Francesco Bandini," p. 435).

102. Ibid., p. 435; Kristeller at p. 415n.

103. Ibid., pp. 422–24.

104. Ibid., p. 432.

105. Ibid., p. 433.

106. Ibid., p. 434.

107. Kristeller (ibid., p. 423n) observes that a related notion of the mind's growing power, which Gondi describes as part of his incipient ascent, can be found, for example, in Ficino's *Theologia Platonica* 9.2 ("Mens quo magis separatur a corpore, eo melius se habet"; Marcel, 2:10–11), which contains some comments on powers of the mind at the time of death.

108. Kristeller, "Francesco Bandini," p. 434.

109. On the tradition of melancholy, and on Ficino's important place in it (via his *De vita*), see R. Klibansky, E. Panofsky, and F. Saxl, *Saturn and Melancholy: Studies in the History of Natural Philosophy, Religion and Art* (New York, 1964), esp. pp. 241–74; L. Babb, *Elizabethan Malady*, esp. pp. 60–61, 74; Lyons, *Voices of Melancholy*, esp. p. 5; R. and M. Wittkower, *Born Under Saturn: The Character and Conduct of Artists: A Documented History from Antiquity to the French Revolution* (New York, 1963), esp. 102–6. These studies, particularly the exhaustive work of Klibansky *et al.*, preclude my need to treat this problem in any detail here.

110. Cf. Chap. 1, n. 52 above.

111. On Hippocratic thought and on Galen, see Klibansky *et al.*, *Saturn and Melancholy*, p. 15; also, on the late medieval period, see the examples they present in their argument that "the notions of 'acedia,' 'tristitia,' and 'melancholia' mingled and interpenetrated during the later Middle Ages" (p. 221n) and, in general, their discussion pp. 217–40. Also see R. Kinsman, "Folly, Melancholy, and Madness: A Study of Shifting Styles of Medical Analysis and Treatment, 1450–1675," in *Darker Vision of the Renaissance*, pp. 273–320 at p. 309. Wenzel discusses the connection between *accidia* and melancholy in high and late medieval theology and confessors' manuals (*Sin of Sloth*, pp. 59, 159–60, 191–94). A pertinent instance of

the term in the French Renaissance vernacular occurs in the translator's prologue to the anonymous translation of Petrarch's *De rem.* made for Louis XII c. 1503. The translator discusses the King's great vulnerability to both prosperity and adversity; he ends the discussion of adversity by saying: "[E]t tous autres infortunes à quoy estes subject et vous pevent advenir, comme il est advenu à plusieurs aultres empereurs, roys et grans princes, ne vous puissent troubler ne mener à disperance, trouble d'esperit ne melencolie, mais puissez porter la fortune prospère ad adverse d'ung mesme courage" (Delisle, "Anciennes traductions français du traité de Pétrarque," pp. 273–304 at p. 298.)

112. For example, in 1378 the Bolognese chancellor Giuliano Zonarini wrote Salutati complaining of his melancholy, presumably referring to his depression. Salutati's response treated the term both as a humoral and a psychological malady (see Chap. 4, n. 39 above). For Nicolaus of Modruš' use of the term in a humoral context in his *De consolatione*, see Chap. 6, n. 66 above.

113. For Boccaccio's uses of the term in the "Proemio," see *Il Decameron*, ed. A. Rossi (Bologna, 1977), p. 18. On his use of the term in *Ninfale fiesolano* see Klibansky *et al.*, *Saturn and Melancholy*, pp. 218–19. For Alberti's use also of the term as synonymous with lovesickness see, for example, his *Deifira* (*Opere volgari*, ed. C. Grayson, 3 vols. [Bari, 1960–73], vol. 3). Thus the blending that occurred between Petrarch's lovesickness and his "*accidia-aegritudo*" also generally occurred between lovesickness and "melancholy" (cf. following note and nn. 114 and 119 below). As for Alberti's *Profugiorum ab aerumna libri* (in some mss entitled *Della tranquillità dell'animo* [*Opere*, 2]) see particularly Book 3, the subject of which is the cure of "insita e obdurata grave maninconia (*sic*)" (2:159, 166).

114. The term "heroic melancholy" here will be used to describe the malady of the outstanding figure in general. Originally, heroic (from Eros) melancholy, or lovesickness more specifically, referred to a disease of lovers (Babb, *Elizabethan Malady*, pp. 128–29; Klibansky *et al.*, *Saturn and Melancholy*, pp. 16, 86).

115. See Klibansky *et al.*, *Saturn and Melancholy*, for the Greek text and an English trans. (pp. 18–29) and for their discussion esp. at pp. 15–17.

116. Kristeller, *Philosophy of Ficino*, pp. 216–17; Allen, *Platonism of Ficino*, p. 59.

117. For example, he cites the regular abstractions of Plato and Xenocrates: "Plato cum frequenter contemplationis intentione longe secessisset a corpore, tandem in ea ipsa abstractione a corporis vinculis decessit omnino. Eius discipulus Xenocrates singulis diebus integram horam abstrahebatur a corpore" (Marcel, 2:201; Kristeller, *Philosophy of Ficino*, p. 216).

118. Marcel, 2:202; translation in Kristeller, *Philosophy of Ficino*, p. 216.

119. "Hinc Plato scribit in Phaedro Philosophorum mentes praecipue alas quibus ad divina volatur recuperare, quia videlicet semper divinis incumbant. . . . Ob id scribit Aristoteles omnes in qualibet arte viros excellentes melancholicos extitisse, sive tales nati fuerint, sive assidua meditatione tales evaserint" (Marcel, 2:202). Later in the same chapter Ficino also includes the "melancholic humor" as one of the seven types of "vacatio" that facilitate this separation of mind from body. It was thus a melancholic Socrates who had special powers: "Socrates, quem Aristoteles melancholicum iudicavit, daemonis familiaris inspiratione multa praesentiebat, cuius rei testes sunt Plato, Xenophon, . . ." (Marcel, pp. 219–20). Before the

Theol. Plat. Ficino also had discussed amatory frenzy as a cause of melancholy in the *De amore*, completed in 1469 (S. Jayne, "Introduction," in his *Commentary on Plato's "Symposium" on Love* [Dallas, 1985], p. 3; Klibansky *et al.*, *Saturn and Melancholy*, p. 218n). Here, in the ninth chapter of the sixth speech he describes how the rapture of love dessicates the blood, leaving it melancholic (*De amore*, ed. Marcel, p. 214). Thus, both amatory frenzy as well as philosophical abstraction could induce melancholy. On lovesickness as a melancholic disease see Babb, *Elizabethan Malady*, pp. 128–42; one of Robert Burton's chief categories is "Love Melancholy."

120. *Opera*, p. 729; *Letters*, 2:23 and textual emendations at 92.

121. *Opera*, p. 733; *Letters*, 2:33–34; Klibansky *et al.*, *Saturn and Melancholy*, cite this passage (p. 258) and suggest the letter (3.24), probably to be from mid-1470s, given the dates of other letters in this book (p. 258n) (the following two being Oct. and Nov. 1476); the letter to Michelozzi (3.16), cited above, is presumably of the same general period; on views of Saturn see Klibansky *et al.*, *Saturn and Melancholy*, pp. 125–214.

Was this melancholy the extent of Ficino's experience with psychological or spiritual dejection? Ficino's sixteenth-century biographer Giovanni Corsi argued that Ficino became "quadam . . . spiritus amaritudine distractus"; that he sought to assuage this "animi dolor" by composing the *De amore*; that he was cured only through a type of spiritual conversion, in which he turned away from his dangerously pagan ways and composed the highly Christian *Theologia Platonica* and the *De Christiana religione*: "[I]ta per haec nimirum studia quietem consolationemque adeptus, omnem illam animi aegritudinem penitus depulit" (edition of *Vita Marsilii Ficini* in Marcel, *Marsile Ficin (1433–1499)* [Paris, 1958], pp. 680–89, at p. 683). Kristeller disputes the credibility of Corsi's argument in his "Per la biografia," pp. 202–5.

122. The first book (*De studiosorum sanitate tuenda, sive eorum qui literis operam navant, bona valetudine conservanda*) was written in 1480; the second (*De vita producenda, sive longa*) and third (*De vita coelitus comparanda*, originally written as a commentary on Plotinus) were composed in 1489 (Kristeller, *Supp. Fic.*, 1:lxxxiii–vi; Boer, *Book of Life*, pp. ix–x). For the text see *Opera*, pp. 493–572; for an English trans., which I will cite or follow, see Boer, *Book of Life*. For discussions of the work see n. 109 above; also Kristeller, *Philosophy of Ficino*, pp. 212, 310–11, 314, 373; Allen, *Platonism of Ficino*, p. 193; A. Corsini, "Il 'De vita' di Marsilio Ficino," *Rivista di storia critica delle scienze mediche e naturali* 10 (1919), 5–13; D. P. Walker, *Spiritual and Demonic Magic from Ficino to Campanella* (London, 1958; Notre Dame, 1975), pp. 3–72; F. Yates, *Giordano Bruno and the Hermetic Tradition* (New York, 1964), pp. 62–83.

The *De vita* was not Ficino's only medical treatise: earlier, in 1479, he wrote a plague treatise, *Consiglio contro la pestilenza*, later Latinized by a translator as *Epidemiarum Antidotus* (Kristeller, *Supp. Fic.*, 1:lxxxvi–vii; *Opera*, pp. 576–606) (in 1478–79); also cf. the shorter *Ricepte contro alla peste* (*Supp. Fic.*, 1:clxi; 2:175–82).

On Ficino's role as a doctor see Giovanni Corsi's comments in his biography (Marcel, *Ficin*, p. 687; *Letters*, 3:144–45; "Introduction," in *Letters*, 1:20; Klibansky *et al.*, *Saturn and Melancholy*, p. 256n; Corsini, "Il 'De vita,' " p. 7). According to Corsi, he was particularly adept in the treatment of melancholy: "Nonnullos, quod mirabile visu fuit, atra bile vexatos medendi solertia ita curavit, ut ad pristinam redigeret valitudinem . . ." (Marcel, *Ficin*, p. 687; *Letters*, 3:145).

123. *Opera*, p. 497; Boer's trans., *Book of Life*, p. 7; Klibansky *et al.*, *Saturn and Melancholy*, pp. 259–60, 346–47; and, generally, on the role of melancholy in facilitating contemplation and on its benign and pathological forms see Book 1.4–6 (*Opera*, pp. 496–990).

124. *Opera*, p. 497; Boer, *Book of Life*, p. 7.

125. "Hactenus quam ob causam Musarum sacerdotes melancholici, vel sint ab initio, vel studio fiant, rationibus primo coelestibus, secundo naturalibus, tertio humanis ostendisse sit satis. Quod quidem confirmat in libro Problematum Aristoteles. Omnes enim, inquit, viros in quavis facultate praestantes, melancholicos extitisse. Qua in re Platonicum illud, quod in libro de Scientia scribitur, confirmavit, ingeniosos videlicet plurimum concitatos furiososque esse solere. . . . Quod quidem Plato noster in Phaedro probare videtur, dicens poeticas fores frustra absque furore pulsari" (*Opera*, p. 497; cited by Klibansky *et al.*, [*Saturn and Melancholy*, p. 259], who also make this observation: "As far as we know Ficino was the first writer to identify what 'Aristotle' had called the melancholy of outstanding men with Plato's 'divine frenzy' " [*Saturn and Melancholy*, p. 259; but cf. their comments on pertinent medieval and Renaissance discussions prior to Ficino's at pp. 95–97, 255, 259]). As for Ficino's perception of himself, Lorenzo, and his circle as devotees of the Muses and as aspirants of amatory, musical, and philosophical frenzy see *Saturn and Melancholy*, pp. 245, 254, 259n; in Ficino see, for example, his praise of Lorenzo de' Medici's patronage of Poliziano, in which he says "tu sacerdotes Musarum nutris" (*Opera*, p. 618); or his reference to Lorenzo's capacity for frenzy: "Audivi quandoque Laurentium Medicem nostrum nonulla horum similia ad lyram canentem, furore quodam divino, ut arbitror, concitum" (*Opera*, p. 665). As for others in his circle, we should cite Ficino's account of one interesting case of "Discipulus noster nimio Musarum amore ac studio superiore autumno in melancolie morbum incidit" (Kristeller, *Supp. Fic.*, 1:46; *Letters*, 1:202). Becoming delusional and terrified, this figure fled to a monastery. Ficino, already an ordained priest by then, wrote a letter concerning this tragic case to a Dominican, Leonardo Mansueti of Perugia, lamenting that this melancholic victim would be given holy orders for such inappropriate reasons. Ficino's comments here should be compared to those of Salutati to Andrea Giusti and Pellegrino Zambeccari, whose interests in religious retreat also had improper motives (i.e., grief and unrequited love) (see Chap. 5 above).

126. *Opera*, p. 502; Boer, *Book of Life*, p. 20. Ironically, then, music is both a source of divine frenzy as well as a cure for the melancholic afflictions that strike the frenzied.

127. *Opera*, p. 609; cf. n. 65 above.

128. See his discussion in the *De musica* (*Opera*, pp. 650–51); on Ficino's originality in his theory of music and the spirit, see Walker, *Spiritual and Demonic Magic*, pp. 3–29.

129. *Opera*, p. 651; *Letters*, 1:143–44. In letter 1.128 Ficino recounts an instance in which he (unsuccessfully) sought consolation in music in a time of

sorrow: "Nuper Venerande pater [the Sienese Cardinal Francesco Piccolomini] ob egregii cuisudam amici iacturam gravi moerore premabar, neque solari moerentem poterat cithara Calliope sua, saepe mihi alias lenimen dulce laborum" (*Opera*, p. 672).

130. Klibansky *et al.*, *Saturn and Melancholy*, pp. 266–74; on Ficino's complex position on the careful use of astrological medicine, see Walker, *Spiritual and Demonic Magic*, pp. 21–24; Kristeller, *Philosophy of Ficino*, pp. 310–12, 314.

131. See Klibansky, *et al.*, *Saturn and Melancholy*, pp. 217–54; Wittkower, *Born Under Saturn*, pp. 14 ff.; Babb, *Elizabethan Malady*, passim; Lyons, *Voices of Melancholy*, passim; as for the artist, for example, on Michelangelo's melancholy, on Vasari's use of the term in his *Lives*, and on Dürer (who was thought by Melanchthon to have suffered a melancholic disease), see Klibansky *et al.*, *Saturn and Melancholy*, pp. 232, 277 ff.; Wittkower, *Born Under Saturn*, pp. 71–75, 104.

132. Ficino puns an analogy between his "medicus" father and his "Medici" patron: "Ego sacerdos minimus, patres habui duos, Ficinum Medicum, Cosmum Medicen. Ex illo natus sum, ex isto renatus. Ille quidem me Galeno, tum Medico, tum Platonico commendavit; hic autem divino consecravit me Platoni. Et hic similiter atque ille Marsilium Medico destinavit: Galenus quidem corporum, Plato vero medicus animorum. Iam diu igitur sub Platone salutarem animorum exercui medicinam, quando post librorum omnium eius interpretationem, mox decem atque octo de animorum immortalitate libros, et aeterna foelicitate composui, ita pro viribus patri meo Medici satisfaciens. Medico vero patris satis deinceps faciendum putans, librum de Literatorum valetudine curanda composui" (*Opera*, p. 493; Boer, *Book of Life*, pp. 1–2; Klibansky *et al.*, *Saturn and Melancholy*, p. 262; Corsini, "Il 'De vita,' " p. 9).

133. Edited by Kristeller in *Supp. Fic.*, 1:64–65; discussed by him in "Lay Religious Traditions," pp. 117–18.

134. *Opera*, pp. 508–9; Boer, *Book of Life*, p. 35. Also see Ficino's *Epitome* of the *Charmides* (*Opera*, pp. 1304–1307) and his discussion of the work in an *Oratio de laudibus medicinae* (*Opera*, pp. 759–60; *Letters*, 3:22–25). In the latter work, which like the *De vita* 1.26 also develops the metaphor of light, Ficino also argues that the health of the soul must necessarily precede that of the body.

135. He cites light imagery from *Republic* 6.507d, John 1:9, and Ps. 35:10 (identified by Kristeller in *Supp. Fic.*, 1:64–65). Kristeller discusses Ficino's profound interest in light in such works as *De lumine* (*Opera*, pp. 976–86), *Orphica comparatio solis ad Deum* (*Opera*, pp. 825–26), and *De sole* (*Opera*, pp. 965–75) (*Philosophy of Ficino*, pp. 94–98). Also see *Quid sit lumen* (Marcel, 3:370–78). On the role of light in spiritual experience, cf. *Dialogus inter Deum et animam theologicus* (*Opera*, pp. 609–11; *Letters*, 1:35–39); the *Oratio ad Deum theologica* (*Opera*, pp. 665–66; *Letters*, 1:178–81); also the *De raptu Pauli* (Marcel, 3:346–67).

136. *Opera*, p. 509; Boer, *Book of Life*, p. 36; Kristeller, *Philosophy of Ficino*, p. 291.

137. See the preface to Lorenzo (Marcel, 2:35; Kristeller, *Philosophy of Ficino*, p. 253). Perhaps it was this experience of divine illumination that Ficino sought as he played his lyre and sang Orphic hymns to the sun (or to God) (on Ficino's music and songs see Walker, *Spiritual and Demonic Magic*, pp. 19–24; Allen, *Platonism of*

Ficino, p. 60; cf. nn. 75, 128–29 above). Also, cf. the prayer he presents in the *Oratio ad Deum theologica* that opens "O lumen immensum" (*Opera,* p. 665).

138. Marcel, *Ficin,* p. 682; *Letters,* 3:138; could Corsi have drawn here partly on such comments of Ficino's as those cited in n. 132 above?

139. As I argued in Chap. 3, n. 20, there was a detectable difference in Petrarch's use of the terms "anima" and "animus" in some of his writings on spiritual and psychological health. Petrarch hoped to develop (or revive) the role of "medicus animorum" perhaps somewhat in contradistinction to the pastoral "cura animarum." With Ficino, however, this distinction has been lost, as there is no comparable contrast in his use of these two terms.

CONCLUSION
THE ITALIAN RENAISSANCE AND BEYOND

1. On the dialogue see Trinkaus, *Image and Likeness,* 1:178, 297–306; also see John O'Malley, *Praise and Blame in Renaissance Rome: Rhetoric, Doctrine, and Reform in the Sacred Orators of the Papal Court, c. 1450–1521* (Durham, N.C., 1979), pp. 133–35. On Brandolini, also see E. Mayer, *Un umanista italiano della corte di Mattia Corvino: Aurelio Brandolini Lippo,* Biblioteca dell'Accademia d'Ungheria di Roma, no. 14 (Rome, 1938), whose comments would suggest 1489 as the likely date of the dialogue (pp. 27–30); A. Rotondò's entry in *DBI* 14:26–28. After leaving the service of King Matthias, Brandolini returned to Florence and became an Augustinian canon in 1491. On Brandolini (whose eloquence as a preacher Matteo Bosso praised in the 1490s [O'Malley, *Praise and Blame,* pp. 50, 120; Mayer, *Un umanista italiano,* pp. 43–44]) also see further discussion in text below.

2. "Quoniam autem, et disputatio iucundior, et consolatio efficacior esse solet, cum allatis utrinque Academico more rationibus, verum ipsum pervestigatur, et quasi e tenebris ipsis eruitur, ut sermo coram et tanquam ad praesentes haberi videretur, Petrum Ransanum Episcopum Lucerinum, Ferdinandi Regis apud vos Oratorem, gravissimum atque eloquentissimum virum, vobiscum introduxi, hac de re disputantem . . ." (*Dialogus de humanae vitae conditione et toleranda corporis aegritudine* [Paris, 1562], f. 4v).

3. *Dial. de hum. vit. cond.,* f. 13.

4. Brandolini returns to the theme of eloquence at the end of the treatise. There both "Matthias" and "Beatrice" attest to the solace they have taken from the oration of "Bishop Petrus" (ibid., ff. 61–62), and Matthias praises the splendor, gravity, and Ciceronian eloquence of Petrus' oration. Petrus then laments the decline of classical rhetoric and literature and the rise of an unlettered, inelegant, barbaric medieval philosophy. He argues that "Philosophiam sine oratoria facultate, stultam quandam et circularem seu trivialem disciplinam esse. Nunc autem ostendere tantum volui, latine et eleganter pronunciari posse, et veterem illam Ciceronis in disputando (quantum in me fuit) consuetudinem revocavi" (ibid., f. 63; cf. Trinkaus, *Image and Likeness,* 1:305–6).

5. Much more a pure philosopher, Ficino was less rhetorical and less eclectic than his humanist predecessors and counterparts; his most rhetorical *consolatoria* was the vernacular letter to his family on the death of his brother.

6. In a list of favorite books drawn up in the 1330s Petrarch included the *Tusc.* and Seneca's *Ad Luc.* and [Ps.-] Seneca's *De rem. fort.* (Ullman, "Petrarch's Favorite Books"). The influence of Cicero's *Tusc.*, of course, was not merely Stoic in nature but eclectic (see Introduction above); still, as a compendium of philosophical consolation and with its emphasis on constructive psychological healing, this work generally informed Petrarch's highly Stoicizing interests in this area.

7. Epicureanism even had a particular consolatory appeal that suggests its currency was due to more than merely abstract academic debates or intellectual fashion. This is attested to by its unlikely (because of its bad reputation) appeal to the clerics Bosso and Nicolaus of Modruš. Both invoke Epicurean techniques perhaps partly or implicitly in an effort to soften Christian ascetic perspectives or to experiment with more psychologically efficacious consolatory approaches.

8. As Trinkaus suggests, Platina (Bartolomeo Sacchi) also developed the theme somewhat in his *De falso et vero bono*, a self-consolatory Boethian dialogue concerning his imprisonment by Paul II in the late 1460s. Platina's work could perhaps best be described as a combination of the *Cons. phil.* and Cicero's *Tusc.* Bk. 5 (*De falso et vero bono* [and other works] [Paris, 1530]). For a full treatment of Platina's or Brandolini's treatises, particularly in reference to the "dignity" theme, see Trinkaus, *Image and Likeness*, 1:294–321. On Brandolini and the *Dial. de hum. vit. cond.*, published six times between 1498 and 1562, also see n. 1 above.

9. "Scripsi itaque his diebus librum, in quo sum utrumque vestrum non solum de corporis aegritudine, sed de universa quoque humanae vitae conditione, consolatus" (*Dial. de hum. vit. cond.*, f. 4v).

10. Essentially Matthias' speech is an exposition on the philosophical maxim "Optimum esse homini aut non nasci, aut quam celerrime aboleri" (*Dial. de hum. vit. cond.*, ff. 6 ff.), a *locus* Cicero used in his *Consolatio* (see the fragment in Lactantius' *Divine Institutes* 3.19 [*PL* 6:412]), and which he attributed to Silenus (in *Tusc.* 1.48.114); this maxim was also cited in the Preface of Pliny the Elder's *Nat. his.* Bk. 7 and was developed by Ambrose (in his *De excessu* 2.30 ff.), who attributes the saying to Solomon. On Petrarch's discussion of this maxim in his consolation for the fear of death in the *Sen.* 1.5 to Boccaccio see Chap. 2 above. It is possible that in his consolatory refutation of the sentiment *via* "Bishop Petrus" Brandolini was partially inspired by Lactantius' condemnation of the maxim. On this adage as a consolatory *locus*, see von Moos, *Consolatio*, 3:159–61.

Although there are thus classical (e.g., Seneca's *Cons. ad Marc.* 11 and Pliny's *Nat. his.* Bk. 7) and patristic sources for Matthias' lamentation, it would seem likely that, for Brandolini as for Petrarch and Poggio (in his *De mis. hum. con.*), the influence of the *contemptus mundi* (e.g., Innocent's treatise) is also at work.

11. *Dial. de hum. vit. cond.*, ff. 21–23v.

12. Ibid., ff. 23v–44v; for the specifics of Brandolini's praise of man, which invokes certain *loci* found in Petrarch's and Manetti's discussions, see Trinkaus, *Image and Likeness*, 1:300–5.

13. John O'Malley suggests 1485 as a *terminus ad quem* for the *De ratione scribendi* (*Praise and Blame*, pp. 44–45); the *Dial. de hum. vit. cond.* was probably written in 1489 (see n. 2 above). I would like to thank Fr. O'Malley for bringing the *De rat. scrib.* to my attention.

14. *De ratione scribendi* [and other works] (Cologne, 1573), pp. 201–2. He later adds: "Dolorem vero corporis, ad patientiae, constantiae, virtutumque omnium exercitationem, item ad animi praestantiam, ad immortalitatis ac beatitudinis spem atque expectationem revocabimus . . ." (p. 202).

15. Brandolini's impressive endurance of this affliction was cited as an *exemplum* by Giovanni Pontano in a chapter "De caecitate et malis aliis corporis" in his consolatory manual *De fortitudine bellica et heroica* Bk. 2 (*Opera omnia*, 3 vols. [Venice, 1518–19], 1:80r–v).

In general, Pontano's manual warrants notice as a type of consolatory or psychological manual. Dedicated to Alfonso II of Aragon, the work (pub. 1490) opens with a reference to various battles of Alfonso, who in 1480–81 engaged the Turks and in 1482–83 was involved in the conflict between Ferrara and Venice. The first book deals with fortitude in the context of war; the second, with more general situations. In the latter, Pontano offers a type of handbook of consolation and exhortation: in addition to the chapter "On Blindness and Other Bodily Ills," there are others "De toleranda eversione patriae," "De tolerando exsilio," "De toleranda repulsa," "De toleranda paupertate," "De servitute toleranda," "De orbitate toleranda," and "De tolerandis iniuriis et contumeliis." Besides containing various *solacia*, these chapters contain, to an even greater degree, *exempla*, both historical and contemporary. As a manual for misfortune, this part of the *De fort.* is akin to Petrarch's *De rem.* Bk. 2.

16. On the tie between the philosophical notion of (divine) immortality and the cultural interest in (secular) immortality, and on that between immortality and dignity, see Kristeller, "The Dignity of Man" and "The Immortality of the Soul."

17. On Cardano see G. Gliozzi's entries in *DBI* 19:758–63 and in *Dictionary of Scientfic Biography*, ed. C. Gillispie (New York, 1971), 3:64–67; Rice, *Renaissance Idea of Wisdom*, pp. 165–76; Langston, "Tudor Books," pp. 305–23.

18. The *De cons.* was also published in Milan in 1543. The English trans. by Thomas Bedingfeld, *Cardanus Comforte*, appeared in 1573 and again in 1576 (facsimile rept. of the latter published in Amsterdam, 1969) (Langston, "Tudor Books," p. 305).

19. The work was "discovered" by "Francesco Vianello Veneto"; there soon followed attacks on the work's authenticity by such figures as Justus Lipsius. The forgery, either alone or, more commonly, accompanied by commentaries concerning its genuineness, appeared in further publications of 1583–84 in, for example, London, Paris, Frankfurt, and Lyons. See E. Sage, *The Pseudo-Ciceronian "Consolatio"* (Chicago, 1910); also P. Deschamps, *Essai bibliographique sur M. T. Cicéron* (Paris, 1863), pp. 103–4; Kristeller, "Francesco Bandini," p. 421.

20. *Opera omnia*, 10 vols. (Lyons, 1663), 1:618; it should be noted that this edition, with its numerous cross-references to Cardano's corpus (including those that defy the chronology of his works in his *De libris propriis*), thus apparently includes such insertions that he later made.

21. Cardano also cultivated more formal autobiographical genres in his composition of a *De vita propria* and *De libris propriis*.

22. Cardano discussed immortality also in his *De arcanis aeternitatis*; in a *De immortalitate animae* and *De vita et foelilcitate animi post obitum* (two of the dia-

logues included in a larger work titled *Theonoston*); in various sections of the *De utilitate ex adversis capienda*; in the *Guglielmus* (or *De morte*); and most comprehensively in his *De animorum immortalitate*. Cardano addresses issues such as the unity of the intellect, he cites various of the pertinent classical and medieval thinkers, and he comments on some of the contemporary figures in the debate such as Pomponazzi, Gasparo Contarini, and Agostino Nifo (on Cardano's complex and somewhat tentative position on immortality, see Rice, *Renaissance Idea of Wisdom*, pp. 171–72; di Napoli, *L'immortalità della anima*, pp. 352–54; Langston, "Tudor Books," pp. 308–10, 321–23).

23. His writing of the *Guglielmus* (or *De morte*) was inspired by a personal bereavement. As for more general psychological theory, during an illness he wrote the *Theonoston*, a moral and quasi-therapeutic work that included dialogues on tranquility, health, immortality, and the contemplative life (interestingly, the dialogue *De tranquillitate* in this work contains a section on the therapeutic power of music, in which Cardano cites the example of Lorenzo de' Medici's skill with the lyre [*Opera*, 2:345]).

24. In its title, at least, this work was likely inspired by Plutarch's *De capienda ex inimicis utilitate*, though Cardano's treatise transforms the genre to treat a much wider topic in a much more expansive manner (the treatise covering 282 pages in the Lyons *Opera*, 2).

25. Part of the work was written during Cardano's grief over the loss of a son, and, in fact, much of his personal and family difficulties are discussed in the work.

26. See *Opera*, 2:54 ff.

27. *Opera*, 2:67. For Erasmus' work, published in 1534, see *Opera omnia*, 5, pt. 1 (Amsterdam, 1977), pp. 325–92.

As for other noteworthy Cinquecento *consolatoriae*, see (the future Cardinal) Jacopo Sadoleto's substantive, highly classical *Philosophicae consolationes, et meditationes in adversis*, written in 1502 for a bereaved cleric (*Opera quae exstant omnia* [Verona, 1737–38; rept. Gregg Press, 1964], 3:30–66). There were also various sixteenth-century Italian authors, writing in the vernacular, who published consolatory and moral works on bereavement and/or the fear of death. One such work, dealing with the death of a noblewoman, appeared in 1564 in Ferrara from the hands of a Carmelite, Fra Antonio Ricci. This substantive work (426 pages), the *Consolatione della morte: sopra e doppo'l morire della Prudentiss. S. Costanza Austria Gonzaga Contessa di Novellara*, is described by the author as a "parlamento consolatorio." The work relies chiefly on Scriptural consolation but classical and even modern influences are also to be found (e.g., in a discussion of immortality, Ricci cites the *Dream of Scipio* [f. 8]; for a reference to the *Tusc.* and to Petrarch's *Triumph of Fame*, see f. 162v). Various sections of the work use the motif of the dying or deceased figure consoling the living. Besides dealing with bereavement, the treatise also addresses the problem of the proper attitude at the time of death in chapters such as the one titled *Modo di preparare l'animo al morire*. As in the case of Cardano, such sections perhaps reflect the growing influence of the *ars moriendi*.

On the fear of death see Bartolomeo Arnigio's *Discorso sopra disprezzo della morte* (Padua, 1575) (on which see Tenenti, *Il senso della morte*, pp. 316–17) and, more importantly, Fabio Glissenti's *Discorsi morali contra il dispiacer del morire detto Atha-*

natophilia. First published in 1596, this massive work (592 folios in the 1609 Venice edition) was perhaps the ultimate handbook on death in early modern Italy. For the most part it consists of moral and consolatory dialogues (featuring a "Filosofo") concerning the problem of death, though the work also extends into other areas of human life and conduct. The dialogues depict a broad slice of Venetian society; for example, in the second book the "Filosofo" disputes not merely with a "Cortegiano" (his principal interlocutor) but also with a butcher, a mendicant, a servant, and a gondolier, among others. Often these discussions concern the problem of death and, thus, Glissenti seems to provide a manual for death that explores the problem in terms of Everyman. As for sources, the author not only cites copiously from classical and patristic thought but also draws heavily on modern poets such as Dante and Petrarch. (There is an entire chapter concerning Petrarch's negative notion of death in the *Triumphs*: "Si discorre intorno una authorità del Petrarca, la quale pare che mostri, che la Morte sia cattiva; e come si debbia intendere quel luogo" [1609 Venice ed., ff. 22v–24v]. Glissenti seeks to reconcile various of Petrarch's negative comments on death with his own argument that death is not evil, citing here another comment from Petrarch that views death in a positive light. I find no citations from the Latin works of Petrarch, such as the treatment of death in the *De remediis*.) The fifth book is most interesting, because it is built around the specific consolation of a "filosofo infermo" whose imminent death is treated in various contexts. Advice is given concerning the psychological, medical, and spiritual aspects of his dying; there is even advice concerning the problem of grieving for the dead. As for the consolation for the fear of death, Glissenti presents arguments concerning the soul's divinity, and he discusses various philosophical positions dealing with the nature and immortality of the soul (from ancient thought he cites the Pythagorean, Platonic, Aristotelian, Epicurean, Stoic, and Hermetic schools, among others; from modern thought he cites Ficino's view of the nature of the soul [see f. 487v]). He also discusses theological arguments concerning immortality. Finally, this very thorough deathbed dialogue presents a *practica del ben morire*. "Filosofo" offers remedies for all five temptations treated in the *Tractatus artis bene moriendi*—namely, faithlessness, despair, impatience, presumption, and the concern over temporal things (cf. Petrarch's *De rem.* 2.117–32, and Cardano's chapter "De morte" in his *De utilitate ex adv. cap.*). Thus, Glissenti's work represents a fairly thorough integration of the religious *ars moriendi* tradition into a humanistic, vernacular manual for death.

28. *Opera*, 2:16. Cf. Brandolini's critique of modern-day philosophers and theologians (see passage cited at n. 4 above).

29. See *Opera*, 1:503; Rice, *Renaissance Idea of Wisdom*, p. 170.

30. See Langston, "Tudor Books"; L. Zanta, *La Renaissance du Stoïcisme au XVIe siècle* (Paris, 1914); R. Kirk, "Introduction," in his edition *Two Books of Constancie of Lipsius* (Rutgers, 1939); Palmer, *Seneca's "De remediis fortuitorum" and the Elizabethans*; Patch, *Tradition of Boethius*, pp. 66–86.

31. See W. Fiske, *Petrarch's "De remediis,"* pp. 2–48; Heitmann, *Fortuna und Virtus*, pp. 12–13. One must, of course, add to this the work's manuscript currency in the north (concerning which see N. Mann, "The Manuscripts of Petrarch's 'De remediis': A Checklist," *IMU* 14 [1971], 57–90).

32. See Auer, *Dambach*; Tenenti, *Il senso della morte*; M. Spanneut, *Permanence du Stoïcisme, de Zénon à Malraux* (Gembloux, 1937); also studies in n. 30 above.

33. Erasmus' letter is a model Christian humanist *consolatoria* for the loss of a son (fictionally addressed to Antoine Sucket [Sucquet]). This work is a rich blending of classical and Christian *loci* and *exempla*. In the latter part of the letter (in the earlier part he cites, for example, the Stoic notion of *apatheia*) he turns to Platonic notions of immortality and the communion of souls, notions that he complements with Christian arguments concerning immortality. Most importantly, his discussion of the communion of souls recalls somewhat that found in Ficino's *consolatoriae*. He presents the argument that the essence of man is spiritual rather than corporeal and that, therefore, departed souls that cannot be seen with the eyes can be enjoyed in the mind: "Et nobis animo frui licet, quod oculis non cernimus, nihilo secius quam amicis absentibus cogitatione frui solemus. . . . Sic est profecto, bonorum amicitia, animorum, non corporum coniunctione constat. Qui vere amant, animos amant, non corpora. At animorum copulam, nulla vis, nulla temporum, nulla locorum intercapedo potest dirimere" (I use the edition and notes of J.–C. Margolin in *Opera omnia Desiderii Erasmi Roterodami*, 1. pt. 2 [Amsterdam, 1971], pp. 452–53; cf. Margolin's comment at p. 452n). It is difficult to know whether Erasmus knew Ficino's letters, an edition of which had appeared in Venice in 1495; given the ties between Ficino and Colet (see S. Jayne, *John Colet and Marsilio Ficino* [Oxford, 1963]), it would seem likely. Toward the end of the letter Erasmus also uses the motif of the dead figure returning to console the living, a motif probably inspired principally from his earlier translations of Lucian's *De luctu* (on Erasmus' and More's translations of Lucian see C. Robinson, in Erasmus' *Opera omnia*, 1. pt. 1 [Amsterdam, 1969], pp. 363–77). Finally, Erasmus ends his letter with an epitome of a manual of rhetorical responses to the complaints of a bereaved mind: a type of Ps.-Senecan or Petrarchan dialogue of "remedies" for grief. In sum, Erasmus' *De morte dec.* joins a variety of literary, philosophical, spiritual, and rhetorical influences from the Greek, Roman, and Christian traditions.

Though published separately as the *De morte declamatio* (Basel, 1518 [G. W. Panzer, *Annales Typographici*, 11 vols. (Nürnberg, 1793–1803), 6:209]; English translations of the work appeared in England in the 1530s), the work also appeared later as one of the models in Erasmus' *De conscribendis epistolis*, a letter-writing manual. In this handbook Erasmus has a section on the consolatory letter, in which he discusses consolatory technique, offers model letters, culls a "sylva" of *loci* from the letters of Cicero and Pliny the Younger, and presents another of his own (*Opera omnia*, 1. pt. 2 [Amsterdam, 1971], pp. 432–65). Thus as Brandolini had codified the *consolatoria* in the Quattrocento south, Erasmus did so in the sixteenth-century north (I am indebted to Fr. John O'Malley, who brought these two works to my attention and suggested their connection to the dictaminal tradition). Now, also see Pigman, *Grief and English Renaissance Elegy*, pp. 12–16.

34. Despite the humanistic literary structure of the work, More couches the dialogue in highly spiritual terms (see F. Manley's discussion of traditions in *The Complete Works of St. Thomas More*, ed. F. Martz and F. Manley, vol. 12 [New Haven, 1976], pp. cxvii–cxx). His first chapter, "That the cumfortes devisid by the old paynym philosophers, were insufficient And the cause wherfore," argues that

the attempts of the moral philosophers to deal with tribulation and travail are inadequate: "[A]ll their comfortable counsaylles are very farre unsufficient." The true "effectuall medisyns agaynst these diseases of trybulacion" are to be found in Christ (*Dialoge*, in *Complete Works*, ed. Martz and Manley, pp. 10–11; while proclaiming the inadequacy of classical solace, More does not however, as L. Miles points out, completely reject it ["Patristic Comforters in More's *Dialogue of Comfort*," *Moreana* 8 (1965), 9–20 at 10]). The dialogue subsequently explores the spiritual realm of solace (on More's drawing on patristic figures such as Cyprian, see Miles, "Patristic Comforters").

As a rule, Italian consolers (lay and clerical) whom we have examined in this study revealed an Erasmian ease in the blending of pagan and religious thought. An exception anticipating More's attitude could be found in Francesco da Castiglione's *consolatoria* to Cosimo in 1463.

35. On which see Auer, *Dambach*; cf. Tentler, *Sin and Confession*, pp. 114, 159. This remarkable treatise, which must be counted the northern pastoral counterpart to Petrarch's *De rem.*, was completed in 1366, the same year in which Petrarch finalized work on his manual. Whereas Petrarch developed the more patently secular genre of the "remedies of fortune," Dambach, a Dominican professor of theology, chose to adapt Boethius' genre to his contemporary theological context. The work opens with a scriptural definition of consolation—namely, Paul's comment in Rom. 15:4, that "whatever was written in former days was written for our instruction, that by steadfastness and by the encouragement of the scriptures we might have hope" (this same passage opens Gerson's *De cons. theo.* and Luther's *Tessaradecas cons.*; see below in this note and n. 42). But Dambach then identifies a self-consolatory context, saying that just as Boethius wrote his *Cons. phil.* in prison, he too suffers a "quandam exilii speciem" and will thus analogously entitle his work a *Consolatio theologiae*. Invoking Augustine's sanction that classical thought may justly be adapted to Christian ends, Dambach explains that he will draw upon "philosophorum ac rethorum nonnullorum autoritates" (*De consolatione theologie*; I have used the edition [Hain, 15236] in BAV [Strassburg: Georgius de Spira, ca. 1479], unfoliated, Prologue [f. 1]). In comparison to Boethius' rather cerebral dialogue, Dambach's is organized as a manual of consolatory *loci*, consisting of the speeches or "considerationes" of consoling "puellae" who proffer solace for myriad woes. Dambach intended the work to be a very practical manual, systematically arranged so that the "pro qualibet persona ex quibuscunque causis turbata parata consolatio in certo suo loco promptius valeat inveniri" (Prologue [f. 1v]). Besides the fact that "generaliter consistat utilitas [of the manual] in consolacione tristium personarum," Dambach suggested that the manual could also be used for public readings, for preaching, and for private scriptural and moral readings (as an aid) (f. 2r–v). And although Dambach deals with traditional matters of spiritual sorrow, conscience, and sin, the major portion of the handbook concerns worldly matters: frustrations over fortune, glory, health, exile, imprisonment, bereavement, death, social status, carnal pleasures (consider the title of the first book, "Primus liber continet consolationum remedia oportuna contra illa turbativa hominis que opponuntur mundane sue felicitate et prosperatiti"). And though the work speaks sometimes to the particular woes of the clerical or monastic life (e.g., deprivation,

the vows of silence and obedience), it also deals with wider issues affecting the laity (marriage, military life). Dambach's *loci* are drawn from biblical and other religious sources (including, for example, Ambrose, Augustine, Chrysostom, and Bernard of Clairvaux) as well as from classical ones (esp. Seneca and Boethius). The work is thus surprisingly humanistic, and in this, and in its treatment of worldly misery in such thorough detail, it bears a great similarity to Petrarch's contemporary effort to the south. On the *De rem.* and Dambach's *Cons.* cf. Auer, *Dambach*, pp. 241, 256–59. Although Petrarch had ties to Charles IV (to whom Dambach addressed an *Exhortatio* [Auer, *Dambach*, pp. 53 ff.]) and visited his court in Prague in 1356, there is no evidence, to my knowledge, that Petrarch and Dambach knew each other or of each other's projects (on Petrarch's visit in 1356 see Wilkins, *Petrarch's Eight Years in Milan*, pp. 122–24; on Petrarch's letters to transalpine acquaintances such as Charles and Johann von Neumarkt [Jan ze Středa], see P. Piur, *Petrarcas Briefwechsel mit deutschen Zeitgenossen* [Berlin, 1933]). Dambach's work, appearing (either whole or excerpted) in various manuscripts and (fifteenth- and early-sixteenth-century) editions (see Auer, *Dambach*), must have had an appeal similar to, if somewhat more clerical than, Petrarch's *De rem.*

After Dambach, another northern religious development of the Boethian genre was to be found in Jean Gerson's *De consolatione theologiae* (1418). Unlike Dambach's work, however, Gerson's was not concerned with treating particular maladies and misfortunes. Highly spiritual, it instead consciously sought to extend Boethian consolation beyond the limited bounds of philosophy to the higher reaches of theology (see, for example, *Oeuvres comp.*, Glorieux, 9:188–89). Gerson describes the proposed themes treated in his four-book dialogue as discussions "prima de consolatione theologiae per spem in contemplatione divini judicii; secunda, per scripturam in revelatione regiminis mundi; tertia, per patientiam in zeli moderatione; quarta, per doctrinam in conscientiae serenatione" (*Oeuvres comp.*, p. 185). Could early Italian humanist consolation have partly inspired Gerson's interests in theological consolation or certain other currents in his pastoral writings? He knew Petrarch's *De rem.* and, citing Petrarch, he drew upon the *De rem.* Bk. 1, in an Ash-Wednesday sermon of 1389 (see N. Mann, "La fortune de Pétrarque en France: Recherches sur le 'De Remediis,' " *Studi Francesi* 13 [1969], 1–15 at 7–8; *Oeuvres comp.*, Glorieux, 7. pt. 2:973–75). Could Petrarch's treatment of death in the *De rem.* Bk. 2 in any way have inspired Gerson's *De scientia mortis*, which, in turn, became the seed for the *ars moriendi*? (on this, and on other consolatory writings of Gerson, nicknamed "Doctor Consolatorius" [Auer, *Dambach*, p. 194], see Chap. 3, n. 111 above; also cf. his *De remediis contra pusillanimitatem* [*Oeuv. comp.*, Glorieux, 10:374–86]).

As for other examples of religious consolation in the fourteenth- and fifteenth-century north, also see, prior to Dambach, Meister Eckhart's *Buch der göttlichen Tröstung* (*Meister Eckharts Buch der göttlichen Tröstung und Von dem edlen Menschen* [*Liber benedictus*], ed. J. Quint [Berlin, 1952]; trans. in *Meister Eckhart: The Essential Sermons, Commentaries, Treatises, and Defenses*, trans. and intro. E. Colledge and B. McGinn [New York, 1981]). A later and much more important work that perhaps fueled consolatory interests in the north was the enormously popular *Imitatio Christi*. Though this work deals with a wide range of spiritual and contemplative themes, one of its four books, titled the *Liber interne consolacionis*, has such chapters as "Quod temporales miserie exemplo Christo equanimiter sunt ferende" (18), "De tolerancia iniuriarum et quis verus paciens probetur" (19), "Quod homo non sit nimis deiectus quando in aliquos labitur defectus" (57), which are structured as spiritual colloquies between a devotee and Christ (edition in *Le manuscrit autographie de Thomas à Kempis et "L'imitation de Jésus-Christ,"* ed. L.M.J. Delaissé, 2 vols. [Paris, 1956]).

36. In the sixteenth century a greater consolatory concern could be found in the pastoral development of the "art of dying." An example particularly relevant (in one specific) to our study of Italian thought can be found in the Dutch cleric Josse von Clichtove's *De doctrina moriendi*. This work is a perfect blending of the classical consolation for death and the Christian *ars moriendi*. As Tenenti argues, the work draws widely on ancient thinkers, and includes three discrete chapters on the views of death found respectively in Cyprian (*De mortalitate*), Ambrose (*De bono mortis*), and Cicero (*Tusc.* Bk. 1 and *De senectute*) (see Chaps. 3–5 in the *De doctrina moriendi opusculum* [Paris, 1520], ff. 12–24v; Tenenti, *Il senso della morte*, pp. 102–4). In these three chapters and in several others, Clichtove deals with the psychological problem of accepting and not fearing death. With the perspective of the classical and patristic consoler, he complements the sacramental treatment of death (on confession, the eucharist, and extreme unction see Chaps. 10–11) with a humanistic, consolatory treatment. Moreover, in a final chapter examining how "Moderandum esse dolorem recte rationis lege, qui propter obitum cognatorum ac amicorum a plaerisque maior aequo susciptur," Clichtove treats bereavement. Of particular interest here is the fact that, besides drawing on biblical, classical, and patristic thought, he cites Filelfo's *Oratio consolatoria* to Marcello "in qua copiose eleganter et praeclare de animorum immortalitate et non deplorandis iis qui hinc a deo evocantur verba facit" (f. 85v). On Clichtove's many activities as an editor and for many of his prefaces to classical and religious works, see Eugene Rice, *The Prefatory Epistles of Jacques Lefèvre d'Étaples and Related Texts* (New York, 1972), passim.

As for other pastoral treatments, a well-circulated piece (whether in its true or adapted forms) was the Protestant Urbanus Rhegius' *Seelen Artzney fur gesund und kranken zu diesen gefarlichen Zeyten* (Augsburg, 1529), a work translated into Latin as the *Medicina animae*. Natalie Davis has shown how the original work was adapted and partially "Catholicized" in Latin and French editions published in Lyons in 1542 (followed also by an Italian edition in 1549) as part of a general consolatory collection of works on sickness and death. This anthology included *Imagines de morte* [Holbein's cycle on death] *et Epigrammata*, a *Ratio consolandi ob morbi gravitatem periculose decumbentes*, Cyprian's *De mortalitate*, and a dubious sermon of Chrysostom's, *On Patience, the End of the World, the Second Coming . . .* (see N. Z. Davis, "Holbein's *Pictures of Death* and the Reformation at Lyons," *SR* 3 [1956], 97–130, esp. 121 ff.). An English version (by Henry Thorne) of much of this work was published in England (1567?) as *The Physicke for the Soule*.

Also, on the rhetorical, consolatory tone of the Calvinist Thomas Becon's popular *The Sycke Mans Salve* [London, 1561] see Beaty, *Craft of Dying*, pp. 108–56. In the prefatory letter to this dialogue Becon suggests that in his treatise he has "interlased many comfortable exhortations unto the sycke." Though the work is chiefly comprised of biblical *loci*, among the consolations for the fear of death one finds citations of Cicero's *Tusculans* and *De senectute* (in 1561 ed. see pp. 307–8, 339–40); Cyprian's *De mortalitate* is also cited (pp. 154–60).

37. Joseph Hall, *Heaven upon Earth* and *Characters of Vertues and Vices*, ed. R. Kirk (Rutgers, 1948), p. 104. Hall had a French counterpart in Pierre Du Moulin (the Younger), whose *Traité de la paix de l'âme et du contentement de l'esprit* (Sedan, 1660) also dealt with both "divine" and "secular" tranquility. But whereas Hall turned to Seneca for his chief model (*Heaven upon Earth*, p. 84), Du Moulin, who cited Hall in his work, drew principally on Epictetus. Most importantly, Du Moulin's goal in this work was to refute Pierre Charron's charge that theology does not address the affairs of the secular realm. In the preface to the second edition of his *De la sagesse* (Paris, 1604) the cleric Charron had suggested that his work would deal with "l'humaine sagesse," an area neglected by theology. He argued that, compared to moral philosophy, theology is (in terms of form) little suited for and (in terms of content) less concerned with treating secular matters, and he suggested that his work would be not of a divine genre but of a human one treating worldly issues (*De la sagesse*, ed. M. A. Duval [Geneva, 1968; rept. of 1824 Paris ed.], pp. xxxviii–xlii). The consolatory and psychological realm was clearly part of this "human wisdom," as the considerably Stoic Charron dealt with such problems as the readiness of death (for which see the lengthy Chap. 2.11 [*De la sag.*, 2:234–73]) and the remedies for external and internal disquiet (in his highly popular work [39 editions in the first three quarters of the seventeenth century (Spanneut, *Permanence du Stoïcisme*, p. 254)] Charron drew not only on ancient Stoic thought but also on the modern Stoics Guillaume du Vair and Justus Lipsius). In the preface to his *Traité* Du Moulin answered Charron's indictment of theological wisdom; he argued that Charron would deny the theological domain of some of its rightful territory—namely, that area dealing with "the skill of living and dying well" (English trans. of the *Treatise of Peace and Contentment of Mind* [London, 1671], sig. A6). Appropriately, after a first chapter on spiritual issues, Du Moulin's treatise examined the Stoic secular realm of tranquility, the passions, and conduct.

38. Downame quotes extensively from Seneca's moral letters as well as from his *Cons. ad Marciam* and *De providentia*; he also cites Plutarch's *De tranquillitate animi* and Ps.-Plutarch's *Cons. ad Apol.* He also turns to various patristic sources, such as the treatises on patience by Cyprian, Chrysostom, and Tertullian.

39. It is worth noting that in his *On Comfortable Considerations for the Sicke* (1621), also later included in the 1630 *Monument of Mortality*, Day expressed an awareness of the need for revivifying the consolatory role. Referring to the earlier Christian era of Tertullian and Eusebius he says, "So fervent, at those dayes, was the love towards God and their neighbors (which now is waxen cold) in the mindes of Christians, and that true Christian charitie, whose propertie is (as Saint *Paul* saith) to rejoyce with them that rejoyce, to weepe with them that weepe" (*On Comf. Cons.*, p. 2, in *Mon. of Mort.* [London, 1630]; passage modernized in the use of i/j and u/v).

40. Hall, Downame, and Day (in *On Comf. Cons.*) all turn to the classical tradition. But notwithstanding Downame's and Day's drawing on classical thought, they also sometimes criticize it as erroneous or insufficient. Other works that reveal

a sense of competition with classical consolation include William Gilbert's *Architectonice consolationis; or the Art of Building Comfort* (London, 1640), which challenges the Stoic *consolatio* for bereavement. In France, Charles Drelincourt's *Les consolations de l'âme fidèle contre les frayeurs de la mort* (Charenton-le-Pont, 1651) attempts to replace inadequate classical (particularly Stoic) consolations for dying with Christian remedies; see esp. the second chapter, titled "Qu'en toute la Philosophie des Payens, il ne se trouve ni de vraye ni de solide consolation contre les frayeurs de la mort" (Nouvelle ed. [Amsterdam, 1699], pp. 9–19; on Drelincourt and this work, see McNeill, *Cure of Souls*, pp. 212–13). An English translation of *Les consolations* was published in America in 1824, its Protestant editors citing its European popularity and its usefulness as a manual of pastoral consolatory care (*The Christian's Consolations Against the Fears of Death, with Seasonable Directions How to Prepare Ourselves to Die Well* [Wheeling, Va., 1824], pp. iii–iv).

41. On "logotherapy" see Laín Entralgo, *Therapy of the Word*; also M. O'Rourke Boyle, "Erasmus' Prescription for Henry VIII: Logotherapy."

42. The Protestant context of this process warrants further study. The sacramental framework for the consolation of illness was somewhat dismantled by Luther. In 1519 he wrote a *Tessaradecas consolatoria pro laborantibus et onerantis* for the ailing Frederick the Wise at the suggestion of his humanistic colleague Georg Spalatin (who, incidentally, himself a couple of years later helped complete a German translation of Petrarch's *De remediis* [Fiske, *Petrarch's "De remediis,"* p. 32]). As Luther tells Frederick in the dedicatory epistle, the work is a fourteen-part spiritual exercise meant to replace the superstitious cult of the fourteen patron saints of illness: "I have put together these fourteen chapters after the fashion of an altar screen and have given them the name *Fourteen Consolations*. They are to replace the fourteen saints whom our superstition has invented and called 'The Defenders of Evil.' Now this is a spiritual screen and not made of silver. The book is not meant to adorn the walls of churches, but to uplift and strengthen the pious heart" (*Luther's Works*, vol. 42, ed. M. Dietrich, trans. M. H. Bertram [Philadelphia, 1969], p. 123). Heeding the biblical warning in Ecclus. 11:25, that "In the day of prosperity, adversity is forgotten, and in the day of adversity, prosperity is not remembered," he presents two sets of corrective reflections on the human condition, one consisting of seven evils (e.g., damnation, pain, death), the other of seven blessings (man's physical and mental blessings, future beatitude). In some sense, the work is thus a spiritual analogue to Petrarch's remedies for good and bad fortune; also, in joining the themes of misery and dignity in a consolation for illness, the work has some parallel to Brandolini's *Dialogue* to King Matthias (first pub. in Basel in 1498). Most importantly, Luther's *Tessaradecas* shows the effort to move from a sacramental treatment of illness to a more "psychological" one. The work was fairly popular, appearing in several German translations and two English ones (M. H. Bertram's "Introduction" in *Luther's Works*, 42:119–20; on this work cf. Clebsch and Jaekle, *Pastoral Care*, pp. 209–10).

43. Burton's subtitle describes the comprehensive scope of his treatment of melancholy: *What it is, with all the kinds, causes, symptomes, prognostickes, and severall cures of it . . . philosophically, medicinally, and historically opened and cut up* (Facsimile

rept. [of Burton's 1628 Oxford (3rd) ed.], ed. H. Jackson [New York, 1977]). On Burton's well-known work see, for example, Babb, *Elizabethan Malady*; Lyons, *Voices of Melancholy*; Kinsman, "Folly, Melancholy, and Madness."

44. Burton's unusual mixing of roles and interests was not lost on him, as he defends his right as a "melancholy divine" to enter the doctor's province. Citing a figure such as Ficino, "a priest and physician at once," he argues that such a hybrid healer is appropriate to this disease that afflicts body and soul alike. He is up to the measure, because he is "by my profession a divine, and by mine inclination a physician" (*Anatomy*, "Democritus Junior to the Reader," pp. 36–37).

45. The *De vita* is cited in various places; see, for example, the section on "Love of Learning, or overmuch Study. With a Digression of the Misery of Scholars, and why the Muses are Melancholy" (*Anatomy*, First Partition, pp. 300 ff.). Burton also cites, among other of Ficino's writings, his *De amore* and *Theologia Platonica*.

46. If the title of this section was perhaps partly derived from an anonymous British work, the *Remedies against discontentments* (pub. in 1596), this remedy manual was certainly also in the tradition of the Ps.-Seneca's and Petrarch's *De remediis* and Cardano's *De cons.*, all of which are cited (for a citation of Petrarch's *De rem.* 2.3 [*Opera*, Basel, p. 127] see Second Part., pp. 135, 287n; in general in the *Anatomy* there are citations of or references to other of Petrarch's works, including the letters, the *De vita solitaria*, and the *Secretum* [the latter cited as the *De contemptu mundi* (First Part., p. 300)]; Cardano's *De cons.* is cited several times). Like various Renaissance Italian writers, Burton grounds his consolatory endeavor in a larger tradition: "Because in the precedent section I have made mention of good counsel, comfortable speeches, persuasion, how necessarily they are required to the cure of a discontented or troubled mind, how present a remedy they yield, and many times a sole sufficient cure of themselves [see, in this earlier section, Burton's remarkable comments on the medicinal power of eloquence (at Second Part., pp. 112–13)]; I have thought fit, in this following section, a little to digress . . . , to collect and glean a few remedies and comfortable speeches out of our best orators, philosophers, divine, and Fathers of the Church, tending to this purpose. I confess, many have copiously written on this subject, Plato, Seneca, Plutarch, Xenophon, Epictetus, Theophrastus, Xenocrates, Crantor, Lucian, Boethius: and some of late, Sadoletus, Cardan, Budaeus [Guillaume Budé], Stella, Petrarch, Erasmus, besides Austin [Augustine], Cyprian, Bernard, etc." (Second Part., p. 126). Burton's survey here reveals how the consolatory tradition is no longer merely a classical and patristic one principally but also a modern one cultivated by the likes of Petrarch and Cardano. Burton then explains his purpose in condensing material from this tradition and in making it accessible (cf. Petrarch's statement of purpose in *De rem.* 2.117). He also suggests that, in the tradition of Cicero's, Boethius', and Cardano's analogous works, his also has a potentially self-consolatory dimension (Second Part., p. 127).

47. The rich humanistic tenor of Burton's "Consolatory Digression" can be seen in the chapter concerning death titled "Against Sorrow for Death of Friends or otherwise, vain Fear, etc.," where his sources include the *Apology*, *Crito*, *Phaedo*; Lucian's *De luctu*; the *Tusculans* Bk. 3; Ps.-Seneca's *De rem. fort*; Plutarch's *De tranquillitate animi*; Ps.-Plutarch's *Cons. ad Apol.*; Boethius' *Cons. phil.*; Cardano's

De cons.; and a spate of quotations from such as Homer, Ovid, Vergil, and Catullus; his religious sources here, other than the Bible, include writings of Ambrose, Augustine, and Bernard (the *Meditations*).

48. Uniting all facets of "negative" emotion, Burton's treatise affirmed the legitimacy of despair or, certainly, signaled its flowering as a topic of literary discussion and, even, sport. Of the various facets of melancholy that Burton examines, he apparently considered his treatment of "religious melancholy" to be the signal contribution of his work. Though Timothy Bright discussed religious despair in his *Treatise of Melancholie* of 1586 (Babb, *Elizabethan Malady*, pp. 51–52), Burton argued that no one had fully treated this aspect of the disease, which he subsumed under the larger rubric of "love-melancholy" in the Third Partition. Arising from such problems as superstition, spiritual excesses, bad conscience, and fear concerning salvation, "religious melancholy" is accorded the same clinical attention as other types of melancholy. And in prescribing remedies for it, Burton recommends the same regimen he did for general melancholy, including "comfortable speeches." As he did for secular distress, he likewise culls consolatory speeches for religious disquiet (Third Part., pp. 408 ff.). Such an approach perhaps further suggests the influence of humanist rhetorical theory upon pastoral thought.

In a word, Burton united into a single clinical framework the domains of the doctor, the love poet, the moral rhetorician, and the pastor. Moreover, his treatise suggests that the popularization of melancholy in the medical and literary sphere has thus facilitated its partial encroachment even upon the categories of spiritual health. Religious despair is thus somewhat absorbed into, and somewhat dwarfed by, a nonreligious psychological tradition.

SELECT BIBLIOGRAPHY

PRIMARY SOURCES

(Classical and patristic sources are not included. For references to these works, see the Index.)

Abelard, Peter. *Historia calamitatum*. Ed. J. Monfrin. 3rd ed. Paris, 1967.

Acciaiuoli, Donato. Epistola consolatoria to Lorenzo and Giuliano de' Medici on the death of Piero de' Medici. BNC, MS. Magl. XXVII, 115, ff. 14–20v.

Agli, Antonio. Epistola consolatoria to Cosimo de' Medici on the death of his son Giovanni. In *Collectiones Cosmianae*. BML, MS. Laur. 54, 10, at ff. 97–104.

———. Epistola consolatoria to Piero de' Medici on the death of Cosimo. In *Collectiones Cosmianae*. BML, MS. Laur. 54, 10, at ff. 123v–134.

Albertano da Brescia. *Liber consolationis et consilii*. Ed. Thor Sundby. London, 1873.

Alberti, Leon Battista. *Opere volgari*. Ed. Cecil Grayson. 3 vols. Bari, 1960–1973.

Altividus de immortalitate animae (or *Liber Alcidi*). BML, MS. Laur. 84, 24, ff. 204v–234.

Arnigio, Bartolomeo. *Discorso sopra disprezzo della morte*. Padua, 1575.

Arrigo da Settimello. *Elegia de diversitate fortunae et philosophiae consolatione*. In *Henrici Septimellensis: Elegia, sive de miseria*. Ed. A. Marigo. Padua, 1926. *Arrighetto ovvero Trattato contro all'avversità della fortuna di Arrigo da Settimello*. Ed. D. M. Manni. Florence, 1730.

Bandini, Francesco. *Dialogo di messer Francesco Bandini dun ragionamento avuto conlui Simone Ghondi il di avanti morissi*. In P. O. Kristeller, "Francesco Bandini and His Consolatory Dialogue upon the Death of Simone Gondi." In P. O. Kristeller, *Studies in Renaissance Thought and Letters*, pp. 411–35. Rome, 1956.

Becon, Thomas. *The Sycke Mans Salve*. London, 1561.

Bernard of Clairvaux. *Sermones super Cantica Canticorum* 26. In *S. Bernardi Opera*, vol. 1. Ed. J. Leclercq, C. H. Talbot, and H. M. Rochais. Rome, 1957.

Bevilacqua da Lazise, Giorgio. *Excusatio adversus consolatores in obitu Valerii filii*. Verona, Biblioteca Civica, MS. 1472 (B. Lett. 82.4), ff. 7–173.

Boncompagno da Signa. *"Amicitia" di Maestro Boncompagno da Signa*. Ed. S. Nathan. Miscellanea di letteratura del Medio Evo, no. 3 (1909).

———. Chapter "De consolationibus" in [*Rhetorica antiqua* (or *Boncompagnus*)], Book 1. In BAV, MS. Archivio di S. Pietro, H 13, ff. 35vA–43vA.

———. "Il *De malo senectutis et senii* di Boncompagno da Signa." *Rendiconti della R. Accademia dei Lincei*, classe di scienze morali, series 5, 1 (1892), 49–67.

Bosso, Matteo. *De tolerandis adversis*. In [*Opera*]. [Strasbourg, 1509].

———. *De veris salutaribus animi gaudiis*. In [*Opera*]. [Strasbourg, 1509].

Bracciolini Poggio. *Epistolae*. Ed. T. Tonelli. 3 vols. Rept. in *Opera omnia*, vol. 2. Ed. R. Fubini. 4 vols. Turin, 1964.

————. *De miseria humanae conditionis*. In *Opera omnia*. Basel, 1538. Rept. in *Opera omnia*, vol. 1. Ed. R. Fubini. 4 vols. Turin, 1964.

————. *Oratio in funere* (on the death of Lorenzo di Giovanni de' Medici). In *Opera omnia*. Basel, 1538. Rept. in *Opera omnia*, vol. 1. Ed. R. Fubini. 4 vols. Turin, 1964.

Brandolini, Aurelio. *De ratione scribendi* [and other works]. Cologne, 1573.

————. *Dialogus de humanae vitae conditione et toleranda corporis aegritudine*. Paris, 1562.

Bruni, Leonardo. *Epistolarum libri VIII*. Ed. L. Mehus. 2 vols. Florence, 1741.

————. *The Humanism of Leonardo Bruni: Selected Texts*. Trans. and Intro. G. Griffiths, J. Hankins, and D. Thompson. Binghamton, 1987.

Burton, Robert. *The Anatomy of Melancholy: What it is, with all the kinds, causes, symptomes, prognostickes, and severall cures of it*. Ed. H. Jackson. Facsimile rept. of 1628 Oxford (3rd) ed. New York, 1977.

Cardano, Gerolamo. *De consolatione*. In *Opera omnia*. 10 vols. Lyons, 1663.
    Cardanus Comforte. Trans. Thomas Bedingfeld. Facsimile rept. of 1576 London ed. Amsterdam, 1969.

————. *De utilitate ex adversis capienda*. In *Opera omnia*. 10 vols. Lyons, 1663.

Castiglione, Francesco da. Epistola consolatoria to Cosimo de' Medici on the death of his son Giovanni. In *Collectiones Cosmianae*. BML, MS. Laur. 54, 10, at ff. 89v–96v.

Charron, Pierre. *De la sagesse*. Ed. M. A. Duval. Paris, 1824; rept. Geneva, 1968.

Clichtove, Josse von. *De doctrina moriendi*. Paris, 1520.

Conversini da Ravenna, Giovanni. B. G. Kohl and J. Day, "Giovanni Conversini's *Consolatio ad Donatum* on the Death of Petrarch." *SR* 21 (1974), 9–18.

————. *De consolatione in obitu filii*. Oxford, MS. Balliol 288, ff. 51vB–71vA.

Corsi, Giovanni. *Vita Marsilii Ficini*. In R. Marcel, *Marsile Ficin (1433–1499)*, pp. 680–89. Paris, 1958.

Dambach, Johannes von. *De consolatione theologiae*. [Strasbourg, c. 1479].

Day, Martin. *On Comfortable Considerations for the Sicke*. In Martin Day, *Monument of Mortality*. London, 1630.

————. *Meditations of Consolation*. In Martin Day, *Monument of Mortality*. London, 1630.

Downame, John. *Consolations for the Afflicted, or the Third Part of the Christian Warfare*. London, 1613.

Drelincourt, Charles. *Les consolations de l'âme fidèle contre les frayeurs de la mort*. Nouvelle ed. Amsterdam, 1699.
    The Christian's Consolations Against the Fears of Death, with Seasonable Directions How to Prepare Ourselves to Die Well. Wheeling, Va., 1824.

Du Moulin (the Younger), Pierre. *Treatise of Peace and Contentment of Mind* (translation of *Traité de la paix de l'âme et du contentement de l'esprit*). London, 1671.

Eckhart, Meister. *Meister Eckharts Buch der göttlichen Tröstung und Von dem edlen Menschen (Liber benedictus)*. Ed. J. Quint. Berlin, 1952.

SELECT BIBLIOGRAPHY** 289

Erasmus Desiderius. *De morte declamatio.* Ed. In *De conscribendis epistolis,* in *Opera omnia Desiderii Erasmi Roterdami.* Vol. 1, pt. 2. Amsterdam, 1971.

———. *De praeparatione ad mortem.* In *Opera omnia Desiderii Erasmi Roterdami.* Vol. 5, pt. 1. Amsterdam, 1977.

Ficino, Marsilio. *De amore.* In *Marsile Ficin, Commentaire sur le Banquet de Platon.* Ed. R. Marcel. Paris, 1956.

Marsilio Ficino: Commentary on Plato's "Symposium" on Love. Trans. Sears Jayne. Dallas, 1985.

———. *The Letters of Marsilio Ficino.* Trans. Fellowship of the School of Economic Science, London. 3 vols. London, 1975–81.

———. *Opera omnia.* Basel, 1576; rept. Turin, 1959.

———. *Supplementum Ficinianum.* Ed. P. O. Kristeller. 2 vols. Florence, 1937.

———. *Theologia Platonica de immortalitate animorum.* In *Théologie Platonicienne de l'immortalité des âmes.* Ed. R. Marcel. 3 vols. Paris, 1964–70.

———. *De vita.* In *Opera omnia.* Basel, 1576; rept. Turin, 1959.

Marsilio Ficino: The Book of Life. Trans. C. Boer. Irving, Tex., 1980.

Filelfo, Francesco. *Epistolarum familiarium libri xxxvii.* Venice, 1502.

———. *Oratio consolatoria ad Iacobum Antonium Marcellum de obitu Valerii filii.* In *Orationes cum quibusdam aliis eiusdem operibus.* Basel, not after 1498.

———. *Oratio parentalis de divi Francisci Sphortiae Mediolanensis ducis foelicitate.* In *Orationes cum quibusdam aliis eiusdem operibus.* Basel, not after 1498.

Gerson, Jean. *Oeuvres complètes.* Ed. P. Glorieux. 10 vols. Paris, 1960–73.

Giamboni, Bono. *Della miseria dell'uomo, Giardino di consolazione, Introduzione alle virtù di Bono Giamboni.* Ed. F. Tassi. Florence, 1856.

Gilbert, William. *Architectonice consolationis; or the Art of Building Comfort.* London, 1640.

Glissenti, Fabio. *Discorsi morali contra il dispiacer del morire detto Athanatophilia.* Venice, 1609.

Hall, Joseph. *Heaven upon Earth, or of True Peace and Tranquillitie of Minde.* In *Heaven upon Earth* and *Characters of Vertues and Vices.* Ed. R. Kirk. Rutgers, 1948.

Hildebert of Levardin (or Le Mans). *Liber de querimonia et conflictu carnis et spiritus seu animae.* In *PL* 171.

Imitatio Christi. Le manuscrit autographie de Thomas à Kempis et "L'imitation de Jésus-Christ". Ed. L.M.J. Delaissé. 2 vols. Paris, 1956.

Innocent III (Lotario dei Segni). *De miseria condicionis humane.* Ed. R. E. Lewis. Athens, Ga., 1978.

Lawrence of Durham. *Laurentius von Durham, Consolatio de morte amici: Untersuchungen und kritischer Text.* Ed. U. Kindermann. Breslau, 1969.

Lupset, Thomas. *The Waye of Dyenge Well.* In *The Life and Works of Thomas Lupset.* Ed. J. A. Gee. New Haven, 1928.

Luther, Martin. *Fourteen Consolations* (translation of *Tessaradecas consolatoria pro laborantibus et onerantis*). In *Luther's Works,* vol. 42. Ed. M. O. Dietrich. Trans. M. H. Bertram. Philadelphia, 1969.

McNeill, J. T., and Helen M. Gamer. *Medieval Handbooks of Penance: A Transla-*

tion of the Principal 'Libri poenitentiales' and Selections from Related Documents. 1938; rept. New York, 1965.

Manetti, Giannozzo. *Dialogus de acerba Antonini, dilectissimi filii sui, morte consolatorius in monasterio cartusiensium habitus.* In *Dialogus consolatorius.* Ed. A. de Petris. Rome, 1983. BNC, MS. Magl. XXI, 18, ff. 1–45v.

———. *Ianotii Manetti de dignitate et excellentia hominis.* Ed. E. Leonard. Padua, 1975.

Marsuppini, Carlo. *De morte Nonninae matris consolatio.* In P. G. Ricci, "Una consolatoria inedita del Marsuppini." *La Rinascita* 3 (1940), 363–433.

Medici, Lorenzo de'. *L'Altercazione.* In *Opere.* Ed. A. Simioni. 2 vols. Bari, 1913–14.

More, Thomas. *A Dialoge of Comfort agaynst trybulacion.* In *The Complete Works of St. Thomas More,* vol. 12. Ed. F. Martz and F. Manley. New Haven, 1976.

———. *De quatuor novissimis.* Facsimile of 1557 London edition and modern edition of *The Last Four Things* in *The English Works of Sir Thomas More,* vol. 1. Ed. W. Campbell and A. Reed. London, 1931.

Morelli, Giovanni di Pagolo. *Ricordi.* Ed. V. Branca. Florence, 1969.

Nicolaus of Modruš. (Modrusiensis; Nikola of Kotor). *De consolatione.* BAV, MS. Vat. lat. 8764. BAV, MS. Vat. lat. 5139.

———. *De mortalium foelicitate* (or *De foelicitate humana*). Rome, Biblioteca Casanatense, MS. 276 (B IV 13), ff. 2–20.

———. *Oratio in funere . . . Petri.* Rome, 1481–87.

Peter of Blois. *De amicitia christiana et de dilectione Dei et proximi.* In *Un traité de l'amour du XIIᵉ siècle, Pierre de Blois.* Ed. M.-M. Davy. Paris, 1932.

———. *De duodecim utilitatibus tribulationis.* In *PL* 207.

Petrarca, Francesco. *Epistolae variae.* In *Epistolae: De rebus familiaribus et Variae,* vol. 3. Ed. G. Fracassetti. Florence, 1863.

———. *Le Familiari.* Ed. V. Rossi (vols. 1–3) and U. Bosco (vol. 4). Florence, 1933–1942.

Francesco Petrarca: Rerum familiarium libri I–VIII. English translation by A. Bernardo. Albany, 1975. *Letters on Familiar Matters: 'Rerum familiarium libri' IX–XVI.* Baltimore, 1982. *Libri XVII–XXIV.* Baltimore, 1985.

———. *Invective contra medicum* (P. G. Ricci's edition with Italian translation and additional notes by C. Kraus Reggiani). In *Opere latine.*

———. *Opera latine di Francesco Petrarca.* Ed. A. Bufano. 2 vols. Turin, 1975.

———. *De otio religioso* (G. Rotondi's edition with Ital. translation and notes by B. Aracri). In *Opere latine.*

———. *Poëmata minora quae extant omnia.* Ed. D. Rossetti. 3 vols. Milan, 1829–1834.

———. *De remediis utriusque fortunae.* In *Opera omnia.* Basel, 1554.

Phisicke Against Fortune. Trans. Thomas Twyne. Facsimile rept. of 1579 London edition. Intro. B. G. Kohl. Delmar, N.Y., 1980.

———. *Rerum senilium libri.* In *Opera omnia.* Basel, 1554.

Lettere Senili di Francesco Petrarca. Italian translation by G. Fracassetti. 2 vols. Florence, 1869–70.

————. *Rime, Trionfi, e poesie latine.* Ed. F. Neri, G. Martellotti, E. Bianchi, and N. Sapegno. La letteratura italiana, storia e testi, no. 6. Milan and Naples, 1951.

————. *De secreto conflictu curarum mearum* (E. Carrara's edition with Italian translation and additional notes by A. Bufano). In *Opere latine.* *Petrarch's Secret or the Soul's Conflict with Passion.* Trans. W. H. Draper. London, 1911.

————. *De sui ipsius et multorum ignorantia* (P. G. Ricci's edition with Italian translation and additional notes by C. Kraus Reggiani). In *Opere latine.* *On His Own Ignorance and That of Many Others.* Trans. H. Nachod. In *The Renaissance Philosophy of Man.* Ed. E. Cassirer, P. O. Kristeller, and J. H. Randall, Jr. Chicago, 1948.

————. *De vita solitaria* (G. Martellotti's edition with Italian translation and additional notes by A. Bufano). In *Opere latine.* *The Life of Solitude by Francis Petrarch.* Trans. J. Zeitlin. Urbana, 1924.

Platina (Bartolomeo Sacchi). *De falso et vero bono [and other works].* Paris, 1530.

Poliziano, Angelo. *Pro Epicteto Stoico epistola.* In *Prosatori latini del Quattrocento.* Ed. E. Garin. La letteratura italiana, storia e testi, no. 13. Milan and Naples, 1952.

Pontano, Giovanni. *De fortitudine bellica et heroica.* In *Opera omnia.* 3 vols. Venice, 1518–19.

Ricci, Antonio. *Consolatione della morte sopra e doppo'l morire della Prudentiss. S. Costanza Austria Gonzaga Contessa di Novellara.* Ferrara, 1564.

Rinuccini, Alamanno. *Lettere ed Orazioni.* Ed. V. Giustiniani. Florence, 1953.

Rockinger, Ludwig. *Briefsteller und Formelbücher des eilften bis vierzehnten Jahrhunderts.* Quellen und Erörterungen zur bayerischen und deutschen Geschichte, no. 9, pts. 1–2. Munich, 1863; rept. New York, 1961.

Sadoleto, Jacopo. *Philosophicae consolationes, et meditationes in adversis.* In *Opera quae exstant omnia,* vol. 3. 4 vols. Verona, 1737–38; rept. Gregg Press, 1964.

Salutati, Coluccio. *Epistolario di Coluccio Salutati.* Ed. Francesco Novati. 4 vols. Fonti per la storia d'Italia, nos. 15–18. Rome, 1891–1911.

————. *De nobilitate legum et medicinae—De verecundia.* Ed. E. Garin. Florence, 1947.

————. *De seculo et religione.* Ed. B. L. Ullman. Florence, 1957.

Scala, Bartolomeo. *Dialogus de consolatione qui dicitur Cosmus.* In *Collectiones Cosmianae.* BML, MS. Laur. 54, 10, at ff. 104v–122v. Edition forthcoming by Alison Brown.

Tractatus artis bene moriendi. English translation *The Boke of the Crafte of Dyinge.* In C. Horstmann, *Yorkshire Writers: Richard Rolle of Hampole and His Followers,* vol. 2. 2 vols. London, 1895–96.

Traversari, Ambrogio. *Ambrosii Traversarii . . . latinae epistolae* [ed. P. Canneti]. *. . . Adcedit eiusdem Ambrosii vita in qua historia litteraria florentina ab anno MCXCII usque MCCCCXL . . . deducta est* [L. Mehus]. 2 vols. Florence, 1759; rpt. Bologna, 1968.

————. *Hodoeporicon.* In A. Dini-Traversari, *Ambrogio Traversari e i suoi tempi.* Florence, 1912.

————. G. Battelli, "Una dedica inedita di Ambrogio Traversari all'Infante Don Pedro di Portogallo, Duca di Coimbra." *La Rinascita* 2 (1939), 613–16.

Vespasiano da Bisticci. *Vite di uomini illustri del secolo XV*. Ed. P. d'Ancona and E. Aeschlimann. Milan, 1951.

Villani, Filippo. *Liber di origine civitatis Florentiae et eiusdem famosis civibus*. Ed. G. C. Galletti. Florence, 1847.

Villena, Enrique de. *Tradato de la consolación*. Ed. D. Carr. Madrid, 1976.

Vincent of Beauvais. *Tractatus consolatorius ad Ludovicum IX regem de obitu filii*. In *Opuscula*. Basel, 1481.

SECONDARY SOURCES

Allen, Michael J. B. *The Platonism of Marsilio Ficino: A Study of his "Phaedrus" Commentary, Its Sources and Genesis*. Berkeley and Los Angeles, 1984.

Ariès, Philippe. *The Hour of Our Death*. Trans. H. Weaver. New York, 1982.

Auer, Albert. *Johannes von Dambach und die Trostbücher von 11. bis zum 16. Jahrhundert*. Beiträge zur Geschichte der Philosophie und Theologie des Mittelalters, no. 27, pts. 1–2. Münster, 1928.

Babb, Lawrence. *The Elizabethan Malady: A Study of Melancholia in English Literature from 1580 to 1642*. East Lansing, Mich., 1951.

Banker, James R. "Mourning a Son: Childhood and Paternal Love in the *Consolatoria* of Giannozzo Manetti." *History of Childhood Quarterly: The Journal of Psychohistory* 3 (1976), 351–62.

Barasch, Moshe. *Gestures of Despair in Medieval and Early Renaissance Art*. New York, 1976.

Baron, Hans. "The Evolution of Petrarch's Thought: Reflections on the State of Petrarch Studies." In Hans Baron, *From Petrarch to Leonardo Bruni: Studies in Humanistic and Political Literature*, pp. 7–50. Chicago and London, 1968.

————. *Petrarch's "Secretum": Its Making and Its Meaning*. Cambridge, Mass., 1985.

————. "Petrarch's *Secretum*: Was It Revised—and Why?" In Baron, *From Petrarch to Leonardo Bruni: Studies in Humanistic and Political Literature*, pp. 51–101. Chicago and London, 1968.

Beaty, Nancy L. *The Craft of Dying: A Study in the Literary Tradition of the "Ars moriendi" in England*. New Haven, Conn. 1979.

Bec, Christian. *Les marchands écrivains: affaires et humanisme à Florence, 1375–1434*. Paris, 1967.

Becker, Marvin. *Florence in Transition*. 2 vols. Baltimore, 1967–68.

————. "Individualism in the Early Italian Renaissance: Burden and Blessing." *SR* 19 (1972).

Bellemo, V. *Jacopo e Giovanni de' Dondi dall' Orologia*. Chioggia, 1894.

Bernardo, Aldo. "Introduction." In *Francesco Petrarca: Rerum familiarium libri I–VIII*. Trans. A. Bernardo. Albany, N.Y., 1975.

————. "Letter-Splitting in Petrarch's *Familiares*." *Speculum* 33 (1958), 236–41.

Bertalot, L. "Cincius Romanus und seine Briefe." In Ludwig Bertalot, *Studien zum italienischen und deutschen Humanismus*, vol. 2, pp. 131–80. Ed. P. O. Kristeller. 2 vols. Rome, 1975. Originally in *Quellen und Forschungen aus italienischen Archiven und Bibliotheken* 21 (1929–1930).

Beyenka, Mary. *Consolation in Saint Augustine*. Washington, D.C., 1950.

Billanovich, Giuseppe. *Petrarca letterato*. Vol. 1, *Lo scrittoio del Petrarca*. Rome, 1947.

Bobbio, Aurelia. "Seneca e la formazione spirituale e culturale del Petrarca." *Bibliofilia* 43 (1941), 224–91.

Bosco, Umberto. *Francesco Petrarca*. Turin, 1946; rept. Bari, 1973.

Bouwsma, William. "The Two Faces of Humanism: Stoicism and Augustinianism in Renaissance Thought." In *Itinerarium Italicum*, pp. 3–60. Ed. H. Oberman with T. Brady, Jr. Leiden, 1975.

Boyle, M. O'Rourke. "Erasmus' Prescription for Henry VIII: Logotherapy." *RQ* 31 (1978), 161–72.

Brown, Alison. *Bartolomeo Scala, 1430–1497, Chancellor of Florence: The Humanist as Bureaucrat*. Princeton, 1979.

———. "The Humanist Portrait of Cosimo de' Medici, Pater Patriae." *Journal of the Warburg and Courtauld Institutes* 24 (1961), 186–221.

Buresch, Karl. *Consolationum a Graecis Romanisque scriptarum historia critica*. Leipziger Studien zur classichen Philologie, no. 9, pt. 1. Leipzig, 1886.

Cammelli, G. *I dotti bizantini e le origini del umanesimo*. 3 vols. Florence, 1941–54.

Chiappelli, A. *Studii sull'esercizio della medicina in Italia negli ultimi tre secoli del medio evo*. Milan, 1885.

Clebsch, W. B., and C. R. Jaekle. *Pastoral Care in Historical Perspective: An Essay with Exhibits*. New York, 1964.

Cochin, H. *Le frère de Pétrarque et le livre "Du repos des religieux"*. Paris, 1903.

Constable, Giles. *Letters and Letter-Collections*. Turnhout, 1976.

Corsini, A. "Il 'De vita' di Marsilio Ficino." *Rivista di storia critica delle scienze mediche e naturali* 10 (1919), 5–13.

Cosenza, Mario E. *Biographical and Bibliographical Dictionary of the Italian Humanists*. 4 vols. Boston, 1962.

Courcelle, Pierre. *La "Consolation de Philosophie" dans la tradition littéraire: Antécédents et postérité de Boèce*. Paris, 1967.

———. "Pétrarque entre Saint Augustin et les Augustins du XIVe siècle." In *Studi Petrarcheschi*, Accademia Petrarca di lettere arti e scienze di Arezzo, vol. 7, pp. 51–71. Ed. U. Bosco. Bologna, 1961.

Davis, Natalie Z. "Holbein's *Pictures of Death* and the Reformation at Lyons." *SR* 3 (1956), 97–130.

Delhaye, P. "Deux adaptations du 'De amicitia' de Cicéron au XIIe siècle." *Recherches de théologie ancienne et médiévale* 15 (1948), 304–31.

Delisle, L. "Anciennes traductions français du traité de Pétrarque *Sur les Remèdes de l'une et l'autre fortune*." *Notices et extraits des manuscrits de la Bibliothèque Nationale et autres bibliothèques*, no. 34 (Paris, 1891), pp. 273–304.

Della Torre, A. *Storia dell'Accademia Platonica di Firenze*. Florence, 1902.

De Petris, Alfonso. "Il *Dialogus consolatorius* di G. Manetti e le sue fonte." *GSLI* 154 (1977), 76–106.

———. "Giannozzo Manetti and his *Consolatoria*." *BHR* 45 (1979), 493–525.

De' Rosmini, C. *Vita di Francesco Filelfo da Tolentino*. 3 vols. Milan, 1808.

Diekstra, F.N.M. "Introduction." In Diekstra, *A Dialogue Between Reason and Adversity: A Late Middle English Version of Petrarch's 'De remediis'*. Assen, 1968.

Di Napoli, G. *L'immortalità dell'anima del Rinascimento*. Turin, 1963.

Donovan, R. "Salutati's Opinion of Non-Italian Latin Writers of the Middle Ages." *SR* 14 (1967), 182–201.

Durling, Robert. "Introduction." In *Petrarch's Lyric Poems: The "Rime sparse" and Other Lyrics*. Trans. and ed. R. Durling. Cambridge, Mass., and London, 1976.

Errera, C. "Le 'Commentationes Florentinae de exilio' di Francesco Filelfo." *Archivio storico italiano*, series 5, no. 5 (1890), 193–227.

Ettore, I. "Francesco Petrarca e i medici: La polemica con Giovanni Dondi"; "Petrarca e i medici: I medici amici." *Il giardino di Esculapio* 3 (Milan, 1930).

Fabbri, R. "Le *Consolationes de obitu Valerii Marcelli* ed il Filelfo." In *Miscellanea di studi in onore di Vittore Branca*, vol. 3, pt. 1, pp. 227–50. 5 vols. Biblioteca dell' "Archivum Romanicum," Series 1, nos. 178–82. Florence, 1983.

Favez, C. *La consolation latine chrétienne*. Paris, 1937.

Fern, Mary. *The Latin Consolatio as a Literary Type*. St. Louis, 1941.

Fiske, W. *Francis Petrarch's "De remediis utriusque fortunae": Texts and Versions*. Bibliographical Notices, no. 3. Florence, 1888.

Foresti, A. *Aneddoti della vita di Francesco Petrarca*. Brescia, 1928.

Frati, C. "Evasio Leone e le sue ricerche intorno a Niccolò vescovo Modrussiense." *La Bibliofilia* 18 (1916), 1–35, 81–98.

Garin, E. *La disputa delle arti nel Quattrocento*. Florence, 1947.

———. "Una fonte ermetica poco nota: contributi alla storia del pensiero umanistico." *La Rinascita* 3 (1940), 202–32.

———. *Italian Humanism*. Trans. P. Munz. New York, 1965.

———. "Per la storia della tradizione platonica medioevali." *Giornale critico della filosofia italiana*, 3rd series, no. 3 (1949), 125–50.

Gregg, R. C. *Consolation Philosophy: Greek and Christian Paideia in Basil and the Two Gregories*. Patristic Monograph Series, no. 3. Cambridge, Mass., 1975.

Gualdo Rosa, L. *La fede nella "paideia": Aspetti della fortuna europea di Isocrate nei secoli XV e XVI*. Studi storici dell'Istituto storico italiano per il Medio Evo, 140–42. Rome, 1984.

Hain, L.F.T. *Repertorium bibliographicum*. 2 vols. Stuttgart and Paris, 1826–38.

Heitmann, Klaus. *Fortuna und Virtus: Eine Studie zu Petrarcas Lebensweisheit*. Studi italiani, no. 1. Cologne and Graz, 1958.

———. "La genesi del *De remediis utriusque fortune* del Petrarca." *Convivium*, N. S., 1 (1957), 9–30.

———. "L'insegnamento agostiniano nel "Secretum" del Petrarca." In *Studi Petrarcheschi*, Accademia Petrarca di lettere arti e scienze di Arezzo, vol. 7, pp. 187–93. Ed. U. Bosco. Bologna, 1961.

Holmes, George. *The Florentine Enlightenment: 1400–50*. New York, 1969.

Howard, Donald R. "Renaissance World-Alienation." In *The Darker Vision of the Renaissance: Beyond the Fields of Reason*, pp. 47–76. Ed. R. S. Kinsman. Berkeley and Los Angeles, 1974.

Huillard-Bréholles, A. *Vie et correspondance de Pierre de la Vigne*. Paris, 1864.

King, Margaret. "An Inconsolable Father and His Humanist Consolers: Jacopo Antonio Marcello, Venetian Nobleman, Patron, and Man of Letters." In *Supplementum Festivum: Essays in Honor of Paul Oskar Kristeller*, pp. 221–46. Ed. J. Hankins, J. Monfasani, and F. Purnell, Jr. Binghamton, N.Y., 1987.

Kinsman, Robert S. "Folly, Melancholy, and Madness: A Study of Shifting Styles of Medical Analysis and Treatment, 1450–1675." In *The Darker Vision of the Renaissance: Beyond the Fields of Reason*, pp. 273–320. Ed. R. S. Kinsman. Berkeley and Los Angeles, 1974,

Klibansky, R., E. Pansofsky, and F. Saxl. *Saturn and Melancholy: Studies in the History of Natural Philosophy, Religion and Art*. New York, 1964.

Kohl, Benjamin G. "Introduction." In facsimile rept. of Thomas Twyne's 1579 translation of Petrarch's *De remediis utriusque fortune*, the *Phisicke Against Fortune*. Delmar, N.Y., 1980.

———. "The Works of Giovanni di Conversino da Ravenna: A Catalogue of Manuscripts and Editions." *Traditio* 31 (1975), 349–67.

Kristeller, Paul Oskar. "Per la biografia di Marsilio Ficino." In Kristeller, *Studies*, pp. 191–211. Originally in *Civiltà Moderna* 10 (1938).

———. "Byzantine and Western Platonism in the Fifteenth Century." In Kristeller, *Renaissance Thought and Its Sources*, pp. 150–63. Ed. M. Mooney. New York. 1979.

———. "The Dignity of Man." In Kristeller, *Renaissance Thought and Its Sources*, pp. 169–81. Ed. M. Mooney. New York, 1979.

———. "Francesco Bandini and His Consolatory Dialogue Upon the Death of Simone Gondi." In Kristeller, *Studies*, pp. 411–35.

———. "Humanism and Scholasticism in the Italian Renaissance." In Kristeller, *Renaissance Thought and Its Sources*, pp. 85–105. Ed. M. Mooney. New York, 1979. Originally in *Byzantion* 17 (1944–45).

———. "The Immortality of the Soul." In Kristeller, *Renaissance Thought and Its Sources*, pp. 181–96. Ed. M. Mooney. New York, 1979

———. "Italian Humanism and Byzantium." In Kristeller, *Renaissance Thought and Its Sources*, pp. 137–50. Ed. M. Mooney. New York, 1979.

———. *Iter Italicum*. 3 vols. to date. London and Leiden, 1963–83.

———. "Lay Religious Traditions and Florentine Platonism." In Kristeller, *Studies* pp. 99–122.

———. "Matteo de' Libri, Bolognese Notary of the Thirteenth Century, and his *Artes dictaminis*." In *Miscellanea Giovanni Galbiati*, vol. 2, pp. 283–320. Milan, 1951.

———. "Il Petrarca, l'Umanesimo e la scholastica a Venezia." In Kristeller, *Studies in Renaissance Thought and Letters II*, pp. 217–38. Rome, 1985. Originally in *Lettere Italiane* 7 (1955).

———. "Petrarch's 'Averroists': A Note on the History of Aristotelianism in Venice, Padua, and Bologna." In Kristeller, *Studies II*, pp. 209–16. Originally in *BHR* 14 (1952).

———. *The Philosophy of Marsilio Ficino*. Trans. V. Conant. New York, 1943.

———. "The Scholastic Background of Marsilio Ficino." In Kristeller, *Studies*, pp. 35–97. Originally in *Traditio* 2 (1944).

———. *Studies in Renaissance Thought and Letters*. Rome, 1956.

———. *Studies in Renaissance Thought and Letters II*. Rome, 1985.

Kuhn, R. *The Demon of Noontide: Ennui in Western Literature*. Princeton, 1976.

Laín Entralgo, Pedro. *The Therapy of the Word in Classical Antiquity*. Trans. L. J. Rather and J. M. Sharp. New Haven, Conn. 1970.

Langdale, M. "A Bilingual Work of the Fifteenth Century: Giannozzo Manetti's *Dialogus consolatorius*." *Italian Studies* 31 (1976), 1–16.

Langston, Beach. "Tudor Books of Consolation." Ph.D. Diss., Univ. of North Carolina, 1940.

Leclercq, J. "L'amitié dans les lettres du moyen âge: Autour d'un manuscrit de la bibliothèque de Pétrarque." *Revue du moyen âge* 1 (1945), 391–410.

Lee, Egmont. *Sixtus IV and Men of Letters*. Rome, 1978.

Lepori, F. "La scuola di Rialto dalla fondazione all metà del Cinquecento." In *Storia della cultura Veneta*, vol. 3, pt. 2, pp. 559–70. Vicenza, 1980.

Lyons, Bridget G. *Voices of Melancholy: Studies in Literary Treatments of Melancholy in Renaissance England*. 1971, rept. New York, 1975.

McClure, George W. "Healing Eloquence: Petrarch, Salutati, and the Physicians." *JMRS* 15 (1985), 317–46.

McGuire, M. "The Christian Funeral Oration." In *Funeral Orations by Saint Gregory Nazianzen and Saint Ambrose*. Trans. L. McCauley, J. Sullivan, M. McGuire, and R. Deferrari. New York, 1953.

McManamon, John. *Funeral Oratory and the Cultural Ideals of Italian Humanism*. Chapel Hill and London, 1989.

McNeill, J. T. *A History of the Cure of Souls*. New York, 1951.

Mann, Nicholas. "La fortune de Pétrarque en France: Recherches sur le 'De remediis.'" *Studi Francesci* 13 (1969), 1–15.

———. "The Manuscripts of Petrarch's 'De remediis': A Checklist." *IMU* 14 (1971), 57–90.

Marsh, David. "Boccaccio in the Quattrocento: Manetti's *Dialogus in symposio*." *RQ* 33 (1980), 337–50.

———. *The Quattrocento Dialogue: Classical Tradition and Humanist Innovation*. Cambridge, Mass., 1980.

Martha, B. C. *Études morales sur l'antiquité*. 4th ed. Paris, 1905.

Mayer, Elisabetta. *Un umanista italiano della corte di Mattia Corvino: Aurelio Brandolini Lippo*. Biblioteca dell'Accademia d'Ungheria di Roma, no. 14. Rome, 1938.

Mehus, Lorenzo. Traversari, *Ambrosii Traversarii . . . latinae epistolae* [ed. P. Canetti]. *Adcedit eiusdem Ambrosii vita in qua historia litteraria Florentina ab anno MCXCII usque annum MCCCCXL . . . deducta est* [Mehus]. 2 vols. Florence, 1759; rept. Bologna, 1968.

Mercati, Giovanni. "Notizie varie sopra Niccolò Modrussiense." In Mercati, *Opere minori*, vol. 4, pp. 205–67. Studi e Testi, no. 79. Vatican, 1937. Originally in *La Bibliofilia* 26 (1924–25).

Miles, Leland. "Patristic Comforters in More's *Dialogue of Comfort*." *Moreana*, no. 8 (1965), 9–20.

Monfasani, John. *Collectanea Trapezuntiana: Texts, Documents, and Bibliographies of George of Trebizond*. Binghamton, 1983.

Moos, P. von. *Consolatio: Studien zur mittellateinischen Trostliteratur über den Tod und zum Problem der christlichen Trauer*. 4 vols. Münstersche Mittelalter-Schriften, no. 3, pts. 1–4. Munich, 1971–72.

(Moran), Mary Evaristus. *The Consolations of Death in Ancient Greek Literature*. Washington, 1917.

Murphy, James J. *Rhetoric in the Middle Ages: A History of Rhetorical Theory from St. Augustine to the Renaissance*. Berkeley and Los Angeles, 1974.

O'Connor, Mary C. *The Art of Dying Well: The Development of The "Ars moriendi."* New York, 1942.

Oliver, R. "Politian's Translation of the *Enchiridion*." *Transactions and Proceedings of the American Philological Association* 89 (1958), 185–217.

O'Malley, John. *Praise and Blame in Renaissance Rome: Rhetoric, Doctrine, and Reform in the Sacred Orators of the Papal Court, c. 1450–1521*. Durham, N.C., 1979.

Palmer, R. G. *Seneca's "De remediis fortuitorum" and the Elizabethans*. Chicago, 1953.

Patch, Howard R. *The Tradition of Boethius*. New York, 1935.

Patetta, F. "Una raccolta manoscritta di versi e prose in morte d'Albiera degli Albizzi." *Atti della R. Accademia delle Scienze di Torino* 53 (1917–18), 290–94, 310–28.

Pazzini, A. *Storia della medicina*. 2 vols. Milan, 1947.

Pigman, G., III. *Grief and English Renaissance Elegy*. Cambridge, England, 1985.

Ricci, P. G. "Una consolatoria inedita del Marsuppini." *La Rinascita* 3 (1940), 363–433.

Rice, Eugene. *The Renaissance Idea of Wisdom*. Cambridge, Mass., 1958.

———. *Saint Jerome in the Renaissance*. Baltimore, 1985.

Rico, Francisco. "Petrarca y el *De vera religione*." *IMU* 17 (1974), 313–64.

———. *Vida u obra di Petrarca*. Vol. 1, *Lectura del "Secretum."* Padua, 1974.

Robertson, D. W. "A Note on the Classical Origin of 'Circumstance' in the Medieval Confessional." *Studies in Philology* 43 (1946), 6–14.

Sabbadini, R. *Giovanni da Ravenna, insigne figura d'umanista (1343–1408)*. Como, 1924.

Sage, Evan T. *The Pseudo-Ciceronian "Consolatio."* Chicago, 1910.

Seigel, Jerrold. *Rhetoric and Philosophy in Renaissance Humanism: The Union of Eloquence and Wisdom, Petrarch to Valla*. Princeton, 1968.

Sheppard, L. A. "A Fifteenth-Century Humanist, Francesco Filelfo." *Transactions of the Bibliographical Society*, 4th series, no. 16 (1935), 1–26.

Siraisi, N. *Taddeo Alderotti and his Pupils: Two Generations of Italian Medical Learning*. Princeton, 1981.

Snyder, Susan. "The Paradox of Despair: Studies of the Despair Theme in Medieval and Renaissance Literature." Ph.D. Diss., Columbia Univ., 1963.

Soranzo, G. *L'umanista canonico regolare lateranense Matteo Bosso di Verona (1427-1502)*. Padua, 1965.

Sottili, A. "Autografi e traduzioni di Ambrogio Traversari." *Rinascimento*, 2nd series, no. 5 (1965), 3–15.

Southern, R. W. "Peter of Blois: A Twelfth-Century Humanist?" In Southern, *Medieval Humanism and Other Studies*, pp. 105–32. Oxford, 1970.

Spagnola, G. "La cultura letteraria di Arrigo da Settimello." *GSLI* 93 (1929), 1–68.

Spanneut, M. *Permanence du Stoïcisme, de Zénon à Malraux*. Gembloux, 1937.

Starn, F. "Petrarch's Consolation on Exile: A Humanist Use of Adversity." In *Essays Presented to Myron P. Gilmore*, vol. 1, pp. 241–54. Ed. S. Bertelli and G. Ramakus. 2 vols. Florence, 1978.

Stinger, Charles. *Humanism and the Church Fathers: Ambrogio Traversari (1386–1439) and Christian Antiquity in the Italian Renaissance*. Albany, 1977.

Sundby, Thor. *Della vita e delle opere di Brunetto Latini*. Florence, 1884.

Tateo, Francesco. *Dialogo interiore e polemica ideologica nel "Secretum" del Petrarca*. Florence, 1965.

Tenenti, A. *Il senso della morte e l'amore della vita nel Rinascimento (Francia e Italia)*. Turin, 1957.

———. *La vie et la mort à travers l'art du XVᵉ siècle*. Cahiers des Annales, no. 8. Paris, 1952.

Tentler, Thomas. "Forgiveness and Consolation in the Religious Thought of Erasmus." *SR* 12 (1965), 110–33.

———. *Sin and Confession on the Eve of the Reformation*. Princeton, 1977.

Thorndike, Lynn. "Medicine versus Law at Florence." In Thorndike, *Science and Thought in the Fifteenth Century*, pp. 24–58. New York, 1929.

Trexler, Richard. "In Search of Father: The Experience of Abandonment in the Recollections of Giovanni di Pagolo Morelli." *History of Childhood Quarterly: The Journal of Psychohistory* 3 (1975), 225–52.

Trinkaus, Charles. *Adversity's Noblemen: The Italian Humanists on Happiness*. New York, 1940.

———. *In Our Image and Likeness: Humanity and Divinity in Italian Humanist Thought*. 2 vols. Chicago and London, 1970.

———. *The Poet as Philosopher: Petrarch and the Formation of Renaissance Consciousness*. New Haven, Conn., and London, 1979.

Ullman, B. L. *The Humanism of Coluccio Salutati*. Padua, 1963.

———. "Observations on Novati's Edition of Salutati's Letters." In Ullman, *Studies in the Italian Renaissance*, pp. 197–237. 1955; revised and expanded, Rome, 1973.

———. "Petrarch's Favorite Books." In Ullman, *Studies in the Italian Renaissance*, pp. 113–33. 1955; revised and expanded, Rome, 1973.

Walker, D. P. *Spiritual and Demonic Magic from Ficino to Campanella*. London, 1958; Notre Dame, 1975.

Watkins, Renée N. "Petrarch and the Black Death: From Fear to Monuments."
    SR 19 (1972), 196–223.
Weiss. R. "Il codice oxoniense e altri codice delle opere di Giovanni da Ra-
    venna." *GSLI* 125 (1948), 133–48.
Wenzel, Siegfried. "Petrarch's *Accidia*." *SR* 8 (1961), 36–48.
———. *The Sin of Sloth: Acedia in Medieval Thought and Literature*. Chapel Hill,
    1967.
White, Lynn, Jr. "Death and the Devil." In *The Darker Vision of the Renaissance:
    Beyond the Fields of Reason*, pp. 25–46. Ed. R. S. Kinsman. Berkeley and Los
    Angeles, 1974.
Wilkins, Ernest H. *Life of Petrarch*. Chicago and London, 1961.
———. *The Making of the "Canzoniere" and Other Petrarchan Studies*. Rome,
    1951.
———. "On Petrarch's *Accidia* and His Adamantine Chains." *Speculum* 37
    (1962), 589–94.
———. *Petrarch's Correspondence*. Padua, 1960.
———. *Petrarch's Eight Years in Milan*. Cambridge, Mass., 1958.
———. *Petrarch's Later Years*. Cambridge, Mass., 1959.
———. *Studies in the Life and Works of Petrarch*. Cambridge, Mass., 1955.
Witt, Ronald G. "Boncompagno and the Defense of Rhetoric." *JMRS* 16
    (1986), 1–31.
———. *Coluccio Salutati and His Public Letters*. Geneva, 1976.
———. *Hercules at the Crossroads: The Life, Works, and Thought of Coluccio Salu-
    tati*. Duke Monographs in Medieval and Renaissance Studies, no. 6. Durham,
    N.C., 1983.
———. "Medieval 'Ars dictaminis' and the Beginnings of Humanism: A New
    Construction of the Problem." *RQ* 35 (1982), 1–35.
Wittkower, R. and M. *Born Under Saturn: The Character and Conduct of Artists:
    A Documented History from Antiquity to the French Revolution*. New York, 1963.
Zanta, L. *La Renaissance du Stoïcisme au XVIᵉ siècle*. Paris, 1914.
Zippel, G. *Carlo Marsuppini d'Arezzo: Notizie biografiche*. Trento, 1897.

INDEX

Abelard, Peter, 15, 19, 187n.23, 219n.8
Academic school, 9, 102, 134–35
Acciaiuoli, Angelo, 99, 243n.125, 261n.41
Acciaiuoli, Donato, 136, 261n.41, 268n.87
accidia (acedia) 14, 25–29, 46, 54, 55, 58, 69, 70, 149, 174n.53, 205n.18, 269n.111
active life/contemplative life, 27, 50, 86–91, 92, 107–8, 156, 176n.59, 227n.84
aegritudo, 7, 25–29, 46, 54, 55, 56–57, 69, 70, 101, 125, 149, 205n.18, 209n.58
Aelred of Riveaulx, 15, 75
Aeneas of Gaza, 247n.27, 265n.67
Aeschylus, 102
affects. See *pathe*
aging, 30, 42, 61–62, 80, 95, 105, 136, 138, 139, 159, 164, 201nn.71 and 77, 203n.9
Agli, Antonio, 135, 259n.23, 264n.62, 268n.98
Agli, Pellegrino, 142
Alamanni, Andrea, 258n.21
Albanzani, Donato, 40–42, 60, 82, 94, 203n.2, 210n.65, 211n.70, 224n.56, 234n.59
Alberico of Montecassino, 15
Albert of Saxony, 122
Albertano da Brescia, 181n.86, 182n.92
Alberti, Leon Battista, 103, 149
Albizzi, Alberto degli, 76, 77, 221n.28
Albizzi, Albiera degli, 146, 259n.24
Alexander of Hales, 121
Alfonso I, king of Naples, 267n.86
Alfonso II, king of Naples, 276n.15
Alonzo da Cartagena, 245n.7
Altividus de immortalitate animi (Liber Alcidi), 138, 220n.18, 223n.53, 239n.93, 268n.88
Ambrose, St., 15, 99, 101, 102, 171n.35, 185n.15, 219n.8, 281n.35, 286n.47; *De bono mortis*, 176n.59, 201n.75, 282n.36; *De consolatione Valentiniani*, 201n.75; *De excessu fratris sui Satyri*, 43, 94, 172n.39, 176n.59, 201nn.75 and 77, 267n.87, 275n.10; *De obitu Theodosii*, 201n.75; *De*

officiis ministrorum, 13. See also Petrarca: and Ambrose
Anaxagoras, 110
Annibaldeschi, Paolo, 34–37, 39, 41, 42, 94
Antiphon, 5
Antonino, archbishop of Florence, 135, 244n.2
Antonio da Barga, 109
Antonio da Cortona, 83, 224n.56 and 61, 231n.33
Antonio de Ferrariis (Galateo), 206n.26
apatheia, 5, 107, 173n.43, 257n.14, 279n.33
Aquinas, Thomas, 190n.43, 222n.46
Argyropoulos, John, 133, 134, 136, 149, 141, 259n.26
Aristotle, 50, 51, 66, 110, 115, 121–122, 140, 141, 150, 158, 206n.31, 231n.36, 239nn.93 and 94, 249n.35, 256n.5, 258n.16, 259n.26, 265n.66, 278n.27; *Nicomachean Ethics*, 5, 52, 76, 77, 99, 108, 136, 141, 158, 207n.41, 208n.43, 221nn.32 and 35, 240n.101, 249n.35, 259n.26, 261n.43; *Politics*, 108. See also Peripatetic school
Aristotle, Ps.-, *Problemata*, 149, 191n.47, 270n.119, 272n.125
Arnigio, Bartolomeo, 277n.27
Arrigo da Settimello, 17
ars dictaminis, 15–16, 30, 44, 74, 124–25, 130, 131, 218nn.7 and 8
ars moriendi, 65–68, 162, 277n.27, 278n.27, 281n.35, 282n.36
ars praedicandi (art of preaching), 119, 219n.8, 248n.28
astrology, 59, 61, 151, 161
Athanasius, St., 117
Augustine, St., 12–13, 15, 102, 116, 122, 125, 171n.35, 185n.15, 258n.16, 280n.35, 281n.35, 285n.46, 286n.47; *De civitate Dei*, 12, 56, 69, 173n.43, 190n.37, 191n.47, 193n.65, 204n.11, 208n.45, 249n.35, 254n.58; *Confessions*, 12, 23, 34, 68, 101, 126, 243n.122; *Soliloquies*, 23; *De vera religione*, 48–49,

272n.125; *Philebus*, 140, 141, 266n.77;
Republic, 135, 140, 168n.9, 169n.11,
273n.135; *Symposium*, 142; *Theaetetus*,
140, 143; *Timaeus*, 168n.9, 239n.93
Plato, Ps.-, *Axiochus*, 140, 141, 238n.93,
263n.58
Platonic Academy (Florence), 132, 133,
141, 142, 143, 147, 151, 154, 269n.100
Platonism, 5, 9, 24, 43, 64, 65, 110, 132 ff.,
158, 223n.53, 239n.93, 263n.54,
278n.27, 279n.33. *See also* Petrarca: and
Platonism
Plethon, Gemistus, 133, 141
Pliny the Elder, *Naturalis historia*, 56,
193n.65, 275n.10
Pliny the Younger, 185n.15, 279n.33
Plotinus, 64, 132, 201n.71, 271n.122
Plutarch, 102, 162, 170n.23, 285n.46,
193n.65; *De capienda ex inimicis utilitate*,
170n.23, 277n.24; *Consolatio ad uxorem*,
170n.23, 239n.93, 241n.107, 251n.44;
De tranquillitate animi, 170n.23,
283n.38, 285n.47
Plutarch, Ps.-: *Consolatio ad Apollonium*, 6, 8,
109, 134–35, 233n.46, 237n.72,
239n.93, 241n.107, 251n.44, 258n.16,
283n.38, 285n.47; *Vitae decem oratorum*,
168n.6
Poggio Bracciolini. *See* Bracciolini, Poggio
Poliziano, Angelo, 118, 132, 262n.52,
268n.96, 272n.125
Pomponazzi, Pietro, 238n.87, 277n.22
Pontano, Giovanni, 276n.15
Porphyry, 132
Posidonius, 12, 110, 118, 122
poverty, 27–28, 42, 119, 125, 160, 161,
205n.18, 254n.59, 276n.15
prayer, 113, 162, 164
prayers for the dead, 14, 35, 114, 200n.58
Proclus, 132
protohumanism, French, 15, 75
Pythagoras, 110, 132, 151, 266n.74,
278n.27

Quintilian, 15, 241n.107; *Institutiones oratoriae*, 122, 228n.2

Raimonda, Cosma, da Cremona, 237n.83
Razzano, Pietro, of Lucera, 157
René, duke of Anjou, king of Naples, 114,
243n.125, 244n.4

Requiem Masses, 14
resurrection, Christian theme of, 12, 32, 55,
62, 239n.95
Rhegius, Urbanus, 282n.36
Riario, Pietro, 121, 127
Riario, Raffaelo. *See* Sansoni-Riario, Raf-
faelo
Ricci, Antonio, 277n.27
Ricci, P. G., 134
Rice, Eugene, 163
Richard of Pofi, 219n.8
Rico, Francisco, 48
Rinuccini, Alamanno, 135, 139
Robert, king of Naples, 41, 200n.64
Roberto da Battifolle, Count, 223n.53
Roselli, Rosello de', 94, 220n.15
Rossi, Roberto, 221n.28
Rucellai, Giovanni, 266n.78
Rustici, Cencio de', 263n.58

Sabbadini, R., 104
Sacchi, Bartolomeo. *See* Platina
Sadoleto, Jacopo, 277n.27, 285n.46
Sagremor de Pommiers, 205n.17
Salutati, Coluccio, 15, 44, 73 ff., 104, 112,
114–15, 116–17, 156, 160, 182n.90,
243n.125, 270n.112, 272n.125; on the
active life, 86–91, 92, 156; and Aristotle
and Peripatetic school, 76, 77, 79, 92, 97,
106, 107, 108, 115, 134, 146, 158,
257n.7; and *ars dictaminis*, 74, 218nn.7
and 8; and Augustine, 81, 89, 116,
219n.8, 224n.56, 227n.83; and Cicero,
76, 81, 92, 94, 95–98, 102, 219n.8,
227n.84, 230n.27, 237n.79; on divine
providence/will, 81, 83, 87, 94–95, 96,
102, 109; on flight from plague, 80–81,
83, 88, 94; on friendship, 75–80, 82, 92;
and loss of sons Piero and Andrea, 79, 84,
95–98, 99, 104, 105, 108, 224n.56,
227n.84, 228n.4; and loss of wife Piera,
84, 94–95, 224n.56; on monasticism, 85,
91; on physicians and eloquence, 73–74;
on secular renunciation, 86–91, 92; and
Stoicism, 80, 81, 84, 95–98, 108, 112,
134, 158, 227n.84, 228n.5, 231n.27; on
time and consolation, 84, 98; on will vs.
intellect, 96, 108–9; *De fato et fortuna*, 74,
81, 94; *De nobilitate legum et medicine*, 74,
88, 109, 206n.26, 217n.2; *Quod medici
eloquentie studeant*, 73; personal letters, 74

ff.; *De seculo et religione*, 74, 77, 85, 91,
204n.12, 221n.28, 227n.80, 229n.15; *De
vita associabili et operativa*, 78, 88. *See also*
Manetti: and Salutati
Salviati, Jacopo, 147
Sansoni-Riario, Raffaelo, 121
Savonarola, Girolamo, 66
Saxl, F., 149
Scala, Bartolomeo, 133–34, 135–39, 159,
263n.54, 268n.96
scholasticism, 47, 50, 51, 53, 59, 63, 119,
121–22, 123–24, 130, 156– 57, 218n.8,
248n.27
secular renunciation, 43–44, 86–91, 92, 156
Seneca, 7–8, 15, 17, 67, 91, 102, 103, 118,
122, 125, 162, 163, 176n.59, 185n.15,
206n.31, 219n.8, 281n.35, 283nn.37
and 38, 285n.46; *De brevitate vitae*,
170n.23, 214n.104, 215n.111; *De consolatione ad Helviam*, 7, 32, 250n 37. *De consolatione ad Marciam*, 7, 32, 100, 169n.21,
239n.93, 250n.37, 267n.87, 275n.10,
283n.38; *De consolatione ad Polybium*, 7,
32, 239n.93, 250n.37; *Epistolae ad Lucilium*, 7, 28, 52, 60, 65, 81, 127, 181n.86,
192n.56, 195n.4, 196n.19, 197n.25,
200nn.57 and 59, 206n.31, 211n.73,
214nn.98, 103, and 104, 219n.8,
251n.45, 266n.76, 275n.6, 283n.38; *De
sapientis constantia*, 170n.23, 193nn.60
and 65; *De tranquillitate animi*, 28, 69,
170n.23, 191n.49, 192n.55, 209n.58,
214n.104. *See also* Petrarca: and Seneca
Seneca, Ps.- *De remediis fortuitorum*, 8, 52,
54, 62, 63, 122–23, 158, 191n.49,
213nn.87 and 92, 275n.6, 279n.33,
285n.46, 285n.47
sepulchers, 40
sermons, 11, 144. *See also* *ars praedicandi*
Seta, Lombardo della, 230n.20
Sette, Guido, 47, 212n.78
seven deadly sins, 14, 25, 52, 69
"Simonides." *See* Nelli, Francesco
Sixtus IV, pope, 121, 122
Socrates, 5, 138, 140, 143, 149, 152, 153,
223n.53, 270n.119
"Socrates." *See* Kempen, Ludwig van
Sophists, 4–5
Spalatin, Georg, 284n.42
Statius, 176n.59, 185n.15, *Thebais*, 21, 113

Stefano da Bibbiena, 79
Stoicism, 5, 9, 67, 100–103, 106, 107, 108,
114–15, 120, 127, 134, 136– 39, 164,
254n.60, 258n.20, 261n.44, 262n.52,
278n.27, 283n.37, 284n.40. See also *apatheia*; Petrarca: and Stoicism; Salutati:
and Stoicism
studia humanitatis, 134
Stufa, Sigismondo, 146, 259n.24
suffering, Judeo-Christian views of, 9–10,
15, 119–20, 123, 127
suicide, 64, 242n.116, 254n.58
Sulpicius, Servius, 126, 169n.18, 224n.57,
229n.6, 251n.45, 253n.53
sweet grief. See *voluptas dolendi*
Symmachus, 219n.8

Tacitus, 219n.8
Taylor, Jeremy, 66
Terence, 125, 255n.68; *Andria*, 40, 229n.5;
Heautontimorumenos, 224n.57
Tertullian, 171n.35, 283nn.38 and 39
Thales, 110
Theocritus, 257n.11
Theophrastus, 285n.46
Thomas of Capua, 16
Thorne, Henry, 282n.36
Tommaso da Messina, 20
Tommaso di Rieti, 228n.2
Tornabuoni, Lucrezia, 259n.24
Tosetti, Lello di Pietro Stefano dei
("Laelius"), 61, 197n.24, 201n.70
Tractatus artis bene moriendi, 65–67,
201n.71, 216n.120
Traversari, Ambrogio, 99, 117, 131, 133,
246n.11, 247n.27, 257n.5, 262n.47,
265n.67
Trevisan, Zaccaria, 224n.56
Trinkaus, Charles, 57, 109
tristitia saeculi/tristitia secundum Deum, 10,
11, 12, 14, 17, 29, 55, 57, 69, 71, 131,
160, 165, 171n.31, 181n.86, 191n.43,
209n.56
Turchi, Pietro, 220n.15
Twyne, Thomas, 202n.1

Valerius Maximus, 219n.8; *Factorum et dictorum memorabilium libri*, 200n.64
Valla, Lorenzo, 108, 119, 233n.47,
237n.83

45 00
_____
1202